The Culture of Fascism

The Culture of Fascism

Visions of the Far Right in Britain

Edited by
Julie V. Gottlieb and
Thomas P. Linehan

I.B. TAURIS
LONDON · NEW YORK

Published in 2004 by I.B. Tauris & Co Ltd
6 Salem Road, London W2 4BU
175 Fifth Avenue, New York NY 10010
www.ibtauris.com

In the United States of America and Canada distributed by
Palgrave Macmillan a division of St. Martin's Press
175 Fifth Avenue, New York NY 10010

ISBN   HB 1 86064 798 7   32 0 5 33
       PB 1 86064 799 5   G-OT

A full CIP record for this book is available from the British Library
A full CIP record is available from the Library of Congress

Library of Congress Catalog Card Number: available

Typeset in Palatino 10/12 by JCS Publishing Services
Printed and bound in Great Britain by MPG Books Ltd, Bodmin

Contents

Part III: Cultural Confrontations: Foreign Influences and Cultural Exchange

Contributors' Biographies

Claudia Baldoli completed her PhD at the London School of Economics in International History. She is a research fellow in Rome and a visiting Lecturer at Birkbeck College, University of London.

Philip M. Coupland completed his PhD in the Department of History at the University of Warwick in 2000. He has taught history at the University of Warwick and at the time of writing (December 2002) is a researcher on the European Commission funded project 'The Churches and European Integration', based in the Department of History at the University of Glasgow. Dr Coupland has written on British fascism and other topics of British political history in the *Journal of Contemporary History, Twentieth Century British History* and elsewhere.

Julie V. Gottlieb completed her PhD at the University of Cambridge in 1998, was a post-doctoral fellow at the University of Toronto, taught at the University of Manchester and the University of Bristol, and is a Lecturer in Modern British History at the University of Sheffield. Her publications include *Feminine Fascism: Women in Britain's Fascist Movement, 1923–1945* (I. B. Tauris, 2000, paperback 2003) and articles and chapters on gender, culture and British fascism. She is co-editor of the forthcoming *Power, Personality and Persuasion* (I. B. Tauris, 2004) and she is currently working on 'Gendering Appeasement: Women and Foreign Policy in Britain, 1918–1940'.

Roger Griffin is Professor of History at Oxford Brookes University where he lectures on aspects of the History of Ideas relating to ideologies and values which have shaped the modern world. His major work is *The Nature of Fascism* (Pinter 1991, Routledge 1993) which established the first new theory of generic fascism for over a decade and continues to have an influence on the 'new consensus' which is now emerging in fascist studies about the need to take seriously fascism's intent to inaugurate a national or ethnic rebirth in the sphere of political culture. This approach was refined further in *Fascism*, a documentary reader of primary sources relating to fascism published by Oxford University Press (1995), and *International Fascism. Theories, Causes, and the New Consensus*, a documentary reader of secondary sources published by Arnold in 1998. He has also published numerous articles and chapters on the relationship of both inter-war and post-war fascism to such topics as the myth of Europe, time, religion, aesthetics, the New Right, and the theatre. His long term project is a comparative study of fascist culture for Macmillan which will focus particularly on the quest to regenerate the collective experience of history through a transformation of political culture brought about in the classic era of fascism by ultra-nationalist forms of ritual politics.

Richard Griffiths was Professor of French at King's College London from 1990 to 2000. He has written extensively on the British and the French extreme Right, and his most recent publications include *An Intelligent Person's Guide to Fascism* (Duckworth, 2000) and *Patriotism Perverted: Captain Ramsay, the Right Club, and British Anti-Semitism 1939–1940* (Constable, 1998). He is also the author of the ground-breaking *Fellow Travellers of the Right: British Enthusiasts for Nazi Germany, 1933–39* (Constable, 1980).

Matthew Hendley has a PhD in History from the University of Toronto. He has completed a Social Sciences and Humanities Research Council of Canada post-doctoral fellowship at McMaster University, and was the Northrop Frye Postdoctoral fellow at Victoria College, University of Toronto, before becoming assistant professor at SUNY-Oneonta. Hendley's dissertation, 'Patriotic Leagues and the Evolution of Popular Patriotism and Imperialism in Great Britain, 1914–1932', is a study of the impact of the First World War on organized patriotic and imperialist movements. This thesis received honourable mention for the Canadian Historical Association's John Bullen Prize in 1999. Dr Hendley has a strong interest in the intersection of gender with political and imperial culture and has published three articles in *Albion*, the *Canadian Journal of History* and the *Journal of the Canadian Historical Association*. He is currently revising his dissertation for publication.

Thomas P. Linehan read History at the University of York, and later went on to receive his doctorate in History from Royal Holloway and Bedford New College, University of London. He is the author of *East London for Mosley: the British Union of Fascists in East London and South-West Essex 1933–1940* (Frank Cass, 1996) and *British Fascism, 1918–1939: Parties, Ideology and Culture* (Manchester University Press, 2000). Dr Linehan is currently working on a study of the Communist Party of Great Britain during the inter-war years. He is currently a Lecturer in History at Brunel University.

Helen Pussard is a Lecturer in the Social and Cultural Study of Sport and Leisure at the University of Surrey Roehampton. She is currently finishing her PhD thesis on pleasure grounds in the first half of the twentieth century at the University of Manchester.

Dan Stone is Lecturer in Twentieth-Century European History at Royal Holloway College, University of London. He is the editor of *Theoretical Interpretations of the Holocaust* (Rodopi, 2001) and author of *Breeding Superman: Nietzsche, Race and Eugenics in Edwardian and Inter-war Britain* (Liverpool University Press, 2002), *Constructing the Holocaust: A Study in Historiography* (Vallentine Mitchell, 2003) and *Responses to Nazism in Britain: Before War and Holocaust* (Palgrave, 2003).

Richard Thurlow in a Senior Lecturer in History at the University of Sheffield. He has published widely on British fascism throughout the twentieth century. His publications include the seminal *Fascism in Britain: From Oswald Mosley's Blackshirts to the National Front* (I. B. Tauris, 1998), *The Secret State: British Internal Security in the Twentieth Century* (Basil Blackwell, 1994) and *Fascism* (Cambridge University Press, 1999)

Steven Woodbridge is Lecturer in Politics in the Faculty of Arts and Social Sciences, Kingston University, Surrey. He was awarded a PhD from Kingston in 1998, his area of research being British fascist ideology during the inter-war period. His research interests currently include British fascist and neo-fascist ideas during the twentieth century, together with the wider comparative nature of extreme right-wing ideology in Europe. He has given conference papers on the development of the extreme right in the 1990s, British neo-fascist attitudes to culture, and the resurgence of conspiracy theory in the twenty-first century. He is at present working on a study of British fascism during the 1920s. Dr Woodbridge is a member of the ECPR Standing Group on Extremism and Democracy.

Introduction:
Culture and the British Far Right

The historiography of the British far Right has evolved over the past decades from studies adhering to largely empirical approaches, and motivated principally by the need to understand the 'failure' of British fascism according to political and socio-economic explanatory models, to fresher perspectives and more innovative methodological approaches that suggest the relative place of the far Right in larger debates in the fields of both contemporary British history and comparative fascism. The study of the British far Right has long been dominated by investigations of local support for the British Union of Fascists (BUF) or by demographic surveys of membership;[1] definitional discussions of British fascist ideology and political development;[2] studies of the electoral (mis)fortunes of far Right groups and government responses to political extremism;[3] investigations into the formal and informal relations between British 'fellow travellers' and their continental counterparts;[4] and political biography of leading figures or more narrative but no less lively family histories (where the Mosleys and their assorted high-bred relations provide the anecdotal raw material for a veritable cottage industry).[5] Together these approaches – which have benefited a great deal from, and whose proliferation has been justified by, the periodic release of illuminating official documents and the more systematic archiving of personal papers and printed material[6] – have been able to reveal as much as is likely to be known about the BUF in particular; a political movement that has arguably received more retrospective notice and has been the subject of more painstaking historical analysis than its impact on the 1930s alone might merit. The empirical approach has constructed a narrative of the far Right's political marginality, personal eccentricity and quirkiness, and 'otherness'.[7]

However, in the past decade historians have sought to redraw the theoretical and methodological boundaries of the historiography, and thereby revise and renarrate the development and the significance of the far Right. Those conducting their research in this field have of late begun to bring the perspectives of culture (both mass and elite)[8] and gender (both the position of women and the construction of feminine and masculine typologies),[9] as well as the history of ideas to bear on the growing wealth of source material and historical evidence.[10] It is the mission of this volume to offer as representative a sample as possible of these new perspectives, and to supplement the empirical approach by providing close readings of the symbols, the language and the (self)representations of the British far Right.

While our collective approach requires the re-reading of the sources, reflects on newly-excavated primary material and acknowledges the volatility of historical categories, the editors of this collection maintain that any reinterpretation of fascism must remain firm in its fundamental condemnation of the British far Right and its project. All contributors to this volume condemn, without hesitation, the far Right's authoritarianism, posturing elitism, anti-democratic aggression, violence, intolerance, sexism and racism. A cultural approach does not provide retrospective legitimacy to the far Right, nor does it celebrate its production in the sphere of culture, however revolutionary and even 'avant-garde' certain aspects of 'fascist modernity' might have been. It would be myopic to believe that this bid to understand, and this process of imaginative intellectual probing, in any way detracts from the political and moral need to expose the offensive, intolerant and violent extremism of fascism for the present generation.

Taking a cue from the so-called 'consensus' on the 'primacy of culture' thesis in fascist studies, all the essays in this volume share an interest in the relationship between politics and culture.[11] We aim to demonstrate through a variety of specific case studies that British fascism is not merely a political movement, but also a cultural movement, a (failed) attempt at *Kulturkampf* and a culturally-informed expression of political belief. If the British far Right can be understood to be a cultural movement, this inevitably challenges the reigning narrative of fascism's failure in Britain in relation to the political system and in interaction with competing notions of the state and the nation. In other words, however unsuccessful the British extreme Right has been in the course of the twentieth century by the measure of political gain, it has nonetheless often been a reflector and recycler of wider cultural phenomena, and in grudging dialogue with current cultural discourses. The far Right has not developed in a cultural vacuum. However marginal vis-à-vis the liberal–democratic consensus, for all that British fascists have absorbed, appropriated and corrupted from their British socio-cultural and political context, they have also been a vocal participant in that contentious debate, still ongoing, regarding the meaning of 'Englishness' and what constitutes the British 'character'.

In common we consider both the movement's reactions to high and popular cultural forms (film, theatre, music, mass media, visual art and literature), as well as offering readings of political expressions informed by cultural history. We thus seek to provide a cultural history of fascist politics, and not merely another investigation of political culture. Only by re-reading the cultural expressions of the British far Right do we feel that this area of scholarly interest can be revitalized by beginning to engage with innovative theoretical and methodological paradigms through which fascism is represented historically.

Why read British fascism as a cultural phenomenon? Culture was an indispensable feature of fascism's revolutionary project, as is now recognized by many scholars of generic and continental fascism.[12] This was certainly the case with the BUF. The Mosleyites' gloom-laden prognosis that contemporary British life was exhibiting signs of acute ill-health – manifested in a range of imagined decadent features (materialist individualism, rationalism, urbanism, intellectualism, 'cultural Bolshevism' etc.) – stemmed from a world view that, to a large degree, was cultural in origin and inspiration. To the BUF, cultures, like nations and civilizations, were biological organisms with their own evolutionary life cycles. Britain was thought to be nearing the end of its life cycle of creative cultural development that apparently accounted for the 'pathological' symptoms referred to above. As fascist revolutionaries, of course, the Mosleyites believed that they could check and reverse this 'organic' process of biological decline. They would expedite the evolutionary process by initiating a variety of measures (corporate, Faustian-scientific etc.) designed to rekindle the nation's 'life force' and evoke a sense of national destiny similar to that which they believed characterized earlier eras of national advance and cultural attainment.[13]

Thus the British far Right did not confine itself to high political discourse, to economic policy, to street-level provocation and demonstrations, or to formal or more casual relations with soon-to-be-hostile foreign powers. Rather, British fascists developed an extensive and, more often than not, coherent cultural package, complete with suggested readings, suggested theatre and film viewing, recommended 'listening in' and proscriptive ways of understanding modern art and music and modernist art forms. In relation to the latter, one of the underlying questions that this volume is asking is whether there was any validity in the BUF's claim to be a 'Modern movement', and how the fascist definition of the 'modern' appropriated and/or contested our current definition of Modernism (the latter defined as an artistic sensibility, as well as a conglomeration of normative constructions of Modernity).

On the other hand, the BUF developed its own politicized technology – the theatre of the mass meeting, the adaptation of media technology to animate the appearance of Mosley as matinée idol, the production of films, songs and political literature – in flattering imitation of Mussolini's and Hitler's politicized aesthetic experiments, and also in competition with the techniques of mass politics being developed by the mainstream parties. This technological innovation and the distinctive material culture spawned by the movement was due, partly, to legislative prohibitions on fascist activity. For example, the BUF was banned from broadcasting on the BBC, and with the Public Order Act (1936) political uniforms were banned. However, an all-consuming cultural life was also integral to the development of a community of fascist 'fanatics'. The BUF, and later in the century the National Front and British National Party, recast cultural forms in the fascist mould, and an anthropological reading of the fascist movement's own popular culture can thus reveal a great deal about the proximity or the distance between the manners and habits of the mainstream members of the British community and their black-shirted political black sheep relations. We are thus equally interested in investigating the far Right's *own* cultural production, alongside an analysis of its cultural values and ideals.

Spanning the entire twentieth century, the essays offer cultural readings of propaganda, political ideas, racial theories, political aesthetics, gender ideologies, material culture and forms of literary expression that were closely engaged with the political discourse and aspirations of the far Right. The essays are arranged into three thematic categories. In Part I, the unifying concern is with cultural perspectives. The essays in this section consider far Right perspectives on culture in the context of particular cultural and ideological expressions, namely cinema, theatre, music and ideologies of gender and race.

Providing some longer-term perspectives on the British Right and highlighting the blurred boundaries between sections of the Conservative Party and the far Right, Matthew Hendley examines feminized political tropes in Primrose League and Conservative Party propaganda. By taking the Primrose League as the main subject of investigation, he unveils an interesting paradox: that a political movement that was characterized by high rates of female membership, and that sought to politicize women from the Right, referred to a set of images that tended to undermine or subordinate the female role. Nonetheless, the Primrose League continued to attract a dedicated female following. Indeed, it might even be argued that this imagery and rhetoric was the key to its success with women, building as it did on traditionalist and familiar symbolic codes in English politics and on the typologies and aesthetics common to political satire. (George Mosse has argued that the power of the fascist aesthetic was also to create nothing new or original, but to offer continuity with national and nationalist cultural codes.)[14] As Hendley points out, the preponderance during the inter-war period of women members of the British Fascists Ltd (1923–35) and the BUF with Conservative backgrounds speaks for this subjective continuity, and it could even be argued that their transfer of loyalties was facilitated by their comfort with these familiarly gendered nationalist symbols.

Thomas P. Linehan's essay on fascist cinema spectatorship considers the representations of contemporary cinema at play in the film discourse of the British far Right in the inter-war period. Through a range of lively examples culled from the far Right's publications, he shows how fascist writers depicted contemporary cinema, in both its international and home-grown variants, as an agent of encroaching Americanization, as an intellectually bankrupt 'mass culture' object, and as a dangerously seductive site of sexual titillation. Similarly, cinema figured in this critique as a conduit for the circulation of so-called 'international' Jewish propaganda, and as a forum that offered a bastardized view of British history. British fascist film spectators would never be content to restrict themselves solely to such passive 'anti-' observations though. For, as Linehan goes on to show, as 'palingenetic' revolutionaries the fascists imagined and strove to bring into the domain of popular cultural discourse an alternative model of British cinema, one refashioned to serve their goal of national rebirth.

While Linehan analyses the far Right response to the influence of the modern cinema, Roger Griffin surveys the BUF's responses to theatre and music during the 1930s. In his essay, Griffin draws upon his pioneering work into the core of palingenetic myth underlying the fascists' 'regenerative' mission and fascist rebirth ideology. Quarrying the BUF press to discern a British fascist critique of contemporary cultural forms, Griffin fleshes out the emergent fascist canon, and speculates on the nature of cultural politics in fascist-corporatist Britain. But the essay does not merely scrutinize the BUF's cultural preferences or its own hit parade. Griffin also reveals a great deal about the movement's fascistization of cultural forms, from their marching songs, their hosting of musical evenings, to their own 'Aryan bands' offering a play list of popular favourites as well as Anglicized fascist anthems. Griffin's essay convincingly shows, too, that the Mosleyites' diagnosis of the health of Britain's theatre and music was informed by their Spenglerian assumption concerning the organic life cycle of cultures that was so integral to their palingenetic vision of the nation's destiny.

The formation of Aryan dance bands was obviously predicated on a theory of race, and Richard Thurlow's essay provides the wider context for British fascist racial theories and explores the prioritization of notions of culture within these racist pseudo-scientific musings. Spanning the entire twentieth century, considering the long-term resonance of the BUF's contribution to racist discourse and taking an intellectual history approach, Thurlow charts the evolution of racist intellectual constructs and points to key areas of divergence between the British

Nazi genetic racists and the British Mosleyite cultural racists. Thurlow considers the influence and the uses and abuses of science by Britain's leading racists, and leads us to speculate that alongside the fascist appropriation of artistic forms, Britain's far Right also developed its own 'fascist science' that was specific to the British historical context and to the British scientific community.

Part II of the volume is concerned with the cultural representations and the cultural production emanating from within the far Right itself. The essays in this section provide readings of the BUF's 'new fascist men', the uniforms donned by these self-tailored new fascist men, and the playground of the mass meeting arranged to entertain new fascist men and women. The development of their own cultural forms was most often a reaction on the part of the fascists to what they diagnosed as the unrelenting decadence of the age, and Steven Wood-bridge's essay brings the discussion up-to-date, with a thorough analysis of the post-war far Right's cultural diagnostics.

Julie Gottlieb's essay explores the construction of masculinity in Britain's fascist movement, with a focus on the early years of the BUF. The BUF developed its own language of aesthetics and its own cata-logue of symbols that were at once derivative of concurrent continental models, yet distinctive for the movement's stated aim of expressing a quintessentially nationalist and British cultural heritage. She argues that a distinctively British fascist aesthetic was discernible in the BUF's graphic arts, in its political cartooning, in newspaper critiques and editorials on art exhibitions, films and modern literature, in hagiographic portrayals of the 'Leader' and in the development of fascist journalists' own evocative and idealizing language for describing moments of political violence and brutality. She suggests that the aggressively masculine British fascist aesthetic – which first responded to and then inflated normative constructions of masculin-ity – provided a symbolic code to express the aspirations of a fledgling fascist movement in Britain. The British fascist construction of mascu-linity was further defined by a hostility to psychoanalysis and sexology, to the perceived effeminacy of the post-war British state and to the sexual disorder which allegedly characterized avant-garde and Modernist art forms. Nonetheless, she points out that aesthetic resonances with Vorticism and Futurism complicate the BUF's identi-fication with or rejection of cultural Modernism.

The BUF's aesthetic sensibilities and its construction of manliness were most readily visible in the style and cut of the Blackshirt uniform itself. Philip Coupland's essay offers a close reading of the BUF's sartorial culture, examining the meaning of the Blackshirt uniform and its significance to the wearer, the political observer, and its sym-bolic values in the political climate of the 1930s. Coupland provides a factual account of the development of the uniform, insignia and regalia of the BUF. However, his major effort is to detail and analyse the meanings appended to the shirt within both fascist subculture and in wider political culture. This requires outlining and analysing the formal rules governing who could wear which uniform where. Around that basic framework fascist rhetoric and aesthetics built a rich and complex symbolic language. In relation to the ruling dress codes of the day the shirt, as worn by the Leader and his 'brother Blackshirts' on the march or when speaking at, or stewarding, public meetings articulated a force for order, dynamic action, brotherhood and modernity.

Where brother Blackshirts gathered and strutted in their uniforms is the subject of Helen Pussard's investigation. Pussard examines the appropriation of mass culture forms by the Blackshirts. Hers is a tightly focused case study of the BUF's meeting at Belle Vue, Manchester, in 1934, and by turning the microscope to this one meeting she is able to recreate, and then deconstruct, the spectacular theatricality that distinguished the BUF's political technology from other political movements in the period. The Belle Vue meeting was a showcase for the BUF's political marketing and an opportunity to flaunt its showmanship. The uses and impact of noise, lighting, the distribution of propaganda and platform oratory are each examined in this essay, emphasizing the convergence of political and leisure spaces.

If the British far Right developed its own cultural forms as a corrective to what it diagnosed as a decadent culture, then how did the theme of decadence persist after 1945? Steven Woodbridge brings us up to the present day, offering an overview of the discussion of culture by, and the leitmotif of decadence in, post-war British fascist movements. British fascists, in common with European fascist activists and ideologues in general, often took the view that Britain's culture in the twentieth century had become decadent and was showing clear signs that the nation was in serious decline. They argued the need for the 'purification' of the arts, literature and music as part of the political and social project to renew Britain and bring about the rebirth of a healthy polity, leading to a supposedly 'higher form' of civilization. In conjunction with their critique of decadence, they also put forward ideas on the nature of their alternative vision of culture. By concentrating on three extreme Right movements – the Union Movement (formed in 1948), the National Front (formed in 1967) and the British National Party (formed in 1982) – Woodbridge's overall objective is to illustrate some of the common ideas held by all three regarding cultural themes and thus some of the continuities in neo-fascist discourse.

Part III of the volume is concerned with cultural confrontations, the exchange of ideas and practices between fascists in different national contexts, and the British fascist intrusion into wider philosophical

debates. Claudia Baldoli's essay examines the relationship between
Italian Fascism and British fascism, and argues that there was a significant shift in BUF ideology and policy from an imitative reverence for
Italian Fascism to greater admiration for Nazi Germany as the 1930s
unfolded. She is concerned with detecting the BUF's foreign influences and British fascism's place within a universal and pan-European
fascist political culture. In addition to the analysis of original new
material on Italo-BUF relations, she also offers a close reading of the
motivations and cultural activities of the BUF's Italian branches and its
successor, the significantly named Anglo-Italian Cultural Association.

Richard Griffiths also illustrates foreign influence and cultural
exchange between fascists and fascist fellow travellers, but he takes a
less immediately obvious case: that of cultural and intellectual
exchange between the British and specifically the Welsh intelligentsias
and the French radical Right. His essay offers an intellectual history of
the influence of the French radical Right on a handful of British Modernist writers, and on some of the founding members of the Welsh
Nationalist Party. The focus here is on the impact of fascism in elite
cultural circles. While the two parts of the chapter: the influence of the
Action Française on T. E. Hulme and T. S. Eliot among others, and the
interaction between French ultra-nationalism and Welsh nationalists
may appear at first sight only loosely connected, the thread of French
influence ties them together convincingly. The concluding discussion
of the relationship between fascism and literary Modernism is especially illuminating.

Dan Stone also considers the issue of (high) cultural and philosophical exchange, especially the exchange of ideas between those on
the peripheries of Britain's fascist movement and those advocates of a
rural revivalism in inter-war Britain. His essay examines the way in
which the English landscape was central to the concerns of inter-war
British fascists, and demonstrates the way in which representations of
the landscape were key in the development of a specifically English
form of fascism. This had two poles, a negative and a positive one. The
former concentrated on the threat to the landscape presented by
foreigners, especially Jewish immigrants (depicted as *rootless* internationalist cosmopolitans) concentrated in dirty cities, and the second
on a celebration of the health and vitality of the English landscape,
and the rootedness of the people in it. For the back-to-the-land movement, their vision of a culturally homogeneous nation or race,
dependent on the soil and deriving identity and meaning, as well as
food, from it means that the cultural and political aspects of this type
of fascism are inseparable. The anthropological bent in cultural history that stresses representations and the creation of meaning through
symbolic landscapes here comes up against a movement that derived
its symbolic action from (putatively) real landscapes. In his conclu-

sion, Stone considers how this changes our understanding of cultural history and of British fascism.

Indeed, all the essays in this volume seek to do just this: by taking a cultural history approach we each hope to suggest different interpretations of British fascism, as well as offering some insight into the potential of cultural history in this field of historical enquiry.

Julie V. Gottlieb
and *Thomas P. Linehan*

Part I

Cultural Perspectives:

The British Far Right and
Ideologies of Culture

Women and the Nation:
The Right and Projections of Feminized Political Images in Great Britain, 1900–18[1]

Matthew Hendley

As a cultural form, fascism might be considered to be masculinity without civilized restraint. Scholars of gender have looked at the phenomenon of European fascism with a combination of fascination and revulsion. Germany and Italy had National Socialist or Fascist Governments. Naturally enough, these regimes have attracted the most attention from those wishing to examine the link between fascism and gender.[2] The British fascist movement was much less well developed but has attracted a growing number of scholars. The interest in gender as a means of understanding British fascism and the role of women in the fascist movement has led to a blossoming of new and important studies.[3] However, despite these studies there is still much work that needs to be done, especially in tracing the origins of gender constructions on the Right in Britain. As the essays in this volume make clear, there must be a greater effort to understand British fascism on a cultural level. This chapter suggests that the gender analysis of the political culture of British Conservatism will serve as an important foundation for understanding the political culture of British fascism. It will focus on British Conservatism's considerable success in gendering aspects of itself and its ideology to be female. In particular, it will focus on feminized imagery used by the British Conservative Party and its ally the Primrose League towards the perceived threats posed by the Ulster crisis, Liberal reformism, socialism and free trade, as well as the Conservatives' satirical feminization of their political opponents.

Part of the appeal of British fascism for its supporters lay in its use of aggressive masculine political rhetoric. The governing elite was portrayed as effete and the parliamentary system was said to keep in power an 'old gang' that emasculated the nation and left it ripe for a Communist takeover.[4] Certainly, this construction of masculinity was crucial for defining fascist ideology but must be considered in the context of the political culture of the traditional British Right to be properly understood. In fact, the fascist embrace of a culture of hyper-

masculinity was an important move away from the growing embrace
of feminized imagery by the mainstream forces of the British Right
such as the Conservative Party.[5] The continuities and discontinuities
of the gendered aspects of British fascist culture can be best understood, therefore, through an analysis of the pre-war origins of
feminized imagery used by the Conservatives.

The Primrose League was the principal means through which Conservative women could participate in mass politics before 1914.
Originally formed in 1883 after the death of the Conservative leader
Benjamin Disraeli, the League quickly became a mass organization.
Skirting the restrictions of the Corrupt Practices Act of 1883, it was formally independent of the Conservative Party and reliant on its own
funds. The League was pledged to various eternal 'principles' that
included 'the maintenance of Religion, the Estates of the Realm and
the unity of the British Empire'.[6] Though its membership records
tended to be inaccurate and inflated, it is undeniable that the Primrose
League was one of the largest political organizations of the late Victorian period. By the late 1890s, it claimed to have two million members
scattered throughout the United Kingdom in over 2,500 local branches
(called 'habitations'). Studies by Martin Pugh and E. H. H. Green have
shown that before 1902, the Primrose League also served as an important vehicle for political and social integration by freely mixing social
classes and voters with non-voters, as well as by forging links between
'old and new Conservatives'.[7] It was equally notable in its appeal to
women, who formed at least half of the overall membership and often
provided its most active members.[8]

The study of British politics used to be thought of in exclusively
male terms. Almost the sole exception was the well-developed historiography on women's suffrage.[9] Although politically-involved women
were most often to be found supporting the Conservative Party, it is
only recently that historians have given Conservative women their
due.[10] The volumes of new work on women's involvement in politics
has erased any idea that British politics was ever solely a man's game.
The next step is to examine the imagery used by politicians and the
political culture they helped create. It is vital to see how certain cultural assumptions on gender and other matters entered into political
discourse and were deployed by political organizations. National
symbols, tropes used to represent specific issues or people and the
portrayal of ordinary citizens form crucial components of any political
culture. All political parties try to create a political culture to support
their own ideology. It can be argued that the success of any given
political movement is in part linked to its ability to present its ideology in a political culture that is acceptable to a majority of the
nation's citizens.

The Conservatives put special emphasis on feminized imagery well before women could vote. Feminized imagery placed gender at the centre of political debate and served as an important weapon in the Conservative arsenal. Key aspects of feminized imagery included placing political situations in domestic environments, the presentation of women both as political symbols and political actors and the portrayal of issues Conservatives considered to be of importance to women. An interesting omission from the feminized images used by Conservatives and the Primrose League was Britannia, the ancient female symbol of Britain. This image only rarely appeared in Conservative literature.[11] She was slightly more frequently used by the Primrose League but often in a non-political fashion to symbolize the Empire.[12] Britannia appeared only once each in directly political contexts, such as a single anti-free trade image and in praise of the Borden government's offer to help fund dreadnought construction.[13]

The issues Conservatives believed women were most interested in usually centred around food, home and the family. Images of women threatened by political opponents and their ideology played a ready role in popular propaganda. The image of the home is particularly important as it is contested terrain. Women's historians have portrayed it at the heart of ideas of separate spheres for men and women. Radical women's historians have understood the home as 'a site of oppression, gender struggle and/or the privatized reproduction of the labour power required to fuel capitalism'.[14] However, the idea of home is both historically and socially constructed and is a 'profoundly resonant metaphor for psychic needs'.[15] Examining the force of such ideas and images can lead to a new understanding of the dynamic of women and British politics. Conservatives learned at their peril the political impact of food and domestic issues in their defeats in the 1906 and 1923 general elections. Back in office in 1924, their new policies included the creation of an Empire Marketing Board that advertised imperial foodstuffs as well as pensions for widows.[16] This movement towards a more feminized type of politics was foreshadowed by the gradual eschewing of a more masculine-centred Tory populism from the late Victorian period onwards. Rather than defend 'historic male pleasures … in urban popular culture such as the pub and sport' from the interventions of Liberal do-gooders, the Conservative Party moved towards a more domestic-centred politics.[17] It is crucial to remember that the transition within the Conservative Party to the more feminized and domesticated values represented by the post-war leader Stanley Baldwin had its roots in the Edwardian period.[18]

It is also important to compare the use of feminized imagery by the mainstream forces of Conservatism before 1918 with the Edwardian radical Right and the British Fascists of the 1920s. Before 1914, there was widespread concern over the decline of Britain as a nation due to economic competition from Germany and the United States as well as the inept British performance in the Boer War. The Edwardian period has been described as the 'age of leagues'.[19] Before 1914, Britain was beset by a variety of radical Right groups claiming to have a solution to Britain's problems. Radical Right organizations generally rejected a number of the long-held traditions of British political culture, including belief in parliamentary democracy, advocacy of a small professional voluntary army and adherence to free trade. Some organizations such as the National Service League, founded in 1902, and the Navy League, founded in 1895, looked to military solutions to Britain's problems. Some were purely obstructionist like the Anti-Socialist Union founded in 1908. Others, like the Tariff Reform League, founded in 1903, looked to economic means for Britain's salvation such as the abandonment of free trade. Finally, other groups such as the British Brothers' League catered to anti-alienism and opposed immigration. One characteristic common to most of these groups was their strongly masculinist bent. Most had an almost exclusively male leadership and put women in purely secondary roles. Even more importantly, their imagery, arguments and rhetoric were strongly masculine. Groups like the National Service League were perhaps the most masculinist with a focus on military training for men above all.[20] Of all the groups, the Tariff Reformers paid the most attention to feminized imagery and had their own separate organization for women (called the Women's Unionist and Tariff Reform Association founded in 1906).[21] However, none of these groups was as notable in their use of feminized imagery as the Conservatives and the Primrose League. As Richard Thurlow has argued that the Edwardian radical Right was a key foundation for the inter-war fascist movement in Britain, this shortcoming is significant.[22]

The British Fascists of the 1920s forms a curious paradox in the study of political organizations using feminized imagery. It was the most important fascist organization in Britain in the immediate post-war period and had some echoes with the Conservatives and Primrose League. Founded by a woman (Rotha Lintorn-Orman), eager to promote women in its organization and even having female paramilitary units, it nevertheless remained a fringe movement and was later superseded by the British Union of Fascists (BUF) in the 1930s. The British Fascists may have used the Primrose League as an organizational model. Like the League, the British Fascists had a grand council, children's clubs and a strong focus on social activities. It differed from later British fascist organizations because it seemed to embrace 'traditional ideas of gendered behaviour for women' combined with 'a high degree of female activism and propaganda directed at women'.[23] Rotha Lintorn-Orman believed in the 'regimentation of femininity'; she thought women should place their own interests behind those of the nation. Consequently, she had no real interest in issues of female emancipation. However, her thinking was not completely fascist either. Gottlieb has argued that the British Fascists did not meet the definition of the 'fascist minimum'.[24] Despite its grandiose claims, the British Fascists lived on the farthest edge of the political fringe. Compared to the Conservative Party, Primrose League and the BUF, the British Fascists were an organization whose impact on British society and political life has been described as 'marginal'.[25] Their negligible political presence meant that their overall influence in promoting feminized imagery was minimal.

With the power of feminized images in mind, it is none too surprising that the Primrose League as well as the Conservative Party appropriated them. The League eagerly mixed such images with views of threats posed by a host of perceived malignant enemies. Peaceful British domesticity was continually vulnerable. Irish nationalism, Liberal reformism, socialism and free trade formed a formidable group of enemies who threatened the sanctity of the British household.

Conservatives had long demonized Irish nationalists and had aggressively opposed William Gladstone's efforts at disestablishment, land reform and ultimately Home Rule. When the Liberal government of H. H. Asquith began to put forward its Home Rule legislation from 1912 onwards, the Conservatives reacted vehemently. After the Parliament Act of 1911 prevented the House of Lords from killing Home Rule, Conservative behaviour became increasingly desperate. The new Conservative leader Andrew Bonar Law seemed ready to advocate armed resistance against the British government to prevent Home Rule from becoming law.[26]

It is in this context that one must examine the Primrose League's initiative to evacuate Ulster women and children and the use of feminized images by the Conservatives and Primrose League to portray the Ulster crisis. This episode is important as it mobilized female and male supporters into political action with a strong use of feminized political imagery. As an organization pledged to the maintenance of the Empire, the Primrose League had long opposed Home Rule and any concessions to Irish nationalists.[27] As Home Rule legislation became increasingly possible, the League ended its policy of formal independence from the Conservative Party. In 1913, it amended its declaration and tied membership in the League directly to support of the Unionist cause.[28] After a mass meeting of the Primrose League in Nottingham in December 1913, a 'Help the Ulster Women' Committee was formed. This organization was a joint effort of the Primrose League and the Women's Unionist Association.[29] The scheme was to provide 'shelter to the women and children of the Ulster Loyalists in the event of the Home Rule bill becoming law, and of the civil war resulting'.[30]

By the end of 1914, Home Rule legislation was passed through the Commons but remained suspended for the duration of the First World War. This meant that the League's scheme was never put into effect. However, there are several important aspects of the scheme to consider. To begin with, the League took it seriously. By August 1914, the League had secured promises of accommodation for over 8,000 Ulster women and children as well as donations of £17,000.[31] In addition, there were plans for the reception of refugees, hospitality, communications and clothing.[32] The reception of the refugees showed the importance of female domesticity and linked it to hospitality, household comforts and safety.

An additional aspect of the scheme worth noting is the fact that the Irish Unionist women themselves did not always fit the gendered stereotype that had been created for them. At the climax of the Ulster crisis between 1913–14, Ulster women were portrayed as victims of the Liberal government's plans for Home Rule. A number of popular pamphlets issued by the Conservative Party showed Ulster as a solitary young woman wrapped in a Union Jack and threatened by an ominous mob of men.[33] One pamphlet starkly pointed out that political support for Home Rule and the implied military coercion of Ulster would mean widowhood for vast numbers of women in Northern Ireland.[34] For the Primrose League and the British Conservative Party, feminized imagery centred on female victimhood and threats to domesticity seemed most appropriate. For the Ulster women and their organizations such as the Ulster Women's Unionist Council, such imagery was overtly passive. Ulster women were preparing to stay in northern Ireland to work in ambulance and nursing corps, to maintain postal and electronic communications and as medical auxiliaries. If they were to leave Ulster, it was to speak, canvass and distribute literature for the Unionist cause in Britain itself, not to fly as refugees.[35]

A final part of the scheme to consider is its importance as a precedent for wartime work by the women of the Primrose League. During the final preparations for the Ulster refugee scheme, it was mentioned that many of those involved had done similar work during the South African war.[36] When Britain became involved in the First World War, the League turned itself over quickly to wartime philanthropic efforts including hospitality for Belgian refugees.[37] This continued the pattern of female mobilization against a threatening 'other' that had first been represented by the Irish nationalists. Such war work was symbolic of the general movement of Conservatives towards a feminized and domestically centred version of British politics.[38] This work helped keep the Primrose League organizationally active during the wartime political truce between the major parties.

This activity proved vitally important and helped ensure the League's survival into the post-war period.

In addition to opposing moves on Ulster prior to 1918, the Conservative Party and the Primrose League denounced reformism, socialism and, as always, feminized imagery played an important part in these denunciations. Specific Liberal reforms such as National Insurance were targeted, as was the general Liberal ideological commitment to free trade. In addition, a sustained attack was made on the nefarious effects of socialism on family life well before the Russian revolution of 1917 had made such condemnations commonplace.

Conservative propaganda often portrayed the negative impact of specific Liberal reforms and free trade policy on women. The National Insurance Act, a key Liberal innovation that provided contributory provision against illness and unemployment, was criticized with reference to its negative impact on female servants.[39] In feminizing this issue, a cross-class perspective was adopted. Pamphlets from 1911 were directed at both middle-class housewives with servants as well as working-class mothers with daughters in service.[40]

While specific Liberal reforms generated the predictable level of Conservative opposition, the more general Liberal commitment to free trade aroused the fiercest response. The Conservative Party was being torn apart from before the General Election of 1906 by those advocating tariff reform led by the crusading Joseph Chamberlain. While much ink was used to explain the economic superiority of tariff reform over free trade, an effort was also made to show free trade's destructive impact on families and women. E. H. H. Green has shown that tariff reform promised to defend British industry, increase domestic employment, fund social reform and strengthen imperial links.[41] When Joseph Chamberlain first launched his campaign for tariff reform in October 1903 he argued that tariff reform would help the working class keep their jobs and maintain their living standards in the face of foreign competition.[42] Conservative pamphlets amplified this theme by using feminized imagery to show that free trade led to unemployment and domestic suffering. 'The Child's Appeal' of 1910 showed a small child with her working-class father imploring the reader not to 'tax the land that grows the children's bread but tax the foreigner who takes dad's work instead'.[43] A 1908 pamphlet entitled 'Dearer Living and Less Comfort' juxtaposed a British family who sat freezing by an empty fire with a contented fat German and his daughter who sat by a toasty fire and complimented Mr Asquith for allowing them to buy cheap untaxed coal.[44]

One of the major arguments used by the Liberals against tariff reform was that abandoning free trade would increase the cost of living because of food taxes. Conservatives were livid at such attacks. The issue of food taxes was rebutted in Conservative pamphlets using the threat posed to the price of bread (in the guise of the 'Dear Loaf') as an example and showing its negative impact on women. House-wives loomed as important political figures in such propaganda in spite of not possessing a formal vote. One pamphlet from 1910 asked male voters to 'Ask your wife' whether the Liberal commitment to free trade had actually resulted in cheaper bread and provisions.[45] Another pamphlet from the same year directly told housewives that the actual impact of tariff reform on the cost of bread would be mini-mal or non-existent.[46] Conservative housewives were encouraged to confront intrusive Liberal canvassers by pointing out that the price of bread under a Liberal government was now higher than ever. A pam-phlet showing a housewife's fiery rejection of Liberal political entreaties while standing in her kitchen wearing an apron shows a simultaneous commitment to traditional feminine values and Con-servative economics.[47]

It is important to note that the Primrose League, with its less sophisticated ideological framework, did not present such stark images over tariff reform. The Primrose League felt threatened by more radical Conservative organizations such as the Tariff Reform League (and especially its women's organization) and wished to avoid being so divisive. The League was officially neutral on the issue.[48] Nevertheless, some leading members on the Grand Council were active tariff reformers and local workers often lent their efforts to the Conservative tariff reform organizations.[49] With such divisions over the issue, it is unsurprising that the Primrose League's use of dramatic feminized imagery over tariff reform was much rarer than that of the Conservative Party. In all the issues of the *Primrose League Gazette*, only two feminized images were used on tariff reform and one was used to illustrate the need for more effective political cartoons.[50]

The Conservatives' use of feminized imagery against specific Lib-eral reform initiatives as well as free trade is interesting for a variety of reasons. First, it shows that although women did not have the vote, their influence was considered important enough to have specific messages and images directed at them. Such an understanding was explicitly spelled out in the 1912 Conservative Party guide for party workers entitled *Party Notes*. As the guide noted: 'wives are some-times very useful allies; by all means endeavour to enlist their support in their husband's absence.' It did caution, however, the need to 'make a point of seeing him as well'.[51] This advice and the general desire to direct political messages at women and use their talents in canvassing echoes the Primrose League's entire *raison d'être*. The use of feminized imagery also suited their purposes well. Second, it shows a defensive mindset in Conservative propaganda against Liberal reforms. Liberal reforms were criticized for interfering in British households where women held sway. Arguments over the validity of these reforms or their cost to the nation were glossed over in this analysis. Finally, this type of Conservative propaganda argued that Liberal promises to lower the cost of living were empty and that free trade ideology had a destructive impact on women's lives. The struggle to oppose free trade was all consuming for the Conservative Party after 1906. Large numbers of British people believed in free trade dogma with almost religious fervour.[52] The Conservatives produced a great number of economic studies attacking free trade but rational arguments could only go so far against such a deeply held belief. Pamphlet literature often used feminized imagery to reach the same level of emotion roused by Liberal free traders.

Specific Liberal reforms and the general commitment to free trade generated significant Conservative opposition but so did less tangible opponents such as socialism. Although socialism was not a major political force in Britain before 1914, Conservatives recognized it as such. In fact, socialism was never clearly defined in Conservative propaganda. It was presented as an ideology that was an absolute rejection of the political, religious and social status quo. The Primrose League 'believed that it had a special mission to defend the family, especially the working-class family from the demoralizing doctrines of atheistic Radicals and Socialists'.[53] In its more sensationalist form, the League equated socialism with free love and the nationalization of women and children. Unlike other more extremist extra-parliamentary groups such as the Anti-Socialist Union, the Primrose League put the defence of a sentimental view of marriage ahead of property rights in its battle against socialism. For example, an article in the *Primrose League Gazette* of 1908 asked how the socialist state would nurse the babies, wash the children and 'wheel the perambulator'.[54] In a similar light, one cartoon showed Keir Hardie, the first Labour MP, ineptly fulfilling his duties as the Chief State Nurse at the Interior of the State Nurseries.[55] In its popular pamphlet literature, the Conservative Party was even more aggressive in portraying socialism's impact on the family. In 1907, two pamphlets misquoted a number of leading socialist thinkers, including H. G. Wells and William Morris, to show that socialism would substitute the state for the traditional family. Other pamphlets before the First World War put forward the image of the state regulating all aspects of family and personal life, including the choice of marriage partner, living quarters and child-rearing methods. To make matters worse, socialism would lead to meal preparation in central kitchens and the end of all religious instruction.[56]

Overall, the use of feminized imagery for the cause of anti-socialism did not always have the desired impact before the First World War. This was due to the generally weak nature of British socialism at the time as well as the lack of finesse in painting socialism

and Liberal collectivism with the same brush. Furthermore, this technique was of limited effectiveness because 'large sections of the
Conservative Party, including groups such as the Primrose League,
acknowledged the necessity for social reform'.[57] The strongest use of
anti-socialism linked to feminized political imagery would come after
the Bolshevik Revolution in 1917.[58] With the first instalment of
women's enfranchisement in 1918, the Primrose League suffered competition among Conservative organizations as women could join the
Unionist Party directly. Consequently, the League's membership suffered a considerable decline.[59] The League hoped to distinguish itself
as an anti-socialist platform that paid special attention to women voters. As well as sponsoring speaker's classes for women and continuing
canvassing, the League embraced feminized imagery with a vengeance.[60] Women in the fascist movement denounced the Primrose
Leaguers as quaint and unsuited for modern politics. However, it was
partly due to the League's efforts that the Conservative Party would
garner the lion's share of female support after 1918.[61]

A final area of feminized imagery to discuss is its use as a form of
political satire by the Conservative Party and the Primrose League.
Faced with strong reform-minded opponents after the Liberal land-
slide of 1906, the Conservatives and the Primrose League responded
by portraying their opponents unflatteringly dressed in women's
clothing or overwhelmed by family situations. The humour was combined with sharp political criticism and formed a continuum with the
BUF's later condemnation of the unmasculine aspects of parliamentary politics. One key point to remember was that the feminized
images used by the Conservatives and Primrose League were always
directed towards a single party and not the system at large.

The feminization of political figures was not invented by the
Conservatives nor was it a twentieth-century phenomenon.[62] Nevertheless, there was an explosion of these images during the politically-
fraught Edwardian period. From 1900 to 1918, the Conservatives
made use of satirical feminized imagery in two main ways. First,
before the election of 1906, Conservative pamphlets often portrayed
Henry Campbell-Bannerman as a hapless mother or nanny and his
Liberal colleagues as squabbling children. Second, after the election
and the retirement of Campbell-Bannerman, feminized imagery
showed leading Liberals such as the new Prime Minister, Herbert
Asquith, and his Chancellor of the Exchequer, David Lloyd George, as
flighty women or domestics. In addition, the Primrose League made a
special effort to place John Redmond, the Irish Nationalist leader, as
well as Lloyd George, in feminine clothing.

The satires of Campbell-Bannerman rejoiced in portraying Liberal
divisions in a family setting or the Liberal leader as a befuddled
domestic servant. Pamphlets in this vein were ironically titled 'The

Happy Radical Family' or 'A Happy Family'.[63] The latter was particularly evocative, with Campbell-Bannerman presented as a matronly mother resting uncomfortably in the family bed with rambunctious children marked 'Alien', 'Little England', 'Sectarian education' and 'Small army and navy' pulling away at her sheets. Other images included Campbell-Bannerman as a matronly servant or housewife unsuccessfully attempting to serve a sceptical John Bull a helping of 'Radical Pudding'.[64]

After the Liberals had won the election of 1906 and were proceeding with their various reforms, feminized imagery continued. David Lloyd George was the leading spokesman for many of the Liberal reforms and the Chancellor of the Exchequer from 1908 onwards. He seemed to get the most attention in Conservative propaganda. In 1908, Lloyd George was shown as Old Mother Hubbard upsetting a cupboard marked the 'Exchequer' and breaking a number of stored bottles with the words 'budget surplus' marked on them.[65] In another image entitled 'John Bull's Kitchen' there are too many disaster-prone Liberal cooks, including 'Georgina Lloyd'.[66]

The Primrose League generally followed the lead of the Conservatives in their use of feminized imagery, although they reserved special venom for John Redmond. The Primrose League reproduced fifteen feminized images between 1906 and 1914 mocking their opponents. Following the Conservative Party, the majority of these images were employed against the Liberals with Asquith and Lloyd George singled out for special attention. Once again, Lloyd George appeared as an incompetent female domestic and flighty housewife as well as holding a new role as a churlish nurse.[67] Asquith appeared as an old lady named Dame Asquith.[68] Other feminized Asquith identities included Asquith as housekeeper admonishing the clumsy maid 'Georgina Lloyd' and Asquith as a lady with a huge hatpin labelled 'coercion of Ulster'.[69] The most creative anti-Liberal image employed is a 1908 image entitled 'The Dress Exhibition' which had the leading Liberal ministers in drag with their dress types described in terms to echo their failings as politicians.[70] These satirical representations of leading Liberals follow a similar pattern to the Conservative pamphlets. However, an important difference for the Primrose League images is that John Redmond also figured prominently.

One-third of all the images in the *Primrose League Gazette* include Redmond. It is significant that all of the Redmond images appeared after the January 1910 election gave the Irish Nationalist Party unprecedented power to keep the Liberal government in office. This fact, combined with the Parliament Act of 1911, made Home Rule almost inevitable despite Conservative opposition. Redmond was thus shown as a governess restraining a baby Asquith, a matronly dance partner forced upon a reluctant Asquith, a housewife threatening a henpecked Asquith hiding under his bed, an overweight lady in a boat being rowed by a straining Asquith and a nurse forcing a crying child-Asquith into his bath of 'Home Rule'.[71] The image here was of the unnaturalness of Home Rule that was being imposed on reluctant Liberals by the Irish Nationalists. The fact that Redmond was shown as female was a way of undermining the legitimacy of Irish aspirations.

There are some important points about the use of satirical feminized imagery by the Conservatives and the Primrose League. First, it reveals the English cultural bemusement at cross-dressing. The origins of this phenomenon are unclear, though it has certainly remained constant in twentieth-century British popular culture up to and including the comedy of Monty Python and Benny Hill.[72] Second, it highlights the lack of control that the Liberal leadership held over its more divisive party members. It also implies that firm leadership is male. In contrast, the Liberals were led by kindly matrons unable to control unruly children. In combining these ideas, Conservative propaganda showed Liberal unsuitability for office by feminizing Liberals in a mocking manner. This pattern would continue after 1918. David Jarvis has noted the Conservative Central Office 'often satirized Labour leaders, and particularly Ramsay MacDonald, as a female figure – unattractive, shameless and with a difficult brood of children'.[73] Third, the satirical imagery is an effort not to belittle the entire political system but only one party. There are male figures of reason still present in the images, such as John Bull, who usually look on in horror or bemusement. Unlike the fascists, the entire political system was not condemned.

The timing of the pamphlets is also crucial. The Edwardian period was one in which the suffragette movement undertook a powerful and often violent campaign to win female suffrage. The Primrose League occasionally felt it necessary to address the female suffrage issue, although in its editorials it remained steadfastly neutral. It claimed that League members could attend meetings on either side of the issue as long as they did not compromise the chances of any Unionist candidates.[74] Leading female members both supported and opposed the struggle for the vote.[75] The Conservative Party's pamphlet literature also did not portray female suffrage very often. One slight exception is a pamphlet entitled 'Female Suffrage' which focused on Asquith's own inconsistency over the issue rather than the merits of the suffrage cause itself. In this image a unambiguously masculine-looking Asquith is confronted by a sexless spinster who represents the suffrage cause.[76] The use of a spinster figure to symbolize suffrage is important. Lisa Tickner has argued that the suffragette spinster was a key type often utilized by the anti-suffrage movement in addition to other 'unwomanly' figures such as hysterical women and the 'shrieking sisterhood'.[77] Despite the overlap with established anti-suffrage images, the Conservatives did not use these images frequently. As the suffragette campaign became increasingly militant, the satirical feminized imagery became rarer. With women activists using their femininity in a threatening manner, the feminization of opponents could no longer be used as shorthand for the weakness of political opponents.

One important question to conclude with is to ask why female Primrose Leaguers and Conservatives seemed to accept the use of feminized imagery as a form of mockery. Though Conservative feminized imagery often showed women in noble poses, when it satirized political opponents the feminine was used as a source of humour. This fact reveals several things. First, most of the images used were by male artists.[78] Second, it shows that despite the important female presence on the Primrose League, true power lay elsewhere. The main leadership of the Primrose League and the Conservatives was always male and this male power structure led to a political culture willing to use feminized imagery but only in terms suitable to the leadership. Third, it reveals that Conservative women and female members of the Primrose League clearly embraced a gendered political culture that privileged male political domination. Feminized political imagery for Conservatives and Primrose Leaguers never meant feminist political imagery.

The use of feminized imagery before 1918 was useful for a number of reasons. First, it enabled the League and the Conservatives to put on a social conscience, even if for partisan political purposes. The Ulster refugee scheme masked much less benign partisan objectives based on political self-interest. Feminized imagery was useful before 1918 when women would work for Conservative ends in an auxiliary role or after 1918 when they could vote directly. This ability paid particular dividends when the League faced competition from other Conservative rivals for membership. In fact, it might be argued that the use of such imagery helped give the Primrose League a new role in the age of mass democracy after 1918. A final advantage of feminized imagery was to tie Conservatism to the central notion of Englishness through the image of the household. By taking a seemingly immutable image, such as the British family, and presenting the Conservative Party as its protector against political and foreign threats, Conservatism became conceptualized as permanent, natural and necessary. Rather than being one ideology among many to choose from, Conservatism was raised to a more prominent and less politically vulnerable status and equated with the English love of the home.

After 1918, women could vote and feminized political imagery could be directly assessed by female voters. After 1918, the BUF and other fascist groups competed for female support with the

Conservative Party. Although the Conservatives were more fearful of losing male supporters to the BUF than women, the BUF did make some noted gains amongst activists if not the overall electorate.[79] As Julie Gottlieb has noted, British fascism 'attracted women with radically conservative beliefs who sought to play more militant and proactive roles than those offered by the Conservative Associations'.[80] The types of feminized imagery that the Conservatives and Primrose League used after 1918 differed from that of the pre-war period. However, the pre-war gendered imagery used by Conservatives resembled much more closely its post-war counterpart than the aggressive hypermasculine discourse of the fascists. While the wartime experience may have prompted fascists to reject the feminized imagery of old, it may have reinforced Conservative preferences for it. The vast difference between the political cultures of the fascists and Conservatives in the inter-war period was foreshadowed by the pre-war movement to feminine gendered images.

Reactionary Spectatorship:
British Fascists and Cinema in Inter-War Britain

Thomas P. Linehan

In language saturated by nostalgia and anti-Semitism and replete with images of combat and foreign invaders, A. K. Chesterton, a senior figure in the British Union of Fascists (BUF), declared that: 'The cinema was captured by American and Polish Jew financiers and made to contribute to the general demoralisation of the people. It either neglected or befouled the English scene, so full of pageantry and memories of colourful adventure and daring, to superimpose a bastardised Judaic-American pseudo-culture upon a nation with a superb cultural inheritance of its own.'[1] Chesterton's prognosis of the state of the nation's cinema between the wars was one of a number of similar negative representations in the discourse of the far Right.[2] Fascist writers represented the contemporary cinema, negatively, in a number of ways: as an agent of threatening Americanization, as an intellectually barren mass cultural form, as a dangerous site of seduction, as emblematic of encroaching decadence, or as a vehicle which propagated immorality. Cinema figured in this negative discourse, similarly, as a symptom of soulless modernity, as an instrument for the promotion of so-called 'international' Jewish propaganda, or as a forum which presented a bastardized view of the nation's past and imperial heritage. There was another narrative in play, however, which expressed a less critical view of cinema and its role in British society. Britain's far Right fringe imagined a time when American and other so-called 'alien' influences would be exorcized from the nation's cinema, when British cinema would be refashioned to serve the fascists' revolutionary goal of national 'rebirth'. Cinema in service to the fascist revolution would play a different role in society, disseminate a different set of film messages and images, and draw on alternative themes to those circulating in the era of so-called 'Financial Democracy'.

The notion of cinema as agent of an encroaching America figured prominently in far Right film discourse. Fascists disliked the fact that American distribution companies and American films dominated the nation's cinema. In 1926, for example, British films accounted for a paltry five per cent of all movies shown in British cinemas.[3] Despite the passing of the 1927 Cinematograph Films Act, obliging an exhibi- tor to show a proportion of home-grown films, the bulk of movies showing in British cinemas during the late 1920s and 1930s continued to be American.[4] Many native fascists feared the cultural fall-out from the Hollywood motion picture and imagined the piecemeal Ameri- canization of British culture. They deplored the American movie, its thematic content, its perceived ideological message and its signifi- cance for the national culture, British identity and even the native English language. A BUF member complained about those British who 'adopt the strange half-English idioms of the Jew-inspired Amer- ican films', while A. K. Chesterton remarked that Samuel Goldwyn was 'symbolically Lord of the English scene'.[5] Chesterton went on to berate the Britons who spurn Shakespeare yet 'swallow the soporifics of the culture dope-pedlers [sic] or welcome the degrading aphrodisi- acs which they sell'.[6] Another Mosleyite remarked on the glut of American films showing in British cinemas, 'which are no encourage- ment to national pride'.[7] 'Metro-Goldwyn' film products, complained another follower of Mosley, where British men and women were 'being taught to sentimentalize over foreign dope that is totally unlike the life we live', had displaced the 'whole-hearted entertainment of English plays and variety'.[8]

American film images were cast in roles other than that of foreign invader or alien presence. At other times, the Hollywood movie was reviled as a key prop of the mass culture industry, its quintessential expression. Ironically, in a perspective that echoed elements of Adorno's and Horkheimer's mass manipulation theory of the 'culture industry', many on the far Right saw popular cinema as a form of cul- tural debasement and a weapon of mass deception.[9] Undoubtedly, the bulk of contemporary films were consciously designed as mass con- sumer products rather than works of art, 'artifacts for instant consumption and discard' which took their cue from the mass public's seemingly insatiable demand for escapist recreation.[10] In inter-war Britain, cinema, with American products in the forefront, was the pre- dominant form of mass entertainment. By 1938 there were 4,800 cinemas in Britain, boasting an overall seating capacity of four and a- quarter million, catering for this mass audience.[11] In that year alone, 1938, an estimated 987 million cinema tickets were purchased by eager cinema fans. This represented twenty-five times the number of tickets bought by soccer supporters during the same year.[12] A Gallup poll in January 1938 revealed that forty-seven per cent of the popula- tion attended the cinema every week or ten days.[13] Cinema was a cheap and affordable form of entertainment, a cinema ticket costing just 6d., or the equivalent of the price of a pint of beer by the mid-

1930s.[14] The private sphere of the cinema offered plush wall-to-wall comfort, relaxation, temporary pleasurable diversions, a space to dream and an opportunity to engage in narcissistic identification. Films are a voyeuristic exercise where spectators are allowed to comprehend events from a safe position of separation and of mastery.[15] Movies also playfully provoke anxiety but, again, it is an anxiety that is experienced in safety. In general, films are a spectator's unlived life, offering a vicarious experience freed from the peril of consequences.[16]

Fascists, as with other cultural elitists of this ilk writing in Britain between the wars, such as Clive Bell, T. S. Eliot, F. R. Leavis, John Cowper Powys and Aldous Huxley, expressed disquiet about the onset of an apparently all-consuming 'philistine' mass culture. Powerful trends in modern life, which included technological change, the mass democratic suffrage, a mass-based popular press, and increased leisure time and disposable income, were bringing forth a 'mass society' and this supposedly philistine mass populace, the eager consumers of the new mass culture. The charges levelled against mass culture by the elitist self-appointed guardians of the nation's cultural heritage were damning. A mass cultural form like the Hollywood movie, for example, supposedly pandered to the cheap, unthinking emotional response and lowered and homogenized taste. It was also accused of producing standardized mass thoughts and immobilizing minds. 'Uniform mass man' was the outcome, living a standardized mass existence and languishing in a drugged state of mental stupor, the 'unvarying Deltas and uniform Epsilons' of Aldous Huxley's *Brave New World* (1932).[17] Britain's fascists expressed similar views. 'We live in an age of standardisation, not only of things but of ideas and recreations', complained John Frederick Charles Fuller, writing in 1932 just prior to his joining the BUF, adding that the 'film buffoon and heroine are standardised performers'.[18] To its detractors, mass society was an intellectually and spiritually barren cultural desert that signalled the death of authentic self-hood, a bleak place which stifled all noble thought, inspiration and creativity. Britain's fascists, in particular, believed that mass culture lacked a heroic base, and was thus the antithesis of 'true' culture as they defined it. The pursuit of ignoble ends is often concealed by high-sounding rhetoric and this is particularly so with regard to fascist rhetoric on culture. Authentic culture, according to the fascist mind, should be expressive of humankind's aspiration to achieve 'noble' aims in the struggle that is life. The goal of art and culture, in other words, was to inspire and elevate the human soul. Culture should affirm supposedly eternal verities, too, truths which were thought to be universal and in tune with life's higher aspirations.

In the fascists' opinion, such elevated themes were simply not in evidence in mass cultural products and consequently in the bulk of popular films consumed by British spectators between the wars. The offerings of the escapist 'dream palaces' of the Hollywood-dominated mass culture industry, the wearisome round of trite love stories and sensationalistic melodramas, lacked the ability to inspire and uplift the human spirit. One BUF member referred to the prevalence of 'idiot films' on show in Britain's cinemas, while a columnist writing for the far Right journal the *New Pioneer* in 1939 complained about 'all the slush imported into our cinemas from Hollywood' during that year.[19] In a similar vein, a BUF film reviewer considered the standard Hollywood plot to be 'incredibly naïve'. Reviewing two Hollywood adventure yarns, he found the usual stock of 'tough cowboys and bouncing young women, hold-ups and bank robberies' and 'marches through trackless forests, where pools are so crowded with alligators that the intrepid marchers walk over their backs to the other side'.[20] The American motion picture industry, to its fascist detractors, debased culture by simplifying reality in this manner. The celluloid images disseminated by the Hollywood 'dream factory' were perceived to be hollow, bogus and duplicitous, symptomatic of the artificial, synthetic culture that was part of an increasingly 'Americanized' post-war England. In the elaborate prose of one Mosleyite, Hollywood was all 'tinsel artifice and meretricious sentiment'.[21]

'Mass manipulation' outlook fascists believed that post-war Britain's inhabitants were turning their backs on reality and political participation by succumbing to a cinematic escapist world of make-believe and synthetic pleasures. A. K. Chesterton wondered about the Briton who worships 'at the shrine of his favourite shadows of the screen' and mass culture's 'strange preoccupation with unreal things'.[22] Youth, the so-called 'Bright Young Things', were thought to be particularly prone to falling under the spell of cinema's overpowering illusions. James Rudd of the BUF feared that a large segment of Britain's post-war youth generation was caught in the grip of hedonism and had an 'incessant desire to get away from the facts of life'.[23] The young 'pursue pleasure and cease to exist in the outside world', he complained. What particularly concerned Rudd was that 'in their pursuit of pleasure they subject themselves utterly to the influence of the cinema' which, for him, was wholly objectionable. Another Blackshirt, Michael Goulding, attacked those of Britain's youth who, by frequenting the cinema, sought 'adventure by artificial means'.[24] Such sentiments strike one as ironic, of course, given that fascism, too, traded on illusions and the 'imaginary', as we shall discuss below.

To the fascists, the eager consumption of the cinematic mass product by 'Britons', and particularly the nation's youth, was a sure sign of encroaching decadence. The inter-war fascist imagination was characterized by a fear of impending national disintegration, and it was decadence that was assumed to be the harbinger of this decline. To the pessimistic fascist mind, decadence was a spiritual and moral blight that stifled the regenerative urge. The regenerative urge was imagined as a sort of enigmatic Bergsonian inner spiritual 'life force' that, if assiduously cultivated within the national psyche, would ensure the nation's survival and allow it to pass to a higher state of evolution. The cultural stakes were thus very high indeed for Britain's fascists. Fascism had a mission and it was to regenerate youth, a task upon which 'may well depend the moral and physical culture of our race' declared James Rudd.[25] Evidently, Mosleyite fascism had set its face against the destiny of the decline of Europe's 'Faustian' culture prophesied by Oswald Spengler in *The Decline of the West* (1918, 1922), a pessimistic and fatalistic tome which had exerted much influence on the BUF's imagination. In proclaiming that fascism would beget the rebirth of Faustian Europe and its transition to a higher plane of existence, however, the BUF recognized that the struggle would be long and hard. Mosley and his followers were aware, too, that the terrain of aesthetic culture, including film aesthetics, would be the site on which many of the key battles against the scourge of domestic decadence would be fought.

Britain's fascists were convinced that great nations and empires passed away as a result of domestic decadence. A British Fascisti member, writing in 1926, claimed that it was the destructive power of internal 'immoralities' which brought Rome, Egypt, Carthage and Greece to heel, rather than the power of external foes.[26] The onset of 'immorality' terrified the fascists, and to many of them the cinema was heavily implicated in spawning it. Films, declared a Mosley follower, which, along with theatre and novels, 'pervert and distract' Britain's youth with their 'sordid entertainments', are 'now used to destroy our moral conception of social order'.[27] The contemporary cinema, therefore, would provide some British fascists with an anti-phenomenon to juxtapose with their own moral paradigm.

In the same vein, palingenetic fascists accused films of being excessively 'sex-conscious' which, for them, served to encourage the seemingly ever-increasing tendency towards sexually promiscuous behaviour and 'unnatural' vice in the wider society. Reviewing *The Gay King*, a historical period piece dealing with the *Risorgimento* produced in Mussolini's Fascist Italy, a BUF writer thought it a 'great relief' from the 'fantastic and erotic thing usually offered from Hollywood'.[28] The senior BUF official Robert Gordon-Canning, also, was disapproving of Hollywood films, which too often 'appeal to the cruder sex emotion of the audience' and whose narrative content contained barely concealed ideas 'bordering on the pornographic'.[29] This imagined link between many of the offerings of contemporary cinema and apparently unrestrained sexual indulgence within the wider society mirrored a deeper anxiety of course: the fascist fear of sexuality-out-of-control.

The cinema ignited another fear. Apparently movies glorified, and rendered heroic, those thought of as society's permissive, delinquent, darker and marginal characters. A BUF member wrote of 'the gross glorification of thieves, murderers, adulterers, swindlers, and prostitutes, which are frequently the themes of films'.[30] It was a characteristic thought to be most apparent in the incoming American films. A fascist writing under the pseudonym 'Junius' saw American films as 'lauding of just those spectacles of barbarity to which the falling Roman Empire was a constant witness in the arena of the Colosseum. Horrific pictures, animal fights, torture, gang fights, swindling and gladiatorial combats displayed between one low criminal and another'.[31] The American gangster film became the principal focus of this anxiety. To its far Right critics, the gangster film stylized gangsterdom and glamorized crime. Fascist reactions to the gangster film are partly linked to far Right sensibilities concerning authority, order and discipline. The American gangster flouted authority and displayed a casual irreverence for the rule of law. Fascists feared the gangster melodrama's seditious message, its potential to shape audience disposition towards established authority, and its encoding of gangster as hero. Unwitting young male spectators in British cinemas were presented with 'an inversion of values, whereby the gangster, the killer, the man who challenges the authority of the state becomes the hero', observed James Rudd.[32] Fascists conflated gangster films with juvenile criminality. Motion pictures 'glorify the gangster and the gunmen, who, well armed, show their heroism in shooting the defenceless in the back', complained the Blackshirt Michael Goulding.[33] Youth 'has little chance in face of this insidious disruption' and is thus 'taught crime from the first time it sees a film', he continued.[34] The 1930s film gangster hero not only signified social menace and moral subversion to the fascists, he encoded highly individualistic principles of a type which they found repugnant. As a vulgarized 'Horatio Alger' type who craved easy riches and upward social mobility, the screen hoodlum was the embodiment of individual self-aggrandizement, a character who spurned the principle of obligation to the collective, an ideal which fascists believed was fundamental to the maintenance of a stable ordered polity.[35]

The American gangster genre may have disturbed fascist sensibilities in other ways, triggering a whole cluster of phobias in the fascist mind concerning the modern city. The city was cast in numerous negative roles by fascist writers in inter-war Britain. In a reactionary narrative informed by degenerationist, eugenic and Spenglerian ideas, the modern city or 'Megalopolis' featured as a place of formless criminal and sexual anarchy, as a centre of devitalized existence, as an agent of biological retrogression and physical and spiritual enfeeblement, and as 'daemonic stone-desert' which threatened the more 'authentic' rural way of life.[36] The 1930s urban gangster film has been read as a dark allegory for the menace of the modern city.[37] The screen gangster was at home in the heavy claustrophobic atmosphere of the city, a forbidding presence that moved menacingly through its shadowy mean streets. In the same vein, the 1930s urban gangster movie has been read as an allegory for America's deviation from a truer path back to the 'garden', conceived as pre-modern, artisanal and rural-pastoral rather than urban.[38] The screen gangster, who inhabited a violent and unrelentingly dark expressionistic urban environment that seemed to mirror his violent persona and dark soul, apparently signified this fall from grace and deviation from the path back to the garden.[39]

The theme of city as negative presence was not confined to American gangster movies during the 1930s. It featured in Frank Capra's screwball comedy masterpiece *Mr Deeds Goes to Town*, a 1936 Columbia production that starred Gary Cooper and Jean Arthur. Unlike the urban gangster hero, however, who was content to inhabit the modern city's dark spaces and was a symbol of its corruption and 'decadence', the hero of Capra's movie, Longfellow Deeds, was a small-town outsider who sought to redeem the city by bringing to it the values of the country.[40] Capra's film illustrated a moral lesson about big city greed, cynicism and corruption, the clash between metropolitan and rural values, and the capability of an incorruptible, honest individual to ultimately bring about a urban-rural reconciliation. Britain's fascists found Capra's message about the wise-guy corruption, hypocrisy, cynicism and greed of the big city and its clash with the incorruptible hero figure from outside much to their liking. One BUF reviewer described *Mr Deeds* as 'a picture of supreme merit' which was 'staggering in its truth and sanity'.[41] Breaching the urban-rural divide was not the only mode of narrative closure sought by comedies like *Mr Deeds Goes to Town*. Capra's ultimately upbeat comedies resolved to heal social-class tensions, a perennial fascist preoccupation, and to mend fractured gender relations though the latter was framed, narrowly, in terms of a reassertion of patriarchal privilege. These themes were certainly evident in Frank Capra's other contemporary screwball comedy classic, *It Happened One Night* (1934), which starred Claudette Colbert and Clark Gable, and may partly account for the BUF's reference to it as a 'delightful, well-balanced film'.[42] Of course, Capra's films served up aesthetic delights as well as social and moral messages. His witty, romantic, screwball films displayed an effervescence and verve that even Britain's fascists, ever suspicious of Hollywood's power of mass seduction, found difficult to resist. Henry Gibbs, one of the BUF's foremost movie critics, was evidently dazzled because, for him, Capra was 'one of the world's greatest directors'.[43]

If Capra's screwball comedies engendered pleasure in the fascist spectator, the same could not be said for many of the historical films shown to British audiences during the inter-war period. For the far Right, too many Hollywood and native films offered up parodies of the past, cinematic caricatures which not only vilified esteemed traditions and injured national pride but created permanent misconceptions in impressionable minds, the mass of British film-goers being 'usually deficient in all historical sense'.[44]

Although there were a few exceptions, as we shall see below, historical films were accused of maligning Britain's past and its imperial heritage. Far too many films 'purporting to show events in our national life', bemoaned Anne Cutmore of the BUF, 'show us a nation of crafty plotters, without honesty or charity'.[45] Similarly, claimed 'Junius', with whom we are already acquainted, the soldiers and sailors who 'fought with cutlasses' to win an empire for Britain were depicted in American features as 'bloody pirates' and Cecil Rhodes as 'building an Empire with a cheque book and murder'.[46] The 1936 Gaumont-British production, *Rhodes of Africa*, which sought to cast Rhodes as a stoical, compassionate imperial hero, did not go nearly far enough for 'Junius' who thought it an 'awful film'.[47] To 'Junius', Walter Huston as Rhodes looked 'like Ramsay MacDonald' rather than an imperial hero, while the film's director, Berthold Viertel, was 'an Austrian Communist'.[48] *Rhodes of Africa*, declared another disgruntled Blackshirt, 'will add nothing to the reputation of the great hero' of Africa, because the 'task of making a film to illustrate the building of empires is not compatible with the mentality of those who have more usually to present the tragedy of Jazz'.[49]

Historical features were charged with ridiculing cherished institutions, too, particularly that of monarchy. The 'so-called historical films' pouring out of Hollywood 'have for their motive the belittling of the Monarchy as an institution', complained the far Right proto-fascist journal, the *Patriot*, in 1926.[50] Citing a cluster of historical films that had monarchy as one of their principal themes, the *Patriot* proclaimed that 'every weak, mean, discreditable feature' of the monarch depicted therein 'is enlarged and emphasized'.[51] Villains of the piece included Universal's *The Hunchback of Notre Dame* (1923), the mid-1920s version of *Scaramouche*, a light-hearted swashbuckler set in revolutionary France, and *The Eagle* (1925), United Artist's period romp about Cossacks in pre-revolutionary Tsarist Russia, starring Rudolph Valentino. The implication of these representations of the past, Hollywood-style, and others like them, the *Patriot* continued, 'is purely anti-monarchical – that is, to depict the Crown as cruel, unjust, ridiculous, and obnoxious', an image that could easily be imprinted on impressionable minds.[52]

The BUF, a decade later, could be just as scathing about movie representations of monarchy. Reviewing the 1936 RKO historical costume drama, *Mary of Scotland*, the Mosleyite Anne Cutmore slammed this Americanized version of the national past where Elizabeth I, 'the greatest queen of our history is compared to her disadvantage with a trollop of little wit'.[53] In a similar vein, Robert Gordon-Canning lambasted two Alexander Korda productions, *The Private Life of Henry VIII* (1933) and *Catherine the Great* (1934), on the grounds that 'in not one of these has the greatness of monarchy been shown'.[54] Korda's depiction of monarchy in *The Private Life of Henry VIII*, in which Charles Laughton played Henry, evidently touched raw fascist nerves. Laughton's irreverent characterization of Henry, with its multiple signifiers of monarchial self-indulgence and courtly excess, sent fascist tempers soaring. Anne Cutmore was appalled by the film where 'one of our greatest kings is held up to ridicule as a glutton and a sot'.[55] Leigh Vaughan-Henry writing in the BUF press thought that Korda had reduced the Tudor king to 'an inflated "Sugar Daddy", philandering flatulently' in the manner of any 'regular guy' or 'moron'.[56] It was the parliamentarian demagogue, the 'mediocrity' and the 'levellers-down' who would draw comfort from such images, declared Vaughan-Henry, 'when history's outstanding figures are presented as sub-human pathological types, belchingly uncontrolled creatures of every low instinct'.[57]

If motion pictures like *The Private Life of Henry VIII* shamelessly fictionalized monarchy, other inter-war history film narratives supposedly trivialized the historical process. Revolutions, which the far Right took very seriously, were reduced by Hollywood film magnates to dewy-eyed romances complete with 'mysterious damsels, stucco palaces, and armed pasteboard soldiery'.[58] When Hollywood offered up more earnest treatments of revolutionary sagas, it promoted, for the *Patriot*, the unsavoury and potentially inflammatory notion that revolutions 'produce noble leaders'.[59] It was a theme clearly discernible, thought the *Patriot*, in D. W. Griffith's 1921 epic about the French Revolution, *Orphans of the Storm*, and MGM's 1926 version of *Ben Hur*.[60] *Orphans of the Storm* and *Ben Hur* also illustrated the equally unpalatable political lesson 'that empires are necessarily tyrannous'.[61] The encoding of revolutionaries as noble and empires as oppressive was particularly evident in the latter film. *Ben Hur*, with its images of 'brutal and oppressive Roman civil government' not only sought 'to slander the Roman Empire' but was 'a sermon against Imperialism, made in USA'.[62]

Ben Hur's greatest calumny, in the eyes of the *Patriot*, however, even more heinous than its anti-imperialist message, was its casting of a

Jew as hero. Inter-war fascists were forever indulging in extravagant rhetoric to camouflage fascism's dark and destructive character. Similarly, they were ever eager to present themselves, piously, as warriors embarking on a noble mission of cultural regeneration and rebirth. Not surprisingly, therefore, there were frequent references to heroes and heroic values in fascist discourse. Following Carlyle, Nietzsche and Shaw, the BUF, for example, celebrated society's supposedly 'highest types', the aristocratic leader-figures who, like the 'god kings' of Greek mythology, were imagined to be part human and part divine.[63] In the far Right's highly personalized elitist account of history, it was the heroic exceptional individual, the creative 'will-to-achievement' type who, at history's pivotal moments, acted decisively to move the historical and evolutionary process forward. History's heroic figures, particularly those native-born, were thought to embody the fascist character in its supreme form, in that they epitomized the ideals of duty, service, responsibility, stoicism, and self sacrifice to a higher ideal. Heroes functioned as convenient figures of symbolic identification for the far Right. British Rightists had their own pantheon of heroes: Clive of India, Cecil Rhodes, T. E. Lawrence to name but a few, but Jewish heroes did not figure. *Ben Hur*, by presenting 'a heroic Jewish figure' in the young Jewish patrician Judah Ben Hur was 'consequently forced to falsify Roman history and even the plain narrative of the New Testament'.[64]

For Jewish figures to be cast in positive roles in historical movies, as in *Ben Hur*, was anathema to the British far Right. Thus a BUF film critic slammed Warner Brothers' 1929 biopic, *Disraeli*, a 'bastard biography of California' which portrayed the famed Tory prime minister as 'an angelic and virgin-souled' figure.[65] Even greater scorn was heaped upon Twentieth Century Fox's lavish 1934 costume drama *The House of Rothschild*. The Rothschild banking dynasty loomed large in the inter-war British fascists' anti-Semitic, mythically charged view of a world in sway to an allegedly all-powerful self-interested 'international Jewish finance'. Not surprisingly, then, the fascists' preferred image of a Jewish high financier was darkly anti-Semitic. Instead, in the Fox movie, Nathan Rothschild is interpreted by George Arliss simultaneously as a Union Jack waving super-patriot and as 'a dear old fatherly gentleman in everything but mutton chops'.[66] For the BUF reviewer, the historical distortion was compounded by C. Aubrey Smith's presentation of the Duke of Wellington in the same movie as a 'bluff old imbecile war-horse'.[67] The BUF's contemporary, the Imperial Fascist League, also deplored this supposedly 'whitewashed' treatment of the house of Rothschild in the Fox film and of its portrayal of 'our wonderful leader, the Duke of Wellington, as a veritable clown'.[68]

To anti-Semites on the British far Right, the positive images of Jewish heroes contained in historical films were the carefully crafted creations of 'international Jewry', as were the negative interpretations of Western institutions and the British national and imperial experience. Conspiratorial anti-Semitism and the myth of a Jewish 'hidden hand' financing and orchestrating a global network of pro-Jewish, anti-British, anti-imperial, anti-Western and anti-Christian intrigue via cultural institutions such as the cinema was rampant on the far Right fringe during the inter-war period. Writing in the 1920s, the *Patriot* pronounced that the motion picture industry was almost wholly in Jewish hands, and that imported films were being 'used on a large scale to further the objects which the Protocolists have described, and are being so employed with special designs against our Empire'.[69] The belief that the new so-called 'Jewish' film medium, particularly the Hollywood movie, was being used to damage imperial prestige in the Empire was common. 'No wonder, when the Empire is saturated with Judaic American products year in and year out, that it is beginning to think England is finished', bemoaned 'Junius' of the BUF.[70] The East was thought to be the most vulnerable to these allegedly Jewish orchestrated machinations. What effect the 'decadent materialism of Hollywood' has had 'on India and the East I dread to say', declared 'Junius'.[71] British far Right imperialists feared the Orientalist East's metamorphosis into a vapid Americanized simulacrum of the spiritually bankrupt materialist West. In this gendered narrative of loss, the recast Americanized East would be divested of its allure and mystery, no longer the exotic inviting virginal place of the Western imagination which signified both threat and object of sexual desire.[72]

Jews impregnated themselves in the world of cinema, and then used it to further their own ends, according to the far Right, for various reasons, one of which was commercial self-interest. Indeed, within the fascist mind-set, the pernicious presence of the Jews lurked behind the modern phenomenon of commercial mass culture, in that they profited from the crude 'dumbing down' of aesthetic taste supposedly associated with it. The commercialization of the arts by the Jews was an 'attempt to mould our thoughts', declared one BUF activist, so as to increase the potential for economic exploitation.[73] When the cinema was not being exploited for commercial gain, it was apparently utilized as an instrument for the promotion and dissemination of 'international' Jewish propaganda. Thus Twentieth Century Fox's *The House of Rothschild* (1934) contained a message, that is 'to threaten Hitler with dire financial consequences' if the Nazi dictator proceeded to persecute the Jews.[74] Similarly, London Films' rousing swashbuckler about Elizabethan England's triumph over the Spanish Armada, *Fire Over England* (1937), was interpreted by the same BUF writer as an allegory about the fate awaiting continental tyrants should they step out of line.[75] In the movie, Raymond Massey's King Philip of Spain functions as the textual representation of the modern fascist dictator, while the unquestioning conformity demanded by a pious and intolerant Catholic Spain was a metaphor for the Nazi suppression of Jews and others' religious and personal freedoms. The intention of *Fire Over England*, according to far Right semioticians, was to not only throw out a warning to Hitler, but to create bad blood between the Third Reich and Britain and to stir up already troubled political waters in Europe.[76] The Mosleyites claimed that 'international Jewry', for reasons of communal and financial self-interest, sought war between London and Berlin. Even more than *Fire Over England*, Charlie Chaplin's satire of Adolf Hitler, *The Great Dictator*, was adjudged to be guilty of fanning the flames of war. Emblematic of the worst type of anti-German, pro-war propaganda, Chaplin's film was an 'insult to the German nation and Herr Hitler' complained a BUF reviewer, who urged that it should not be exhibited in Britain. For this Blackshirt, 'the Chaplin film is the most dangerous piece of celluloid ever to come into this country. It may set all Europe on fire, and every theatre exhibiting it will be selling Jewish propaganda and endangering the relationships of England and Germany'.[77]

Britain's far Right luxuriated in the idea of a national cinema that would no longer be dominated by the Hollywood film industry nor be under the alleged aegis of Jews, and which would cease to churn out movies that supposedly sapped national vitality, corrupted Britain's youth, appealed to base instincts, ridiculed cherished institutions and caricatured or maligned the national and imperial past. The fascists determined to re-appropriate the national cinema and to reconfigure it to serve fascist ends. 'One of the first duties of Fascism will be to recapture the British cinema for the British nation', declared A. K. Chesterton.[78] A reconstituted national cinema would perform a different role in society, disseminate a new set of images, fashion a different film aesthetic, and draw on alternative themes and paradigms to those of the epoch the fascists sought to 'transcend'. British cinema screens would be filled with native sights and sounds, for example. The British people should derive their impressions and suggestions from films which 'present British life and ideals', urged the *Patriot* in 1925.[79] The BUF would harbour a similar desire. 'In heaven's name, why don't they [British film producers] put Britain on the screen?' asked Henry Gibbs.[80] For Gibbs, British studios should 'make films which present the true, living vital Britain'.[81] Movies should express national life and ambition and only when they were 'supremely national' in this way, would Britain create a film industry that would gain the respect of the outside world.[82] If Gibbs had had his way, documentary films and similar realist fare would have formed part of the diet of films offered to British audiences. The documentary genre's gritty realist thematics and distinct stylistic features seemed well suited to the task of telling the national story. British cinema screens should feature stories about the perils of coal mining, the varying fortunes of the domestic cotton industry and the drama of life in the merchant fishing fleet, according to Gibbs.[83] Robert Flaherty's 1934 British documentary film, *Man of Aran*, chronicling the lives of crofters and fishermen in the west of Ireland, pointed the way forward for Gibbs, as did a later home-grown documentary film, *Edge of the World* (1937), portraying love, life and death on a remote Shetland island.[84] Gibbs also admired John Grierson's classic 1929 documentary film, *Drifters*, profiling the life of the North Sea fishing fleet.[85] British audiences should also see film adaptations of 'grand novels about tillers of English earth'.[86] Throughout his sojourn as a fascist, Gibbs would remain attached to the view that cinema should get 'nearer to life' in order to remain popular and truly national.[87]

It is tempting to suggest that Gibbs's predilection for realist documentaries and the themes contained therein are connected to fascist sensibilities and preoccupations. *Man of Aran*, *Edge of the World* and even Grierson's *Drifters* contain themes which fascists liked to identify with. In all three filmic accounts, we find hardy types inhabiting remote places in close touch with a nature relatively uncontaminated by modernity, confronting the challenge and rigours of the elemental. Here, vitality is associated with man's struggle against a forbidding, untamed environment, where the physical world suggested both threat and uplifting challenge. It should not surprise us that Gibbs's favourite movie for 1937 was MGM's account of a Chinese peasant and his family, *The Good Earth*. For Gibbs, *The Good Earth* was a moving story of man and woman 'united in their never-ending struggle against the force of pitiless Nature' and as such was an epic that 'rises above time and place'.[88] A similar fascist sub-text can be detected in the sentiments of another BUF review of a foreign film. Appraising the 1936 Italian Fascist film *Lo Squadrone Bianco* (*The White Squadron*), which depicted life in an Italian garrison in Libya, the Mosleyite reviewer enthused that it 'has all the enduring greatness of simplicity. There is no affection, only a plain recounting of Man's eternal battle with Nature'.[89] To Britain's fascists, particularly those of a neo-Romantic persuasion, nature was a special, timeless place far removed from the alienation and duplicity of liberal-capitalist modernity. Like their continental counterparts, they would indulge in a nostalgic yearning for nature, imagined as a site of purity and redemption lost to liberal-capitalist modernity and as a metaphysical source that nourished the spirit, the latter thought to be a vital well-spring of the individual's and the nation's cultural expression. Similarly, nature was perceived by 'blood and soil' racial fascists to be a vital repository of the nation's racial essence. Nature was also considered to be the only source of life and truth. 'Only from nature could the truth arise', declared the Mosleyite Henry Williamson.[90]

British audiences would not be treated exclusively to documentary and other realist genre films, though. No longer under foreign dominion and cleansed of imagined alien impurities, British cinema would be relocated in the vanguard of the fascist cultural and spiritual revolution and serve the goal of national regeneration. It would be a cultural forum where 'the finest creative genius and artistic talent of Britain may find its true expression independently of present-day box office assessments and in service to the ideal of enriching the life of a great people'.[91] Films in service to the fascist revolution would have firm contours, spiritual substance and convey reassuring messages. Such films would be interspersed with morally uplifting themes and endeavour to instil national pride in the movie spectator. Reflecting favourably on the 1938 Warner Brothers' version of *The Dawn Patrol*, dealing with the exploits of Royal Flying Corps officers in France during the First World War, Henry Gibbs remarked: 'we would welcome more films, wherever they may come from, recalling our people to a proper pride in their nationhood'.[92] Like the heroic themes and characters in *The Dawn Patrol*, the latter being 'specimens of British fighting-men which nobody would wish to disown', Gibbs yearned for film narratives that sought to express the 'best' of the national past and the British character.

Fascist histories were mythic constructions, of course, fictionalized narratives imposed on the past that aimed to align the spectator with the far Right's preferred version of the national past. The national past was an idealized space, or other, that fascists cherished as an uncontaminated place of spiritual and moral purity lost to liberal-capitalist modernity. The national past had a more overt political function, however. Within the far Right mind-set, the past should act as a source of inspiration for the present and serve as an instrument to mobilize sentiments in the quest to attain the fascist revolution. Fascists believed that historical films, rather than malign or parody the national past as the bulk of inter-war historical movies allegedly did, should play their part in this national project. Film representations of the British past, therefore, should always celebrate national achievements and supposed national virtues. They should be reassuringly nostalgic and suggest a common cultural heritage which the present could draw upon. Historical films should serve the needs of the fascists' rebirth revolution in other ways, too, in that their themes and messages should arouse patriotic emotions and mobilize support in the present. As Eric Rentschler has noted, fascist films imputed to historical material 'a timeless authenticity for a timely calling'.[93]

Ironically, given that many on the far Right adopted a 'mass manipulation' perspective on the American motion picture, a few Hollywood historical films seemed to provide a model worthy of emulation by a future fascist film industry. These 'model' Hollywood historical epics, many of which were eulogies to British imperialism, were frequently acclaimed in the BUF press. After watching Paramount's 1934 historical spectacular *Lives of a Bengal Lancer*, one Blackshirt reviewer wrote that, 'It takes America to put the British spirit on the screen'.[94] This BUF film critic could barely contain his excitement as he surveyed the grand cinematic extravaganza unfolding before his eyes, 'It is magnificent!', he gushed.

> The scenes in India baffle description when it comes to technical difficulties. ... Intense pity, breath-taking admiration, pride of race, all combine to thrill. That is how I felt sitting amongst a packed and delighted house, watching Sir Guy Standing, Gary Cooper, Aubrey Smith, and Richard Cromwell giving us the return of the Briton. The people gasped. Could it be true? Dare anyone eulogise the soldier, dare anyone remember the North-West Frontier...[95]

Another BUF film critic was equally enthralled by the 1936 Warner Brothers' blockbuster, *The Charge of the Light Brigade*, which catapulted Errol Flynn to superstardom. Commenting on the famous charge at Balaclava, he enthused that 'it is impossible to be British, to watch it, and not to be proud'. Overcoming his irritation at the film's numerous factual inaccuracies, the Mosleyite pronounced 'that here is a film calculated to thrill every British audience to its marrows and to make the finest type of British propaganda throughout the world'.[96]

Such grand historical epics as *The Charge of the Light Brigade* drew squeals of delight from fascist cinema spectators because they found such overt expressions of manly valour and the martial values impossible to resist. More pointedly, however, the far Right praised these Hollywood historical films because the representation of British history depicted therein conformed more closely to its preferred image of the national past, an image that was heroic, celebratory and unashamedly nostalgic. Occasionally, a British-made historical feature film elicited similar praise. Whereas one BUF film critic, as we have seen above, interpreted London Films' *Fire Over England* as a Jewish contrived anti-Hitler parable, another thought it virile, 'full of inspired patriotism' and 'one of the finest and most inspiring films yet seen'.[97] This was a celluloid image of England and the English past that Britain's far Right preferred British audiences to gaze upon. 'This is an England which considers reputation well risked for Empire in America, and it is an England of splendid patriotism, untouched with snivelling and ineffective remonstrance and accusation', opined the BUF writer.[98] Similarly, Flora Robson's Elizabeth I in *Fire Over England*, unlike the 'purely politically minded, vicious harridan' portrayed in RKO's *Mary of Scotland*, was motivated by high ideals and selfless patriotism.[99] 'This may be Elizabeth idealised', admitted this BUF film critic, 'but it is the Elizabeth we prefer to see'. Another patriotic offering from London Films, Alexander Korda's 1939 adaptation of

A. E. W. Mason's *The Four Feathers*, a rousing imperial yarn about cow-ardice and redemption set against the backdrop of the war in the Sudan, inspired similar feelings. Some of its scenes, including that showing the story's hero Harry Faversham 'fighting with Kitchener in the bloody sands before Omdurman', were 'filled with breathless excitement' for a film critic of the far Right journal the *New Pioneer*, who thought it 'the finest film of the year'.[100] Historical films that con-tained a patriotic imperialist theme would, no doubt, hold pride of place within a fascist-run native film industry. 'As we have an Empire, gained by struggle and hardship', proclaimed Henry Gibbs, 'it should be the most natural thing in the world to film it'.[101]

Even more than the smattering of American productions and the occasional home-produced feature, contemporary film offerings from Nazi Germany suggested the form that some films might take in a future British Fascist film industry. The BUF would spare nothing in its praise for *Der alte und der junge König* (*The Old and the Young King*) for example, Hans Steinhoff's 1935 period piece about the stormy rela-tionship between a youthful and rebellious Frederick the Great of Prussia as crown prince and his father Frederick William.[102] Eventu-ally disabused of his recalcitrant ways by his father, an unyielding disciplinarian played by Emil Jannings of Weimar cinema fame, the young crown prince forsakes his own pleasures for the sake of a higher obligation to crown and state. Having been brought to an awareness of his duty and 'destiny', the young Frederick repositions himself in a domain 'of straight lines, uniformed masses, and unques-tioned allegiances, joining the masculine space of the parade ground and the state, assuming its language and order'.[103] The BUF obviously approved of the fascist motifs in *The Old and the Young King*, as well as its gendered narrative of temptation and conquest which duplicated the classic horror film's message of a body penetrated by a monster deemed to be sexually and biologically different. Its suggestion, for example, that the young Frederick's inner self was being invaded by 'alien', foreign bodies associated with degenerative, feminine, lustful pleasure, which must be ruthlessly expunged if he is to re-enter the 'masculine' world of disciplined self-control and social responsibility signified by his authoritarian father.[104] The BUF also applauded *The Old and the Young King*'s desire 'to show the stark reality of national destiny' and express 'great themes of national and social purpose' in its narrative.[105] Calling it a film 'in the best Fascist spirit and Fascist temper', it mused 'would we had a national film industry in this coun-try capable of doing the same for ourselves, instead of pursuing the trivialities and obscenities of post war decadence!'[106]

Another production from the Third Reich, Veit Harlan's *Der Herrscher* (*The Ruler*) which won the 1937 German Film Prize and which again saw Jannings in the lead role, elicited a tribute from the

BUF similar to that for *The Old and the Young King*. Like Hans Stein-hoff's film of Frederick the Great's passage to leadership, *The Ruler* transparently reflected fascist ideology in its message of the resolute lonely leader determined to fulfil his higher duty to the *Volksgemein-schaft*. One BUF reviewer pronounced *The Ruler* 'an extremely fine film' and a 'drama of human passions' which 'possesses all the intrinsic dignity of simplicity', while another thought it 'a full depiction of the leadership principle in action'.[107]

It is evident from the glowing appraisals of *The Old and the Young King* and *The Ruler* that the far Right would have favoured exposing British audiences to fascist message movies in a future fascist Britain. If Mosleyites like Robert Gordon-Canning had had their way, fascist principles would have been embedded in the narrative structure of many a film. In the 'debased' cinema world of 'Financial Democracy', complained Gordon-Canning, the supposedly fascist 'ideas of service, responsibility, duty, are buried out of sight'.[108] It is very likely, however, that British fascist cinema would not just deal in fascist propaganda, reflect ideological impulses, or display signs of fascist revolutionary imperatives; nor would it aspire to be exclusively heroic, celebratory, and unashamedly nostalgic and patriotic. The empirical evidence from regime fascisms in Italy and Germany suggest that such films would represent only a percentage of the output of a native fascist film industry, and probably a small percentage at that. In Fascist Italy, propagandist and other such 'virile' and celebratory films, represented just five per cent of national film production during the twenty-year period of Mussolini's rule.[109] Escapist films, melodramas, and sentimental and often frivolous comedies for the most part, which bore a striking similarity to Hollywood features of the same era, dominated Italian Fascist cinema. In the Third Reich, too, the vast bulk of films were 'un-political' light-hearted escapist fare, with not a swastika, well-proportioned machine body, lonely leader-figure, or choreographed massed bloc of inanimate human subjects in sight. Indeed, around fifty per cent of the films on show during the Nazi era were comedies and musicals.[110] As in Fascist Italy, many of these escapist entertainment films would bear the mark of the Hollywood 'dream factory'. Nazi cinema was above all, in Eric Rent-schler's phrase, 'a Ministry of Cheer and Emotion': it was not 'an elaborate dance of death, a prolonged exercise in violence and devastation', nor did its films exhibit the 'customary tropes of the uncanny and the horrendous'.[111]

In all likelihood, a British fascist film industry would have presented a similar menu of escapist entertainment films to the British cinema public, many of which would have probably mimicked Hollywood formulas. Despite the elitist cultural rhetoric and the disparaging comments about mass cultural taste on the part of those who harboured a 'mass manipulation' perspective on the cinema, many native fascists acknowledged the seductively attractive power of popular cinema. 'What a blessing are films!' exclaimed Henry Gibbs, 'for a shilling, eighteen-pence, we escape drab realities, inherit worlds of make-believe, ... attain various forms of Utopia, Atlantis, where life achieves poetic, if unhappy, conclusion'.[112] Gibbs understood that the appeal of mass cinema was to a large extent based on its ability to create these captivating 'worlds of make-believe', compelling illusions that tugged at the emotions and orchestrated desire. He also recognized that this aspect of cinema was perfectly compatible with fascism, fascist ideology, and fascist film aesthetics. Astute observers of fascism like Walter Benjamin and Siegfried Kracauer recognized that its rule was based as much on illusion, mass seduction and appeals to the imaginary, as on terror.[113] 'Reality' and aesthetics became virtually interchangeable in fascism because it sought to break down the traditional divide between political experience and aesthetic experience. In the realm of fascist film aesthetics, too, the wiser practitioners of fascist propaganda knew that, because of cinema's unique capacity to transcend the boundary between the real and the aesthetic and create warmly reassuring imaginary experiences, mastery could be gained over the subject through means other than overt external coercion. Rather than bludgeon the subject or spectator into submission with heavy-handed propaganda messages, therefore, a fascist cinema could serve fascist goals best by entering a private, inner emotional space and subtly manipulating imaginations and desires. In so doing, this cinema of seemingly harmless illusions created the ultimate illusion, the illusion of freedom, the perception that there existed a private inner space beyond the remit of the party and state.[114] As one historian has noted in relation to cinema audiences in the Third Reich, contented subjects who believed that a measure of personal freedom was being preserved were more malleable and less prone to question the authority of the state.[115] In Mussolini's Italy and Hitler's Germany, the escapist entertainment film was symbiotically related to the more overt fascist message movie. The former was the Dr Jekyll to the Mr Hyde of the latter, the more acceptable public face behind which fascism concealed its real, darker and more malevolent character and intentions. In the future fascist Britain that the British far Right sought, it is reasonable to assume that a native fascist film industry would have taken on a similar dual and contradictory persona.

'This Fortress Built Against Infection'

The BUF Vision of Britain's Theatrical and Musical Renaissance

Roger Griffin

Britain's Forthcoming Artistic Renaissance

The ideologues[1] of the BUF produced no equivalent to Rosenberg's *Myth of the Twentieth Century* as a comprehensive statement of its vision of cultural renewal and artistic palingenesis, nor any monographs on individual spheres of artistic endeavour.[2] Nevertheless, its diagnosis of the health of Britain's theatre and music can be reconstructed as a relatively coherent 'discourse' from what is, for an abortive political movement which lasted a mere seven years, an abundance of publicistic[3] references to them in the movement's newspapers and periodicals.[4] It was a diagnosis informed by a cluster of axioms about the arts that were broadly consistent with the 'Spenglerian' view of the organic life cycle of cultures that became so central to the Leader's palingenetic vision of Britain's imminent destiny after 1932.[5]

The first premise was that the state of the arts was a direct expression of the 'greatness' of the nation conceived in a way typical of the patriotic mind-set of inter-war Europe as a synergy between military, political, and imperial strength on the one hand, and the ability to produce achievements in science, technology and the arts on the other. The profoundly patriarchal nature of such an assumption, already implicit when 'great men' alone are listed as having incarnated the qualities of an age actually named after a queen[6] or in the constant references to 'man', becomes explicit when Mosley calls for the 'new Britons' to embody virility'[7] or a 'manful appreciation of life'.[8] Before the days of feminism and political correctness such chauvinist language could be generated by the patriotic pride in the cultural achievements of the nation's artists and intellectuals that, in liberal democracies, so often coexists with a recognition of the deeply private, unpredictable and mysterious nature of human creativity. What made it specifically fascist,[9] or at least ultra-nationalist, in orientation in the BUF context was the insistence that all such achievements were to be seen as direct manifestations of the national genius, as revelations of what Herder called the 'Volksgeist' or essential spirit of the people. Hence there were such pronouncements as the following: 'art is the expression of the whole community, or it is nothing but neurotic self-exhibitionism';[10] 'art must have roots: when it is uprooted, when the deadly disease of cosmopolitanism sets in, it ceases to be the trumpet of man's spirit and becomes the gangrened emblem of the spirit's death';[11] 'culture is the supreme achievement of a nation's conscious communal effort'; 'a healthy civilisation in which culture flourishes and art is alive, beautiful, is a civilisation in which men may lift their eyes to something nobler than themselves',[12] 'politics has lost the one quality which could make it eternal: its close association with the arts and with the culture of man'.[13]

A second axiom was that Britain had once achieved a totality of political and cultural greatness which eclipsed that of any other nation, namely in the Elizabethan era (occasionally referred to as the Tudor Age). The flowering of England's contribution to the European Renaissance coincided with her emergence as a great naval and colonial power, thereby lending a specious empiricism to the BUF's organic theory of culture, its patriotic belief in Britain's genius and world civilizing mission, and the sense of the lamentable decline from a Golden Age of art and culture so essential to the movement's core myth of imminent rebirth. Indeed, whereas the Italian Renaissance flowered at a low-point in Italy's history as a unified nation-state, the Elizabethan Renaissance (like the ones which took place in sixteenth-century Spain and seventeenth-century Holland) perfectly embodied for a twentieth-century fascist the lost Atlantis when thought and action, culture and empire were inextricably bound up as expressions of a young national community growing in self-awareness and organic strength.

Anchoring Britain's future in nostalgia for the Tudors played a major role in the 'naturalization' of continental fascism by enabling BUF ideologues to develop an internally consistent metapolitical discourse in which to articulate the diagnosis of contemporary Britain, one that went considerably beyond slavish imitation of continental role models. Indeed, both Italian Fascists and Nazis could only point to 'Golden Ages' which long predated their emergence as a modern nation-state. To the Fascist mind-set of a Spenglerian persuasion, the fact that Queen Elizabeth, Marlowe and Purcell were roughly contemporaries and that the creation of the greatest empire ever seen began in the lifetime of William Shakespeare, the greatest dramatist of English, if not world, literature, had to be more than a coincidence. Dowland's madrigals, the first dawning of the British scientific, mathematical, and technological revolution, the colonization of the

Caribbean, the defeat of the Armada were all 'obviously' manifestations of the same fundamental reality: an organic culture in the full bloom of its first spring.

Seen through a mythic lens of palingenetic ultra-nationalism Elizabethan society allowed what Mosley described in *The Alternative* as the 'thought-deed man'[14] to hold sway untrammelled by a democratic conscience which makes cowards of us all. Hence his statement in *Tomorrow We Live* that 'Our new Britons require the virility of the Elizabethan combined with the intellect of and method of the modern technician'.[15] Hence the conviction of one of his rank-and-file supporters that 'Fascists have an opportunity to bring about a Renaissance of British letters comparable to Elizabethan splendour',[16] and that when Hitler launched the purge of modernist art in 1936 it was a call to German artists to restore the 'national function of art' that existed when Shakespeare encapsulated in dramatic prose the soul of Tudor England.[17] The resolute confidence displayed by A. L. Glasfurd in the profound compatibility of fascism with the 'English tradition', not least in the sphere of culture, should thus come as no surprise:

> The vigorous patriotism, the advanced social conscience, the idealism and the vital spirit of endeavour that characterised the Elizabethan is also typical of the Fascist. Both, in a word, are men of action. Both belong in a different world from that of the intermediate liberal-bourgeois type. The complacent Old Party politician, who regards our new insurgent Fascism with numb horror or attacks it with hysterical abuse, is also congenitally incapable of understanding the spirit of the Elizabethan age. Those who see in Fascism a force destructive of culture should examine this period of history. Like the dawning Fascist era, the age was an age of popular dictatorship and national integration, an age when individualism was not suffered to degenerate into anarchy, an age when men did not hesitate to meet force with force. It was the epoch of Hawkins, Drake and Raleigh. And yet it was in this 'barbarous' period that England experienced a cultural Renaissance unequalled in her previous or subsequent history. The Elizabethan had hot blood and a ready hand, but he was none the less not a great artist.[18]

The third vital premise of the BUF's discourse on the contemporary British arts was that they were now afflicted by the same pathological symptoms which were affecting the whole of the West. One of the most comprehensive statements of this conviction came, appropriately enough, from the Leader himself in the first flush of his conversion to Spenglerism:

> [W]e have reached the period, by every indication available to the intellect, at which each civilisation and Empire of the past has begun to traverse that downward path to the dust and ashes from which their glory never returned. Every fatal symptom of the past is present in the modern situation, from the uprooting of the people's contact with the soil to the development of usury and the rule of money power,

accompanied by social decadence and vice that flaunts in the face of civilisation the doctrine of defeat and decline.[19]

Another characteristic jeremiad about the state of the nation's art came
from the pen of the most Spenglerian of the BUF's ideologues, Raven-
Thomson:

> Culture in literature bitterness, cynicism and Gertrude Stein; in music
> sensuality, swing and Stravinsky; in painting introspection and surreal-
> ism; in sculpture puerility and Picasso, excrescences and Epstein. No
> longer does the artist seek to capture elusive beauty, rather does he
> make it his business to worship the transient futilities spewed up by
> modern life, glorifying the misbegotten and pandering to the pervert.[20]

Though the profound decadence of contemporary culture was axiom-
atically assumed by all BUF ideologues, they might cite as its root
cause one of a number of factors familiar in fascism's catalogue of the
blights and woes of modern civilization.[21] These included the 'disease
of Industrialism, with its accompaniments of excessive mechanisation
and urbanisation',[22] the presence among 'the people of Britain in the
dark days of their eclipse' of 'cosmopolitan geniuses willing to make a
burlesque of their noble cultural heritance';[23] the 'sorry mess of egotism and greed' which results 'when man ceases to be an individual
and becomes a democrat that is, when he forgets the soil',[24] or when
'money dictates the damning of the founts of English culture'.[25] Other
factors adduced were the rise of leisure, which, according to A. Raven-
Thomson, initiated 'the decline of Rome';[26] usury, which Ezra Pound
was convinced had brought down not just the Roman Empire but the
Chinese one as well;[27] the 'excessive individualism' that 'appeared
with particular violence at the Reformation, which is one of Disintegration's land-marks';[28] the collective 'harking back to the ideals of the
tribe' comparable to a garden reverting 'back to the jungle';[29] or the
spread of democracy with its 'Philistine majorities'.[30]

    A major result of such pathological processes was a fundamental
change in the relationship between the 'people' and artists, who have
formed 'a rebellious Bohemian community, intent mainly upon shock-
ing the hippopotamus that crushes their talent, but seldom succeeding
in penetrating its thick Philistine hide'.[31] 'Looking from the ugliness
without to the ugliness within'[32] in the search for recognition, their art
no longer unconsciously articulates the values of the people which
they have internalized as members of the national community, but
expresses 'that extreme mental extroversion which is ultimately
responsible for the chaos – social, political, economic and cultural – in
which the West now finds itself'.[33] As a result it cannot help but be
'artifice – synthetic and barren, deadening to the soul'.[34] The anti-type
of the true artist were the 'Bloomsbury intellectuals' who had made it
fashionable to assert that 'Fascism is anti-culture',[35] thereby per-

versely missing the point that Fascists were committed only to destroying *decadent* art: 'Are we to destroy all the works of art in Great Britain, or the little muddied stream of forced and warped thinking emanating from long-haired men and sandalled women in Bloomsbury's dirtier boarding-houses?'[36]

An even more ominous symptom of the 'whole rotten intellectual mess of the present day'[37] was the alleged domination of the arts by Jews, which was presented as the outward manifestation, not of an alleged loss of racial purity (as Nazi ideology insisted), but of the growing power of money. Thus 'the Jew' is accused of being eternally preoccupied with gold 'causing him to drive Western civilization down to the standards of Eastern barbarism in his quest for profit'.[38] One consequence of this was the commercialization of art, the eagerness to pander to the taste of the lowest common denominator for the purpose of pure profit. Another was the unscrupulous employment of foreign artistes at the expense of British ones. As a result of Jewish infiltration, aesthetic canons themselves had been degraded and public taste corrupted. In short, the BUF perceptions of cultural decadence were dominated by the feeling (reminiscent of the science-fiction film *The Invasion of the Body Snatchers*[39]) that British culture was being infiltrated by alien forces and destroyed from within, a paranoia epitomized in Chesterton's graphic warning that the statues of Shakespeare and Nelson might be one day replaced by ones of Samuel Goldwyn and Hore-Belisha.[40]

The final axiom was that one of the principal missions of the BUF was to reverse this deplorable state of cultural collapse: '[Fascism] is a new and revolutionary creed of national and cultural regeneration, come with a two-fold purpose: to check the rapid decay and corruption produced by the illusion of democracy, and to restore a deeper purpose to national life.'[41] 'Fascism will sweep away that cult of ugliness and distortion in art, music and literature which is the product of neurotic post-war minds, sickened by long incarceration in dim cities.'[42] It would defy Spenglerian laws of inexorable decline by acting as the catalyst for national awakening. For, as Raven-Thomson put it: 'a revolutionary urge that restores the national spirit of the British people may well recover the Tudor atmosphere that gave us Shakespeare and the greatest triumphs of English poetry and drama.'[43] The BUF press makes it clear that two key areas of British culture where the battle to combat the syndrome of pathological degeneration promised to be particularly fierce were the theatre and music.

The 'Death' of the British Theatre

As is implicit in Raven-Thomson's words, Shakespeare was a gift to the cultural pundits of the BUF as the epitome of everything that

Britain once stood for and was now under threat. Indeed, the only other literary genius who can be directly compared with him for his value to fascists as a cultural icon, and who could be selectively quoted to underpin their ultra-nationalist agenda, is Dante, whose call for the unity of the Italian nation Mussolini's Blackshirts could claim they were finally answering in a new age of faith.[44] Not only is Shakespeare an 'immortal' dramatist of indisputable world renown, and the embodiment of the glories of the English language, he was a man 'of the people' about whose private life remarkably little is known compared with the outstanding figures of the Italian Renaissance. Moreover, his plays 'work' linguistically and dramatically entirely within the bounds of the shared world view and iconography of his contemporaries just at the time when England was emerging as a self-conscious nation-state with its own unique cultural and political 'destiny'. As a result they are replete with eminently quotable sentiments rooted in a vitalistic, mythically charged world view that patently pre-dates the secular individualism of liberal democracy, or, for that matter, socialist egalitarianism, materialism, hedonism, artistic modernism, or any other of the 'isms' whose proliferation is, for a fascist, synonymous with cultural putrefaction. In short, Shakespeare supplied irrefutable evidence of the fact that 'the theatre ... was not created out of the fortuitous desire of a small section of humanity, but it grew spontaneously from the whole of the people'.[45]

A. K. Chesterton thus spoke for many in the BUF movement when he invoked Shakespeare as proof of the superior truthfulness of art compared with science, and of the need for 'vision' in the life of a people, before going on to deplore the modern values that have caused the immortal bard's place to be taken by the likes of Aldous Huxley and H. G. Wells.[46] The BUF's appropriation of Shakespeare reaches Monty Pythonesque heights in the article 'Shakespeare would have been a Fascist', in which he is presented as the embodiment of patriotism, the hatred of communism, total loyalty to the monarch, and the celebration of war. What is more, he had understood that only by 'wounding herself' could England become vulnerable to foreign conquest. One phrase from John O'Gaunt's speech, suitably cut, acquires a fresh resonance in the context of the BUF's campaign to put 'Britain First':

> This fortress built for nature by herself
> Against infection and the hand of war.[47]

For BUF columnists, convinced that the days when the Globe played Shakespeare to houses packed with audiences drawn from all social strata represented the high-point of the British theatre, the symptoms of its advanced state of decay in the 1930s were plain to see. Instead of being 'an expression of the spirit and the feeling of the people', the play had too often become 'merely the hobby of a man whose money has been made in a purely utilitarian pursuit, and is seeking diversion and the possibility of more profit in the theatre'. In other words it was reduced to being 'the vehicle for the flaunting of some entirely worthless small personality which has in some ways touched ... the pocket of the wealthy'. The 'spontaneous expression of mental life in the people ... has been 'delivered over to cupidity and avarice'. There is thus 'great danger that an impoverished and unworthy theatre may be completely superseded by the cinema'. No wonder 'the theatre today is said to be dying'.[48]

A major cause and symptom of this lamentable situation (in fascist discourse causes and consequences of decadence are mostly indistinguishable) was that both the management of theatres and the system for engaging professional actors had fallen into the hands of Jews. Predictably, BUF columnists had no scruples in enlisting Shakespeare as propagandist of anti-Semitism. Thus a BBC broadcast of excerpts of Shylock's speeches becomes a pretext for citing Antonio's pronouncements on the impossibility of ever reasoning with a Jew in an article that finishes with the threatening words: 'It is fortunate perhaps for Jewry that we have not in England one of these ancient laws of Venice called into execution by Portia!'[49] Another assures readers that 'There is many a stirring message for National Socialists in the works of Shakespeare', an assertion which it illustrates by citing words from *Romeo and Juliet* as an indictment of the suffering and degradation inflicted on the poor by 'Financial Democracy', usury, and the 'greed for gold'. It proceeds to offer a 'description of modern England' which consists of a passage from *Richard II*, interpreted as the portrait of a country crippled by the interest on foreign debt and the influx of 'cheap foreign goods' which are 'condemning thousands of our fellow countrymen to the miseries of unemployment': 'Shylock must have his pound of flesh, cost what it may'.[50]

There is little doubt that BUF journalists struck a deep chord with readers on this issue. One letter to *Blackshirt* complains that what was once 'the Theatrical Profession' had now degenerated into a '"racket" almost totally controlled by Jewish managers and agents, who exploit the artistes, force them to starvation salaries, and import foreign and Jewish artistes in preference to our own and the public have no say in the matter.' He called for Fascists to sit in silent protest whenever a foreign or Jewish act was on stage.[51] Such complaints recur time after time in the BUF press. In 'The Blight of the Jew', a former actor claims he lived well until Jewish theatrical management and agencies established their 'stranglehold' and forced out British actors like him. He concludes with a memorable racial stereotype: 'Now, in my opinion, large brown and soulful eyes gleam brightly on either side of Jewish noses and the whisper is "Television". Observe and see if I am wrong.'[52] In another article a cabaret dancer recounts the immense hardship and humiliation she has experienced in her profession due to the fact that 'foreigners' have taken over the music hall.[53] Such personal testimonies were grist to the BUF's satanic mills. A leading article ascribed the crisis in the theatre to 'Exploitation run mad, exploitation carried to a point of destruction that only a Jew knows. The net result was that the theatre faltered and failed, with the life of it being slowly choked out.'[54] Another claims that in 1935, while British variety artistes joined the dole queues, 1,600 permits for foreign acts were issued and the BBC signed up a growing number of foreign acts, a situation attributable to the fact that 'nearly 90% of the booking agencies are controlled and owned by Jews'.[55] The point was summed up in what was hardly the best example of the national genius for writing headlines containing outrageous puns: 'British Artists Shall not Starve that Foreigners May Staff'.[56]

According to the BUF press the Jewish theatrical 'racket' meant not only a flood of foreign artistes and unemployed British actors, but a flood of vulgarity as well:

> The English theatre is dying, and the cinema is not responsible. It is the people who dictate that overworked, half-naked chorus girls, queasy-weasy sex philosophy and corpses shall constitute theatrical entertainment and art. But people get tired of blatant stage sex and bright young men and women, devoid of all pretence to humanity, to hurl cheap witticisms at each other from behind the footlights.[57]

Serious drama was not the only victim of the crisis. The great British pantomime had fallen on hard times because it was in the hands of 'aliens' culturally incapable of understanding it.[58] The BBC was taken to task for preferring to give airtime to comedy served up by 'four coloured Americans, one Chinese, the usual surfeit of Semites', rather than choose the 'eminent' (and presumably pro-Fascist) English humorist, Mr Gillie Potter.[59] Even when 'true art' was staged, there was another sinister sign of the desecration of the British theatre: the foreign infiltration of Shakespeare. A. K. Chesterton wrote a scathing critique of Hollywood's rendition of *Romeo and Juliet* and of the decision to allow Russian director Komisarjevsky not only to stage *Antony and Cleopatra*, but to invite him to produce yet more plays in the very Mecca of Shakespeare, Stratford-upon-Avon. But what appears to have stuck in his throat above all else was the casting of the Austrian Jewess Elizabeth Bergner in the role of Rosalind in *As You Like It*, especially since it was stipulated in her contract 'that the name of Bergner should take precedence over the name of Shakespeare'.[60]

The Eclipse of British Music

For a British fascist obsessed with national decline, the state of music was no more encouraging than the state of the theatre. As with drama, the recurrent BUF premise was that healthy art is a spontaneous expression of the people, unmediated by artifice or idiosyncrasy, so that 'music is an integral part of the social life, not of a few, but of the nation. It should be allowed to grow and flourish on the natural soil of its country'. The very idea that the natural home of music was Germany or Italy was 'astonishing when one thinks of the Elizabethan age when England was almost, if not the, leading musical nation in the world', and could still boast having in Elgar 'the greatest living composer'.[61] Here, too, history had smiled on Fascism by imparting some empirical objectivity to the myth of an era from which Britain had so palpably declined. To quote one of the BUF's resident musical experts, Selwyn Watson, 'in the Elizabethan Era – the Golden Age of Britain – we were the supreme and acknowledged masters of the art of music'. It is a matter of record that a cluster of outstandingly original composers, such as William Byrd, Tallis, Gibbons, Wilby, Weelkes, John Dowland, Robert Jones, and one giant, Purcell, created a distinctly 'English' dialect of Renaissance music. However, Watson's claim that 'the men who defeated the Armada prided themselves on their singing of madrigals' owes less to academic research than to wishful thinking about the intimate link between military might and musical genius in that 'organic age'.[62]

British music and the theatre may have been equally moribund, but the cleavage which existed in the coverage of 'classical' and 'popular' music was more apparent than for 'theatre' and 'variety hall'. As far as 'high-brow' music was concerned, a major cause for concern for the Fascist intelligentsia[63] was the neglect of British composers such as Elgar, Bax, Delius and Vaughan Williams,[64] who had been crowded out by foreign operas. In his plea to 'Rescue British Music' the BUF musical pundit, John Porte, goes so far as to dismiss the Grand Opera season at Covent Garden wholesale as a 'spectacle of international rubbish' staged by those who fail to realize that 'Grand Opera is not part of the life of English musical people': 'We are a nation of singers and players, as well as masters of theatre work, but opera, that muddled mixture of bad plays, bad acting and good music and singing, is not English.'[65] In another scornful attack on the Covent Garden season – 'foreign operas performed by foreign singers and supported by a motley audience of aliens and Society folk who consider Grand Opera Seasons as variations of Goodwood and Ascot' – Porte claims that in France, Germany and Italy audiences hear operas performed in their own language, and calls for British operas to be written which reflect 'the spirit of our own people'.[66] At least Captain Cuthbert Reavely, of whom more anon, could not disapprove of the main fare in the 1935 Grand Opera season, which was Wagner's Ring Cycle. Nevertheless, he took the opportunity to criticize the inclusion of a Rossini festival alongside the works of the master – Wagner – to deplore the 'almost complete absence of any British singers', and to express relief that audiences were spared 'the threat of "Wozzeck", another modern Jewish perpetration'.[67] Berg's expressionist opera epitomized the fascist equation of Jewish creativity with an ugly, unintelligible modernism, or what Nazis called 'Cultural Bolshevism' (a phrase whose very absence from the BUF press again underlines the fact that we are not dealing with the simple cloning of Nazi aesthetics).

If the BUF's high-brow critics were reduced to carping from the wings, the popular music scene offered a contemporary phenomenon which its more populist cultural purists could really get their critical fangs into: jazz. For Arthur Reade, who set out the principles involved in the defence of Western civilization, the 'passion for jazz' was a symptom of regression,[68] while the music critic who called himself 'Bluebird' accused the Jews of literally being able to call the tune thanks to the cultural domination they had achieved in Britain, and of imposing 'primitive "native jew" [sic] tunes with only that weird jumble of rhythm once associated with the half-civilized'.[69]

The most extreme indictment of jazz stems from the vitriolic pen of an anonymous columnist in Blackshirt who portrays jazz as a modern form of St Vitus's dance, which originally arose as a hybrid cultural product of two races singing for a lost homeland, the Jews and America's negroid population. Broadway (like Hollywood, a Jewish financial empire) then turned it into a powerful weapon in the Jews' cultural war against the Gentiles. He claims that not only does constant exposure to jazz's subversive rhythms undermine racial differences, but the cynicism and resignation of its texts sap the young of courage and vitality, thereby inducing a collective 'neurasthenia' calculated to make the host nations more likely to succumb to Jewish influence.[70]

As with the theatre, the BUF believed that the corrupting influence of the un-British contents of the art form went hand in hand with the pernicious economic dimension of its performance imposed by Jewish ascendancy. There is some evidence here of the growing virulence of BUF anti-Semitism (much more apparent in the more overtly political and economic pages of the BUF press) as the decade wore on. In 1934 a piece entitled 'Music in the Gutters' claimed that only 4,500 out of 40,000 British musicians were in employment and blamed the arrival of the talkies for ruining the profession without any mention of Jews, not even their domination of Hollywood. By 1936 the diagnosis presented in such articles had taken an ominous turn. According to one purporting to expose 'The Menace from the East', 'our Press and leading publishing houses, all our cinemas, and even the radio, are either owned or at least controlled to a large measure by Jewish finance', so that now 'the musical profession is entirely in Jewish hands, and, whilst hundreds of English musicians are unemployed and in dire want, hundreds of German Jews have been allowed to come here and gain employment'.[71] The direct causal link between the alleged Jewish domination of the entertainment industry and its high levels of 'indigenous' unemployment was emphasized in numerous articles. One of the more effective, 'Behind the Saxophone', used personal testimony to bring home the hard times inflicted on a British bandsman by the rise of alien jazz.[72] It was a situation summed up in the hardly very poetic ditty 'Yiddles play their fiddles on the wireless, Gentiles play their brass-bands in the gutter'.[73]

In case the economic crisis for British musicians might be thought to affect only dance bands, 'The Tragedy of the Concert Hall' described in vivid detail the humiliations and penury suffered at the hands of agency sharks by a gifted soprano attempting to break into the world of concert performance in terms reminiscent of *They Shoot Horses, Don't They?*[74] The BUF's campaign against the BBC (a foretaste of some of the more hysterical episodes of government paranoia in the Thatcher years) shows how far it too was considered an extension of the same 'racket', as well as acting from within the establishment as the Trojan horse for the (Jewish) destruction of British culture on all fronts. A steady drip-feed of articles in *Action* and *Blackshirt* pilloried its exploitation of British artists; employing too many foreigners; putting on variety acts, drama and music which were out of touch with the people; broadcasting too much jazz; and of acts of such flagrant cultural subversion as hosting a Bessarabian orchestra which played music in 'truest kosher style' ('Was it a cat fight or an Abyssinian funeral? It was not music'),[75] and desecrating Christianity by scheduling 'Louis Levy and his Jewband' for Christmas Day. In one singular fit of cultural paranoia a columnist raises the spectre of the BBC selling 'British ether' to the highest bidder.[76] In this context an article by Ezra Pound on how 'mercantilism rots the arts' and how usuriocracy' has been destroying English music from within ever since the well-remunerated 'Handel' (George Friederic Händel!) first crossed the Channel does not seem out of place in content, despite the idiosyncrasies of style.[77]

The Panacea

The doom and gloom that pervaded BUF diagnoses of the pitiful state of Britain's theatre and music, no matter how unrelenting, were far from pessimistic. They were an intrinsic part of the rugged palingenetic logic behind Fascist mythic thinking in every sphere of political analysis, and hence dialectically linked to the vision of rebirth in a revolutionary new order. According to the logic of cyclic rather than linear time, the darker the night, the closer the dawn; the worse the current plight, the more imminent the rebirth. Hence the heady 'cultural optimism' displayed after grim evocations of the present state of the arts in such assertions as 'Nothing short of a national revival, an awakening of the national consciousness, can rescue the national art from slow expiration';[78] 'Release our natural genius in all directions and music in this country would flourish as it did in the Elizabethan era';[79] 'We are, as it happens, on the verge of a tremendous musical renaissance'.[80]

The organic laws of culture mean that once the people were stirred politically from their slumber by the gathering momentum of Mosley's movement the drama too would be awakened.[81] The same law (even if incomprehensible to the minds of art experts and intellectuals still in the thrall of decadent liberalism or modernism) will banish discord from popular music and allow melody to return home from exile. It is only when 'the rapidly rising British Union ... arouse[s] once again full-blooded feelings in the minds and bodies of full-blooded British men and women ... we may hope to hear really great tunes again'.[82] Yet even the most manic Fascist ideologue recognized that the process of cultural rebirth could not be left simply to a process of osmosis: as in other spheres it had to be induced. National life could only start becoming 'organic' once more if the new government created an all-pervasive structure capable of reintegrating the key areas of activity that had become so fragmented and corrupt under 'Financial Democracy'. In practice, this meant some radical institutional and constitutional innovations.

The first concerned the function of the Second Chamber with which Mosley proposed to replace the 'unworkable anachronisms' of the House of Lords. There is documentary evidence here to suggest that the influence which Spengler exerted on Mosley's thinking after 1933 led him to place culture much closer to the centre of his scheme for the new national order than it had been when his diagnosis was couched in mainly economic terms. In the first (1932) edition of *The Greater Britain* Mosley envisages the new Chamber as a technocratic body, the 'National Corporation, which would function as an effective Parliament of Industry'.[83] The second edition of 1934 talks of the House of Lords being replaced by a Chamber 'which represents in a special sense every major interest of the modern State', though the ensuing list makes no reference to cultural matters beyond 'religious thought' and 'education'.[84] But in 1936 Mosley's *Fascism: 100 Questions Asked and Answered* specifies that the Second Chamber will represent the industry, culture, and ability of the nation, including outstanding personalities from the fields of education, religion, the services, science, art and every aspect of the people's spiritual life. 'From this pool of culture and ability Government will derive a real assistance.'[85] E. D. Randall, composer of the words to the BUF anthem 'Britain Awake', reflected the shift in Mosley's thinking when, as early as 1934, he wrote 'In the Second Chamber of the Fascist Parliament will sit elected representatives of the national culture – men distinguished in their service of the arts and sciences, philosophy and religion, so that for the first time in our history men of creative genius will receive their rightful share of public honour, hitherto reserved for politicians and soldiers – ministers of deceit on the one hand, and on the other, of destruction'.[86]

The main organizational framework for the regeneration of British culture, however, was to have been provided by the Corporate State. Just how the arts would have been regimented in the new Britain is a matter of speculation. By 1937, when Raven-Thomson, the BUF's main theoretician of British corporatism, published *The Coming Corporate State*, there were two full-scale contemporary experiments in the fascist incorporation of culture on which he could draw: the cultural sections of Italy's 'Corporativist State' whose structural and legislative apparatus was still evolving on paper, however minimal its effectiveness as an organ of Fascistization, and the far more rigorously hierarchical and ruthlessly 'coordinated' *Reichskulturkammer* which Goebbels ran as his personal empire. Yet in the mere four pages dedicated to the *Gleichschaltung* and revitalization of British culture in Raven-Thomson's blueprint for the new Corporatist Britain, little specific on culture emerges other than the crudely utilitarian equation of art with a parlour-game such as backgammon (one which would have raised the hackles of J. S. Mill). According to the section 'the problem of leisure', every corporation would have been responsible for organizing the leisure facilities in its productive sector, which meant encouraging 'sport and athleticism' as well as 'less strenuous forms of recreation of equal value' such as 'music, dramatics, literature, debate and indoor games of skill'. This was followed by an even more laconic chapter entitled 'The Patronage of the Arts' which tells us 'a special corporation' for the artist would ensure 'him' (of course) 'self-governing powers' and 'training' while securing 'his' own honoured place in national life.[87] However, when Anne Cutmore's blueprint for the 'reawakening of British drama'[88] promises that there will be a Corporation just for the theatre we can assume that detailed planning of the new structure was still in its early stages.

The same is true of the third major organizational innovation on which Britain's cultural rebirth was to have depended: 'Afterwork', a nation-wide capillary movement for filling the nation's free-time with healthy productive purpose which was explicitly modelled on the Fascist 'Dopolavoro' and the Nazi 'Kraft durch Freude' organizations. Its highly invasive impact on the private lives of the 'New Britons' is implicit in Raven-Thomson's pronouncement that within the Corporate State 'leisure must be directed into developing the cultural standards of the masses by recreational activity', and that 'the mass, in their recreational hours, will be encouraged, by reduced prices and special facilities, to visit concerts and opera, theatres and exhibitions of pictures and sculpture'.[89] Anne Cutmore's scheme for drama's rebirth confirms that the BUF saw 'Afterwork' as a vital means both of healing Britain of its cultural malaise and of solving the problem posed by the increasing amount of leisure that she assumed would be generated by the Fascist mastery of science, technology and planning and the subsequent reduction in working hours.

While the Second Chamber, the Cultural Corporation(s), and Afterwork were being put in place, a raft of new legislation and measures could have been expected from a Mosley government aimed at regenerating the theatre and music. For one thing the new state would ensure that no artist was forced to live in poverty. Not only would the arts be heavily subsidized, but the existing agency system would be swept away and replaced by a national organization run by paid professionals.[90] On paper this meant that at a stroke not only would exploitation and the profit motive be taken out of the arts, but that it would be possible finally to regulate centrally the number of foreigners working in Britain while guaranteeing jobs for (registered) British artistes. Moreover, the aesthetic content of theatre programmes, classical concerts, and light entertainment (not forgetting the BBC, which would finally become a 'British' Broadcasting Corporation) would be strictly controlled – through mechanisms of censorship never spelt out – so as to eliminate any art which smacked of the cynical, the prurient, the vacuous, the sensationalist, or the cosmopolitan. In the case of the theatre, for example, this system would have ensured a steady supply of 'edifying plays and suitable variety acts to be performed in a national network of Municipal Theatres subsidized by a special tax so that tickets were affordable'.[91] Afterwork would, presumably, have seen to it that their seats were always full.[92]

But, such measures were within the BUF mind-set only the pragmatic, 'material' aspect of a deeper spiritual process which lay at the heart of the Fascist 'reawakening': the healing of the rift between the artist and 'his' people, the rerooting of the artist's inspiration in the common experience and aspirations of 'his' nation from which it had been torn, the reharnessing of artistic talent to the collective destiny of Britain. It is in this sense that Raven-Thomson announces that 'The Corporate State will maintain a much closer contact between artist and people'.[93] The organic, idealist vision of culture which is second nature to fascists made it self-evident to BUF cultural commentators that any constitutional or institutional innovations it introduced would fail miserably if it did not succeed in spreading a sense of higher communal purpose. This they saw as vital to the synergy between the nation's material and cultural power that they believed had existed in its Golden Age some three centuries earlier. For Fascists it was axiomatic that the real revolution commenced 'in the hearts and not on the barricades'.[94] 'It will be in rediscovering the Age of faith of Christendom and the vital energy of Tudor England that we may realize in part the great future of our nation'.[95]

The Ambiguities of Britain's Cultural Rebirth

For those imbued with the 'decadent' mentality of scepticism it is patently obvious that the BUF's seven years of intense ideological activity had been insufficient to resolve many crucial issues raised by the perceived need to reverse the decline of Britain's theatre and music. Not only were the mechanisms of the control and organization of the arts still at a rudimentary stage of forward planning and described in nebulously mythic language, but a close study of the BUF press reveals that major differences in interpreting the Fascist vision of Western civilization persisted at the highest level on such issues as the role of Christianity or religion in underpinning the West's past and future 'greatness', the part played in its decline by Jews, and the centrality of culture rather than technocracy to its regeneration. A comparison of the 'philosophy of history' of Mosley with that of major ideologues such as Raven-Thomson, A. K. Chesterton, Arthur Reade or E. D. Randall suggests latent conflicts and potential personality clashes on Britain's reborn culture at least as profound as the ones which existed between Hitler, Goebbels, Darré, and Rosenberg. For instance, Raven-Thomson's Philistine view of art as a glorified leisure activity was incompatible with Chesterton's more genuinely 'organic' (and far more virulently anti-Semitic) view which owed much to fin-de-siècle aestheticism both in the supreme value it put on art as a gratuitous expression of human spirituality, and in its fascination with putrefaction.

Also latent in BUF publicism on the arts was an impenetrable vagueness about precisely what the aesthetic forms and contents of Britain's reborn arts would be. *Blackshirt* and *Action* are frustratingly devoid of the detailed theatre criticism or surveys of contemporary drama which might have allowed inferences to be drawn about the sort of British and continental plays from the past which would have become the basis of an expurgated 'British' repertoire, and what kind of new ones would have been encouraged – presumably with the competition prizes and generous grants of the sort instituted in the new Italy and Germany. It is not even clear if all forms of experimentalism or theatrical modernism would have been banned, since Leigh

Vaughan-Henry's article strikes a stridently Futurist note when he insists that:

> We cannot carry over the effects of a new spirit and a new mental trend in the garbage of outworn thought or expression. We live in an age of aviation, telegraphy, radio, and electricity. Only in equivalent types of thought and expression can we voice the spirit of our time.[96]

In similar vein, another commentator declares that 'The world is moving forward to a new and strange age, and Fascism must be ahead of, not behind, the times. There is no place for the reactionary'.[97] Translated into terms of theatre management such pronouncements imply that at least some elements within the BUF might actually have encouraged the emergence of a British Pirandello or Marinetti (though tributes to Vorticism or a BUF attempt to emulate Wyndham Lewis's *Blast* are conspicuous by their absence).

In music, too, the case for a Fascist modernism had its proponents. Indeed, it was the main music critic of the BUF, Selwyn Watson, who must have shocked many a reader with his article 'In defence of Modern Music: its causes and its future'. It not only stressed that music is constantly evolving, so that over time what seems jarring comes to be heard as melodious, but praised Debussy, Stravinsky and Schönberg as 'revolutionaries of immense talent'. The unfamiliar harmonies and atonal qualities of modern classical music, like the syncopated rhythms and strident discords of jazz, reflected a world, which with the outbreak of the First World War had simply 'gone mad'. Yet he insisted that even British composers whose sound to many was 'unwelcome', such as William Walton and Benjamin Britten, had 'definite points of contact with the past', and that in their day Bach, Beethoven, Schumann and Wagner were trail-blazers and mould-breakers.[98]

The decadence or health of musical modernism was not the only nettle a BUF regime would have had to have grasped. There was also the dispute between those advocates of radical cultural cleansing who would have banned opera sung in a foreign language (and even opera altogether as 'un-British'), and those who, true to a sense of belonging to a Western and not just British civilization, vigorously defended performances of opera in the original as long as the British public saw the best that foreign musicians could offer.[99] It would also have had to decide whether to give in to calls for a total ban on foreign artists working in Britain or to introduce some sort of quota or exchange system.[100] If extreme xenophobes and anti-modernists had won the *Kulturkampf* over the interpretation of the slogan 'Britain First!' when applied to theatres and music halls, it would have led to a cultural revolution which smacked more of Chairman Mao than of Queen Elizabeth I.

There is slightly more to go on in the case of music than of the theatre when trying to hazard a guess as to what the new regime might have promoted in practice. In popular music the marching anthems of the BUF are on several occasions welcomed as signs of the rebirth of British tunefulness after the cacophonies of jazz, despite the fact that the tune of E. D. Randall's 'Britain Awake!'[101] was cribbed from the Nazi Horst Wessel Lied. Yet Fascists in whom Elgar's 'Land of Hope and Glory' induced shivers of ecstasy were on a collision course with the many advocates of British swing. One self-styled 'Christian' bandsman even wrote to *Action* claiming that British dance music was actually pioneered by 'white men', but that 'the Jews, true to their character, soon copied the original brains'.[102] This mythic narrative left the door wide open to a 'de-Judaised' jazz scene persisting under Mosley, and adverts offering the services of BUF and Aryan dance bands suggest that, as in Germany, 'decadent' rhythms would have continued to be heard in the new Britain, as long as they were played by Gentile hands.[103]

As for classical music, the presence of a fundamentalist xenophobic lobby is suggested by the inordinate praise heaped on *Iernin*, a Cornish opera of 'phenomenal brilliance'[104] composed by George Lloyd [*sic*], 'a young composer of genius', and on Sir Edward German's no less obscure *Merrie England*, which, we are told, pointed the way towards 'a real national opera in a future national England'.[105] John Porte's scheme for 'rescuing British music' within the Fascist state also involved an unmistakable *völkisch* element in his emphasis on revitalizing 'our great heritage of folk singing and dancing, and our amateur choral societies, so returning Britain to its 'natural State'.[106] A more reliable glimpse of the musical shape of things to come in a Fascist Britain is probably afforded by the concert held on 18 December 1935 at the Aeolian Hall in London by the BUF. The programme consisted of orchestral pieces by Elgar, Schubert and Wagner performed by the All British Orchestra in a display of 'uncompromising, joyful virility'. These were supplemented by Carmen's 'Toreador Song' and 'In the Gloaming' sung by Captain Cuthbert Reavely (described as 'in the forefront of living baritones'), who also helped organize the concert and was a contributor of several articles on music to the Fascist press. In the sphere of classical music at least, the ascendancy of safe, bourgeois, 'middle of the road' music over the avant-garde seems to be a law-bound feature of all modern revolutions whatever their political complexion,[107] and the same would have undoubtedly been true of the 'reawakened' British theatre as well under Mosley.

Yet in British Fascism, following another apparent 'law' of modern revolutionary movements, a mystifying rhetoric routinely papered over any ambivalences concerning aesthetic modernism and the profound contradictions between the BUF's utopian promises and the banality of what probably lay in store for audiences. A classic example of this rhetoric is provided by the short speech that Mosley made after the hardly earth-shatteringly innovative Aeolian Hall concert. In it he announced that, since great ages of creative activity foreshadow rather then reflect the periods of action, from his movement there would emerge an art, pure, original and higher than anything so far conceived: 'Fascism will bring to the new age the inspiration that is lacking today, for any creed which affects the human spirit so profoundly, and which fuses all human things in a white heat, can never fail to bring an art and a culture which shall be the glory of mankind'.[108]

Yet Mosley's bombast euphemized something much more sinister than a Philistine misunderstanding of the anthropology of culture, the nature of artistic creativity, and the impossibility of inducing cultural rebirths without creating aesthetic abortions. Latent in so much of the BUF's coverage of theatre and music, and perhaps made more insidious by the absence of explicitly eugenic or biological rationale, is the hidden agenda of ethnic cleansing in the name of cultural regeneration. The BUF may have started out as a movement trying to emulate Fascist Italy, but it is clear from its cultural criticism that, for most of its active supporters, its heart lay in Berlin rather than in Rome. In July 1935 we are told that Jews 'only have themselves to blame' for the decision to eliminate their culture from German life, given the fact that 'the infusion of alien thought and repulsive forms of "art" into the culture of a nation is infinitely more harmful' than economic domination.[109] The following year, on the occasion of the opening of the Haus der deutschen Kunst and the Decadent Art Exhibition in Munich, we are informed that Hitler is 'superbly suited to put an end to the infantile meanderings of the "Modern Art" of international Jewry'.[110] But as early as July 1933 the *Blackshirt* published what is, in the wake of the Holocaust, a chilling article in its series 'Letters of Lucifer' entitled joyfully 'Cleansing England!' It vilified the hostility of 'decadent' 'Bloomsbury' intellectuals to the draconian literary censorship recently introduced by the Third Reich and to the book-burnings that accompanied it:

> While the Nazis are cleaning out the sewers of the Kurfürstendamm and burning the productions of German intellectual decadence, the 'enlightened' government of Parliamentary England allows handbooks on opium-smoking to circulate among the young generation of our country. It is high time that Fascism applied the stomach-pump of common sense to the unclean stomach of English intellectualism.[111]

Thus the call in 1936 for a 'cleansing flame' to purge Britain of vice as effectively as Hitler has done in Berlin, Hamburg, and Munich',[112] or the warning two years later that 'it will need the iron grip of National

Socialism to loosen the Semitic stranglehold on the arts',[113] suggest that the BUF's 'economic' and 'cultural' variant of anti-Semitism might well have led to a use of state terror to 'remove' Jews from civil society indistinguishable in practice from that imposed by a more overtly biological, eugenic variety.

Even in this crucial area of BUF ideology ambiguities persisted, however. The article lamenting the 'death of tunefulness' and the readiness of the British to 'dance with no heart to any little yiddish tune that any little yiddish dance band cares to give them', makes the very un-Nazi admission that 'many of the great tunes which we all sang in 1914–18 were composed by Jews', explaining that 'the jew then was the servant and not the master'.[114] Arthur Reade argued that Jews should lose all citizenship rights and be physically removed from the West if its civilization was to be saved. But he went on to debate where they should be moved to, suggesting that Palestine was too small, and that the most likely candidates were Uganda, Biro-Bidjan (in a far Eastern province of the former USSR near the Chinese border), and Madagascar (by the late 1930s a favourite imagined location for a Jewish homeland among non-exterminatory anti-Semites). The article closes with another sentiment unthinkable in a Nazi context that, once secure in their own territory, the Jews' drive towards world domination may well be channelled into 'developing an all-round national life which would constitute their own special contribution to the human race'.[115]

Nevertheless, even if the BUF's anti-Semitism stopped short of being genocidal, there is ample evidence in its press that, despite the steady flow of information about what was happening to the 'enemies of the Third Reich', in the main its supporters' admiration for the escalating Nazi programme of ethnic cleansing was sustained right up to the outbreak of the war. For example, one article published in the summer of 1939 expressed unqualified enthusiasm for the cultural and spiritual rebirth which would ensue from a 'de-Judaised' Europe.[116] It is thus difficult to see how when push came to shove the BUF would have avoided collaborating in the Final Solution just as whole-heartedly as Pétain's Vichy or Szálasi's Hungary in its pursuit of a ritually purified and regenerated culture, no matter how 'unbiological' its racial theories. With hindsight, then, *Blackshirt*'s reference to England as 'a fortress built against infection' manages to contaminate Shakespeare's turn of phrase with anachronistic eugenic connotations of industrialized mass-murder using chemical pesticides. As Goethe (another of Mosley's cultural heroes) once put it, 'real events cast their shadow before them'.

Conclusion: The Nemesis of One Faustian Man

Denied political space by Britain's stable liberal democracy and sated nationalism, deprived of a structural crisis profound enough to spark off an epidemic of palingenetic political myth, British Fascism could never gain critical mass as a charismatic revolutionary movement.[117] The Corporate Britain was thus destined to remain a figment of utopian fantasy. It must therefore remain a matter of counterfactual speculation what would have become of the theatre and music within a Mosleyian new order. Were it to have retained political autonomy I suspect that a typically British compromise (no doubt dignified by the euphemism 'synthesis') would have resulted: a botched blend of Italian Fascist 'hegemonic pluralism' in which the state associated itself with any outstanding acts of creativity (even by non-Fascists) without imposing an official aesthetic or indulging in racial persecution,[118] and Nazi-style 'totalitarianism', complete with attempted purges of 'foreign' modernism and Jewish 'cultural bolshevism' from British society and impressive state-sponsored revivals of Elizabethan drama and music (not to mention madrigals and morris-dancing). On the other hand, there is every indication that the new Britain, had it been incorporated into the Nazis' New European Order, could have supplied enough home-grown collaborators who sympathized with Nazi aesthetics and art policies to ensure the sort of cultural convergence with the Third Reich that was witnessed in occupied France. It is far from inconceivable that stage-managed book-burnings outside the British Museum and the spectacle of the front rows of London theatres and concert halls filled with Nazi uniforms might one day have become part of the British way of life within the 'European New Order'.

As for Mosley himself, it is perhaps a tribute to the extraordinary tenacity of palingenetic myth (not to mention the human capacity for denial and self-delusion) that in the last phase of his life he did not recognize how badly he had misjudged the revolutionary potential of Britain's political situation in the 1930s. Nor did he contemplate with relief the systematized mass murder in which he would have been forced to collude had circumstances turned him into an English Quisling. Instead, he withdrew into a highly aestheticized 'meta-political' world of his own extrapolated from his pre-war Spenglerian vision. His essay 'Wagner and Shaw: A Synthesis' suggests that towards the end of his life he cast himself (at least subliminally) in the leading role of a cosmic opera in which his consummate failure in reality was simultaneously dramatized and lyricized, transfigured poetically into a heroic self-sacrifice which opens up for others the possibility of eventual triumph. In it he suggests that Wagner chose to follow the portrayal of Siegfried's triumph in the eponymous epic with the depiction of his failure in *Götterdämmerung* in order to convey the message (one that he believes was too subtle for Shaw to have grasped) that beyond all human striving, whether successful or not, a higher cyclic law of nature is at work. The opera's theme is 'the presage of rebirth in the recurring motif of destiny proving, affirming, and heralding another great upsurge in the life force'.

In this cosmic, aestheticized vision of the historical process Mosley has indefinitely postponed the paradise of a new Britain until another turning point in history occurs at some unspecified point long after his death. He now clearly identifies with those men he feels are the true subject of Wagner's opera, ones 'who will be ready to renounce the lesser order to achieve the greater, who will yield joy to serve destiny because some are called to strive greatly that higher forms may come'. To be worthy of this higher calling such a man:

> must have within him 'die ewigen Melodien' (the eternal melodies) and be 'at one with all high things'. Otherwise the synthesis of life and love would not be there. He would not be the final hero, the symbol of that generation of higher men which is ready to give all that all may be won.[119]

In 1933 Mosley had proclaimed his bid to create a new breed of 'Faustian Man' in the 'sceptred isle', seemingly oblivious of the cycle of murder, destruction, and self-deception into which the legendary Faust was drawn by his drive to conquer the realm of total experience. But, as in Goethe's version, he had now found a way of narrating his own redemption at the last minute, even if he had to play the part of the 'eternal feminine' himself: the ultimate patriarchal fantasy.

The Developing British Fascist Interpretation of Race, Culture and Evolution

Richard Thurlow

The British Union of Fascists (BUF) synthesized strands of radical right, national socialist and racial populist thought in Britain into a unified idea whose dynamism would sweep away the 'united muttons' of the 'old gangs' and create a 'new order'.[1] This chapter will explore the ideological divide in British fascism which made Mosley's project of a united British fascist movement a forlorn utopian dream. At root it was the different conceptions of race, culture and evolution which reinforced the personal divisions between competing 'leaders' and movements.[2] It will be argued that there were two viewpoints, which evolved in different directions between the inter-war and post-1945 periods, the Mosleyite and racial nationalist traditions. Although the BUF was more important than its rivals in the 1930s, Mosley was turned into a pariah figure by the war, and racial nationalism became far more significant after 1945, with the National Front (NF 1967–) and British National Party (BNP 1983–) having important backward linkages to the extremist inter-war movements like the Britons Society and the Imperial Fascist League (IFL).[3] In essence Mosleyites argued that culture created national and racial difference, while racial nationalists believed that race determined culture. Mosleyites believed in a neo-Lamarckian evolutionary process, while racial nationalists were genetic determinists influenced by Social Darwinism.

The differences between the Mosleyite and racial nationalist interpretations of race, culture and evolution invites a more thorough examination than those who would simply dismiss both as 'racist'. In general, it may be said that the Mosley tradition was closer to the Italian idealist fascist view of race, while the materialist British racial nationalism bore similarities to Nazism. Italian Fascist views on race derived from the theory of ethnocentrism of the Austrian-Jewish sociologist Ludwig Gumplowicz, and the concept of the nation as a race cradle suggested by the English anthropologist, Sir Arthur Keith.[4] The argument was that race formation was a dynamic historical and political process within the confines of the nation-state and that the defining characteristics of a people were acquired by the interaction of heredity, environment, culture and evolution over historical time. The Nazi conception of race, justified in both mythic and scientific terms, was a static, taxonomic, materialist view which was entirely dependent on heritable biological traits. Each of the main races had its own mental and physical attributes which were not subject to change except by racial mixture. Miscegenation would lead to the degeneration of the qualities of the supposed 'higher' race.[5] For Mosley culture developed as the spiritual and artistic achievement of the evolution of a people, influenced by history, environment, nationality and genetic endowment. Racial nationalists saw culture as determined by alleged innate characteristics of the 'nation' which led to inevitable decay and decline if influenced by outside forces imported by 'inferior' races.

For Italian Fascists and the BUF, provided there was not too wide a variation from the original 'stock', race-mixing within the nation state was not discouraged because it broadened the gene pool for future development. To Nazis and the IFL this view was absurd. For the BUF, most British citizens could not be racially categorized as superior or inferior to one another. For the IFL, the Nazi conception meant the ascribed superior-inferior dichotomy was fundamental with all non-'Nordic/Aryan' groups being viewed with disdain. Other ethnic categories ranged from the 'submen' of the Slav, black and aboriginal races, to the 'anti-nature' of the Jew, who was not even categorized as a human being.[6]

Although there was a generalized xenophobic nationalism built into much BUF propaganda, there was little attempt to turn it into an explicit racist philosophy. The official line was that the existence of a multi-racial empire made that impractical. However, Mosley talked about 'African savages', as well as stereotyping Jews during his anti-Semitic campaign, but his nationalism, unlike Joyce and BUF East End speakers, avoided biological images for the most part. Mosley believed that 'the great third factor of education is added to heredity and environment in human affairs, and the consequent evolution of a culture increases rather than diminishes difference'.[7]

Thus, for Mosley, culture remained more important than race as the basic unit of group categorization. Genetic arguments were used on occasion but they were always subsidiary to culture. In 1936 he warned of the possibility of a 'brother's war' in Europe, a metaphor based on his conception of the cultural and spiritual unity of Europe, when the real enemy was the 'Oriental barbarians' of another culture, Soviet Russia. After 1945 he developed this idea by using a racial metaphor to describe his basic cultural conception: 'The idea of kinship is the true idea, the reaching out of our hands to those who are kindred of the same kind ... As a family of the same stock and kind Europe should always have been united in this ideal.'[8] By this he meant that all Europeans possessed the spiritual attributes of an evolutionary vision and the ceaseless striving of Faustian man. This, however, was not to be viewed as a characteristic that was superior to those of another culture, merely a difference which was innate and not subject to transmission.

In contrast, the racial nationalist tradition developed a pseudo-scientific theory of a much lower order of thought than Mosley's. This was similar to Nazism, although it developed from a Nordic 'Anglo-Saxon' intellectual tradition. Both the minuscule Britons Society, which published *The Protocols of the Elders of Zion* in Britain after 1920, and the IFL made minimal political impact.[9] The Britons, with a small middle-class membership, held meetings on racial and nationalist themes and published a monthly newspaper-journal in the 1920s, although its print run was only 150.[10] Although its typical content was the political pornography of a scurrilous gutter anti-Semitism, Professor G. P. Mudge of London University outlined the basic philosophy of racial nationalism in a series of articles in *The Hidden Hand*, entitled 'Pride of Race'. The Britons described him as 'one of the first scientists to lecture on the importance of the Nordic and Mediterranean races in Britain and the danger of race mixture with Jews and Negroids'.[11] Mudge argued that:

> The greater contest in which we are all engaged is a conflict between races or nations. We must accept it as an axiom that this conflict is inevitable. The circumstances of nature and the impelling motives of human kind are such, that struggle and battle are as certain as the setting and rising of the sun, and are indeed part and parcel of the same universal laws.[12]

He stated: 'The English nation is the most homogenous of the nations of Europe' and from an anthropological point of view it was 'peopled by Nordic and Mediterranean types'. Mediterranean peoples were purportedly vivacious, versatile, impulsive and sociable, but they lacked the virtues of discipline, truthfulness, personal loyalty and leadership.

In contrast to the 'Mediterranean', the 'Nordic' allegedly possessed the personality features which the former lacked. Nordics supposedly combined beauty, brains and nobility, being typically blond, blue-eyed, tall and strong with a strong character reference as being sporting, sociable, loyal with steadfast and enduring qualities. Mudge then concluded from his analysis of the two 'great races' that history shows us, 'that the Nordic race has formed the administrative and organising caste and supplied the national leaders in classic, medieval and modern times, while the Mediterranean has constituted a great part, perhaps in the same nation as the bulk of the people'.[13]

Mudge also emphasized that 'a nation should be populated by a people as similar in blood and race as it possibly can be'. If racially divergent strains were allowed to enter the country then 'this is to invite national disaster in the struggle for existence, particularly if they were Jews, Chinese, Mongols, Indians or Negroes'. Mudge considered the majority of Englishmen were Nordics, although, given his favourable view of the English blend, he then partially contradicted himself by arguing that no Nordic should marry a Mediterranean as this would dilute the quality of the race.[14]

Today Mudge's views read like a classic case study of nineteenth-century racism. The mixture of social Darwinism, the categorization of national and racial types, the reading of personality from physical attributes, primitive eugenics, and the attribution of an aesthetic ideal of beauty and Victorian value judgements to specific 'races' were symptomatic of this. So too was the ascribed superiority of Nordic man and Anglo-Saxon nations. (Particularly significant, despite the Nordic's supposed love of liberty, was that his more authoritarian qualities were emphasized. There appeared also to be a shift from the traditional assumption of Anglo-Saxon authority over colonial peoples to a more elitist anti-democratic control by 'Nordics' over 'Mediterraneans' in British society.) This transition from nineteenth-century 'Anglo-Saxonism' was to be completed by Arnold Leese.[15]

Leese, a member of the Britons, became Director-General of the IFL in 1930.[16] Its active membership of a few dozen individuals were the main British fascist alternative to what Leese called 'kosher fascism' and the 'British Jewnion of Fascists' in the 1930s.[17] He argued that Mosley was a Jewish plant to discredit fascism in Britain, and wrongly accused his first wife of Jewish ancestry (Cimmie Mosley's grandfather, Levi Leiter, was an American millionaire with Dutch Calvinist roots). Although he changed his tune following internment, in 1940 he criticized Hitler for attacking 'Aryan' Norway.[18] He was also scathing about Mosley's failure to understand the primacy of race and his supposed failure to understand the 'threat' the Jews posed to British society; for Leese, Spengler was the enemy of fascism and national socialism.

In the *Fascist* he demonstrated his obsession with anti-Semitism but his garrulous style exhibited a perceived racial philosophy. For Leese, 'Race as a guide for statesman to future political events is a neglected study; breeds of men have characteristics just like breeds of dogs and there is no equality either in men or dogs'.[19] He possessed a Manichean view of society in which the future of civilization depended on the outcome of the struggle between the Nordic and the Jew. For Leese 'the Nordic may claim with justification that his race has ever been the greatest force for civilisation in the history of man's life on the globe'. The Nordic was responsible, according to Leese, for 'the great cultures of the ancient world'.[20] While for Leese there were no pure races, 'race mixing' could be of two kinds. Where the parents were of radically different types this led to the degeneration of the qualities of the 'higher' race, but if the racial outcross was between individuals whose characteristics were supposedly complementary, then it was bene-ficial. Like Mudge, Leese thought 'that there were far too many Arabs, Negroes, Somalis and Chinamen contaminating the white blood of our race with the assistance of the lowest of the low of white women'.[21] This, however, was secondary to the real problem that 'the acceptance of the Jew as a citizen of this country' meant that the 'poi-soning of our Anglo Saxon blood by this yellow negroid horde is proceeding apace'.[22] For Leese the Nazi defeat in 1945 meant the destruction of the Nordic race and Anglo-Saxon civilization: '*Europe is dead and gone* never to rise again ... as the Nordic race merges with the scrub population'.[23]

Leese's views on racial nationalism derived mainly from an 'Anglo-Saxon' tradition. He mentioned Hans Guenther, *The Racial Elements of European History*, L. A. Waddell, *The Makers of Civilisation in Race and History*, Madison Grant, *The Passing of the Great Race* and three books by Lothrop Stoddard, *The Revolt against Civilisation*, *The Rising Tide of Colour against White World Supremacy* and *Racial Realities in Europe*. From Waddell, the Professor of Tibetan at the University of London, he took the myth of the 'Aryan' origin of civilization and the bearer of culture throughout history. This view of the Nordic as the creator of culture owed much to Hans Guenther. For Leese, Guenther shows that middle-class moralizing and aesthetic value judgements could be incorporated into scientific endeavour. Guenther's pseudo-scientific rationale for race thinking and Nordic supremacy deeply influenced Leese as well as the Nazis. Madison Grant and Lothrop Stoddard applied Social Darwinism to 'Nordic' man and to Leese they demon-strated the importance of heredity over environment in history. They attacked Lamarckism and argued that mankind had made no 'racial progress' in either physical or brain capacity. For Leese the aim would be to preserve the innate qualities of the Anglo-Saxon 'Nordic' stock and to save them from degeneration rather than strive towards Mos-ley's higher form.[24]

Since 1945 race has been a key issue in the attempt to resuscitate neo-fascist movements in Britain. Although the National Socialist Movement (1962–8) and the British Movement (1968–) were blatant mimetic Nazi organizations, other racial populist and neo-fascist groups distanced themselves from fascism. The League of Empire Loyalists (1953–67), the British National Party (1962–7) and Mosley's Union Movement (1948–67) were attacked as 'fascist' by their enemies but did not see themselves as such. They and their most important successor organizations, the NF (1967–) and John Tyndall's BNP (1983–) were racial populist organizations which exploited public con-cern about 'black' immigration. Although the anti-Semitic obsessions of some leading members of the NF and BNP, and the racist influences on a new generation of British 'nationalists' have been pronounced, it would be more correct to see radical Right racial populist movements since 1945 as hybrid movements which incorporated neo-fascist and racist anti-immigrant themes. Other European countries have experienced similar developments.[25] Although a 'Jewish conspiracy' has often been invoked to explain the alleged plot to destroy the 'Anglo-Saxon' race through immigration, in both the NF and BNP, anti-black racism rather than anti-Semitism has been the main propaganda for recruitment purposes.

Perhaps the most sophisticated mixture of prejudice and 'racial science' was the racist propaganda of the NF. This incorporated the idea supposedly derived from socio-biology, that it was a natural instinct to be racially prejudiced, with the traditional inferior-superior dichotomy of racism. In a range of publications, but particularly in John Tyndall's *Spearhead*, the ideology of a British racial nationalism was developed. While the most scurrilous projection of racial fantasies onto black immigrants was left to Martin Webster and *National Front News*, Tyndall, and his editor, Richard Verrall, from 1976 to 1980 developed a range of arguments which incorporated influences from the British racial nationalist tradition, American anti-Semitic and anti-black literature, and the European neo-fascist New Right, although the latter mainly influenced a younger generation of NF activists. Also both Tyndall and Webster were ex-members of Colin Jordan's National Socialist Movement. If Richard Verrall was the link to contemporary academic racial nationalism, then John Tyndall was the main remodeller of old traditions. He developed a full blown theory of Anglo-Saxonism out of xenophobic British nationalism. This fulfilled the same functional role as the Nordic in the Mudge–Leese tradition, with Anglo-Saxons throughout the world being accredited with much the same values and character as the older tradition. However, for Tyndall, the weakness of the ruling class and the decay of racial values in the population at large meant also the decline of Britain.[26]

For Tyndall, British nationalism needed 'unity as a people … linking all in a dynamic upsurge of creative vigour in every field of work and leisure'.[27] If this unity can be achieved then the 'resurgent spirit of Nationality and Race, with its promethian ideals of Genius, Beauty, Nobility, Destiny and Heroism' may transform the future of the nation. This 'resurgent spirit' was 'Anglo-Saxonism'. Tyndall believed that the Anglo-Saxons were one of the two 'truly great and leading races in the world – the other being the Germans'. In Tyndall's view, Anglo-Saxondom was defined as the people of British stock in the world. Together they comprised 150–60 million inhabitants and if they were united they would be 'indisputably the strongest power on earth'.[28] Without the Anglo-Saxon inheritance 'our land would be a wilderness. Our villages and towns would consist of mudhuts. Our art would consist of primitive scrawlings. Our literature would speak to us in grunts. We would have no feats of engineering and science.'[29] The racial fascist conception of high culture derived from supposed innate qualities inherent in the racial and national origins of the artist, which ascribed favoured characteristics such as classical form to the Nordic race, and negative traits, such as all forms of 'modern art', as typical of other inferior races.

To Tyndall the British political establishment was corroded by liberal ideals which had produced weakness and national decline. Even the racial quality of the Anglo-Saxon heritage of Britain was in doubt as 'racial downbreeding and a society without discipline are increasing our population of useless slobs'. Tyndall was referring not only to the racial problems posed by black immigration but also to the supposed 'inferior strains within the indigenous races of the British Isles', particularly football hooligans and skinheads.[30] This was coded language for those who had forced his resignation from the NF, leading to his formation of the New National Front in 1982, and its change of name to become another British National Party in 1983. Tyndall attacked them because he believed only a movement of discipline and authority under strong leadership, with an elite cadre of members, could arrest the forces of decay. The strategy of 'national bolshevism', with its attempt to recruit alienated unemployed youth, was total anathema. The idea that these shock troops were the new barbarians who would destroy the effete decaying bourgeois values of British society, offended against Tyndall's Anglo-Saxonism with its roots in Victorian ideals of respectability and authority. His old chums were now part of a racially heterogeneous rabble, which he repeatedly referred to as the 'gay National Front' as a result of alleged homosexual activities by leading members.

Tyndall's Anglo-Saxonism also has to be viewed in terms of his own political development. Tyndall tried to synthesize the British fascist tradition. For a time he was deputy leader of Jordan's National Socialist Movement, before he formed his own more British form of 'national socialism' in the Greater Britain Movement, the title of Mosley's original BUF manifesto. During his probation in the NF, he learned from A. K. Chesterton the art of cloaking racism and anti-Semitism in more moderate and rational language. Tyndall attempted to fuse both the racial nationalist and Mosleyite inheritance of the British fascist tradition, together with concealed Nazism and extreme racist American influences in the NF and BNP. In spite of his tactical ability and ambition, his extremism and Nazi background forever tainted his attempts to move 'British nationalism' into the political mainstream and in 1999 he was ousted from the leadership of his own creation, the BNP.

Unlike the racial nationalist tradition, for Mosley culture rather than race was the unit of categorization. Genetic arguments were used but they were always subordinate to the main cultural case. For Mosley cultural achievement developed from a variety of historical, environmental and artistic influences and was not dependent on a narrow genetic or national endowment. During the 1930s Mosley argued that British history and culture provided the tradition which, if harnessed under fascist leadership, would lead to the rebirth of British civilization; after 1945 the spark of Faustian culture needed to be relit to defend Europe from the threat of internal and external barbarians.[31]

The BUF argued that British fascism was embedded deep in British history. For the BUF, fascism linked feudalism, the guild system, Tudor centralized authority and the winning of Empire to the conception of the Corporate State. In particular, 'the vigorous patriotism, the advanced social conscience, the idealism and the vital spirit of endeavour that characterized the Elizabethan is also typical of the Fascist'.[32] This peak of British history was reached again in the eighteenth century when much of the Empire was added to Britain's domain. Others, like A. K. Chesterton, saw in the Elizabethan age and the dramas of Shakespeare the aesthetic values which could guide political action.[33] These achievements had been undermined by the allegedly stultifying effects of the victory of parliament over a centralized authority of monarchy: 'As it was the bourgeois class dictatorship, and not the functional state emerged from the chaos of the parliamentary wars, which saw the overthrow of the Tudor Nation state conception.'[34] As a result, liberal capitalism and powerful vested interests replaced the needs of the state as the paramount influence on government.

For Mosley the British ruling class has been characterized by two basic types:

> The man of life enthusiasm and achievement with the capacity of Hellenism, charm and cultural expansion, alternates with that cautious, restricted, inhibited prig who conceals his main interest, which is money, behind a mask of smooth piety that is rendered the more effective by the fact that he has deceived himself before deceiving others. These two forces are the age-old contenders for the soul of England. They are proved incapable of effective synthesis, despite all attempts and observations to the contrary; so the conflict for some time past has been almost completely, if temporarily resolved by the victory of the latter.[35]

To Mosley, the victory of the Puritan spirit and the emergence of the 'will to comfort' type, who evaded rather than grappled with the great political problems, meant that the British parliamentary system was no longer capable of solving the great historical crisis now facing the nation.

Mosley's fascist thought developed from heroic vitalism and creative evolutionism. For Mosley fascist idealism meant the synthesis of Nietzschean and Christian values, of the will to power exemplified by the athleticism and discipline of the individual striving to become Superman, being harnessed into the service of the community.[36] The BUF represented the Spartan heroic elite teaching a muscular Christianity which would indoctrinate society with the values of the new fascist man.[37]

The BUF saw Spengler's *Decline of the West* (1914) as the 'greatest expression of the bourgeois mind' whose cyclical view of history supposedly outlined the cause of the rise and decay of societies. Mosley was deeply influenced, too, by his concept of Caesarism, his morphology of culture in general and the incompatibility of the Faustian (European) and Magian (which included the Jews) culture in particular. Mosley also argued, following Spengler, that the great cultures were not for export and that attempts to impose values on others were doomed to failure. For Spengler 'race' was a feature of all cultures, and meant the classic expression of the symbols and values of a culture. Where Spengler was mistaken was in his pessimism. As Mosley saw it, fascist man would be inculcated with the values and energy to end the organic decay of European civilization and the British Empire and to rejuvenate society.[38] After 1945 Mosley made 'Europe-a-Nation' rather than the British Empire his utopian dream through an 'extension of patriotism'.

The significant differences between the Mosleyite and racial nationalist traditions over race and culture also had implications for their views on human evolution. For whereas the BUF viewed evolution in neo-Lamarckian terms, racial nationalists interpreted it as a perverted form of Darwinism. Such differences were accentuated because Mosley and the BUF argued from cultural premises, whilst racial nationalists developed their views from 'scientific racism'.

The major implication of a neo-Lamarckian view of human evolution was the belief that characteristics acquired during a parent's lifetime could be inherited by offspring under certain conditions. A biological organism was able to respond to environmental change by adaptation in the interest of the survival of the species. The mechanical application of this belief led to the disastrous experiments in Soviet agriculture by Lysenko. However, Mosley and the BUF emphasized willpower as the prime agent of evolution rather than the influence of the environment.[39] Accordingly, humanity had the capacity to control its own destiny and to plan evolution. As this could be accelerated by will power and education, the main force for change could be social and cultural factors rather than physical. Hence what mattered for Mosley was not alleged racial characteristics of a people but cultural values. These enabled adaptation as a response to events and the will to transform reality. Thus, in theory, the social implications of Mosley's vision had more in common with Marxist ideas about the malleability of human nature rather than racial determinism. Mosley, however, followed the assumptions of most nineteenth-century Lamarckians who limited their theory of inheritance of acquired characteristics to those of European stock, by arguing that evolution had come to an end amongst the 'lower races', and that they could no longer respond to the challenge of the environment.[40] This form of pseudo-biological culturalism was very different to Boasian cultural relativism because the assumptions of late nineteenth-century neo-Lamarckism explicitly denied the transfer of values outside a very limited range of cultural and physical difference.[41] This reinforced Spengler's cultural morphology, which insisted that the defining features of a culture could not be grafted on to another, particularly if in the case of the Faustian (European, early autumn) and Magian (Jew, winter) they were in different phases of development. This belief led Mosley to support apartheid in his 'Eur-Afrika' dreams of the 1940s.

The major contrast between Lamarckian and Darwinian theories of human evolution was that the former emphasized the interaction between the mind and will of man and the environment, whilst the latter argued that adaptation through random mutation and natural selection was the chief motor of change. Today Lamarckism is not taken seriously as a theory of evolution, although acquired characteristics obviously are an important feature of the transmission of culture and education in human development. Nevertheless the obscure backwater of British fascism has shed some interesting light on the arguments and played a small bit-part in a significant scientific debate.

The root of BUF ideology saw a dichotomy between an optimistic view of the evolutionary potential of man and the performance of the British governing class. For Mosley the potential for man was almost limitless:

> Biology begins again to teach that the wilful determination of the species to rise above the limitations of material environment is the dominating factor in evolution. ... In fact every tendency in modern science assures us that in superb effort the human spirit can soar beyond the restraint of time and circumstance.[42]

The future belonged to the 'thought-deed' man, the apotheosis of the 'will to achievement' type who would control human evolution. This belief was raised to a religious principle when Mosley argued that aiding the 'progressive movement from lower to higher forms' meant serving the 'purpose of God' and that his life was dedicated to that purpose.[43] He wished to create a new man in a new society with new values.

For Mosley, 'every Blackshirt is an individual cell of a collective Caesarism. The organised will of devoted masses, subject to a voluntary discipline and inspired by the passionate ideal of natural survival, replacing the will to power and a higher order of the individual superman.' The dynamic leadership, authority and spiritual idealism of fascism would create the necessary prerequisites that would ensure future prosperity. Mosley argued that 'Caesarism and Science together could evolve Faustian man'.[44]

Mosley derived his Lamarckian ideas from George Bernard Shaw, particularly from the preface of *Back to Methuselah* (1922). For Shaw the failure of reconstruction after the First World War confirmed his doubts, 'whether the human animal, as he exists at present, is capable of solving the social problems raised by his own aggregation, or as he calls it his civilisation'. This failure led him to believe that the rulers of society were 'all defectives'. If society was to progress, man would have to change: 'What hope is there then of human improvement? According to the neo-Darwinists, to the Mechanists, no hope whatsoever, because improvement can only come through some senseless accident which must, on the statistical average of accidents, be presently wiped out by some other senseless accident.' Shaw argued that this was far inferior to the Lamarckian belief that living organisms changed because they wanted to and that 'consciousness, will, design, purpose, either on the part of the animal itself or on the part of the superior intelligence controlling its destiny' was the motive force behind evolution in a species. Vitalism, with its concept of will to power through self control and creative evolution, offered far more hope to man than the 'dismal creed' of Darwinism.[45]

Like Mosley, as a result of his enforced leisure during the Second World War, Shaw's interest in Lamarckian evolution partially derived from Goethe's morphological view of nature. This utopian optimism needs, however, to be kept in perspective; the dark side of Mosley's wrestling with the implications of the Faustian riddle illustrated his descent into the political gutter with the adoption of political anti-Semitism after 1935, and the anti-immigrant campaign in Notting Hill in 1958–9. As Nicholas Mosley pointed out: 'that while the right hand dealt with grandiose ideas and glory, the left hand let the rat out of the sewer'.[46]

In marked contrast to the Mosleyite tradition, post-war racial nationalism in the NF and BNP has developed an extreme form of Darwinism and genetic determinism as the basis of its racist outlook. Like Mudge and Leese these included the ascription of psychological characteristics to physical classification, ethnocentric middle-class moralism and the use of aesthetic values to create a racial hierarchy. These arguments were sometimes used as a cloak for the resurrection of Nazi ideas, or to advertise the more academic presentation of the Nordic tradition in the publications of the Historical Review Press or the physical anthropology journal, *Mankind Quarterly*. Such influences buttressed the conclusions of 'scientific racism' which included 'proofs' from phrenology, the blending theory of genetic inheritance of the biometricians, intelligence testing and the alleged findings of socio-biology.[47]

Prime among these assumptions were the alleged superiority of 'Anglo-Saxon' stock over other racial groups, and the threat to the 'racial purity' of 'white' Britain posed by 'black' immigration. This was usually portrayed as a 'Jewish' plot, engineered by 'Jewish' finance and 'Jewish communism', and vigorously propagated by 'Jewish' scientists. Somewhat ironically, the 'Science for the People' critics seized on the NF interpretation of the alleged conclusions to accuse the socio-biologists and 'Selfish Gene' kin selectionists of genetic determinism with racist implications, an accusation which was refuted by Ed Wilson, Richard Dawkins, Bill Hamilton and other biologists.[48] While conversely, the social sciences have successfully resisted being reduced to a branch of biology, nevertheless population genetics is now a reputable science, despite the long shadow engendered by Nazi atrocities. Both the socio-biology/evolutionary psychology and 'science for the people' disputants accept that population genetics and Mendelism do not support racist ideas. The range of variation in mental and physical characteristics are greater within a population than between different ethnic groups. Culture, language and human interaction with the environment was thought to differentiate man from other life forms, and dominant and recessive genes make genetics far more complex than any determinist model.

Like fundamentalist evangelical Christians, racists have tried to exploit the divisions between evolutionary biologists. By misinterpreting what socio-biologists and evolutionary psychologists were claiming about human nature and relating it exclusively to social Darwinism and instinctivist psychology, Richard Verrall of the NF claimed that human actions were genetically determined and that racial prejudice and nationalism were natural programmed instincts.[49] For Verrall both Lamarckian theories of evolution and the importance given by social scientists to human culture represent the work of 'scientific hoaxers', leading to the absurdities of Lysenko's experiments in the Soviet Union. Lamarckism is depicted as the Marxist theory of evolution, because it encourages social engineering: 'it held out the prospect of giving certain physical treatment to human beings which could turn them into equal communist zombies whose acquired characteristics could be inherited by succeeding generations'.[50]

For Verrall although men have some free will, and the environment plays a minor role in influencing development it is the genetic inheritance which determines his potential: 'Against this destructive theory we racialists declare that man and society are the creation of his biological nature. We insist not only that genetic inheritance determines inequality – not social environment – but that social organisation and behaviour are essentially the product of our biological evolution.' Verrall argues that it is 'the modern science of sociobiology that has finally buried Marxism', and that Crick and Wilson have put the seal of scientific approval on this 'biologically determinist view of man and society'. Their significance for the NF was that they had, allegedly, rediscovered 'Darwinian evolution in micro-biological terms'. The implication of this for Verrall was that 'Sociobiology has shown us that evolutionary processes have genetically and therefore immutably programmed human nature with instincts of competitiveness, territorial defense, racial prejudice, identification with integral behaviour within one's kin group (nation), instincts which the Marxist fantasy said were socially determined which would and should be eradicated'.[51] Some of the intellectual 'young Turks' in the NF were influenced by the French neo-fascist 'New Right', especially Alain de Benoist, and the Italian Julius Evola. The 'differentialist' emphasis that each cultural group should retain its own identity was advocated in such ultra-nationalist publications such as *Scorpion*.

While this misinterprets the beliefs of most socio-biologists and geneticists, even in 1980, nevertheless there is still significant scientific disagreement over the implications of socio-biology and evolutionary psychology. While such racist (and indeed sexist) ideas as projected by the NF have no scientific basis or moral or social validity, controversy over the human genome project, or other forms of genetic engineering, make this still a highly contentious area. What can be said, however, is that there have been flights of rhetoric in the language of socio-biologists and ethnologists which has sometimes led to misinterpretation, as in the case of the NF. So little is known about the relationship between individual genes, or groups of genes, and behaviour, indeed the programming of the genetic code, the relationship between mind and the genes and the role of culture, that some of the most influential population geneticists have urged caution in interpretation of data. While some of the most important and well funded scientific research is taking place in this area, much of it remains highly controversial.[52]

Although both the Mosleyites and racial nationalists within British fascism developed racist ideologies, there were significant differences, which help explain why the divisions became so bitter and impeded unity. At root these views were determined by the opposing views of the role of culture and the nature of human evolution. For Mosley culture created race while racial nationalists argued that racial characteristics determined culture. Mosley's fascism was based on vitalist and idealist traditions whilst racial nationalists were materialists and determinists. Whereas the evolutionary debate in British fascism began in nineteenth-century traditions of neo-Lamarckism and crude Social Darwinism, Mosleyites developed a synthesis of creative evolutionism and Spenglerian cultural morphology, whilst racial nationalists evolved from Nordic man, to genetically programmed men (and women).

I would like to acknowledge the financial assistance of the British Academy and the comments of Liz Harvey on an earlier version of this paper.

Part II

Cultural Representations:

Cultural Histories of British Fascism

Britain's New Fascist Men:
The Aestheticization of Brutality in British Fascist Propaganda

Julie V. Gottlieb

In a much-quoted passage from *The Greater Britain* (1932), Sir Oswald Mosley stated that 'we want men who are men and *women who are women*'.[1] Mosley's gendered perception has traditionally been read as a clear statement on the type of woman the British Union of Fascists (BUF) intended to recruit, and as an articulation of an uncompromising vision of bifurcated sex roles in British fascist ideology and practice. While the historiography of British fascism has begun to address the history of women in the BUF,[2] the scholarship has still tended to take for granted that the construction of a culture of 'feminine fascism' was a subaltern complement to an aggressively masculinist fantasy of national palingenesis, and a counterpoint to a pervasive glorification of male violence and male sexualized fanaticism.

This chapter will gender the history of British fascism from another perspective – from that of the creation of 'masculine fascism' in Britain – by examining patterns of male hegemony from the founding of the New Party; by demonstrating the institutionalization of an aesthetic of brutality in the paramilitary hierarchies and in the mobilization of the male civilian combatant; and by exploring the images and mission of British manhood as they were inscribed in the movement's visual culture, rhetorical flourishes and leadership cults. Walter Benjamin famously diagnosed that the power of fascism was to 'render politics aesthetic',[3] and it is intriguing to explore how this process functioned within a fascist movement on the peripheries of power.

It has only been very recently that historians have begun to examine the British extreme Right through these thematic and methodological lenses. Other authors in this volume are now doing just this, and Tony Collins has rightly observed that 'little has been written about the relationship between British Fascism and masculinity', and that 'this is curious since it was the BUF's commitment to manliness and its construction of a distinct masculine identity which provided a crucial element in the underpinning of its paramilitary politics'.[4] While the project to 'gender' British fascism is a relatively new one, the historiography of international fascism(s) has paid close attention to gendered representations in fascist iconography, literature and propaganda, and a growing body of literature is concerned with providing generic definitions for the new fascist man, and exposing the fallacy and farce of 'fascist virilities'. Historians acknowledge that 'as with any revolutionary movement that aims at fundamental change, in its consecration of the Superman political icon, Fascism had as its ultimate goal the creation of a new human being, *Homo fascistus*'.[5] George Mosse has identified the new fascist man as 'a warrior-crusader in the service of a faith'; 'this new man must be disciplined, at one in spirit with like-minded men through a way of perceiving the world, of acting, of behaving, based upon a sober acceptance of the new speed of time and a love of combat and confrontation'; he is 'forceful, energetic, hard and proud'; he is identified by his generation for 'to have experienced the war led to true manhood ... Yet, this idealized veteran was no individualist, he was one with his squad and his people'; 'the new man's body represented his mind as well'; he is torn between a triumphant masculinity and the ideal of family life, most often leading to a rejection of family responsibility and a scorn for women. Notably, there is little historically unprecedented nor exceptionally original in this stereotype. Nonetheless, 'never before or since the appearance of fascism was masculinity elevated to such heights: the hopes placed upon it, the importance of manliness as a national symbol and as a living example played a vital role in all fascist regimes'.[6] Drawing on national traditions of artistic expression, 'the aesthetics of fascism used both a pseudo-classical ideal, if not consistently, and the instrumentality of that part of established religion which ever since the baroque had represented the "beauty of holiness"'.[7] Examining the discourse of Italian Fascism, Barbara Spackman has argued that 'virility is not simply one of many fascist qualities, but rather that the cults of youth, of strength and stamina, of obedience and authority, and of physical strength and sexual potency that characterize fascism are all inflections of that master term, virility'.[8] BUF propagandist A. K. Chesterton's analysis of the originality of fascism certainly conformed to the general exaltation of virility. In 1936 he explained: 'In Fascism there appears once again on the world scene, vigorously contending for world masterdom, the great creative urge of the masculine spirit which through the ages has sped man forward to the heights of his achievement ... It is the spirit of the man of action, the conqueror and the law-giver.'[9]

While Chesterton was reflecting on the universal ethos of fascism, we need to take a more nationally focused approach and examine how the BUF adopted and adapted these masculinist paradigms. As a movement, and never a regime, did the masculine culture of British fascism adhere to these continental typologies? Was there anything unique about the cultural construction of manliness in the case of British fascism? Indeed, this chapter will argue that the BUF represented a nationally-specific response to perceived imperial, cultural and bourgeois decadence, building on the particular and peculiar manly traits of Britain's answer to charismatic leadership in the person of Sir Oswald Mosley – the 'Rudolf Valentino of Fascism'.

Masculinity in Crisis: Blackshirts to the Rescue?

Furthermore, during the 1930s the BUF forcefully intruded into current national debates on gender roles, the future of British youth in crisis, the permission for political violence, and the appropriate ways and means of commemorating the men who died in the trenches, debates which each depended on competing and conflicting images of masculinity. Joanna Bourke has observed that 'a generation of men who had been too young to be actively engaged in military services grew up in a world in which certain aspects of "being a man" were believed to be threatened, and their aesthetics of the body reflected this perception'.[10] Certainly, there was a general recognition that the Blackshirts were appealing to just this generation of young men by 'suggesting that it is manly to dress in uniform, to march and countermarch, and to give a swaggering impression of strength and force'. However, few of those engaged in the enterprise of rebuilding the fortress of British manhood were convinced by the Blackshirts' approach. Indeed, A. V. Alexander identified as the alternative to Blackshirt masculine aggression the Brotherhood Movement which would 'lead the way in educating our youth to the fact that it is far more manly ... to stand for the principles of brotherhood and liberty'. While the late Inspector of Army Physical Training, E. L. W. Henslow Clate, disagreed that the Brotherhood Movement was the best distraction from Blackshirt violence, he also rejected the BUF's attempted resurrection of British manhood, instead offering as the solution 'a more vigorous outlook' in education, religious teachings and in their leisure.[11] Similarly, Lord Rothermere's provocative and ageist support for the Blackshirts spawned a lively debate in the British press on the best solutions to this crisis among the nation's youth.[12] As these examples suggest, the BUF was not far off the mark in its own diagnosis of a national mood of a crisis of masculinity. What British fascists offered to each of these debates was an extremist position that inflated normative masculine stereotypes.[13]

British fascists argued in favour of the bifurcation of male and female political activism; they prophesied that the male youth of Britain would provide the leadership for a fascist revolution in the name of the return to British pre-eminence; and they constructed models for their coming fascist state in the form of gangs of paramilitary men, a nationwide system of political activity organized around sport, regular rehearsals for the greater violence to come and strict hierarchies crowned by the infallible leader. One of the BUF's marching songs, 'Come, All Young Britain' (the music composed by Lord Berners), described the mission, bodies and consciousness of this British fascist vanguard:

> We are men of the modern age,
> We are steadfast and proud and strong;
> We believe in our heritage,
> We are eager lithe and young!
> We've a plan of courageous revival
> For the problems and needs of to-day.
> We must fight for the right of survival;
> We must turn from the things of decay.
> – Come all Young Britain, and march with the
> Blackshirt Battalions![14]

These gangs of fascist men were encouraged to use violence not only "Gainst vested powers, [the] Red front, and massed ranks of Reaction',[15] but were also sanctioned to deal brutally with dissident members. The inner life of the BUF foreshadowed the purges of disillusioned sycophants, the staged 'court martials', and the very public scenes of humiliation that might have been practised at the national level had the movement ever come to power.[16] However, as is well known, British new fascist manhood was denied its ultimate expression by the reality of marginality and political failure.

In the British case then, how does such an intrusive and chauvinist masculinism respond to political and personal bankruptcy? This chapter will examine the extent to which the discourse on the British fascist new man acknowledged unconquerable political opposition first and foremost in the form of a stable parliamentary system and, on a daily basis, in the form of communist and socialist hecklers. Further, it will be seen how Mosley's men were impotent in the face of cultural resistance as it manifested itself in literary parodies of their Leader, in journalistic mockery of their political and sexual immaturity, and in a healthy dose of British humour. In terms of energizing the fascist manly stereotype in Britain, there was a great gulf between aspiration and political consequence.

New Men for a New Party

The masculine body and the trope of the male-identified body politic drove the first movement of Mosleyite dissent. Founded in 1930 and folding in 1932 before the launch of the BUF, Mosley's New Party called for the country to 'brace itself as a man to face new thoughts, new sacrifices and new adventures.'[17] The New Party also marked the boundaries of the generational conflict that was to be so prominent in BUF discourse, and on the eve of the 1931 General Election Mosley called upon his supporters to provide some youthful contrast to 'the scene of an old men's battle.'[18] The New Party established its own youth organization, the NUPA (New Party youth movement), whose members wore a uniform of grey shirts with black trimming – significantly only the trim was black, and it would not be until the formation of the BUF that the whole uniform was stained black with the fascist spirit and colour. In the NUPA the benefits of the political uniform were explained as follows:

> A uniform has a leveling effect. It will also make every member, and particularly the new recruit, feel that he is in the ranks of an army in which all classes are combined with but one purpose: the achievement of a great ideal – the greatest ideal that has been offered the people of our country since August 4, 1914.[19]

As a further inducement to this great ideal, the NUPA organized its own boxing classes, cricket teams and fencing demonstrations and classes, and were in force to steward the New Party's meetings. While New Party membership was open on the same terms to both men and women, the NUPA was an exclusively male affair. NUPA's internal organ, the *New Times*, exposed the male-obsessed attitudes of a group of restless youth as they sought to entrench homosocial relations and reassert male supremacy in government. As E. Hamilton Piercy wrote to the editor:

> Mr Editor, if you have any power at all in presenting opinions, I beseech you always to cry with hefty lungs and a mighty pen against this move [of allowing women to join NUPA]. I firmly believe that a youth movement, such as ours, will lose its manhood the day the first woman enters as a member … We know that, to the woe of this country, women have the vote but any thinking man knows that it is not a woman's job to have anything to do with the running of the country.[20]

The Political Technology of Virility

The same fixation on male camaraderie and male-defined spaces was transported into the BUF.[21] While the Women's Section was formed in March 1933, half a year after the foundation of the movement in October 1932, the BUF was designed in the image of a private army (or storm troop division), with the aim to re-enliven the *esprit de corps* of the trenches, and complete with military ranks and hierarchies, barracks, organized physical activities and drilling and camps. Masculine fascism reached its apotheosis in the summer of 1933 with the conversion of the former Whitelands Teacher Training College in Chelsea into the Black House. (The BUF ran the Black House from 1933 to

1935). Indeed, the formation of the Women's Section, and the establishment of its separate headquarters at 12 Lower Grosvenor Place, was necessitated as much by the politically expedient motivation to attract women to the movement, as by the homosocial desire that the Black House retain its exclusively masculine character. This was exemplified by a directive in the *Fascist Headquarters Bulletin* of 1933 which stipulated that 'ladies are no longer allowed access to NHQ premises, except to attend mixed classes and concerts at such times as may be from time to time authorized'.[22] As one journalist reported of his visit to the BUF's new Black House:

> After being questioned by a black-shirted sentinel at the door ... I was taken along torturous passages, past painters and cleaners and electricians, all displaying tremendous activity. We passed doors marked 'Defence Force Control' and 'Guardroom' in the regular W.D. style of lettering. Eventually we came to a room labeled 'O/C. Propaganda.' Here I was handed over to a young man who told me all about everything – or nearly everything. 'About 150 men will be quartered here permanently,' he said. 'But should an emergency arise we have accommodation for 5,000 men, who could be fed and provided with sleeping quarters here. As you can see, we maintain military discipline, and the men undergo a certain amount of simple drilling, more in the nature of exercise.'[23]

Nor, apparently, was the BUF reluctant to display its paramilitary equipment to its most fierce opponents, and upon a visit to the Black House in July 1934, *Daily Worker* reporters were 'shown the "Riot Squad" cars, the motor workshop, [and] the sleeping quarters of the standing army (with the beds made "spare bed" fashion)'.[24]

The Blackshirts claimed that drilling was an unarmed activity, and merely the 'first step towards an ideal of a nation of young men "living like athletes"'.[25] This command to live as athletes was central to the BUF's vision of the present and the hopes it invested in the future. Blackshirts often repeated the claim that the movement upheld 'a belief in physical and mental fitness'.[26] Alexander Raven-Thomson, the leading ideologue of the movement, remarked that: 'The British people must be led back to the playing fields. They must learn that physical fitness apart from being a pleasure to themselves is an obligation which they owe to the nation. The first effort of the organisation of leisure, especially for the young, will be devoted to sport and athleticism.'[27] This Spartan model was institutionalized by the movement's organization around sport – fencing, boxing, rugby, football, cricket, tennis, golf, swimming, rowing, cycling, flying, motoring and motorcycling – as a means of building the male body and promoting team spirit. Collins's extensive research into the BUF's sporting activities and body culture demonstrates just how important these activities were for recruiting across class lines, for tempting recruits away from the other social clubs run by other parties, and for elevating testosterone levels among Mosley's men and for recruiting.[28]

Like drilling, sport was an integral part of the Blackshirt spectacle and trademark theatricality. For example, the BUF's White City rally on 5 August 1934 was stage-managed as follows: 'From 3 p.m. until the leader speaks at 6 p.m. the arena will be given over to physical training displays, inter-area athletics, boxing matches and fencing. There will sometimes be eight boxing matches taking place simultaneously [and] the blackshirt band will be augmented to 100 performers.'[29] Indeed, the Blackshirts had their own jazz bands (significantly enough, one of these was called 'Jazz without Jews'), their own choirs, and hosted many dances, cabarets and balls. As sport was at the service of building a movement of new fascist male bodies, cultural forms – music, art and design, dance and politicized theatre – were at the service of providing recreation and politically appropriate leisure for this British new fascist man.

Further, from an early stage, the BUF hosted its own christenings and weddings, bringing within its fold – and within the folds of the Blackshirt uniform itself – every stage of the life cycle.[30] Mimicking military weddings, the grooms were always dressed in their full Blackshirt uniform, and the newly-weds were greeted by the fascist salute and a guard of honour made up by fellow Blackshirts. Nor were the very young excluded from this process of fascistization, from this aestheticization of politics, and at BUF bazaars among the items available for purchase were 'dolls dressed in the traditional blackshirt.'[31] The BUF's cultural programmatism extended to art and architecture, and in keeping with Hitler's and Speer's grand blueprints for Nazified German cities, BUF writers were quick to offer their own suggestions for appropriately fascist British architecture. Writing in the *Architects Journal*, a 'Number of Fascist Architects' inveighed against the 'mean and meaningless', the 'false and pretentious', and the 'soulless' in modern architecture, and offered as the fascist alternative architecture that was 'hopeful', encouraged 'vitality' and offered 'new virile styles'.[32]

What will already be clear from these examples is that the movement's vision transcended the aspiration to electoral success. Instead, its aim was to create, while still in political exile, the cultural apparatus that would accompany a British fascist state, and to have ready, for the moment of conquest, a fully formed civic-religious liturgy, an inventory of rituals, and a distinctive style of art, dress and movement. British fascism represented more than a political party; it was also a cultural movement, however misconceived or unsuited to the British terrain.

What were the stylistic influences and the historical parameters for this British fascist cultural project, this British fascist version of

Kulturkampf? While masculine fascism looked back to the past for its models of social formation and military ennoblement (the exaltation of the Merrie England of serene manhood), Mosley repeatedly claimed that his was 'the modern movement', and the BUF derived its aesthetic idiom from Futurism, including the exaltation of speed, new technology and science. This fascist–Futurist paradigm complemented a preference among Mosley's men for fast cars, armour-plated vehicles, motorbikes, and speaker vans. Indeed, the exploitation of modern technology was important both symbolically and practically, and their 'Black Maria' speaker vans served as improvised platforms for BUF orators, especially during more disorganized meetings. For example, at Battersea Park in September 1935, from the roof of their van 'Fascist speakers held forth with the aid of microphones and amplifiers'.[33] Similarly, in the East End in June 1936: 'Mosley has suddenly appeared, as if sent up through a pantomime trap, and is getting the Fascist salute. It is answered by hundreds of hands clustered around the vans.'[34] Further, this embrace of the new and the modern was projected onto the model of the future Corporate State, a state run by Blackshirt experts who were already preoccupied with 'scientific research work into the multifarious problems of Britain's trade and industry – the preparation of carefully thought-out plans to cope with unemployment and housing'.[35]

Visualizing the British New Fascist Man

The dream of a fascist Britain captivated the ageing press baron Lord Rothermere, who led his newspapers' campaigns in support for the BUF with the article 'Hurray for the Blackshirts'.[36] It is worthwhile to make a close reading of the images plastered across the pages of the *Daily Mail* and the *Sunday Dispatch* from 1933 until the summer of 1934 to illustrate the development of a British Blackshirt aesthetic, an aesthetic of virility and implied brutality, which was deemed marketable to the general public.

In word and in image the Rothermere press latched on to Mosley's call for the revival of British manhood, and ran with it to great lengths. Rothermere himself was impressed by the youthful and youth-worshipping ethos of the movement, asserting that 'the Blackshirt movement is the organised effort of the younger generation to break the stranglehold which senile politicians have so long maintained on our public affairs', and believing that 'the new age requires new ideas and new men'.[37] The newspaper photographs were all of young men in uniform, caught in seemingly candid shots at work, play and on the march – together they represented the regimented youth gang. These new fascist men were shown in obviously staged poses as solid despatch riders: foregrounding the might and machismo of the

motorcycle itself, offset by the heft of the rider. They were shown as
telephone switchboard operators: suggesting their ability to harness
the modern technology of mass communication for their own purposes. They were pictured as svelte and elegant buglers – placing
emphasis on the glory of a military tradition and symbolizing the fascist clarion call to the nation. They were photographed as *Fascist Week*
journalists – claiming as a fascist type the hard-nosed propagandists
with an intellect. Mosley's new fascist men were represented as officers commanding their men – giving a foretaste of the confident
appearance of Britain's future leaders. The Blackshirts were represented as disciplined paramilitarists partaking of their simple fare in
the mess halls of the Black House, conveying the unambiguous message of camaraderie, classless brotherhood, and unity in sacrifice.
They were also depicted as animal-lovers communing with 'Dusty'
the canine mascot at Blackshirt headquarters – an allusion to the fascist love of animals, especially their affection for a big virile dog.
Apparently, this emphasis on the love of animals was meant to negate
allegations of fascist brutality and hooliganism, and in another *Sunday
Dispatch* article it was reported that anti-fascists had released white
mice at the Olympia meeting, but this had not achieved the desired
effect of sending 'women into hysterics'. Rather, 'one indeed was
caught and kept as a pet by a Blackshirt'.[38]

Violence, while never explicitly depicted, was suggested in each
Daily Mail image, as Mosley's men were a synecdoche for an ordered
and regimented nation that would rise from the ashes of economic
chaos, imperial decline and cultural decadence. The aesthetic was
defined by straight lines of ordered humanity, the angularity and
unity of male forms, a seething readiness for manly physical assertion,
and a sense of the classlessness and the essential equality of sculpted
and tended male bodies. These were healthy male bodies that had tri-
umphed over the adversity of history, intact young bodies that
represented a recovery from the mutilation and carnage of the First
World War. Nor did these male bodies have anything in common with
those that had been under-nourished, ravaged and rotted by economic depression. These were not the men whose 'bodies bear
witness to their crushed souls, to the grim torture that they are suffering from prolonged unemployment, from tramping the hard streets in
search of work; to the agonising but unheard appeals for a job so that
they might keep alive'.[39] The British new fascist man of Rothermere's
design was healthy, vigorous, immune to disease, and the antithesis of
cultural decay.

In the Rothermere press the representation of the female body in
Blackshirt uniform was also tailored to conform to this suggestively
martial masculine aesthetic. Women were on display in contradictory
portraits, and in images of conflict. Significantly, there were among

these images those of actual physical violence between women, insin-
uating the titillating catfight. Carefully choreographed, the women
were represented practising their ju-jitsu on one another, and standing
on guard with fencing sabres; they were shown standing at ease in
Blackshirt columns, and training to be public speakers to expound fascism on the streets; and they were pictured enjoying a moment's
pause at their own barracks, and working in their offices for the
greater Britain. Like the men, the emphasis was on single-sex gang
formation, active resistance in the face of public opposition and vigorous health and athleticism. Indeed, Ann Page remembered that
women's activities, both their political and leisure pursuits, conformed to the male ideal of athleticism and games of mock violence:
'Believing as we did in the equality of the sexes, we took part in the
same political activities as the men ... And in much the same leisure
activities too: cycling, cricket, swimming, athletics, fencing and judo
(with Japanese Budokwai instructors), even football and flying. Boxing was one of the few exceptions.'[40]

However much the women themselves may have been male-
identified on the subjective level, in the Rothermere press the utility of
women to the movement was exploited much more directly as a sexual and erotic inducement to recruitment, catering to the male gaze.
This can be illustrated by the *Sunday Dispatch* headlines reading
'Beauty Joins the Blackshirts'. Further, this objectification of the sexualized female fascist culminated in a special beauty contest organized
by the *Sunday Dispatch* to select the most attractive woman in Blackshirt uniform.[41] Although this beauty contest never took place – with
Mosley explaining that Rothermere 'was staggered not to receive a
single entry; and I was embarrassed to explain that these were serious
minded women dedicated to the cause of their country rather than
aspirants to the Gaiety Theatre Chorus',[42] it is still significant that
Blackshirt women were enraptured by the rhetorical tide of masculine
resurgence and pubescent vengeance on a 'hag-ridden' Britain ruled
by 'old women'.[43] It was a woman who wrote to the *Evening News* that
she liked the Blackshirts because 'they stand for the ideals of manhood: courage, honour and chivalry, and those ideals alone can save
England from breaking faith with "those who sleep in Flanders'
fields"'.[44]

The Aestheticization of Brutality

While the *Daily Mail* and *Sunday Dispatch* demonstrated restraint in
their depiction of male violence in an attempt to downplay the criminality and hooliganism of the Blackshirts, the fascist press itself
developed a far more explicit and imagistic idiom to describe
moments of physical confrontation, cultural combat and brutality.

This linguistic was unequivocally articulated by BUF journalists who set the tone, prescribed the suitable style, and decreed the literary qualities required of all contributions to the fascist press. Hitler's *My Struggle* and Mussolini's autobiography of 1935 were the most obvious literary prototypes for a British fascist writing style. Regarded as the twin epics of the modern age, 'the twentieth century *Iliad* and *Odyssey*', these two texts were lauded for 'the utter absence of anything woolly or half-hearted [which] is the essence of Fascism'.[45] In order to represent faithfully what the BUF diagnosed as 'the rapid disintegration of the British people', writers for *Action* were advised that: 'It will not be required of us that we should attempt to find a mellow style or strike a reassuring note. This is no time either for *belles lettres* or for the utopian policies of the flaneur.'[46]

While the rhetorical tools of BUF propaganda were provided to members as accessories almost as made-to-measure as the uniform itself, there are some distinctions to be drawn between the application of this rhetorical stencil to the description of violence inflicted on anti-fascists, as opposed to the language used to describe violence suffered by the Blackshirts themselves. Interestingly, this evocation of an aesthetic of brutality was most apparent in BUF reports on the violent tactics employed by their opponents at rallies, mass meetings and street pitches. The aestheticization of male violence followed a two-tiered formula: a (disingenuous) attack on their attackers as un-British for introducing force into an ideological conflict, followed by a process of emasculating and de-sexualizing the opponent by taking cheap shots at physical imperfections, at presumed sexual orientation, at the cowardice of anti-fascist men who allowed women to do their bidding[47] and at the stereotyped racial traits of hecklers. Only in such rhetorical flourishes was a sense of humour (or rabid sarcasm) at all in evidence, and BUF propaganda was strikingly lacking in self-irony or the ability to laugh at itself.

The BUF certainly imagined itself as an army awaiting a showdown with domestic enemies. The lyrics of the 'Blackshirt Marching Song' are as follows:

> We lead the fight for freedom and for bread!
> The Streets are still, the final struggle's ended,
> Flushed with the fight we proudly hail the dawn!
> See, over all the streets the Fascist banners, waving –
> Triumphant standard of a race reborn![48]

The streets of England were imagined as a battlefield after a Blackshirt victory, with the faces of the men bloodshot as if in a post-orgasmic state following transcendent physical and spiritual exertion.[49] Their enemies were a sundry assortment of Jews, foreigners, Reds and Pinks, and the shape-shifting hermaphrodites who governed Britain such as:

> Mrs Baldwin, the PM, [who] offers to masculinity only the odors of a pipe. Mrs MacDonald, the Lord President of the Council, [who] differs from orthodox femininity by talking eternally without saying a word. Tart Miss Eden [who] pits her flapper brains, without the accompanying charm, against the real men like Mussolini and Hitler. The nation whirls and faints amidst these oppressive feminine vapours.[50]

The emasculation of political opponents was a common linguistic turn in BUF discourse, and a ready means to assert fascist dominion over characteristics of virility and hardness. This was also reflected in Blackshirt techniques to disarm anti-fascist hecklers. Blackshirt stewards would pull down a man's trousers so that he would be unable to fight with his hands. One such victim remembered that at Olympia '"he got thrown down four flights of stairs, 'ah bleading trousers torn off, 'is arse"'.[51] Blackshirt hoards symbolically castrated their opponents.

Blackshirts preferred to represent themselves as the victims rather than the aggressors in scenes of hand-to-hand combat. As one former member recalled: 'Because we defended our meetings from orchestrated attacks we were called thugs. You certainly needed to be tough of body and resolute in spirit to stay in the BUF.'[52] However, British fascists were clearly on the attack against the alleged purveyors of degeneracy. The movement abhorred the aesthetic sensibilities and 'neurotic self-exhibitionism'[53] of British Modernism, the ample round-edged sculptures of Jacob Epstein, the loose literary qualities and diseased morality of the 'Bloomsbury bacilli',[54] and demonized the International Surrealist Exhibition (held at the New Burlington Galleries in June 1936) for its eroticism, absence of decency, and its vulgarity.[55] Bloomsbury intellectuals were assailed as much for their role in fomenting so-called cultural decadence as for their apparent physical frailty. One BUF journalist described the British intelligentsia camped in Bloomsbury as 'a motley crew of middle-aged softies, whose contribution to revolution is carefully priced at 5s, and who would probably think that "things were going too far," if any one of them had his black velour hat knocked off in the street'.[56] A. K. Chesterton defined the British fascist aesthetic as one of health, unity, joy through strength, and the celebration of the *élan vital*, positioning as its antithesis the deformity and fragmentation internalized by the Modernist sensibility. Chesterton explained:

> [o]nly in a decadent age do people argue that life is well-served by an art which feeds on deformity. In an age of health art must surrender deformity to the psychological clinic ... Fascism extends no welcome to the dilettante or the prig. The measure of a man shall not be his pretensions but his worth. A sane-thinking, virile nation, safe-guarded against every process that rots – here is the Fascist ideal.[57]

And yet, while the Blackshirt aesthetic was safe from being labelled 'degenerate' as the Nazis might define the term, the BUF's own artistic preferences were neither slavishly traditionalist nor quixotically anti-modern.

The graphic images of men in action disseminated in their news-papers, journals and even their cartooned images of young Blackshirts maintained a simplicity of line, a classical composition, a cutting edge linearity, and blade-like brush-strokes reminiscent of the Vorticist and fascist-sympathizer Percy Wyndham Lewis or of Fillipo Marinetti, Italian author of the 'Futurist Manifesto' (see the cover of *Blackshirt Policy* (1933)). The development of an iconography of dissent as an essential accessory for the British new fascist man was dependent on the identification of an anti-aesthetic, and on the stigmatization of counter-types. The imagined traits of the counter-type were most often projected onto the faces and postures of British Jewry, well illus-trated in the BUF's cartoons drawn by Bowie.[58] Especially rampant were representations of the male Jew as a sexually degenerate blood sucker; immune to the spirt of British sportsmanship and fair play;[59] far removed from rural England due to physical weakness and effem-inacy; the source of moral disease through the dissemination of pornography and indecent literature; and a warmongering anti-patriot about to launch vulnerable British men and women into yet another world war.

While the BUF was clearly on the attack, the movement empha-sized its own status as a fascist 'defence' force, buttressing their (untenable) argument that Blackshirts never incited violence but were more than prepared to meet force with force and protect (their) free-dom of speech.[60] Nonetheless, Eric Hamilton Piercy (National Officer Commanding Defence) – the former NUPA member who had once made the heartfelt plea that women should be barred from intruding in men's social and political spaces – was able to boast publicly that not only had he 'never had charge of a meeting that was broken up – bar one …' but that he also kept as a souvenir from a raucous meeting an 'old original Blackshirt Union Jack. It now hangs over his desk, tat-tered and bloodstained.'[61] Collecting the memorabilia from episodes of cathartic violence – a practice continued at the notorious Olympia Rally where Mosley gathered up the chair legs, knuckle dusters, and rubber truncheons allegedly used by anti-fascists in their organized opposition – speaks for the ceremonialization and romanticization of the so-called defensive violence of the Blackshirt.

These improvised symbols added to the BUF's treasure chest of party paraphernalia, including distinctive newspaper typography and etching-like graphics, political cartoons drawn by Bowie, the fasces, and later, the BUF lightning symbol emblazoned on everything from brass-ware to bathing costumes, to notepaper and, of course, the uniform itself, which underwent a number of redesigns before the implementation of the Public Order Act in January 1937.[62] Alongside its stated mission of rescuing the young manhood of Britain from the decadence of the party system, from the governessing state, from the perniciousness of Hollywood films and from the hours of idleness caused by mass unemployment, the BUF was also in the business of merchandising and peddling the image of the new fascist man for its own political and economic profit. By implication, the British new fascist man was also a conspicuous consumer, a steadfast fanatic who could be counted upon to fill BUF coffers in exchange for the honour of identifying himself with Oswald Mosley, 'the matinee idol among politicians'.[63] The Blackshirt aesthetic was commodified for an age of political consumerism.

The Quintessence of British New Fascist Manhood

The Blackshirts' confidence that they held sole proprietorship to virility and heterosexual potency was invested in their fanatical admiration for their supremely masculine Leader, Sir Oswald Mosley. The BUF's marching song 'Mosley!' made it perfectly explicit that the movement was an organized gang of fanatics devoted to just one man, and to one conspicuously manly man: 'Mosley! Leader of thousands! / Hope of our manhood, we proudly hail thee! Raise we the song of allegiance, / For we are sworn and we shall not fail thee. / Lead us! We fearlessly follow / To conquest and freedom – or else to death.'[64]

Mosley's own stress on masculinity was obsessive, his fear of softness and pliability pathological. His fascism was 'the steel creed of an iron age' – the most potent force. His pitch differed from the mainstream parties precisely because he identified this as the 'time that we substitute a system of manhood for the interference of the universal grandmother'.[65] Supported by a family tradition of Royalist dissent, he identified the historical precedent for the BUF's attitude as the manly 'the Merrie England of gay and serene manhood';[66] his band of new men would have to measure up to the brawny figure of the Elizabethan yeoman. 'Our young, hard Fascism springs from the hard facts of a testing and turbulent age ... it brings also a new type of manhood to government,'[67] he explained. Mosley warned potential adherents that 'we want men, not eunuchs, in our ranks ... In fact, in our movement we seek to create in advance a microcosm of national manhood-re-born.'[68]

Through the starry eyes of his followers, Mosley was the anti-type to the effeminate, loquacious and perverse members of the ruling class in Depression-era Britain. Defying the matriarchal hold on his nation, Mosley was a man who 'thinks and feels for Britain as a man, and all true men, all true women, recognize his lead and follow him unfalteringly through ordeals which only they can face and they can survive'.[69] He was portrayed as a model of virility and masculine endowments as 'his tall athletic frame, with its dynamic force and immense reserve of strength; his unconquerable spirit, with its grandeur of courage and resolve [made him] an outstanding leader of men'.[70] As a 'leader of men' it was Mosley's task to define the new fascist men who would follow him.

By 1932, after the humiliating defeat of his New Party, mainstream politics could no longer sate Mosley's masculine appetite. The BUF was formed in Mosley's image as a paramilitary organization in which the Leader could finally synthesize his two great talents and life-long ambitions – to be a leader of his generation and to become a 'professional man'. In the BUF Mosley 'reverted to type and lived in the spirit of the professional army where I began; I was half soldier, half politician'.[71] The new British fascist man was Mosley in miniature, also 'half soldier and half politician, partly a tough warrior in hard and practical tests, and partly an inspired idealist who marched for the stars with his feet firmly on the ground'.[72]

Cultural Resistance to Britain's New Fascist Men

In the eyes of anti-fascists, however, Mosley's and his new fascist men's magnified machismo, their penchant for aestheticized politics and their attempt to mould fascism to an age of consumption, represented not the BUF's strengths but its points of weakness. Indeed, it was just these Mosleyite innovations in political organization and in civic imagery which were seen to jar with true Britishness. Significantly, in many of the following examples, it can be observed that anti-fascist objections were predicated on a distaste for the formal qualities of British Blackshirtism, perhaps in equal measure to protestations based on the content and the political implications of Mosley's project. Gerald Barry remarked that Mosley's appeal was superficial, using the 'adventitious aids of the Tattoo organiser and the dog-track promoter', and suggested that if his followers be deprived of wearing the black shirt, Mosley's 'present campaign will fall as flat as his last'.[73]

The BUF's own aesthetic of brutality was frequently turned against them, as exemplified by the many symbolically resonant and evocative reports on the violent tactics they employed at Olympia. For example, A. J. Cummings witnessed a scene where an anti-fascist, after trying to ask a question,

> was immediately pounced upon by a pack of human wolves and dragged out of the arena … half-a-dozen Blackshirts frog-marched their victim to an exit, another burley ruffian walked at the side and with true bull-dog courage repeatedly jabbed the helpless man's face with his leg-

of-mutton fist. It was a noble English spectacle for an Englishman to watch.[74]

The implication was that the political man turned beast was foreign to British notions of fair play.[75]

While the BUF was notoriously unable to laugh at itself, the movement was easily undermined by humour. During a 1934 revue performance 'the warmest applause went to the comedian whose song indicated that Englishmen have no liking for shirts of any particular colour and on the whole the British public is inclined to look upon politics which require dressing up as belonging rather to the realm of comic opera than of public affairs'.[76] J. A. Spender recognized that 'in nine cases out of ten the British habit of laughing at these movements and letting them run on is the right way of dealing with them'.[77]

The BUF's leadership cult was also a ready target for derision and ridicule. Hannan Swaffer remarked that Mosley 'sits alone, saluted and fawned by on amid mediocrities and boneheads ... At Chelsea, an almost oriental subservience surrounds him. "General salutes", raised arms, bowed heads – the whole incense of worship is offered him all day long.' Of Mosley's much vaunted gang of new fascist men, Swaffer described it as 'the refuge for many men too silly to work with their heads and too "proud" to work with their hands'.[78] Already in 1934 the *Daily Worker* discerned that

> Mosley's love for theatricalism at his meetings when, surrounded by his thugs and flags, he calls for the spot light, is quite in keeping with the scenery at his headquarters ... Hollywood can teach him nothing. He has made gangsterdom legitimate, and has converted an old-time school ... into a happy hunting-ground for filibusters, swashbucklers, adventurers, and, to use Mosley's own phrase, 'hucksters of the political marketplace'.[79]

In 1939 Wegg-Prosser resigned from the BUF in disgust at Mosley's dictatorial style and his exploitation of his celebrity among his gang members. In his letter of resignation Wegg-Prosser accused Mosley of having 'introduced a hierarchy of unnecessary ranks and grades, headed by a small narrow-minded group of ex-army officers. You never moved without a retinue of these persons, scampering to open doors for you and do small favours. At your meetings you had spotlights, hymns, chants of praise directed to you alone.'[80] In the end, the BUF's aestheticization of male brutality, so carefully stage-managed, so shrewdly marketed, and so expertly accessorized, failed to sell in the British political marketplace.

In conclusion, British fascism, like its continental counterparts, relied on delivering an aesthetic experience by way of ordered and disorderly marches, full regalia, and images of sublime transcendence through the worship of national symbols and a cult of the leader. The aggressively masculine British fascist aesthetic – which first responded to and then inflated normative constructions of masculinity – provided a symbolic code to express the aspirations of a fledgling fascist movement in Britain. On a microcosmic scale, the BUF created a prototypical *mannerbund* at the service of the charismatic dark horse of inter-war politics, Sir Oswald Mosley. The successful exploitation of aestheticized politics, at both the discursive and organizational levels, gave the BUF its force and guaranteed its hold on the popular memory and the historical imagination. However, a rhetoric of undisguised erotic charge, the magnified manliness of the lecherous Mosley,[81] and the banalization of male brutality at Blackshirt meetings, also guaranteed the bankruptcy of fascism in Britain. At a National Government rally in 1936 Lady Astor was quoted as saying that 'the British people could not stand fascism – it was too farcical, if ever it came we should die laughing',[82] and it can be seen how Mosley's puerile new fascist men were an irresistible target for the British sense of humour.

The Black Shirt in Britain:
The Meanings and Functions of Political Uniform

Philip M. Coupland

The black shirt of the British Union of Fascists (BUF) is the foremost icon of fascism in the 1930s, a palimpsest densely written and over-written with contending meanings constructing fascism as a movement, as an ideology, and the fascist as an individual. However, despite the importance of what Walter Benjamin described as the 'aestheticisation of politics'[1] to fascism as a modern movement, comment on this topic has tended towards bare description.[2] Hence, in what follows, this chapter is concerned primarily with the meanings and functions of uniform in the discourse of the BUF and among its opponents.

Indicating the visibility of BUF uniform, one critic commented on how 'the germs of political violence in contemporary England do not take much detecting. Their blackshirts are plain enough even when there is not a "monster demonstration" to attract them.'[3] At the simplest level the shirt, as a 'vestimentary' sign, signified a political allegiance.[4] However, in addition to simply making the BUF visible, the shirt was seized on by fascist and anti-fascist discourses to denote, and rhetorically connote, meaning. In BUF discourse and the dramaturgy of its marches and meetings, uniformed bodies articulated fascist ideology, whilst donning the shirt recast the wearer in the mould of the new fascist man (sic). At the same time, anti-fascists appropriated the simple sign of the shirt as a point of reference in a negative representation of Blackshirts and the BUF.

The Birth of the Shirt

Geoffrey Gorer described it as 'a practical-looking garment ... somewhat like a fencing jacket'.[5] Although the dress of fascists varied and evolved, the original black 'shirt' cut in the form of Mosley's fencing jacket was used from the first BUF meeting until the Public Order Act banned uniforms at the end of 1936.[6] Buttoning at the neck and shoulder, it was robust in service as well as permitting the easy identification of friend and foe. Unlike the conventionally cut 'undress' shirt worn with a black tie by both uniformed activists and – beneath a lounge suit or sports jacket – inactive members, and the 'Action Press' uniform of breeches, military tunic and peaked cap introduced in 1936, the original uniform shirt remained the designated wear for stewarding meetings.[7]

The need for a 'trained and disciplined force' at meetings lay behind the initial move towards adopting a uniform by the proto-fascist New Party.[8] However, the decision to create a uniformed fascist movement entailed more than this defensive function and was not taken lightly; as W. E. D. Allen indicates, Mosley took this step against the 'advice of some of his closest adherents, who were obsessed with the idea that the Englishman does not like uniform'.[9] Another reason was to 'put a big new case over in a hurry' which demanded 'a new means of propaganda and of attracting public attention'.[10]

Political uniform was novel; 'something entirely new to this country'.[11] For a sympathetic observer Blackshirts '[i]n their simple, close-fitting modern uniform, … were themselves a visible expression of the businesslike but straightforward spirit which marks this up-to-date movement'.[12] More ambiguously Winifred Holtby included 'Black Shirts' with 'sport', 'artificial light', 'quick transport', 'Red flags', 'the Great Wheel at Blackpool and Broadcasting House' as symbols of modern change.[13] Looking backwards from 1933, Beverley Nichols suggested the shock of this intervention: 'Fascism, in those days, was mercifully confined to Italy. The youth of England had not yet begun to prance about the street in blackshirts, like perverted Morris dancers, pushing the palms of their hands in the faces of the startled bourgeoisie … No – the Black Shirt … was still a distant menace. It flashed across the screens when Mussolini was in evidence.'[14] An antenna ever sensitive to unwelcome novelty quivered in the form of a *Punch* cartoon imagining the consequences should this practice spread.[15]

Dressing for 'Action'

Robert Bernays believed '[e]very young man swaggering round the purlieus of Westminster or Chelsea was a walking recruiting poster for Fascism.'[16] However, the black shirt was also a way to set the BUF apart from democratic politics, as an agency of radical intervention and revolutionary transformation. Mosley claimed the shirt as the 'outward symbol' of a 'moral force … which aims at nothing less than the creation of a new civilisation'.[17] For A. K. Chesterton the shirt reflected an unequivocal mission: 'Fascists … are no less enlisted on behalf of their country's service than soldiers fighting for its security in times of war, and are, therefore, proud to wear no less unequivocal a uniform.'[18]

This desire to present fascism as a radical alternative is indicated by the choice of black. Grey shirts had been suggested for the New Party in 1931 and were issued – albeit with significant 'black trimmings' – the following summer,[19] and a 'Greyshirt Anthem' was penned for the emerging fascist movement.[20] In rejecting grey for uncompromising black, Mosley made a deliberate choice as to how the new movement was to present itself. As John Harvey shows, black has almost always been implicated in 'power dressing', as the dress of the powerful, evocative of strong emotions and weighty qualities. Black was the colour of the cleric, the prince, the assassin, and the devil. Black connoted asceticism, restraint, gravity, seriousness and industry but was also associated with plague and decay, death and mourning, sin and evil.[21] Lewis Broad and Leonard Russell asked whether Mosley's black indicated '[m]ourning for his lost consistency, or ... despair?'[22] More probably the choice of black reflected a belief that national politics were on the brink of revolutionary change; indeed Mosley's gamble in renouncing democratic politics was premised on the assumption that the 'crisis will deepen sufficiently to break the present party system' or 'new forces will have no opportunity whatsoever'.[23] Underlining both the gamble entailed in this choice and its radical quality, he explained: 'In symbolism as in our creed we are more full-blooded people and literally as well as metaphorically we have put our shirt on Fascism.'[24]

Certainly to one outsider the message of the *form* of fascist politics overrode the BUF's claimed adherence to constitutional practice. Ivor Brown wrote of how 'these devotees of democracy insist on wearing the uniform ... of the Italian Fascists who have, as they boast, "trampled on the stinking corpse of liberty"'.[25] In 1932–4 in particular, the BUF's democratic protestations stood alongside statements that it was ready to fight in the streets if necessary.[26] Reporting the 1933 Maxton–Mosley debate during which the latter promised 'Fascist machine-guns' to meet the Red threat, the *New Clarion* wrote of Mosley as 'dressed for the slaughter ... in his black shirt and tie'.[27] In this context, as was remarked at the time, 'a uniform in politics symbolizes force either to be used now or in the future'.[28] Fascist 'pacifist' proclamations might be better understood as a precaution against prosecution for sedition whilst the uniform articulated the BUF's true nature; '[t]he outward sign ... proved in keeping with the inward "grace"', as *G. K.'s Weekly* wrote.[29]

Black Shirt and Tail Coat

The *black* shirt expressed Mosley's hope for a time when grey ambiguities would be swept aside in the polarization of left and right; red against black. The shirt also articulated fascism's claim to be a 'revolutionary' 'modern movement' by its rejection of the ruling sartorial code: the silk hat and morning coat that Mosley had worn as a junior minister and the archaic court dress of the minister of state. It was better to risk 'defeat, disaster, better by far the end of that trivial thing called a political career than stifling in the uniform of blue and gold, strutting and posturing on the stage of little England'.[30] Just as black expressed a steely dedication foreign to the 'old-gang' parties – it could not 'fade to pale pink or a light primrose hue' or 'become pale black'[31] – the novelty of the shirt distinguished fascism from the politics of the democratic party man garbed in bourgeois respectability: 'the detestable top-hat and frock coat that symbolizes a Victorian mugwumpery offensive to any decent thinking Englishmen'.[32]

In rebutting criticism from Duff Cooper, Gordon-Canning declared that '"fancy dress" ... would probably be more applicable to the court dress of a Cabinet minister than to a Fascist shirt'.[33] In fascist rhetoric references to the ruling sartorial code were also used to articulate a critique of the 'old gang' parties. In BUF discourse the silk hat and frock, or morning coat were the 'uniform of the Democratic party'[34] to which all of the 'old gang' – Labour, Liberal or Conservative – belonged.

Commenting on proposals for state planning as 'fake Fascism' *Fascist Week* linked such policies to their reactionary origins, adding that Lord Lloyd, 'the best-dressed man in the Carlton Club[,] addressed a big rally of Starched Shirts ... the other night'.[35] Looking to the left, the BUF pointed out that whereas the socialist activist before the First World War 'wore a red tie' Labour's descent to respectable impotence had seen them adopt the 'black coats and striped trousers' of the 'old gang.'[36] Mentioning that John McGovern, 'Labour supporter of the Means Test', 'once wore a silk hat' signified hypocrisy and betrayal.[37] Turning to Labour's radical wing, when Stafford Cripps advocated 'dictatorial' powers for a future socialist government, *Blackshirt* applied the old rule of 'judging a man by his shoes', describing Cripps as a bourgeois intellectual 'who had risen in spats to heights to which the ordinary hobnailed Trade Unionist has never ventured to aspire.' Cripps with his comic spats – P. G. Wodehouse's *Young Men in Spats* was published in 1936 – thereby joined the lumpen 'old men of the TUC' in Labour's force for inertia. Next to Cripps, with his 'town-bred physique' and archaic 'great big powdered wig' of the barrister, was juxtaposed the image of 'Mosley – Fascist Leader' as the quintessence of the new fascist man.[38] It was the 'Black shirt which annoys the Black Coats and Fat Bellies' which was 'more symbolic than a million red ties' because there was 'an intense patriotism, purpose, discipline, determination, fearlessness behind it.'[39]

Mosley à la Mode

E. D. Randall juxtaposed 'Youth, clamouring at the Gateway of Life. Youth in black shirted legions' with 'the old men of yesterday, who are still immersed in the squalor of Victorianism.'[40] The black shirt articulated the modernity of fascism. In a cartoon captioned 'Father Christmas is Up-To-Date!' Father Christmas dons 'something modern' – a black shirt, to deliver the *Fascist Week* to Ramsay MacDonald.[41] Appropriating one of the hoariest symbols of patriotism for fascism, another image portrayed John Bull admiring his black shirt, with the book of 'New Ideas' at his side, old thinking discarded along with his top hat and frock coat as 'relics of an old system'.[42]

In this way the shirt played its part in the reified engagement with modernity integral to fascist ideological syncretism. Whilst fascists condemned materialism, they simultaneously drew on machine aesthetics, gloried in power and speed. Supporting Susan Sontag's observation that 'fascist style at its best is Art Deco',[43] the Blackshirt who appeared in the BUF press and elsewhere was the man-machine, a close cousin of Jacob Epstein's Vorticist *Rock Drill* (1913–14). This new man was drawn with the square edges of machine-manufacture, the dense, unrelieved black of the shirt thrusting towards the viewer in an expression of fascist will-to-power. The force of dark space was also apparent in practice, one report of the BUF's Albert Hall rally indicating the effectiveness of 'the black bulwarks' of fascists *en masse*.[44]

Mickey Mouse versus the Black Plague

Debating with James Maxton, Mosley used the imagery of colour to articulate a critique of the party he had left, speaking of the 'pink terms of the ILP'.[45] In fascist discourse 'the colour Black' denoted 'the iron determination of Fascism in the conquest of red anarchy' in a situation when unequivocal hues would saturate the scene and the 'modest primrose' of the Tories and the 'red ties ... faded pink' of Labour were blotted out or washed away.[46] In oppositional discourse the colour and form of fascist uniform were also important points of reference, albeit used in widely different ways indicative of the divergence of anti-fascist tactics. Hannan Swaffer wrote that 'if, whenever they saw a Fascist dressed like Walt Disney's world-famous character ... readers called out "Mickey Mouse" that would be an end of it.'[47] From the confrontational tradition of anti-fascism the *Daily Worker* ridiculed the idea of 'chirping "Mickey Mouse"'; black shirts made the BUF the 'Hitlerite Black Guard, the SS to the very life,' a foe to be 'fought and smashed'.[48]

Democratic socialists and liberals preferred to try to drown fascism in a wave of ridicule, in the 'English way.'[49] Explaining this strategy, J. B. Priestley wrote of how violence 'turns comic storm troops into real storm troops. It transforms the wearing of uniforms from a mere week-end hobby into what seems a stern and noble affair.' He advised: 'If you see a black shirt, smile and pass on.'[50] In parliament it was 'fancy dress'[51] and Vyvyan Adams frivolously suggested 'taxing the wearing of this exotic haberdashery' to determine 'the precise number of uncertified lunatics in the country.'[52] P. G. Wodehouse's 'Roderick Spode', led the 'Black Shorts', clad in 'footer bags' as there were no shirts left.[53] The spirit of the schoolyard responded with the catcall: 'dirty shirt'.[54]

Even an otherwise positive article wondered at Mosley's 'black theatrical garb.'[55] For the unsympathetic the black shirt was a costume in a superficial charade. *Time and Tide* described Mosley as 'a stage figure, a sort of cardboard hero who calls in the limelight, the costumier.'[56] Whereas fascist discourse made the shirt a symbol of its ideology, anti-fascism reduced fascism to a shirt clothing a vacuum. Fascism with its 'romantic if theatrical leader', the 'Blackshirt Harlequin', was all display 'without the policy to justify it.'[57] Alan Herbert, MP, made the same point, noting that a party once 'took its name from its ideas and ideals. Now we have leaders who name themselves after their lingerie – black shirts or blue braces, pink pants or dirty drawers.'[58] In a more considered piece *G. K.'s Weekly* asked whether the absence of the 'soil' which had made fascism flourish abroad made the shirt the BUF's 'sole symbol and ... big idea.'[59]

Reflecting on events at Olympia, E. M. Forster was critical of the dangerous conceit of the 'English sense of humour' which represented Mosley as 'a figure of fun. He is the Wicked Baronet of melodrama ... He even wears black, and as a final absurdity, he is opposed by a second Wicked Baronet in red.'[60] For those who did not take fascism so lightly the shirt was a rhetorical gift. The BUF became a pathogen, a 'black plague' threatening to 'infect the blood-stream of our national life.'[61] The shirt was 'the symbol of death' presaging 'the end of all freedom and the reign of poverty and tyranny.'[62] The 'Blackshirt' promised 'blackguardism.'[63] In the ILP's *New Leader* the shirt clothed the working-class hate figure, the blackleg: 'What are those funny little men / In Shirts as black as ink? ... "Why do they put in [*sic*] fancy dress / In dress that no one likes?" / "Oh, that's because of dirty work, they're kept for breaking strikes."'[64]

However, Arthur Wragg linked both black *and* red to death, picturing a skeleton in the form of a gent's outfitter's assistant offering a choice between two shirts: on the left, 'cheerful tone (rather faded)' and on the right, 'very dressy (rather soiled).'[65] Amongst the defenders of liberalism, condemnation of the black shirt was subsumed within a wider critique of anti-democratic movements. The Conservative *Truth* mentioned 'the coloured shirt menace',[66] and condemning both 'Blackshirts and the Redshirts', Alan Herbert declared '[a] plague on both your blouses!'[67] In actuality, whilst communists, ILPers, and other anti-fascist groups were seen in party shirts, their use was relatively insignificant.[68] Despite this, not only was the notion of a visual indicator of a shared anti-democratic tendency common to 'left' and 'right' rhetorically convenient, but the suggestion that the country was threatened by a wholesale militarization of politics was also an important justification for the Public Order Act.[69]

'Union Jack Shirts'

Whereas Nancy Mitford satirized the ultra-nationalism of the BUF with her 'Union Jackshirts'[70] the black shirt was an obvious resource for those wishing to refute fascist patriotism. For Broad and Russell success for Mosley would see him 'running up the Black Shirt in *place of* the Union Jack.'[71] References to BUF uniform provided effective means of denying fascism's claim to the foundational myths of British identity, of a nation bound and protected by an ancient constitution, of a peaceful and polite people.

In a culture in which national identity reflexively took the foreign Other as its point of reference, the BUF was easily criticized for what J. R. Clynes called its 'alien practices.'[72] Speaking of what 'Shirts ... signify and what they are intended to denote', Clynes believed that uniform 'brings into our political activities alien elements making for conflict and disorder.' He continued: '[t]hey have acquired foreign symbols, foreign salutes, foreign names and foreign dress.'[73] For Herbert Morrison too the black shirt and fascist dramaturgy were 'contrary to all that is best in the British political traditions.'[74] *Everyman* suggested that form mirrored substance: 'Mosley ... is more like a Continental politician than an English one; even his appearance suggests the Europe of the sixteenth century.'[75] Promoting a bill to prohibit uniforms, Oliver Locker-Lampson cited the shirt as indicating a 'wish to drop the old English weapon of persuasion for something else.' Underlining this representation of uniform as inimical to Englishness, he associated it with 'the new spirit of foreign force.'[76]

One of the components of this model of Englishness was an abhorrence of a costly standing army, licentious soldiery and the abridgement of the rights of the freeborn Englishman through conscription. Hence Percy Harris, MP for Bethnal Green South-West, suggested that '[t]here is something in our free traditions ... that dislikes military organisation. The very fact that the members of this body wear uniform and march in military formation is provocative in itself to the public at large.'[77] In the same vein, the day before the 'Battle of Cable Street' (1936) the *Daily Worker* depicted the BUF as an 'army' invading the East End and Mosley as 'the general' of that 'militaristic' force.[78] The cartoonist 'Vicky' preferred to criticize this 'breach of the peace' whilst mocking the Leader's breeches.[79] The Action Press uniform introduced that year undoubtedly amplified the identification of the BUF as a 'foreign' and 'military' force. Aside from the chromium highlights of belt-buckle, buttons and badges, the blackness of the uniform was relieved only by a scarlet armband and, although cut in the style of the Brigade of Guards, for many observers it shouted 'Nazi'. Malcolm Muggeridge wrote of Mosley's uniform having acquired 'a strong Storm-Trooper admixture.'[80] Calling fascism 'the most un-British weed that has ever pushed itself above British soil,' Vyvyan Adams saw it as appealing to 'adolescents by means of uniforms borrowed half from the German Nazis and half from the Italian Fascists.'[81]

For a movement which claimed to put 'Britain First' such constructions on the shirt were a significant threat. In response, one fascist commented 'Britain … must be FIRST in so far as its own Nationality is concerned, and so we don't need BLACK shirts.' As 'our own distinctive colour for British Fascism', he suggested 'a WHITESHIRT with the Union Jack boldly displayed on the left breast.'[82] This suggestion may have intended to refer to the white surcote of the crusader or to draw on the patriotic and masculine connotations of the sports field – James Arbuthnot chose 'cricket shirts with a Union Jack on the breast pocket' for the 'Cricketshirts' of his anti-fascist satire.[83] In the light of what he saw as the 'similarity between the spirit of the Cromwellian revival … and the Fascist Movement' another Blackshirt suggested wearing olive-green shirts.[84] Ironically, according to Unity Mitford, Adolf Hitler also questioned importing the black shirt, preferring a reference to the Ironsides.[85]

However, the black shirt remained and fascism claimed patriotic credentials for it regardless. For Robert Gordon-Canning it was 'certainly patriotic', 'a symbol which stands for the regeneration of England for the benefit of every man, woman and child.'[86] Mosley sought to reinvent the shirt as a 'universal symbol' and then inscribe patriotism onto this neutral space: 'we wear on every Blackshirt the Union Jack, and our Fascism is British through and through.'[87] Indicating the salience of the flag in this bid to nationalize fascism, behind the speaker at all 'Mosley meetings' hung what was reputed to be the largest union flag in the country. The size of this flag claimed a similarly emphatic patriotism; as a sign it linked the BUF, whose symbols flanked it, to patriotism; its spatial relationship to the Blackshirt in front of it connoted that he spoke *for* it, and thus for the nation for which it was the metonymic symbol. Fascist rhetoric also pointed to the medal ribbons sometimes sewn onto the shirt. In a short story about Armistice Day, the unconverted 'Jack' notices with irritation 'another of those Blackshirts' and asks himself: 'What right had that fellow, this Blackshirt to appear in that mockery of a uniform to-day of all days?' However, as 'he looked at the black-shirted figure ... his eye was caught by the row of medal ribbons on his shirt.'[88] The contradiction between the patriotism connoted by war medals and Jack's anti-fascist reading of the black shirt forces him to question his assumptions.

The pursuit of authentic native providence for the fasces symbol which appeared on BUF banners, flags, insignia, and propaganda also prompted a flood of writing pointing to examples of the Lictor's rods on neo-classical public buildings and elsewhere.[89] Seeking a grand historical and ancestral pedigree suitable for an ultra-nationalist movement Mosley described the fasces as:

> a symbol used in Britain for the last 2000 years and are to be found on most of our great monuments. The symbol was brought to Britain by our Roman ancestors who were here for four centuries and their stock remained for ever. The Fasces were the symbol of the Roman Empire. What more fitting that they should be used by the Empire which succeeded and surpassed the Roman Empire?[90]

The BUF also intervened in the symbolic language of the movement to present the fasces against the background of the national flag in order to produce insignia of 'an unmistakably British Appearance' and thereby 'emphasise' the 'patriotism of the movement.'[91] However, in the end the fasces was more or less displaced by the 'circle and flash' symbol that first appeared daubed on walls all over Britain during the BUF 'Mind Britain's Business' campaign in 1935 and then became a plated metal badge.[92] The chromium finish on the pin was not only practical but also evoked modernity, and the circle and flash also appeared on armbands, tie pins, rings, brooches, cufflinks and belt buckles in patriotic red, white and blue.[93] Stressing its qualities and explaining its meaning Mosley wrote: 'This is our modern symbol which belongs exclusively to British Fascism. It portrays the flash of action in the circle of unity. National action can only come for national unity, which in turn can only come from Fascism that ends the strife of Parties.'[94] Opponents preferred to impute a showy transience to Mosleyite fascism by calling it the 'flash-in-the-pan'.

The Black Shirt Brotherhood

Fascists promised that their corporate state would replace the divisive frictions of class with a harmonious organic unity and held up the BUF as a 'microcosm of the national manhood reborn.'[95] Indicating the role of the shirt in this process, Mosley wrote that 'the Blackshirt has achieved within our ranks that classless unity which we will ultimately secure within the nation as whole.'[96] The shirt was a 'visible symbol' promising fascists an 'unfettered chance according to their abilities; [that] class prejudice, which has kept sections of the community apart in watertight compartments for so long, will be obliterated.'[97] It eliminated 'distinctions of dress as between the well-to-do and the poor.'[98] In relation to the prevailing sartorial class code, uniform cancelled 'the distinctions that wealth normally procures. Men who in private life wear Yorkshire worsted can start on a level footing within the organisation as those who can afford to buy suiting of Scottish tweed.'[99] The BUF was 'one great brotherhood' which had 'broken down class barriers by wearing a common uniform.'[100] In this way, the uniform(ity) of individual bodies repaired the fractured social body, albeit only at a symbolic level.

Whilst the *Daily Mail* wrote of how Mosley 'dressed exactly like the humblest of his followers',[101] as with other sartorial sub-cultures where subtleties of cut, label and fabric compose a rich symbolic language, fascist uniform and insignia varied widely according to the status and function of the wearer. Insignia distinguished official speakers and members of the Fascist Union of British Workers (FUBW), and coloured armbands indicated particular functions at Black House.[102] Established on a military model, the BUF had a complex hierarchy of ranks. Except for the chief of staff and the commanding officer of the Defence Forces who wore crossed fasces, rank was indicated by horizontal bars for 'other ranks', and bars with a lightning flash for officers. Initially the colour of the insignia indicated the wearer's role in the organization.[103] Mosley asserted his supremacy as unquestionable Leader, transcending hierarchy, with an unadorned shirt.

Whilst the black tie and epaulettes of the BUF's youth organization and the FUBW linked them chromatically to the movement, their grey and brown 'undress' style shirts differentiated them from Blackshirts.[104] To reserve the 'privilege' of the black shirt to full members, 'probationers' also originally wore grey and later new members were only permitted initially to wear the undress shirt.[105] Even for full adult members, uniform increasingly became a special privilege. In 1935 it was announced that the BUF would be divided into a 'Political Organisation' and a 'Blackshirt Organisation', with uniform 'a privilege reserved for those who perform conspicuous service' in the latter.[106] To wear the black shirt, a minimum of two evenings' service a week was required but there was also a further elite who, by giving five nights, could wear the uniform previously restricted to 1 Division Fascists at Black House. The 'political' wing of the movement would wear plain clothes although it was allowed that they might wear the undress shirt.[107] Similarly, the privilege of wearing the Action Press uniform was earned by selling a set number of the fascist paper.[108] Indicating the degree to which uniform became a repository of status, deprivation of the right to wear the black shirt was among the punishments meted out to members.[109]

In BUF discourse, the hierarchy of rank and status expressed in these differences was one which reflected only service to the cause.[110] Nellie Driver wrote of how 'rank and file members came from all ranks of life, from dockers to doctors; miners to office workers; and factory workers to big business men. When on active duty they all wore the same uniform, so that there were no class distinctions, and all had the chance of gaining rank.'[111] In contrast, Labour Alderman Joseph Toole noted how Mosley was 'in a black shirt – but in a silk black shirt', suggesting the wearer's upper-class background and perhaps imputing an effete quality to those origins.[112] In actuality fascist shirts were not equal either. '1st' and '2nd' quality shirts were available at 7/6d. and 5/6d., as were velvet shirts and a costly 'buttonless type' garment 'only made to measure' at 30/–.[113] Least it be imagined that these differences were merely nominal, former BUF photographer Kay Fredericks, writing of the class-consciousness belying the 'brotherhood of fascism', claimed that '[s]ome of the members who could afford it had their shirts tailored of a better material than those obtainable in the Quarter Masters stores. These shirts immediately became known as boss-class shirts. Mosley was one of the first to wear one of these boss-class shirts.'[114]

Black Blouses

In fascist discourse at least, the black shirt symbolized a classless brotherhood of British 'youth', covered healthy and muscular male bodies, articulated the courage and fortitude of the soldier, the loyalty of the patriot and the self-sacrifice of the true disciple. Inasmuch that the Blackshirt was such an emphatically male figure, this asks a question of the meaning of female bodies in fascist uniform. In her anti-fascist dystopia Storm Jameson imagines the misogynistic reaction of Hillier, the fascist Prime Minister, to the 'National Service Women'. He 'was struck by the extraordinary appearance of a line of women in uniform, their female hips swelling out behind and their breasts pouting in front', achieving 'the comical effect of a parade of penguins in clothes.'[115]

In reality, too, a cult of youth and masculinity naturally denigrated its Other: the fascist revolution would see Britain 'served by young men in black shirts instead of being ruled by old women in trousers.'[116] However, as has been discussed elsewhere, whilst men remained firmly on top in the BUF, attitudes to the feminine and women's role were not without ambiguity.[117] On one hand, an alternative hierarchy of ranks marked with distinctive insignia indicated the separateness of the Women's Section.[118] Women's Fascist uniform also faithfully obeyed, rather than challenged, the ruling codes of respectability. Ironically, the form of the men's uniform shirt encouraged one parliamentary wag to enquire whether it might not 'be more decent to limit the wearing of blouses to the female sex.'[119] Women wore a decent calf-length grey skirt and, unlike the men, who except from an optional and seldom seen forage cap and the peaked cap of the Action Press uniform ignored polite convention and went bareheaded, female fascists wore a black beret.[120] The movement's symbol was also available 'for the ladies' as jewellery in the form of scarf pins in gold or platinum studded with rose diamonds and brooches with paste diamonds or marcasites.[121] On the other hand, unlike BUF cadets and others denied the black shirt, women could wear both the undress garment and the uniform shirt.[122] Perhaps as a concession to feminine 'delicacy', a pullover in wool or cashmere could be substituted during the winter.[123]

Whilst the austerity of women's uniform contrasted with mainstream female fashion, one observer noted that BUF women did not embrace Nazism's rejection of cosmetics.[124] Concerning women's attitude to the shirt, a male fascist suggested that it was 'a sacrifice, when she reluctantly lays aside her latest creation in favour of the Black shirt.'[125] However, for Nellie Driver emblems and uniforms were part of the 'romance' of the movement which had a 'strong appeal'.[126] Another indication of female attitudes came at the time of the movement's reorganization which sought to include all women in the 'plain clothes' political wing of the movement.[127] Suggesting a significant degree of protest, Mosley had to write rebutting the 'mistaken idea ... that women were to have their Black shirts taken away.' Nonetheless whilst allowing that women *could* form uniformed units, Mosley made clear that his wish was that they devote themselves to plain-clothes electoral work.[128]

Clothes Maketh (New) Man

In fascist discourse dress also signified the malign influence of Hollywood: 'outside the local "super" cinema' young men wore 'plum coloured "pork-pie" hats, long tight fitting coats, patent shoes and silk mufflers.' Each one was 'pale and undersized'. the 'typical product' of a 'decadent democracy'.[129] The ideal Blackshirt was a Spartan and self-disciplined figure: another author envisaged 'the bright young things' of the jazz age discarding 'tinted metal finger nails for the more practical black shirts.'[130] The shirt not only signified radicalism, patriotism and classlessness but was also implicated in fascism's transcendence of both the bankruptcy symbolized by 'the tail coat of financial democracy'[131] and the decadence of 'C-3' youth.

The Blackshirt was to be the prototype of a new type of man essential to achieving the fascist revolution.[132] Speaking on the 'spirit of the "Blackshirts"', Mosley made clear that whilst democratic politicians might propose similar reforms of the 'machinery' of state they lacked the essential ingredient of the fascist new man: 'Any such machinery ... would be useless without the spirit and driving purpose of a Fascist movement behind it'. Mosley stated:

> it is the wearing of the Blackshirt, and the spirit of those who wear it, which have been by far the biggest factors in the early success of Fascism. The Blackshirt is to us the symbol of service to, and love of, country; it is the emblem of men and women who are not afraid to stand up before all the world and to proclaim their faith. Throughout modern Europe it has become the outward expression of manhood banded together in the iron resolve to save great nations from degeneration and decay.[133]

Even within the BUF Mosley distinguished between those 'who have the purely political mind as distinct from the dedicated Blackshirt spirit.'[134]

Archibald Crawford, in his novel *Tartan Shirts*, satirized the symbolic power of the shirt with garments whose actual dye imbue the wearer with a political attitude. The 'Pink and White Shirt' of the 'British Nazis or Fascists or Shirtists' makes its wearer 'literally scream with Political rage and dance around ... like a Dervish.'[135] In actuality, too, the act of donning the black shirt was represented as having transformative power. Anne Preston wrote of 'Our Blackshirt Sons': 'They get into black shirts and at once they are in a fine new world. The transformation of a bored and aimless youth into an active Fascist is nothing short of a miracle. From a slouching, apathetic and selfish young cynic he is changed as if by magic into a keen confident lad with a will and mind of his own. His eyes grow steely and his flabby muscles seem to harden overnight.'[136]

In uniform, Blackshirts were ordered to be of irreproachable appearance and conduct, to communicate publicly the traits of discipline and dignity.[137] However, the wearing of the shirt was also represented as an act which assayed the mettle of the member, tested whether they possessed the 'Fascist spirit of courage, comradeship and duty.'[138] Mosley noted that 'it takes a little courage to wear it; ... it picks out the fighters from the shirkers.'[139] The shirt made its wearer glaringly visible. A 'Blackshirt Graduate' wrote: 'As I pass along the crowded pavements I hear uttered almost continually the word "Blackshirt", and I become conscious of the attention I am attracting.'[140] Concerning the nature of this reaction, Robert Saunders mentioned 'the abuse, the scorn and the ridicule and even violence with which we are faced when wearing the Black Shirt.'[141] Saunders recalled the part that the shirt played in him becoming a fascist: 'I applied for membership of the BUF, was accepted. ... It was then suggested that I should don a blackshirt and join ... in selling our papers on the streets.' To pass this test Saunders had to overcome an acutely debilitating shyness. He continued: 'That I should go out and sell papers on the streets ... was unthinkable. But somehow I did so.'[142] This signified the 'deep commitment' of BUF members and Saunders's advice to a fellow activist concerning a possible recruit suggests the shirt's place in fascist political socialization: 'Let him fill in an enrolment form, put on a Black Shirt and join with us in determination to build a "Greater Britain".'[143]

By this visible rejection of bourgeois norms and mores fascists demonstrated that they were worthy of the cause. Writing at a time when many fascists believed that the BUF was being turned into a glorified branch of the Conservative Party by an influx of *Daily Mail* readers, W. J. Leaper proclaimed that:

> Courage is the acid test of political worth. To put on a Black Shirt will test your courage. We hope you have the courage, but if you have not, then you are made of the stuff of the old gangs.
>
> If you should join us, we promise you this: When you have put on the Black Shirt, you will become a Knight of Fascism, of a political and spiritual Order. You will be born anew. The Black Shirt is the emblem of a new faith that has come to our land.

The BUF welcomed patriots and those convinced intellectually, '[b]ut the Black Shirt is the test', Leaper concluded.[144]

Paralleling the religious convert's act of 'witness' which separates them from their old life and seals their new allegiance, the shirt was 'the emblem of men and women who are not afraid to stand up before all the world and to proclaim their faith.'[145] Uniforms were 'not whimsical creations for the beaux amongst us. They are the hallmark of the idealists. They represent an active striving after the best and highest.'[146] In this way, fascist representations of the shirt could acquire a quasi-religious aura. John Hone described his as 'a symbol of my political faith;' Richard Bellamy's comment that '[m]any [shirts] showed bloodstains, honourable marks' of a 'respect ... hardly earned', evokes the martyr's relic.[147]

Richmal Crompton's characters gazed on a Fascist in boyish awe: 'he looked very noble and magnificent, perched up aloft on his wooden box, in his black shirt, shouting and throwing his arms about.'[148] Other commentators were less willing to preserve the myth of the new fascist man. The short and rotund H. G. Wells described Mosley as 'dressed up like a fencing instructor with a waist fondly exaggerated by a cummerbund and chest and buttocks thrust out.'[149] Wells later renewed this attack against 'Horatio Bohun' and his

'Purple Shirts'.[150] George Lancing made a similar point, describing the leader of the 'Purple Vests' as 'clothed to the lower limbs in the close-fitting black tights, worn by figure skaters and fencing masters. A regrettably rebellious tummy was preventatively detained in a gorgeous cummerbund of gold coloured silk.'[151] George Scott portrayed Blackshirts whose seedy physiognomy and poor posture conspired with the ironic caption 'In England's green and pleasant land!' to deflate claims for the Blackshirt.[152] In choosing to make a home movie featuring 'pinkshirts' in 1934 the Marquess of Anglesey may have hoped to satirize the hyper-masculinity of fascism.[153]

Other opponents pointed to other less selfless psychological functions of the shirt. Exploring the 'delights of wearing a uniform', Aldous Huxley suggested that it was a salve for inferiority, making its wearer conspicuous and boosting 'his sex appeal'.[154] No uniform is entirely bereft of an aura of power and violence linked to the intertwined drives of Eros and Thanatos. When the uniform is the black shirt of fascism this can only be more so. In a fascist cartoon the Blackshirt is proudly erect under an admiring female gaze whilst the tail-coated politician looks on jealously,[155] and 'Hamadryad' wrote of 'A bounding Blackshirt in a buckled belt, / My mien is ferocious but my form is svelte; / The ladies blow me kisses as I go, / But do the statesmen love me? Oh, dear, no!'[156] Even Viscountess Rhondda described Mosley as the 'Beauteous Blackshirt' whilst Clynes disapproved of 'youths in black shirts and tight trousers.'[157] More generally, just like 'fancy dress', uniform allowed its wearer to evade the morally constrained persona constructed by their everyday attire to enjoy a 'moral holiday'.[158] Huxley suggested: 'we put on a different character and are able to do things which we should never have the nerve to do in grey flannel trousers and a tweed jacket. A coloured shirt and top boots can go a long way to transform the mildest and most timid of Jekylls into a strong and silent Hyde.'[159]

Bye, Bye Black Shirt?

Dower and Riddell mockingly enquired in 1937 '"Baa, Baa, Blackshirt, have you lost your wool?"'[160] Following the Public Order Act the BUF were permitted to wear no more than a lapel badge.[161] In this way fascists were denied the aura of power which uniforms endowed. Alderman Toole explained that an earlier decision to force fascists to march in Manchester in plain clothes was intended to reveal the BUF as a 'motley crew'[162] and in 1937 an opponent relished the contrast between the 'hefty British bobbies' and fascists as 'raw young recruits ... their dignity much diminished by flannel trousers and tweed skirts.' With uniform banned and its myths dissipated, Mosleyites 'picked their C-3 way over the cobble stones of Kentish Town Road.'[163]

However, the assertion that the uniform ban finished the BUF off is not supportable:[164] some members left but others formerly put off by the uniform joined.[165] In fact the black shirt continued to haunt the fascist imagination and to stand metonymically for the individual activist and the movement collectively. Fascists were instructed carefully to store their uniforms and *Action* depicted the fascist man putting his shirt away 'till the day'.[166] Unable to supply a badge for a member's shirt, Saunders referred to the same fascist future commenting: 'No doubt you will receive one on THE DAY!'[167] In actuality too, whilst full uniform disappeared, Ronald Crisp recalled that 'most people wore black shirts of some description.'[168] The most visible wearer of the shirt was Mosley himself who challenged the authorities to prosecute him[169] and as a synecdoche connected the BUF to its revered and excoriated symbol. Even in wartime, uniforms appeared at a secret ceremony on Mosley's birthday.[170] As late as the 1960s members of Union Movement visited Franco's Spain in uniform[171] and in 1999 Mosleyite Ian Souter Clarence was buried in a black shirt.[172] More widely, the shirt remains an eloquent symbol of a time, an ideology, and a movement.[173]

*   *   *

An unambiguous conclusion concerning the place of the black shirt in the history of British fascism or the political culture of the 1930s would be inappropriate. On one side, it played a central role in the construction of the BUF's myths of classlessness and dynamism and was crucial to the creation of the Blackshirt political identity and a functional militarized movement. For many men and women in the fascist movement the shirt transcended its material form and utilitarian functions to become an honoured and richly symbolic garment. By donning the shirt they truly changed not only their appearance but themselves. At the same time, Mosley's Fascists were all dressed up with nowhere to go; dressed for a struggle that never happened. Just as the old gang parties continued to dominate political space, stranding the BUF's radical proposals on the periphery, so the bourgeois vestimentary code remained intact; crisis did not make respectable opinion forget its qualms about the novelty and militarism of the black shirt. Seen against a backdrop of business-as-usual, fascists were not only extravagantly overdressed for quotidian politics but perfectly attired to play the role of the alien menace in the anti-fascist discourse negating the Blackshirts' most vociferous claim: 'Britain First'.

The Blackshirts at Belle Vue:
Fascist Theatre at a North-West Pleasure Ground[1]

Helen Pussard

Introduction: The Lancashire 'Cotton' Campaign

The relatively peaceful 'Blackshirt rally' of 29 September 1934 at Manchester's principal pleasure ground, Belle Vue, marked the climax of the so-called Lancashire 'cotton' campaign by the British Union of Fascists (BUF) to secure support in industrial north-west England. Stuart Rawnsley has argued that in contradiction to the view that fascism was based in the West End of London and the southern suburbs, by 1935 the north of England had 'proved to be the most important area of fascist expansion'.[2] Lancashire, in particular, held a symbolic place in BUF literature during the 1930s illustrating the deficiencies of the National Government's economic policies in exposing the county's cotton industry to international competition and tariffs. In answering the question 'Have you any special policy for cotton?', Oswald Mosley's written reply was: 'Fascist Government alone can save Lancashire, because Fascism alone is prepared to take strong measures against Oriental coolie competition which is ruining the industry.'[3] Fascism, in this context, sought to 'save' the cotton industry, its 65,000 workers and thus Lancashire itself with a 'swashbuckling Fascist programme'.[4]

The Lancashire 'cotton' campaign was, therefore, a significant initiative for the BUF, highlighting regional contexts, some of which have featured within the historiography on British fascism in the twentieth century.[5] The BUF itself recognized regional variations in its approach to campaigns. In a pamphlet, *The BUF by the BUF* (c. 1939), the Director of Propaganda, A. C. Miles, described how the organization varied its propaganda from area to area: in east London, Leeds and Manchester anti-Semitic tactics were used; in Edinburgh the tone was anti-Catholic and in East Anglia, anti-Protestant.[6] The opposition also made use of regional issues to establish meanings outside national discourses. In distributing pamphlets on the BUF's presence in the north-west, the historic wealth of the Mosley family from land around Manchester was highlighted, giving a personalized dimension to the 'cotton' campaign.[7]

This chapter therefore seeks, on one level, to redress the regional imbalance of work on inter-war fascism by focusing on a specific event in the Lancashire 'cotton' campaign. The choice of Manchester's pleasure ground, Belle Vue, to host the Blackshirt rally of 29 September 1934, however, represented more than a regional diversification for the BUF. It highlights the use of popular cultural forms by the BUF to secure support and, moreover, to enact fascist spectacle. The relationship between the BUF and popular cultural forms is the focus of the first section of this chapter. It argues that the BUF was one of a number of political organizations using commercial sites for meetings during the inter-war years. While the Blackshirt Rally at Belle Vue can be contextualized as part of a general trend towards the commercialization of politics, the BUF adamantly rejected many forms of popular culture at a rhetorical level. The BUF's ambiguous relationship with popular culture therefore provides the backdrop to the third aim of the chapter, to deconstruct fascist theatre at a north-west pleasure ground.

The acknowledgement of the performative nature of the BUF is an important contribution to fascist historiography. The Blackshirt rally at Belle Vue is rarely mentioned in histories of British fascism, which have focused overwhelmingly on Olympia and Cable Street in ways that firmly reproduce the traditional concerns of political history in issues of organization, policing and resistance.[8] The use of spectacle by the BUF has not only been neglected in histories of British fascism. Recent work on the performance and political aesthetics of fascism in Europe has predominantly been focused on fascist states. Cultural formations have been understood as part of a 'total system of control' in fascist states.[9] This methodological approach fails to address the aestheticized political techniques used by fascist movements not in power. The second part of the chapter, therefore, seeks to undertake a cultural analysis by illustrating the use of performative techniques by the BUF. It offers a close reading of the Blackshirt rally at Belle Vue to argue that the BUF was engaged in both a symbolic and material appropriation of space, indicating a level of theatre and 'theatricality' not normally associated with British fascism.[10]

Politics and Pleasure Grounds

The staging of the Blackshirt rally at Belle Vue raised the BUF's profile and arguably allowed for a more theatrical performance than at other municipally-owned venues, such as Manchester's Free Trade Hall or local parks. These aspects of fascist theatre will be examined in the following section to demonstrate the performative techniques used by the BUF. It is important first, however, to contextualize the BUF's presence at Belle Vue. Rather than offer a comparison between European forms of fascist theatre and the Blackshirt rally, I would argue that the meeting needs to be understood as part of the wider commercialization of politics occurring in twentieth-century Britain. From this perspective, fascist theatre is placed in a British context of political performance, moving away from the historiographical 'fascination' with fascism and the 'failure' of the BUF compared with its European counterparts.[11]

The movement of meetings and demonstrations from city centres in England to alternative sites during the inter-war period signalled the erasure of civic spaces for political purposes. After Olympia in June 1934, for example, fascist meetings were not allowed to be held in municipally-owned halls in Manchester unless police were there as stewards.[12] Pleasure grounds such as Belle Vue can be interpreted as one of the beneficiaries of this, as they were able to offer large spaces for social, political and religious rallies. The 1930s therefore witnessed an increase in the number, and scope, of meetings staged at Belle Vue. The pleasure ground diversified its market by hosting these events but, moreover, was instrumental in the concurrent politicization of leisure in the first half of the twentieth century.

Belle Vue emerged initially as a zoological garden in 1836 with a few popular attractions and grew steadily in size and popularity for most of the nineteenth century.[13] The pleasure ground was owned and managed by the Jennison family who developed strong links with the growing railway infrastructure that ensured a flow of excursions and visitors.[14] The first decades of the twentieth century witnessed a slump in attendance at Belle Vue and during the First World War the grounds were utilized for the war effort. The pleasure ground was, therefore, sold to a newly formed company, Belle Vue (Manchester) Ltd, in 1925. Under this new management, and aided by technological advances during the 1920s and 1930s, the grounds were extended and developed. Belle Vue came to offer an extensive amusement park, enhanced exhibition facilities and introduced new forms of spectator sports, such as greyhound racing and Speedway, consolidating its position as a key leisure site for the industrial north.[15]

On one level, Belle Vue encapsulated the changing forms of popular culture in the first half of the twentieth century. It also incorporated social, political and religious events into its leisure provision, offering a venue for the groups displaced from civic centres in the north of England. The inter-war years witnessed the large scale promotion of the pleasure ground for meetings, demonstrations and rallies and a spectrum of groups staged events at Belle Vue.[16] Lloyd George spoke to a crowd of 50,000 at the 'Great Liberal Demonstration' in 1924 through loudspeakers, recorded as the first political meeting to benefit from this innovation. From communist to fascist and diplomatic to nationalistic, Belle Vue hosted numerous political organizations, leading one contemporary guide to comment '[p]erhaps the Ku Klux Klan will be found in session there some day, for Belle Vue is nothing if not catholic.'[17]

The forms of popular culture offered at the leisure site were diversifying during this period and it is interesting to note that political events were becoming part of the pleasure ground's attractions. The decision to allow the Blackshirt rally to be staged at Belle Vue by the pleasure ground's management must, therefore, be understood as commercial pragmatism. John Maxwell, Chief Constable of Manchester, had advised the management of the danger of 'serious riot or disorder' presented by the Blackshirt presence. Belle Vue's operators agreed to the rally, 'provided that the fascists insured the Belle Vue Pleasure Gardens Co. Ltd against all risks, and arranged with the Chief Constable for the supply of an adequate number of police'.[18]

The money gained through admission fees or ticket prices cannot be underestimated in understanding why Belle Vue's management allowed the fascist rally to occur. In one BUF account of the indoor rally at Olympia on 7 June 1934, 'the Reds' were described as 'occupying strategic positions' in the arena 'even in the most expensive seats'.[19] *The Times*, reporting the Blackshirt rally, drew attention to Belle Vue as 'the home of a zoological collection, and a pleasure resort to which admission was obtainable only on payment'.[20] Newspapers also drew attention to Oswald Mosley watching the 'real' Belle Vue fireworks after his speech. On this occasion 'The Siege of Delhi' was staged.[21] This normalized the fascist rally in many ways, presenting the Blackshirts as part of the fabric of the pleasure ground which accommodated political meetings as much as day-trippers in the inter-war years, both providing sources of revenue for Belle Vue.

The Blackshirts were, therefore, one of a number of political groups staging meetings and rallies at Belle Vue. I am not suggesting that commercial sites replaced all forms of BUF activity. Sharon Gerwitz has drawn our attention to smaller, less organized meetings than the Belle Vue rally as important to understanding fascist activity. In Manchester, for example, '[w]eekly meetings were held at such places as Stevenson Square, Miles Platting, Alexandra Park and Platt Fields'.[22] The BUF's choice of venues in 1934 for large rallies, however, reflected an engagement with sites of popular culture. Oswald Mosley's 'slogan', 'Albert Hall, Olympia, White City, Wembley, then Power' demonstrates the commercial spaces that political organizations were occupying.[23] This could be interpreted as the use of advanced mass media within fascism in the seemingly 'unpolitical' world of entertainment, as Reinhard Kuhnl has suggested, thus demonstrating the increasing politicization of leisure.[24]

The BUF's relationship with popular culture can be viewed as part of the wider commercialization of politics in the inter-war period. As a marginal political movement rather than a totalitarian regime, this perspective provides a British context for approaching fascist spectacle in the Lancashire 'cotton' campaign. There are two elements of BUF activity, however, that differed from many of the other political organizations hosting events at Belle Vue. First, the BUF was involved in an ambiguous relationship with popular culture. Although the BUF used popular cultural sites and techniques associated with mass media to increase its public profile, on a rhetorical level the BUF firmly rejected these new forms of mass entertainment. In celebrating the 'inspiring' commitment of the Blackshirts to defend their meetings against the 'Red mobs', A. K. Chesterton argued that the Blackshirts were engaged in a form of self-sacrifice. It is interesting to note that this rested on their withdrawal from forms of popular culture rather than any detachment from family or work obligations:

> Night after night for weeks and months and years the devoted young Blackshirts have given up their ease, spurned the cinema and the dance hall and all other recreations in order to defend Blackshirt speakers from the arguments of cosh and razor and broken bottles.[25]

Moreover, in BUF propaganda a link was made between many of the emerging forms of mass media and entertainment and Jewish influence. A. K. Chesterton stated that '[t]he whole capitalist racket, the whole of the national Press, the whole of the "British" cinema, and the whole bunch of purely parasitical occupations were found to be Jewish-ridden.'[26] The BUF, therefore, sought continually to distance itself from the forms of popular culture Belle Vue encapsulated on a rhetorical level. This was contradicted by the use of the pleasure ground that arguably stood proxy for the 'capitalist racket' of mass entertainment.

Secondly, the Blackshirt rally at Belle Vue on 29 September 1934 displayed forms of spectacle that could not be attributed to other political demonstrations at the pleasure ground. The appropriation of space by the BUF to stage fascist spectacle occurred, and was contested, on symbolic and material levels. The debates that surrounded the Blackshirt rally at Belle Vue and the BUF's attempts to demarcate and dominate space within the pleasure ground were unprecedented. To this extent, fascist theatre and 'theatricality' were achieved and the following section unravels the elements of both. A British context, therefore, for the performative and aesthetic nature of fascism can be constructed. The micro-dynamics of the Blackshirt Rally, however, must be understood within the changing forms of political activity in Britain, as argued above, rather than viewed as a second-rate or a merely imitative form of European fascist theatre or evidence of the 'failure' of British fascism.

Theatre: The Symbolic Appropriation of Space

The Blackshirt rally at Belle Vue was part of a series of open-air meet-ings in non-civic venues in 1934, marking a departure for the BUF from the indoor gatherings in city-centre locations. This departure had the effect of increasing the level of both opposition and police presence at the meetings, leading to greater media reportage. Through newspaper cuttings it is possible to chart the various interest groups and the debates involved in this meeting. The media coverage in the month before the meeting highlights the wider circle of interacting players mobilized by the presence of the BUF in Lancashire, but more importantly must be viewed as a form of 'theatre', setting the stage for Oswald Mosley's entrance. The use of mass media stimulated an enhanced idea of dialogue between the groups, attaching a variety of meanings to the rally before it was staged. The first approach to the Belle Vue meeting will therefore explore the geographically specific issues of the rally through the 'theatre' of contemporary media. This symbolic appropriation of space is significant as it projected both a context and an audience on to the open-air event.

The issue of policing the Blackshirt rally at Belle Vue raised the BUF's profile in Lancashire at the end of its 'cotton' campaign. In the aftermath of events at Olympia and Hyde Park, the Manchester Watch Committee approached the Chief Constable of Manchester, John Max-well, to undertake the policing of the rally 'subject to the cost being met by the Belle Vue authorities'.[27] Belle Vue refused and outrage was expressed in various papers that '£1,000' was to be passed on to 'rate-payers'.[28] It is unclear how this figure was calculated, but the argument put forward was that Belle Vue was a private venue and therefore did not come under the *Report on the Duties of the Police*.[29] There are no policy-making documents from Belle Vue (Manchester) Ltd on this issue, but the following statement was released:

> We obviously cannot undertake financial responsibility for any number of police brought into the gardens. The prior question of payment, how-ever – which is a new issue so far as such meetings at Belle Vue are concerned – will have to be gone into carefully.[30]

The pleasure ground employed its own stewards to 'patrol' the site, but the Blackshirt rally was one of the few occasions when the police were drafted in. A petition was signed by 'the residents around Belle Vue' demanding, therefore, that the BUF be refused entrance to the grounds.[31]

The fortnight preceding the Blackshirt rally witnessed the issue of policing move from a regional discussion to a national debate. John Maxwell, Chief Constable of Manchester, visited the Home Office to discuss his concern at the numbers of fascists involved. These were wildly overestimated at 20,000 fascists, 2,000 anti-fascists and 'as it would be a Saturday', 'ordinary' visitors resulting in 50,000 or more people at Manchester's pleasure ground.[32] The Home Office, and subsequently the Manchester police, were seen to favour the fascists in allowing the rally to take place, securing 'freedom of speech', while banning counter-demonstrations at Belle Vue.[33] The National Council for Civil Liberties, for example, sent a telegram to the Chief Constable condemning the 'serious infringement of the liberty of the subject'. It argued that the Chief Constable's decision to ban anti-fascist processions set 'a dangerous precedent' and would be 'vigorously challenged'.[34]

Within the opposition, numerous interest groups were mobilized on a symbolic level in protest to the BUF's presence in Manchester, from the unemployed at labour exchanges to 'University Men'.[35] The *Daily Worker* turned the question of policing into evidence of the strength of the opposition to the BUF, claiming that police were needed to 'protect Mosley and his gang of thugs from the wrath of the workers'.[36] Unions and their leaders, however, were divided in their support of the 'physical' counter-demonstration. J. R. Clynes, ex-Labour MP and General Secretary of the National Union of General and Municipal Workers, advised against involvement at the same time as one of the NUGMW branches voted in favour of demonstrating against the BUF.[37] Joan Leighton has argued that '[r]esulting from the authorities' handling of this affair, both fascists and anti-fascists were able to claim a moral victory, and this mutual sense of optimism to some extent encouraged further civil disturbance.'[38]

Questions of policing, procession, violence and opposition were therefore raised, discussed and commented on by civic alliances, 'workers' groups, trade councils, the BUF and Belle Vue's management. This constructed an idea of dialogue between these various groups played out in the arena of regional and national newspapers. In reading this form of dialogue, and charting the interest groups involved, attention should be paid to the symbolic place that Belle Vue came to occupy within this discursive arena. The expression '[w]orking-class Manchester' was frequently used to describe the industrial landscape within which this fascist meeting was to occur.[39] Furthermore, Belle Vue came to be referred to as a 'working-class entertainment centre', invoking ideas of workers at play.[40]

That the Trades Union Council's 'Clarion Call' poster encouraged anti-fascist demonstrations against the Blackshirt rally is indicative of the ways in which Belle Vue came to symbolize a workers' playground which needed protecting. Signed by representatives from various trade unions and political parties, the poster urged the 'workers' to unite against fascism as the trade unions had done. The poster implied that the fascist rally at Hyde Park at the beginning of September 1934 had failed in some sense and the Belle Vue meeting was interpreted as Oswald Mosley attempting to 'retrieve his political prestige in the heart of industrial Lancashire'. It also claimed that Belle Vue 'can do more than Hyde Park' and could be an 'even bigger defeat for Fascism'. This description of Belle Vue as the nucleus of an industrial region is central to the construction of the pleasure ground as a 'workers' stronghold' and the poster described the forthcoming rally as 'a threat to the whole working-class movement'.[41]

The 'Clarion Call' poster clearly demonstrates the rhetorical use of notions of class and region within opposition literature. The image is ambiguous, however, as the workers are portrayed as both vulnerable to the Blackshirt presence and yet fully able to resist Oswald Mosley's entrance into Lancashire, Manchester and the inner sanctum which became Belle Vue. The issue of policing and protests operated as a form of dialogue in the newspapers around which these additional layers of meaning were attached. Belle Vue, within this process, was therefore symbolically appropriated before the Blackshirt rally was staged on 29 September 1934 as a pivotal space for the industrial working class in the region and nation. The *Daily Worker* commented, for example, that 'Belle Vue will be like an island in a sea of workers'.[42] References to 'entertainment' and 'playgrounds' can be interpreted as strategic within this symbolic appropriation, highlighting sites where workers would be both united in numbers but vulnerable at play.

The use of mass media to debate the issues involved in a Blackshirt meeting was advantageous to all the interest groups involved. It raised the profile of the rally and opposition to the BUF's presence and dialogue was instigated and recorded for the newspapers' readership. It also attached meanings to the rally before it was staged and thus became a form of 'theatre'. Belle Vue came to symbolize the industrial working class, Manchester and Lancashire, all under threat by the BUF's presence.

Before analysing the meeting itself, it is worth noting here that many fascist meetings held in this period were accompanied by physical attempts to demarcate space. The *Daily Worker* noted that in 'every factory and workshop, in the streets and at the Labour Exchanges, intensive preparations are going on'.[43] The language used in the contemporary media was not mere hyperbole and the anti-fascists in particular were engaged in 'chalking' slogans and distributing leaflets in the Gorton area which Belle Vue was situated in.[44]

> The whole of Manchester is agog with excitement over the proposed visit of Mosley on September 29. The whole town is chalked white with anti-Fascist slogans … [s]pecial leaflets are being distributed at the factories and over 50,000 sticky-backs have been pasted up throughout the area.[45]

On some levels this was symbolic, but it also leads on to a second reading of the Blackshirt rally as 'theatricality' and the ways in which this was staged.

Theatricality: The Material Appropriation of Space

Alice Bellamy has argued that the fascists and anti-fascists in inter-war Manchester appropriated sites of particular strategic significance in constructing their 'publics'.[46] In this case, as examined above, Belle Vue stands proxy for northern 'workers' at play. If newspaper coverage represented the symbolic appropriation of Belle Vue, Alice Bellamy's work calls for an analysis of the material appropriation of space by political groups. Given the transitory nature of political spectacle and the absence of recorded decision-making on fascist performance in Britain, much of this analysis will have to rely on contemporary and retrospective written accounts.[47] It is extremely difficult to recreate the 'experience' of the rally, but an analysis of the use of clothes, barriers, light, noise, water and language reconstructs a sense of fascist theatre. By utilizing these material dimensions, the BUF presented a spectacle that can be interpreted as 'theatricality'. The BUF was able to physically appropriate space within the pleasure ground and, thus, the symbolic meanings attached to Belle Vue. As we will see, however, the material conditions of fascist theatre could also be contested and subverted in meaning. The symbolic and material appropriation of space in constructing fascist theatre and a degree of 'theatricality' was, therefore, never static or complete.

A. K. Chesterton listed, among many, the following reasons for adopting the black shirt as a 'political uniform':

> the strictly utilitarian reason that when meetings are attacked by mobs of alien thugs and Red razor-slashers, it is undeniably useful as a means of enabling the Blackshirts, sometimes outnumbered by hundreds to one, to act together as a disciplined body. It serves admirably, too, in eliminating distinctions of dress as between the well-to-do and the poor in a movement which seeks to break down all barriers of class. Finally, the blackshirt requires courage to wear.[48]

It is therefore interesting to note that the material appropriation of Belle Vue by the BUF on 29 September 1934 was, at first, carried out in a covert fashion. The newspaper coverage stressed the 'import' of Blackshirts from 'Northern centres', distancing the city of Manchester from this event.[49] These Blackshirts, however, attempted to pass as 'the usual crowds of Belle Vue day trippers' in entering the pleasure ground.[50] The following excerpt from the *Manchester Guardian* is indicative of the covert method of clothing employed by the BUF to gain entry to Belle Vue:

Between four and seven-thirty the Fascist forces arrived almost unnot-
iced at the gardens. Many of them slipped through the turnstiles with
macintoshes over their uniforms, and there was little to distinguish
them from the ordinary holiday-makers ... scarcely anyone except the
policeman at the Longsight gate stopped to look at them.[51]

In pragmatically disguising their Blackshirt uniforms, the BUF
entered the pleasure ground inconspicuously and this, ironically,
drew attention only to the number of police present who were physically visible.[52] The use of clothes was therefore significant in ensuring
not only entrance to the grounds but in eliminating the distinctions
between the BUF and 'hundreds of workers milling around' in Belle
Vue.[53] It is unclear from the accounts at what point the 'macintoshes'
were discarded but by the time the meeting started the Blackshirts
were in 'uniform' and thus clearly visible as an organized group using
space within the pleasure ground.[54]

The Blackshirts were 'shepherded' by the police present into a
'square enclosure' in an outdoor area near to the lakes at Belle Vue.[55]
A platform had been erected for Oswald Mosley's speech and the
space in front of this 'grandstand' was demarcated for the Blackshirts
by 'stout wooden barriers'.[56] A 'ring of policemen' stood inside the
square enclosure while other fascist 'hearers', the opposition and visitors to Belle Vue stood outside this arena.[57] The numbers in the
audience vary in contemporary media and retrospective accounts, but
taking an average it would seem that around 500 Blackshirts stood
inside the barriers and approximately 3,000 people were assembled
outside this area.[58] It is difficult to gauge whether this spatial arrange-
ment was organized at the request of the BUF, the police or the
pleasure ground management. The impact of the policy appears to
have been a clear appropriation of some space within Belle Vue by the
Blackshirts but also an ambiguous use of space around the lakes by
the interest groups involved. The opposition, for example, transcended the physical boundaries by throwing 'a handful of anti-Fascist
handbills' into the square enclosure.[59] An interesting gender division
of the Blackshirts was noted in the *Manchester Guardian* between the
men, who stood within the square enclosure, and the women 'selling
copies of the official Fascist paper' to those outside the wooden
barriers.[60]

The distinction between those within the square enclosure and
those outside it was blurred by the use of light at this meeting. Speaking at 7.50 pm on a late September evening, it is probable that some
form of illumination was required by Oswald Mosley. The method of
lighting chosen, however, was a searchlight that seems to have been
operated not by the BUF members to enhance 'theatricality' but by the
police to control the crowd:

> A powerful searchlight was mounted on the roof of the gallery from the centre of which Sir Oswald spoke. Its beam frequently raked the audience below and could at any moment have been directed on a group that was deemed to need the attention either of the police or of the firemen.[61]

The operation of the searchlight responded to the noise generated by the audience, turning 'a spotlight on parts of the audience where the noise was greatest'.[62] It was reported that this 'was received with cheers and the raising of a forest of clenched fists'.[63] The use of light, therefore, blurred the material distinction between the Blackshirts and the rest of the crowd and affected the levels of noise.

As we have seen in examining clothes, barriers and light, the techniques employed by the various interest groups could be subverted in meaning or create unclear boundaries between people inside the pleasure ground. Noise generated from the meeting, however, seems to have been the most obvious and sustained way in which conflict was played out between the Blackshirts and the anti-fascists. As soon as Oswald Mosley appeared on the platform, the Blackshirts began 'cheering' and the 'rowdy opposition force declared itself'.[64] It would appear that the first quarter of an hour of his speech was inaudible except to those on or near the platform. Oswald Mosley then began to use the loudspeakers and was able to make himself heard but the 'shouting, jeering, booing and chanting slogans' continued throughout his hour-long speech.[65] The following account clearly demonstrates the use of noise made by both Oswald Mosley and the opposition in attempting to appropriate space within Belle Vue:

> The interrupters stood shoulder to shoulder at one corner of the square, yelling systematically. 'One, two, three, four, five – we want Mosley dead or alive', was repeated continuously in chorus for minutes together. 'Murder made in Germany!' 'Heil Hitler!' and a more cryptic allusion to the fact that 'Mosley stole the lion's dinner!' were other opposition cries. One group sang the 'Internationale'. Another followed it with an attempt at the 'Red Flag'. After about fifteen minutes of this, a 'score' of policemen filed in to the crowd and stood close to the interrupters who continued shouting as before but gradually Mosley's voice 'amplified by a battery of loudspeakers' began to assert itself. He became progressively more audible but the shouting never stopped going in waves of volume.[66]

The visual elements of fascist theatre are often stressed, but this form of conflict through noise is extremely significant in establishing control. Obviously the accounts differ in interpretation of the impact of the noise, but it is clear that in attempting to render the Blackshirt presence inaudible and Oswald Mosley's 'lashing' of the microphone, the groups were both aiming to dominate the demarcated and wider spaces within the pleasure ground.[67]

The newspaper accounts in the days following the Blackshirt rally stressed the weather variable as contributing to the relatively peaceful nature of this meeting. The expression 'Much Noise but No Disorder' was used and the 'four hours' of rain preceding Oswald Mosley's entrance were viewed as 'damp[ing] the enthusiasm of both Fascists and Communists better than any show of authority could have done'.[68] It is interesting, therefore, given the presence of so much rain that fire engines were in place near to the meeting. Hoses had been connected to the Belle Vue lakes and '[t]he polished nozzles poked ominously from the edge of the water, flanked by firemen wearing oil-skins'.[69] This water supply was not, in fact, used during this meeting but it demonstrates an attempt to control both space and the audience by the municipal authorities, the physical presence of the police. The idea that the rain would alleviate conflict, and that water from the lake would dissipate violence, also indicates external forces that could affect the BUF's appropriation of space.

If the Blackshirt rally was characterized by much noise and water with little physical clashes between the fascists and anti-fascists, the language used by Oswald Mosley has been interpreted as 'stronger' than in previous speeches. The Belle Vue rally marked the turn towards a more violent anti-Semitism by Oswald Mosley in his speech at the pleasure ground, seen by some contemporaries as a result of 'the removal of the restraining hand of Lord Rothermere's advertising clients'.[70] He referred to the 'would-be interrupters' present at the meeting as the 'sweepings of the Continental ghettoes, hired by Jewish financiers', 'an alien gang imported from all quarters of Britain by Jewish money to prevent Englishmen putting their case'.[71] It is difficult to know whether Oswald Mosley decided to adopt more anti-Semitic language given the media interest in the policing and opposition to the rally, the large numbers present or its timing as the finale of the Lancashire 'cotton' campaign. In terms of appropriating space, however, the explicit anti-Semitism in his speech at Belle Vue ensured that this relatively peaceful rally received national as well as regional media attention.

The use of clothes, barriers, light, noise, water and language enabled a number of different groups to establish forms of material appropriation of the space within Belle Vue. This can be interpreted as a form of spectacle and 'theatricality', in particular by the BUF. The utilization of the material surroundings was, however, by no means straightforward. The Blackshirts disguised their uniforms to gain entry to the pleasure grounds. The physical presence of the barriers was subverted by movement within the audience outside the square enclosure and the deployment of light, noise and, potentially, water. The language adopted by Oswald Mosley arguably alienated rather than gained the support of the reporters of the rally. Furthermore,

Belle Vue continued to provide entertainment for its day-trippers and Saturday visitors, ensuring that the appropriation through different media was never static nor comprehensive. The attempts to appropriate space through the manipulation of material conditions by the BUF, the police and the opposition were, however, greater than at other political meetings and demonstrations during the inter-war period at Belle Vue. The Blackshirt rally therefore contained a level of 'theatricality' not normally present at the pleasure ground. The choice of Belle Vue arguably enabled a more theatrical performance than at other venues for the BUF in terms of demarcated space, numbers of visitors and symbolic meanings attached to the pleasure ground and the rally before the event was staged.

Conclusion

In choosing to focus on the Blackshirt rally at Belle Vue, this chapter has sought to broaden fascist historiographies in a number of ways. It has drawn attention to a significant regional initiative, to redress the bias towards studies of the BUF in London and the south of England. The Lancashire 'cotton' campaign was part of a move in 1934 by the BUF towards rallies at sites of popular culture, rather than civic spaces. This can be contextualized within the wider trends of commercialized politics and politicized leisure occurring in Britain during the inter-war period. From this perspective, the BUF was one of a number of political organizations using commercial sites to attract larger audiences in the absence of alternative spaces.

The BUF did differ, however, from other groups in their rhetorical rejection of mass media and mass entertainment, while using these sites of popular culture. Moreover, the Blackshirt rally used performative techniques that were rarely associated with Belle Vue and remain unacknowledged in many histories of British fascism. A sense of theatre was created in the build-up to the meeting as various groups sought to appropriate symbolically the space of, and meanings attached to, Belle Vue. On 29 September 1934, these groups were engaged in a battle for control over the material appropriation of space. Clothes, barriers, lights, noise, water and language were utilized to dominate space and enact fascist spectacle. The 'theatre' and 'theatricality' of the Blackshirt rally have been analysed to argue that a British context for the performative and aesthetic aspects of fascism can be constructed. I would, however, situate this form of fascist theatre within the changing forms of politics and popular culture in Britain during the 1930s, rather than in the political aesthetics of fascist states in Europe. This approach shifts the emphasis, as Roger Griffin has called for, from fascism itself to British society.[72]

Purifying the Nation:
Critiques of Cultural Decadence and Decline in British Neo-Fascist Ideology

Steven Woodbridge

Introduction

In 1972, Richard Verrall, writing in the National Front journal *Spearhead*, expounded views on the relationship, as he saw it, between 'Art and Nationalism'. He explained:

> As Nationalists, we of the National Front are committed to a total regeneration of the nation in every sphere, a purification of our political and social, moral and cultural life. In this task, therefore, one of our primary concerns must be the renaissance of art, so important an element in the spiritual existence of our race.[1]

He continued: 'Art is the test and strength of a civilisation. A great and vigorous culture will always produce a great and enduring art, while those in decline produce works that manifest a kind of neurosis at first, followed by decadence and decay.'[2] The article went on to argue that the 'spiritual temper' of a race or society was mirrored in its creative activity: 'healthy and secure, lofty and serene, as in the sculpture of classical Greece'.[3] A nation inspired by 'base ideals' would have an art 'at best frivolous and shallow, at worst wholly decadent'.[4] Verrall claimed that the nations of the West were in a state of 'political, moral and cultural putrescence', the expression of this 'sickness' lying in 'the nihilistic perversion' identified as 'abstract art'.[5]

Verrall's discourse was very similar to Adolf Hitler's critique of 'Degenerate Art' during the 1930s. Hitler had seen his task as one involving the 'cultural cleansing of the people's life' and he referred to the need for the 'purification of art'.[6] The Nazis were determined to engage in a *Kulturkampf* – a cultural war – to realize these objectives.

Verrall's detailed article, with its graphic description of 'healthy' and 'decadent' cultural forms, captured recurrent ideas in post-1945 far Right ideology in Britain concerning representations of culture. In common with the ideology of inter-war generic fascism,[7] a cultural crusade was envisaged. There was a belief that liberal and Marxist cultural forms had resulted in decadence, suggesting the nation was in serious decline. Consequently, there was a call for the 'regeneration' of the nation, together with a conviction that national culture required purification or cleansing as part of this project. Far Right texts put forward explicit views on what constituted a true, legitimate and authentically British culture. They sought to explain how 'healthy' cultural representations informed and reinforced a unique national identity. Thus, although fascism and neo-fascism emphasized political action, we should not underestimate the extent to which far Right ideologues also endeavoured to engage in the intellectual arena, particularly concerning debates over cultural representations. Moreover, in their desire to define the 'wholesome' version of culture, far Right texts since 1945 were at times replete with (sometimes competitive) concepts of identity.

It is intended in this chapter to illustrate the far Right's prescription for political and cultural renewal through a brief exploration of the intellectual texts of three neo-fascist movements operating after 1945: the Union Movement (UM), formed in 1948, the National Front (NF), formed in 1967, and the British National Party (BNP), formed in 1982. The aim is not to attempt an in-depth analysis of all three movements but, rather, to provide a general overview of the common ideas expressed in their discourse regarding cultural and aesthetic representations and how these shaped identity. It would be a mistake to read complete homogeneity into the far Right's ideas. At the same time, therefore, the discussion will also point to certain moments of tension in their texts, enabling us to better understand the rivalry between movements and the interplay between neo-fascist text and potential audience. The chief objective of this chapter is to help in the clarification of these ideological configurations. This is carried out by textual analysis of some of the main journals, books and ideological statements published by the three movements in question, texts written for both internal party consumption and for dissemination to the general public.

The Importance of Cultural Representations in Post-1945 Far Right Ideology

The British far Right in the post-war period was determined to link cultural activity with national and racial identity. Its definition of what constituted 'true' or 'eternal' culture was designed to furnish actual and potential supporters with a grasp of the essence of 'Britishness'. In the eyes of the far Right, an understanding of national, and Western, identity was intimately bound up with delineating which cultural representations were legitimate and which were not.

National identity could be comprehended through an appreciation of the supposedly distinctive nature of British and white Western cultural creativity: the works of 'high' art, literature, poetry, music and architecture that were rooted in 'classical', non-Modernist forms. Pre-twentieth-century cultural representations were often pointed to as models. These had once made Britain 'great', given her an Empire and Europe a 'superior' civilization. This claim was particularly evident in the ideology of the BNP, the largest far Right party in Britain in recent years. BNP ideologues offered, in their estimation, an authentic version of culture and history, cleansed of those forces which had allegedly engulfed the British people in a 'swamp' of decline and loss of national identity. Avant-garde and Modernist cultural forms were demonized as 'decadent', corrupting and ugly. They were the results of the 'anarchy' created by political liberalism.

From 1981 to 1999, under John Tyndall's leadership,[8] the BNP's cultural pessimism concerning the future of the British nation and the West, partly derived from the writings of Oswald Spengler and other 'Conservative Revolutionaries',[9] provided an ideological continuity with both UM and NF writers and, from the inter-war period, the British Union of Fascists (BUF).[10] This pessimism concerning the cultural aspects of liberal society was combined with an optimism about the potential of decisive political action: a modern non-liberal political movement could save the nation, it was claimed. History had not ended and, as one BNP writer put it in 1996, decline was 'not an inevitable process'.[11]

Indeed, the Spenglerian prognosis on the decline of civilizations proved a source of ambivalent fascination for ideologues in all the three movements under investigation here. In line with inter-war fascist critiques of Spenglerian pessimism, British neo-fascists were convinced that the symptoms of national illness could be cured and decline reversed. They resolved to purify or cleanse 'decadent' cultural representations. This was in order to not only halt decline but help bring about the rebirth of the nation, race and 'British' identity.[12] Above all, in common with their inter-war predecessors, British neo-fascists envisaged a cultural crusade to bring about this new dawn. This critique was combined with attempts to create and institutionalize their own cultural forms. While no single neo-fascist culture emerged, cultural activity still entailed a variety of alternatives to liberal ideas, including the promotion of an interest in 'real' history and literature, and policy statements on aesthetic issues. Study groups, book-lists in journals, articles by leading ideologues and, more recently, web-sites, were all designed to instil in members a sense of their own cultural identity, a sub-culture separate from mainstream liberal and decadent society.

Mosley and the Union Movement: The Rebirth of Culture

Cultural pessimists in Britain had admired the calls for cultural 'renewal' made in inter-war fascist texts. One of the factors involved in men such as A. K. Chesterton and Henry Williamson becoming attracted to Oswald Mosley's movement was the BUF's 'transposition of supposed aesthetic values to the political sphere'.[13] Despite his resignation from the BUF, Chesterton never discarded his Spenglerian cultural ideas and they continued to inform his post-1945 world view. They were present during his leadership of the post-war pressure group the League of Empire Loyalists and, later, his chairmanship of the National Front.[14] Similarly, Williamson continued to develop his aesthetic form of fascism after 1945. He sought to keep it 'alive' in contemporary culture via his fiction.[15] It was often conflated with the desire to purify and cleanse.[16]

Indeed, the theorists and men of letters involved in the far Right in Britain during the post-1945 period very much echoed pre-war ideas concerning the fascist intention to recover and reclaim national culture from the forces of decadence and decline. They were not shy to set themselves up as arbiters of national cultural taste and to set out the processes involved in rebuilding an authentic and 'eternal' British identity.

As soon as he felt safe to resume political activity after the end of hostilities in 1945, Mosley sent out strong signals to his old BUF supporters that the struggle to reverse national decline would continue. The modernization of Britain by a 'modern movement', as opposed to a mere 'party', was still the primary task of politics. At an 18B Detainees reunion held in December 1945, Mosley maintained that his own ideas had not changed during internment but had been 'greatly strengthened'.[17] He asked Jeffrey Hamm to 'spread the ideas'[18] and began to supply suitable texts. These were distributed through a loose network of 'book clubs' during 1946. The book clubs held discussion meetings where literary, cultural and philosophical questions were addressed but the underlying political agenda was an attempt to permeate mainstream culture with new Mosleyite ideas on a post-fascist 'European' identity.[19]

British identity, while still important, was now to be enhanced through 'Europe', a 'Third Way' which would be neither liberal, capitalist nor communist. In *My Answer* (1946), Mosley argued that, as 'we turn our eyes toward the future, we may discern – rising like Phoenix from these ashes – the undying soul of England and the European man'.[20] In his next book, *The Alternative* (1947), which functioned as an ideological launching pad for the Union Movement, Mosley further claimed that he was showing how, via the 'Will to Achievement',

Western civilization and European culture could free itself from the 'Great Negation' and achieve regeneration and 'rebirth'.[21] In this sense, veteran activists would be encouraged to welcome a new cadre of young supporters in order to resume the work pioneered by the pre-war BUF. Surveying post-war conditions, Mosley stated: 'This generation must play the midwife to Destiny in hastening a new Birth.'[22] He warned that it was 'vitally important that the culture and life of Europe should continue', and this would 'depend on the highest type of Europeans giving all, and daring all, as an order of men dedicated to the great rebirth'.[23]

As with the BUF's political project, cultural considerations continued to play an important part in Mosleyite post-war texts. Articles in the *Mosley Newsletter* warned that the maintenance of 'three thousand years of European life and culture' was under threat from 'Oriental Communism'.[24] One writer attacked the British Left for always being ready 'to hail Moscow as the seat of World Culture'.[25] In his opinion, it was important to remember that 'through the blunders of our statesmen and the hypocrisy of our intellectuals, the Tartar is now saddled across the cultural heritage of the West'.[26]

However, a Western and, in particular, 'European' identity, proved controversial among UM supporters, creating tensions in UM texts and within the movement itself. Much to the dismay of some of his former comrades, a number of whom defected to more explicit 'racial nationalist' groups,[27] Mosley's post-BUF creed stressed increasingly that 'British' identity would now be better realized through a wider transnational framework, which involved a greater awareness of the common culture of Europe and its kindred peoples. Alexander Raven-Thomson, who had been the BUF's equivalent of the Nazi ideologue Alfred Rosenberg,[28] was particularly concerned in 1948 to reassure Mosley's older supporters on this issue. The new emphasis on European cultural integration did not mean the replacement of 'our imperial heritage' or an attempt 'to sink our identity as a great nation into any cosmopolitan international system'.[29] He rejected opponents' claims that Mosley's 'Union of Europe' idea contradicted the UM's British patriotism and its desire to preserve the 'noble traditions of our race'.[30] It was, rather, a case of the 'Extension of Patriotism', 'not a repudiation of patriotism'.[31] Employing the imagery of purging and cleansing the nation, Raven-Thomson argued:

> Let us above all be British, for that title has, at least until recently, been one of high honour in the affairs of the world. We have every right to preserve that honourable name, and to eliminate from the life of the nation those alien influences which have already begun to bring discredit upon us.[32]

He also asserted: 'One of our greatest contributions to the future Union of Europe will be to clean up our own country, so that Britain speaks with her own voice ...'[33] UM publications continued, however, to reflect uncritically Mosley's core message in *The Alternative* and pointed to how Britons could find a 'kindred spirit' in wider European aesthetic achievement, such as painting, music and architecture. Jeffrey Hamm, for example, writing on the 'Heritage of Europe', claimed that the high points of European cultural history were to be found in classical Greece, Imperial Rome and in the Renaissance.[34] During the later period, according to Hamm, the 'creative genius of the European soared to fresh heights in every realm of art – in music, poetry, sculpture, and drama'.[35] This 'revival' of culture was 'common to all Europe' and art 'knew no frontiers'.[36]

Hamm argued that a good example was the work of Shakespeare. The great writer was the 'very personification of England' and, furthermore, Shakespeare was held in high esteem on the Continent. Hamm asserted that, in the new Europe 'struggling to emerge' from the ruins of the old, 'national pride is merged with that of the German adoration of Goethe, or that of the Italian admiration for a Dante or a Michael Angelo'.[37] As Europe arose, united around the 'New Idea', Hamm declared:

> we do not speak of this British poet, or that German composer, or of some Italian composer. Our proud boast is that these men were Europeans, born of the culture and civilization of two thousand years of Latin-Teuton genius, itself the product of the three thousand year old Greek spirit.[38]

Europe was now threatened by the 'Asian barbarism' of Russia, which meant the possible 'extinction' of the 'genius of Shakespeare and of Goethe' and 'the inspiring majesty of Wagner'.[39] He asked whether Europe would 'awake in time', remember its 'proud heritage' and enable Mosley to lead 'the Defence of the West'.[40]

The Hellenic and Elizabethan roots of both British and wider European cultural achievements were referred to and promoted in UM articles, with an assertion that contemporary society had lost these original and 'Higher' cultural forms. Often this material was given an anti-Semitic sting. One writer in 1950, exemplifying the UM's desire to purge society of allegedly inappropriate cultural activity, complained about the 'Degradation of Taste'.[41] He argued that the UM would enforce a higher standard of public entertainment, 'taking its management out of the hands of aliens with no understanding of or respect for European culture'.[42] The UM would engage in 'generous patronage' of artistic development and create the means for training in the 'classics'.[43]

An anti-Semitic approach to culture was also evident in the UM's condemnation of the Hollywood film *Sword In the Desert*, which *Union* viewed as a 'Zionist propaganda film' and 'anti-British', causing some UM activists to disrupt screenings.[44] UM newspapers ensured that political news was also supplemented with occasional analyses of cultural representations for the mass membership.[45]

The UM's cultural fascism ultimately remained, however, very much in the hands of Mosley. Two key cultural themes emerged in the UM leader's philosophy. Firstly, he was determined to reclaim and promote 'beauty' in all aesthetic achievement. In his vision of a 'new type' of man 'in the service of a higher purpose', set out in *The Alternative*, Mosley said that what he meant by this was a man who was endowed by 'the accumulated culture of three millennia of high civilisation'.[46] One recurrent preoccupation in Mosley's writings on this new type of man was the desire for some kind of cultural fascist elite. This would lead the way, educate the many and banish representations of 'ugliness' in society.

His reflections on the 'Function of Beauty' captured this well.[47] He argued that in a 'really civilized community' gifted people would be wholly dedicated to the 'development of fresh forms of the beautiful'.[48] The task of such people would be to 'show the world how beautiful life could be. The Artist in life would be honoured only less than the Artist of eternal beauty in music and the plastic arts.'[49] This idea was returned to in the 1960s. Reflecting on 'Beauty and Truth', Mosley stated that a society which had resolved the 'basic needs' should be ready to reward those who had shown 'any form of creative gift' in literature, music or the arts.[50] He wanted to build not only new amenities but also to beautify cities on a scale 'inconceivable today'.[51] Mosley claimed that 'the values of the classic Greeks ... remain the original and continuing inspiration of Europe'.[52]

Secondly, although he recognized a requirement to convert the mass membership of the UM to a 'higher' level of life and culture, Mosley also decided that the UM needed to target the 'gifted people'. He believed that the permeation of his ideas in a cultural struggle in society required a specialist publication designed to reach out to the highly educated. This was the rationale behind the creation of the literary journal the *European*, launched in March 1953. Robert Row, a UM ideologue, said that Mosley wanted the UM newspaper *Union* to win over the masses but he needed the *European* 'to pull in the intellectuals'.[53]

The *European* attracted some 'serious writers'.[54] These included Desmond Stewart, Ezra Pound, Roy Campbell, Henry Williamson, Hugo Charteris, A. J. Gregor and Richard Aldington. Edited by Diana Mosley, the journal was a curious mixture of poetry, book sections and theatre reviews, together with commentaries on politics by Oswald Mosley. UM lieutenants such as Row, or sympathizers such as Gregor, contributed more explicit political essays. The *European* folded in 1959, but the remnants of the UM (now called the Action Society) attempted to create another journal of politics and 'high' culture, *Lodestar*, during the late 1980s. The launch issue contained a combination of articles on political issues and reflections on 'Britain's Traditional Cultural Heritage'.[55] This heritage was allegedly expressed in old landscape and pub names, English folk songs, northern sword dances and native British plays.[56] Subsequent issues included analyses of the writings of Colin Wilson and Henry Williamson and the music of Vaughn Williams. The desire to claim cultural and intellectual legitimacy evidently remained an important part of the UM's political ambition to expunge the nation's life of decadent representations.

The National Front: Cleansing the Nation

Soon after its formation in 1967, the National Front also began to articulate its fears about Britain's alleged decline, the reasons for this, and the political prescription for 'saving' the nation and its citizens' identity. The political modernization and regeneration of the country would entail a systematic cleansing at the cultural level, banishing 'ugliness' and restoring the 'beautiful', an outlook we encountered earlier in the writings of Mosley. NF texts put forward a range of ideas on culture and warned of the 'un-British' cultural threat to national and general Western identity. As with the UM, the NF saw the main threat to British culture as deriving from international communism and its 'twin', liberal capitalism. NF texts emphasized the importance of educating future leaders, echoing Mosley's stress on the need to appeal to a younger generation of activists.

While the NF claimed in 1970 to be recruiting 'ever greater numbers of promising young men and women', one difficulty was that, in NF eyes, both academic life and the main publishing houses in Britain were supposedly 'under almost total control of liberals, internationalists and leftists of every shade'; the NF therefore recognized the need to provide a guide to alternative material giving a 'nationalist and rightist point of view'.[57] Recommended reading for young NF activists included not only familiar books on politics and race but also more obscure titles such as *The New Morality* by A. Lunn and G. Lean, which was described as 'a brilliant demolition of the permissive creed', and *Rhythm, Riots and Revolution* by D. A. Noebel, which dealt 'with the way in which folk and pop music are exploited by communists to disrupt society'.[58]

Cultural sections began to appear in NF publications, giving significant indications of the party's attitudes towards cultural representations. The NF was keen to forge its own non-liberal culture, educating members in a more positive 'Nationalist' world-view. Reviews of cultural activity were sometimes cues for NF theorists to make dire predictions about the future of national culture, echoing the aesthetic pessimism of A. K. Chesterton, the NF's first chairman.

In 1968, for example, in an article that started by attacking the stage show 'Hair' and 'other extravaganzas of sewer life', John Bean warned of 'The Assault on Western Culture'.[59] He claimed that this was exemplified in the changes being witnessed 'not only in the theatre, but in the cinema, in television plays, in the "best-selling" novels, in painting, sculpture and even modern architecture'.[60] He asserted that all these changes had one common factor: 'they are an attack upon all that is beautiful and aesthetically pleasing, and an effort to substitute the cult of ugliness.'[61] Bean continued: 'What we are seeing is the supplanting of the western art form ... by a rootless non-form, symbolising the "one-world" outlook of its promotors.'[62] Warming to his theme, Bean warned that 'modern art' was preparing the way 'mentally and culturally' for a 'de-nationalised world'. Sounding decidedly Spenglerian, Bean argued: 'If this happens mankind will pass into a spiritual night that will last for centuries – if not forever.'[63]

Nearly two years later, Bean returned to his engagement with Spengler's cultural ideas when he reflected on 'Nationalism and the Meaning of History'.[64] He warned that Spengler could 'only give us a message of defeatism' with his view that civilizations rise and disintegrate. Bean decided, as did other NF theorists, that a distinctive cultural identity involved an awareness of history: 'To become aware of our heritage and to develop an innate desire to preserve it from destruction by assimilation with alien cultures is ... one result of searching for the meaning of history.'[65]

The desire for a 'healthy' rebirth of culture was also illustrated in an article on 'Sub-Culture', the title clearly aping Nazi terminology.[66] Written by Eddy Morrison, a nineteen-year-old described as leader of the growing Leeds branch of the NF, the article warned of the 'gradual distortion and replacement of the British way of life and of European culture', the first channel of attack being music. Morrison complained that, in a society already soaked with 'pop' music, the new 'culture-bearers' had now introduced the cult of Indian music and 'more lately, electronic music'.[67] The young activist claimed that folk-music, poetry and literature were all under attack and concluded: 'I believe that a National Front government, on being elected to power, should encourage the rebirth of real culture, at the same time stopping the rot of subculture.'[68]

The link between rebirth and a 'real' culture in order to defeat decline was repeated in a special issue of Spearhead in early 1972. One article called for a 'Renaissance of Western Man'.[69] The anonymous author warned readers of the 'deep moral and spiritual sickness' engulfing the peoples of 'Western civilization and culture, and nowhere more than in Britain'.[70] There was a requirement for 'real youth' and a condition of mind that rejoiced in radiant health. The article claimed: 'Real youth is the moving spirit of every culture in its upward surge of life ...', and stated that the symptoms of sickness were there for everyone to see: 'the spiritual exhaustion of the old art-creating stratum ... is reflected in the familiar excrescences of modern painting, sculpture, architecture, music and poetry – excrescences which seek to reduce those things that should exhibit life's noblest experiences down to a form which expresses only a tortured intellectualism ...'[71]

The author complained that no allowance was being made for 'the deeply mystical and spiritual processes that move men and nations, as well as all great art', especially 'heroic' values.[72] This mystical crusade would be a cultural and political revolution. The article asserted that an appreciation of the 'inner sickness' must lead to the conclusion that Western man could only rise again to become a 'great' cultural force through a 'revolutionary change in existing institutions and values', a change which embraced 'an utter repudiation of everything that is meant by Liberalism'.[73] Engaging in the far Right's recurrent pre-occupation with Spengler, the author stated that the ultimate task was 'to prove wrong the Spenglerian thesis that every civilization meets its moment of irreversible decline and death'.[74]

Later in the year *Spearhead* carried one of the most detailed statements of NF theory on national culture, written by Richard Verrall. Verrall was the NF's main intellectual, who held a first-class honours degree in history from London University and later sat on the NF Directorate.[75] The article, referred to at the outset of this chapter, claimed that the first real manifestations of 'culture distortion' appeared with the invention of 'Cubism', the parent of 'abstract art'.[76] This branch of art had supposedly exhibited 'all those perverse inclinations that characterise a society in decline'.[77] From this moment, Verrall argued, sprang all the 'isms' and the 'anti-art' that had 'eaten away at the foundations of Western aesthetic values, debasing all standards and eradicating the desire for truth and beauty' which had animated the European soul.[78]

In language notably similar to the Nazi approach to degenerate art, Verrall claimed that the 'liberal repudiation of our racial and cultural heritage' had led to the rejection of all inherited traditions in art:

> Art is the activity by which through representational means, we give form to feeling. Representational art and the classic form it has taken in the West are not simply things that have descended to us from the past. Through their age-long association they have entered the very bloodstream of our culture, and, like race itself, they cannot be denied.[79]

Verrall went on to describe the 'true meaning' of art, which could be derived from 'experience in the real world', the 'traditions of the West' and in the 'beauties of existence'.[80] In order to build a new world, Verrall argued, 'we must recover an old spirit' which would be found in the 'civilisation of classical Greece'.[81]

Providing a clear political reading to culture, Verrall claimed the political ideal of the Greeks was an identification of the individual 'with the corporate life of the nation', and that, to the Greeks, 'a work of art was great in so far as it represented, in its most beauteous form, the highest aspects of the national ideal'.[82] Verrall asserted: 'Healthy and aspiring nationalism … has provided that unity of belief and purpose in which all great art has arisen.'[83] This unity had been destroyed by liberalism but a 'regenerative movement' would restore it, 'sweep away all the rubble of cultural decadence', and 'liberate creative minds, so that the true artist once more may flourish'.[84]

During the rest of its existence in the 1970s, the NF sought to provide further cultural material in its texts, repeating the calls for the protection of 'national' art and culture[85] and, in particular, applying such analyses to the medium of film.[86] Moreover, NF writers often repeated the message that the necessary cultural changes were part of a wider revolution. Drastic 'surgery' to cure the 'disease' of national crisis and decline was required.[87] The youth wing of the NF was continually encouraged to develop an alternative internal far Right culture. This institutionalization of NF cultural activity resulted in the formation of groups such as the Viking Cultural Society in Surrey, which met in a local library and discussed Norse 'Kulture' and mythology.[88]

Even when the NF found itself in radical decline during the 1980s, the leadership still adhered to the conviction that Britain required a purification at every level of society, including the cultural. To realize this, the defence of British identity was vital. Ian Anderson stated in 1985: 'We believe in a monoracial society', and he urged that 'White British people should reclaim their country'.[89] This racist imagery was taken up with relish by the BNP, which sought to reinvigorate the far Right's cultural crusade as the NF disintegrated into rival factions.

The BNP: The Centrality of Race to National Culture

Earlier in the chapter the discussion considered briefly the BNP's perspective on culture and identity. Conceptions of culture and racial identity were often inextricably linked in BNP texts. From its formation, John Tyndall was the dominant BNP ideologue. Although he borrowed numerous phrases and ideas from Mosleyite discourse, Tyndall also derived much from Arnold Leese's racial ideas.[90] From early on in his career, he placed himself firmly in the 'racial nationalist' tradition and shared, along with most other far Right activists, a deep suspicion that Mosley had placed too much faith in 'Europe' in his desire to reclaim the past and 'modernise' the future.[91]

Tyndall was convinced that the project to restore European and Western identity involved first and foremost the defence of 'British-ness'. He briefly joined Chesterton's League of Empire Loyalists, a group which retained a strong belief in the British Empire. Tyndall subsequently moved further to the Right, wanting a more radical philosophy. This initially involved an openly neo-Nazi perspective on culture, very similar to Hitler's ideas on degenerate art noted previously. In one of his earliest known published articles, written for the journal of the far Right National Labour Party (founded in 1957), Tyndall reflected on 'The Jew In Art'.[92] This adopted a highly anti-Semitic stance on the 'purification' of culture, reminiscent of Leese's racial obsessions.

Such ideas remained in Tyndall's discourse during his period as leader of the Greater Britain Movement in the 1960s, his chairmanship of the NF during the 1970s, and his leadership of the BNP during the 1980s and 1990s. His journal *Spearhead* was employed as a theoretical publication for each movement he led.[93] The journal frequently carried evidence of Tyndall's conviction that the far Right in Britain was not just a political ideology and movement. It was also a movement for cultural change. 'Nationalism' thus put forward an all-embracing 'revolutionary' creed which placed a great deal of importance on the cultured expression of political belief. Crucially, so BNP texts claimed, the task of winning the 'cultural war' in wider society was a necessary precursor to ultimate success at the political level, an idea which echoed Mosley's original strategy, NF policy, and contemporary far Right ideas in Europe.[94]

At times, the desire to banish enemies in the political arena was equated with a cultural struggle to cleanse 'ugliness' and restore 'beauty' to the nation, an image also in part derived from Mosley's discourse. Indeed, this preoccupation with perceived 'ugliness' and a desire to contain it had deep inter-war roots.[95] Tyndall's belief that liberal culture was 'ugly' remained in place after he had left the official NF and set up the New National Front (later the BNP) in 1981. As he explained in *Spearhead* at the time:

> I want to see the great glories of European art return and to achieve their renaissance here in Britain, so that we may again see a flowering of beauty throughout our land. I see no possibility of this happening except by means of a cultural revolution, and if intolerance of artistic trash is a necessary commodity in the carrying out of such a revolution then let us accept that and get on with it.[96]

In *The Eleventh Hour: A Call For British Rebirth* (1988), which the author described as a 'political manifesto' with an 'autobiographical element',[97] Tyndall wielded both Mosleyite oratory and Leeseite imagery to persuade readers that Britain was 'in a condition of long and continual decline', requiring measures that would 'reverse the process and bring about regeneration'.[98] At one point he stated: 'If I am asked to define our ideal in a few words, it is that of a noble race, attaining the highest possible standards of character, health, strength and beauty, living in a land cleansed of disease, dirt, ugliness and degeneracy and in complete harmony with the natural order.'[99] Developing this theme, he continued: 'We want a nation … surrounded by an environment of great art and culture which will provide continual nourishment for the national spirit.'[100]

As with the NF's ideologues, Tyndall's political ideas were underpinned by a systematic cultural reading of history, repeated by other BNP writers.[101] In his view, the twentieth century was an historical 'aberration', while the nineteenth had kept the patterns of cultural change 'within the parameters of the European cultural tradition', which in its turn was accepted, Tyndall argued, 'without question as the highest to which man could aspire'.[102] Cultural decline ensued in the twentieth century, but Tyndall believed that the Modernist and progressive cultural 'con-trick' of that century was now in the process of 'being massively rejected' via a cultural 'counter-revolution'.[103] It was not a matter of putting the clock back: 'on the contrary, the rhythm of the clock' was now 'simply being restored' as the twenty-first century approached. In a 'Return to Culture', the new century would, in Tyndall's estimation, 'rediscover what is true art, true music and true literature, just as it will return to sanity in other related cultural fields'.[104]

Like Mosley and the UM, Tyndall sought to emphasize how his movement was a 'modernising' movement. Political modernization was often conflated with cultural 'modernisation'. In a use of language designed to claw back the 'modern' mantle for the BNP from liberalism and its Modernist aesthetic representations, Tyndall argued: 'The "progressives" will become reactionaries and the "reactionaries" progressives.'[105] He concluded: 'Our civilisation is awakening from a nightmare, and is ready to resume history's road!'[106] This cultural reading of British history, and dogmatic assertion that the BNP could expurgate and cleanse contemporary culture, restoring the 'High' culture of the past, led to BNP articles on music,[107] literature,[108] art[109] and architecture.[110] Wagner, Elgar, Tolkien, Dickens and – in particular – Henry Williamson were all variously pointed to as representatives of the White race and 'quality' cultural production in the past. Tyndall asserted: 'Everything possible should be done to preserve and nurture the national heritage in music, art, the theatre, literature, and all other creative fields.'[111]

Essentially, however, an unbreakable connection to the British 'Race' was required in all cultural activity. Especially desirable, in Tyndall's view, were films which promoted 'outstanding creative works by members of the British Race'.[112] Employing Mosleyite discourse on national rebirth, Tyndall argued that the 'recovery' of the 'national character' involved a 'mission of total regeneration of a people – in mind, body and spirit – as a necessary prerequisite of political recovery'.[113] This entailed the avoidance of 'reading degenerate books and listening to degenerate music'.[114]

Again, in 1992, Tyndall attacked what he called 'the debasement of culture, manifest in the elevation of ugliness and depravity in every conceivable artistic form'.[115] In images notably similar to both the UM and NF's highly mythical interpretation of the values and cultural representations of Ancient Greece, the BNP habitually attacked Modernist architecture and pointed to the beauty of Ancient Greek cultural achievement.[116]

The purification of national culture was thus always of paramount importance to the BNP leader and his lieutenants, particularly in the face of the threat from 'Globalisation'. Above all, in common with the UM and NF, the BNP sought the 'renewal of our civilisation' and was out, as Tyndall put it, to 'prove Spengler wrong in his assertion that the West is finished'.[117]

Conclusion: A Continuing Cultural Crusade?

The historiography on generic fascist and neo-fascist ideology has engaged in important debates concerning fascism's ambivalent and complex relationship to cultural representations and national identity.[118] Historians have raised the question of whether fascism was a 'traditional reactionary phenomenon' with essentially conservative ideas, or a 'genuine revolutionary movement' that sought the total re-ordering and modernization of national life.[119] Inter-war fascist ideology tried to be a synthesis of both, combining a reactionary conservative attitude to contemporary culture with an attempt to construct a radical and alternative modernity rooted in 'traditional' constructs and representations of culture.[120] Fascists adamantly asserted that culture must be 'disciplined', becoming an instrument of the state or race. Fascist theorists therefore defined what was acceptable and unacceptable, legitimate and illegitimate in terms of cultural and aesthetic creativity.

This chapter has argued that the ideas of British neo-fascists towards cultural production showed very similar patterns. Significantly, John Tyndall's reference to a 'cultural revolution' in 1981 was indicative of a core theme in post-1945 British far Right intellectual publications. All the three movements discussed above, while sometimes differing over the precise details of the ideal way to bring this about, broadly held in common the desire to purify national, racial or European culture, interpreting this in terms of a social and political revolution. As with inter-war British fascism, all three movements saw the impetus behind their project as lying in their critique of liberal, democratic and Enlightenment Western values. Neo-fascists were united in their determination to radically 'cleanse' the diseased cultural symptoms of contemporary liberalism, 'save' the nation, and restore cultural identities which they viewed as traditional, healthy, real and qualitatively superior.

Herein lies the key to the neo-fascist approach to culture and the struggle against 'decadence': it was and is to be a restorative revolution, continuous and all-embracing, reviving selected cultural representations from the past and reinserting them into the present. In this sense, British neo-fascists wanted to reclaim society from the 'alien' values of liberalism and Enlightenment Modernism and to prove Spengler was mistaken in his cultural pessimism. They envisaged 'real' culture as representing solidity over abstraction, beauty over ugliness, and national identity in preference to international otherness. In one sense, these ideas had much in common with the neo-conservative wing of the new Right and journals such as the *Salisbury Review*.[121] However, whereas neo-conservatives mainly wished to preserve 'high' culture from contamination by the 'masses' and, moreover, tended to accept Spenglerian cultural pessimism, neo-fascist theorists were more optimistic. They saw their task as more revolutionary, involving the radical re-education of 'the people' in non-liberal cultural values. A correctly educated mass membership would be a first step towards political revolution.

The attempts to institutionalize alternative far Right cultures did not always go to plan. The aesthetic pretensions and emphases on high culture were often lost on the 'street' activists, engendering tensions between leaders and their grassroots members. As we have noted, evidence of these tensions occurred in the UM over British and European identity. Similarly, NF leaders were sometimes unable to control their members' desire for less 'respectable' cultural forms,[122] and internal conflict broke out in the BNP concerning the party's relationship to the skinhead 'White noise' music movement.[123] Some in the BNP, such as Tyndall, were unable to fully appreciate the extent to which neo-fascist youths had developed their own popular sub-cultures which, ironically, drew heavily on 'decadent' and materialist liberal capitalism – these were built around mass life-style icons, fashion, alcohol, football and rock music. Such sub-cultures displayed more potential to mobilize disaffected youth in the inner cities than the bland reassertion of classicism and high culture often pedalled by far Right ideologues.

Nick Griffin, who replaced Tyndall as BNP leader, was more pre-pared to recognize and exploit such trends. He attempted to tap more effectively into the disaffection and anti-establishment rebelliousness of white working-class youth culture by encouraging the creation of, for example, a 'Young BNP' website and 'Camp Excalibur' activity weekends.[124] In addition, a cultural merchandise service aimed at the wider party membership was launched.[125] Its glossy pictures on the internet were designed to reinforce a sense of deeper cultural and racial identity within the BNP and sympathetic groups. This institu-tionalization of culture for the party was also reflected in the BNP's adoption of annual 'Red, White and Blue' family weekends, an idea inspired by the French Front National.[126] Past and current evidence from far Right texts and activity thus suggests that the cultural dimen-sion remains pivotal to understanding British neo-fascist political discourse.

Part III

Cultural Confrontations:

Foreign Influences and Cultural Exchange

Anglo-Italian Fascist Solidarity?

The Shift from Italophilia to Naziphilia in the BUF

Claudia Baldoli

> Set we forward; let a Roman and a British ensign wave Friendly together ...[1]

The first book issued as part of the 'foreign fascisms collection' by the publishing house La Nuova Europa, in 1933, was dedicated to British fascism. Italian Fascist-Universalism considered it a duty to support British fascists, who professed to believe in the 'universality of Roman ideas'. Only two years later, the same Italian publisher, Asvero Gravelli, began to distinguish between a Protestant (German and British) and a Roman (Italian) type of fascism. Such a variation in the Italian perception of British fascism clearly reflected a shift in the BUF's role model from Italy to Germany. This chapter explores the contacts between British and Italian Fascists and the cultural origins of British fascism in terms of its relationship to the Italian movement, until the identification with a 'Roman' form of fascism became complicated by the growing prominence of Nazi Germany.

The historiography of British fascism has usually identified the contradiction between the BUF's support for fascism abroad and its extreme nationalist propaganda in Britain as one of the major reasons for the BUF's failure.[2] During the Abyssinian War in particular, Mosley's pro-Italian attitude showed that 'BUF beliefs appeared to derive from ideological sympathy with Italian Fascism'.[3] However, during the Abyssinian War the shift toward Germany was already evident.

The first period of the BUF's existence was characterized by the organization of visits to Italy and, though less frequently, to Germany. Peregrinations lasted about a fortnight, and their purpose was to 'see something of the Hitler movement at first hand, as well as to see in Italy the actual working of a Corporate State'.[4] In April 1933, in Rome, the Duce received a group of 200 British teachers who were there to examine the Italian educational system and to observe the working of Italian schools; the British Fascists and the Italian *Fascio* in London had organized this tour jointly, and an Italian Fascist stationed in London, Gino Gario, who was also a journalist of the official newspaper of the Italian *Fasci* in Great Britain, *L'Italia Nostra,* accompanied the group to Rome.[5] British workers who were currently unemployed were taken to Rome to attend exhibitions at the Foro Mussolini, and to visit some after-work organization. They could also see the Colosseum and pay homage to the grave of the Unknown Soldier.[6] During the same period, the London headquarters of the BUF announced to the Italian Embassy its intention to send a team of boy members of the BUF to Rome to play a football match against a team of the Italian youth organization.[7]

Although the fundamental mission of the Italian *Fasci* abroad was the fascistization of emigrants' communities, they also played a role in disseminating propaganda among foreigners and in supporting the growth of foreign fascist organizations. The London *Fascio,* one of the first created outside Italy, in 1921, established numerous contacts with the BUF until 1935.[8] The *Fascio* maintained that it was necessary to respect Mussolini's guidelines to the *Fasci* abroad and not interfere with local politics, yet contact between the two fascist parties had gone well beyond a formal and respectful relationship.[9]

The BUF also invited Italian Fascists to Britain. During the summer of 1933, twenty-seven students from the universities of Aosta and Florence spent fifteen days in London and at Mosley's property in the countryside. As the Italian Ambassador to London, Dino Grandi, wrote to the Italian foreign ministry, they called on him at the embassy accompanied by two representatives of the BUF. Mosley acted as a local 'duce' for the Italians, not only giving a speech but also reviewing them in a military fashion as Mussolini used to do in Italy.[10]

Although the Mosleyites' attitude to these events was sometimes ambiguous, since they had to claim to be a nationalist party above all else, their belief that Britain would be great again only in a fascist Europe encouraged these meetings. In the summer of 1934 a group of British Blackshirts from Bristol walked six miles to the Bristol docks to exchange fascist greetings with the officers and crew of an Italian ship, the *Monte Bianco.* This meeting was followed by another one, when the Italians returned the visit later in the week. In addition, two German vessels also arrived at Bristol and a meeting of unity between Nazis, Italians and British Fascists took place. *Blackshirt* stated that informal gatherings such as these strengthened 'the good understanding' which already existed between fascists of different nations.[11] Continuous invitations from the BUF were followed by visits from Italian Fascists to the British Fascists' headquarters; at the same time, BUF members often visited the Italian *Fascio* in London. Moreover, they both participated in each other's public events.

The events at the famous meeting at Olympia in June 1934, at which the BUF stewards violently counter-attacked an anti-fascist attempt to disrupt Mosley's speech, have often suggested comparison between the Olympia rally (7 June 1934) and the Nazi 'Night of the Long Knives' (30 June 1934); in fact the events at Olympia were not comparable to what happened in Germany, but rather showed similarities with the Italian *squadrismo*.[12] On several occasions *Blackshirt* published a series of pictures of the weapons used by the anti-fascists; it argued that the BUF, like the *squadristi* in Italy twelve years before, was the only assurance of free speech in Britain. Eventually, they suggested that the Olympia disturbance was the end of one period and the dawn of another.

Italian imagery of the BUF represented the latter as a *squadrista* movement, and Mosley as a sort of *ras*, just like the leaders of the Italian Fascist movement.[13] In fact Grandi was uncertain whether Mosley himself would become the future British dictator, but nevertheless saw Mosley as the leader of a British version of *squadrismo*. Although the latter was very weak if compared to the Italian *squadre* of ten years before, it was possible for Grandi to compare the two situations. This comparison was convincing because of the form and hierarchies of their organization and violent style of their activities, such as their brutal attacks on socialists and communist meetings, and the participation of fascist students in anti-democratic attacks against the student unions at British universities. As reported in an article in a German newspaper, it was enough to visit the BUF headquarters to find similarities to *squadrismo*: the room contained 'training instruments, boxing gloves and other tools'. Benches were located near the walls, possibly for the spectators; a wardrobe contained 'swords, masks and fencing clothes. Probably here in the evenings they proceed to the instruction of the blackshirts'.[14] In Grandi's opinion, at that moment Mosley was a kind of 'political Marinetti' surrounded by a mob; this fact, rather than discouraging him, was seen by Grandi as a proof of voluntarism, and brought the ambassador's thoughts back to the age of *squadrismo*:

> Is it perhaps the case that Revolutions are made by saints and gentlemen? During the punitive expeditions I carried out in Bologna in 1920 those who hit harder were not the children of good families. Thus I am not worried by the knowledge that part of the money we give Mosley will be spent in the night clubs of London.[15]

The day after Olympia, *L'Italia Nostra* reported the news of the first meeting held in Rome by the British Fascists in Italy. The Italian sections of the BUF gathered also in other Italian towns to celebrate both the anniversary of Italy's entry into the First World War and King George's birthday. The meeting concluded with the Italian and British anthems, namely the Fascist hymn 'Giovinezza' and 'God Save the King'.[16] Between 1933 and 1934 the BUF formed branches in Genoa, Turin, Bordighera, Milan, Rome and Florence. Most of the members were Anglo-Italian subjects, either British-born and living in Italy or individuals with double nationality, although some of them were British Fascists sent to Italy for propaganda purposes. The Genoa branch was probably the largest, because of the large number of British citizens who traditionally lived in Liguria. John Celli, an Anglo-Italian who in 1934 resided in Milan, was at the head of the national movement. The finances of the party in Italy seemed to have come mainly from the BUF headquarters in London.[17]

The first thing to notice is that these members, instead of being just fascists living in a fascist country, saw themselves as *British* Fascists, who chose to offer their loyalty primarily to Mosley and only secondarily to Mussolini. When they gathered, they usually sent a telegram of greetings to both leaders. The most remarkable distinction between them and Italian Fascists was that they were Anglicans. The main duty of BUF members in Italy was to support the fascist struggle of their fellow countrymen in Britain by seeking to fascistize British subjects living abroad. It is perhaps possible to think in terms of the Italian conception of the pioneer, or cultural colonist, abroad. While in Italy, BUF members not only gathered in Anglican churches, but also 'enjoyed' the fascist atmosphere of the state in which they had the 'good fortune' to live: they dressed in black shirts, paid homage to Italian martyrs of the revolution and sang fascist songs. At a meeting in Genoa in 1934, after the morning service at the Anglican Church, black-shirted, they visited a plaque in memory of a dead hero of the *squadrismo*, showing that fascist martyrs had no nationality in their eyes; afterwards they went to a war memorial arch.[18] The First World War was another common memory for Italian and British Fascists, for their countries had been allies during the war; indeed, Italian university students in London had paid homage to the Whitehall cenotaph the summer before.

The BUF's own historiography reflected the belief that British fascism was part of universal fascism, and that Rome was its origin. The British fascists started writing their own history shortly after the foundation of Mosley's movement. Two main examples of BUF historiography and myth making are James Drennan's *BUF: Oswald Mosley and British Fascism* (1934), and one of the first biographies of Mosley, A. K. Chesterton's *Oswald Mosley: Portrait of a Leader* (1937).[19] These works should be seen as histories of a pre-revolutionary age, written by men who seemed to believe that a revolution was shortly to come: 'we march forward to a victory which is inevitable,' wrote Mosley's earliest biographer.[20] The book by Drennan clearly seemed to emulate the structure of Italian histories of the Fascist revolution,

namely the ones written by G. A. Chiurco, Italo Balbo, Roberto Farinacci and, in Britain, Luigi Villari.[21] As well as those Italian accounts,
which started by describing the transition from the 'old' Giolitti-Nitti-
Facta's Italy to Mussolini's 'new' age, Drennan's book traced an ideal
path that was to lead from Baldwin-MacDonald's England to Mosley's. Once they had demonstrated their political skills during the
years of the parliamentary system, both Mussolini and Mosley
emerged from the chaos of democracy in order to rescue their respec-
tive countries. Just like the Italian books, Drennan's monograph was
filled with quotations from the leader's articles and speeches. Chesterton pointed out that Mosley, just like Mussolini in Italy, 'was planning
the greatest adventure of his career, and the boldest move in the history of British politics'.[22] *Blackshirt* also aimed to appear as a sort of *Il
Popolo d'Italia*, Mussolini's paper since 1914, in the period preceding
the march on Rome in 1922. The faith that fascism would come was
bolstered by the idea of universal fascism: *Blackshirt* frequently
reported fascist successes in other countries, and highlighted the
examples of Italy and Germany. Mosley was often called simply the
'Leader', and he was represented as the British 'duce' in songs and
poems: 'Mosley! Leader of thousands! / Hope of our manhood we
proudly hail thee! / Raise we this song of allegiance, / For we are
sworn and we shall not / fail thee! / Lead us! We fearlessly follow / To
conquest and freedom – or else / to death!'[23]

Many articles in *Blackshirt* focused on the cult of the leader, between
admiration for the Italian and German dictators and the attempt to
create a similar image for Mosley. Mussolini stood as a great leader
until the beginning of 1935, after which, and from 1936 in particular,
the newspaper concentrated its admiration almost entirely on Hitler.
Until then, both leaders were described as examples of supermen: in
1933, Hitler 'became the Chancellor of Germany'; only 'eighteen
months later, he was her supreme ruler. To-day he is the most powerful ruler in German history.'[24] Fascist Italy was interesting in
particular for its architecture and public works; the BUF seemed to
view Italy as a backward country, remade by Mussolini. The new
architecture interested the BUF for its symbolism of rebirth, and the
belief that such a rebirth had been made by one man suggested that
the same could happen in Britain.[25]

However, although the main model was Italy during the first half of
the 1930s, the first step for British fascism was to establish a British tradition. The journalist of the *Rheinisch-Westfälische Zeitung* who
interviewed Mosley in 1933 asked the first question that every non-
English person, according to Mosley, was likely to ask: 'is not the fascist idea too non-English, and will it be able to overcome the
parliamentary tradition?' Mosley made it clear that the existence of an
absolute traditional English model was a mistaken belief, based on the

fact that the English nation was always identified with the average middle-class Englishman. Yet history had shown that the English aristocracy 'had always produced people of daring spirit, who yearn for new adventures. It has given birth to men who have been able to overcome petrified dogmas.' Certain development in English history, asserted Mosley, confirmed his argument exactly: from the lively and prosperous Tudor age, Stuart decadence followed. But from this decadence, the people of England were saved by Cromwell, 'whose appearance can be considered as the first fascist age of England'.[26]

In order to demonstrate that fascism had roots in the British tradition, Mosley's important and first act was to look for an older past than the age of Cromwell. On the first page of both the 1932 and 1934 editions of *The Greater Britain*, he published a drawing of the Roman fasces, and gave the following explanation: 'Fasces are the emblem which founded the power, authority and unity of Imperial Rome. From the Rome of the past was derived the tradition of civilization and progress during the past two thousand years, *of which the British Empire is now the chief custodian.*'[27]

The Roman colonization of the British Isles was thus regarded as the origin of British civilization, and the fact that the Romans came from the Italian peninsula did not mean that it was a foreign civilization. On the contrary, the British Empire now constituted the only example of the continuation of the Roman Empire and its mission in the world. Mosley insisted on those same issues in a small book published in 1936, when he sought to explain fascism through '100 questions asked and answered'. Question five, in particular, explored once again the problem of the 'foreign' roots of British fascism:

> If you do not copy foreign ideas, why do you (1) wear a black shirt, (2) use the Italian Fascist salute, (3) use the Italian fasces?': 'The salute is not Italian nor is it German, but the Germans also use it. It is the oldest salute of European civilization and was used in early Britain many centuries before a Fascist Party was created in Italy. The Fasces, too, are a symbol used in Britain for the last 2000 years and are to be found on most of our great monuments. The symbol was brought to Britain *by our Roman ancestors*, who were here for four centuries and their stock remained for ever. The Fasces are the symbol of the Roman Empire. What more fitting than that they should be used by the Empire which succeeded and surpassed the Roman Empire?'[28]

Since Mosley clarified his theory of the origins of British fascism as a descent from the Roman Empire, which he saw as the first common denominator of European civilization, it would be simplistic to argue that he used the fasces as a purely (Italian) fascist conception. After reading his explanation, it seems more plausible to argue that he did not simply copy Italy, nor did he only seek to find a new symbol for Britain, but for Europe too. The 'Italy of the *fascio*' was in his view not just a 'Britain', but a 'Europe of the *fascio*', which would be led by Britain because the British Empire was evidently the natural successor to Imperial Rome. Mosley's interest in Europe carried on even after the Second World War, and is well documented in his writings.[29] The fact that this exercise was not very successful, that it did not appear persuasive to public opinion, and that those Roman roots might just be invented roots – an invented tradition – should not lead us to dismiss the argument out of hand. Although unsuccessful, the BUF had been able to attract a section of British society. Moreover, the British appeal to a Roman tradition involved the idea of a common European 'fascist' past – and future – which is crucial in the study of the ideological roots of universal fascism, as well as in the understanding of the cultural and political relationships between fascist movements, and fascist countries, during the 1930s.

Richard Bellamy, a BUF member who left four volumes of memoirs,[30] likewise suggested that Mosley was influenced by the knowledge that ties between his country and Italy were deep rooted. They were not limited to the Romans, but continued throughout the centuries, thanks to the traffic in commerce and culture, due to the activities of Christian missionaries, and especially during the Renaissance. According to Bellamy, although 'the spiritual regeneration of the young Germans who followed Hitler won his [Mosley's] firm approval,' the roots of British fascism were Italian and not German: 'some aspects of Nazism, such as the rising tide of hatred against the Jews on the one hand, and the revival of the worship of Thor and Odin and the old Teutonic gods ... evoked no response in him.'[31]

One of the organizers of the BUF's Women's Section, Mary Richardson, underlined the 'parallels between this new imperial Rome and the old Rome'. She also emphasized the parallel between the Roman and the British Empires, both of which, she believed, would eventually be saved by fascism: 'old imperial Rome fell, to be rebuilt again by the power of fascism. Britain shall not "fall", for fascism has come before it is too late ...'[32] However, the most enthusiastic admirer of Mussolini within the BUF was probably Francis J. Burdett. He was only fifteen years old when he wrote a school essay dedicated to the life of the Duce.[33] The sixteen-page essay was then sent to the Italian embassy in London, and rewarded with a signed framed photograph of Mussolini. He soon became a productive journalist, and wrote in the BUF press as well as in the *British-Italian Bulletin*, a supplement to *L'Italia Nostra* published during the Abyssinian War. Burdett was particularly impressed by the way in which Fascism, through the *squadrismo*, faced the post-war chaos. He not only dedicated a few pages in his essay to the subject, but also insisted on it in his articles in *Blackshirt*, where he liked to remember how the blood-red banner of the Soviet arose from the ruins of this once glorious people. The sinister red star of world chaos and destruction appeared to be directing the destinies of the nation .... All seemed lost, all was hopeless confusion, and Italia Bella, the land of the poets, the land of the arts, the home of genius and romance was crushed and dying.

Burdett continued, the 'old men' in power were unable to cope with red terror, and 'Europe mourned the approaching destruction *of the mother of her civilization* ... But a new spirit stirred among the mountains of the North. Like a faint and hardly perceptible breeze, springing from out the soil of the Romagna it spread to every part of the land. Wherever it appeared the ruin and smoke was cleared away.' However, according to Burdett, Mussolini's tasks were not necessarily confined to Italy: 'this new and greater Caesar has arisen in the twentieth century to lead his country, and who knows, perhaps Europe, to her highest plane of civilization.'[34]

John Beckett, another BUF official who wrote his memoirs, revealed that he became a fascist as a consequence of his visit to Italy in 1929. He claimed to have found in the Fascist state the realization of the Labour programme he had unsuccessfully sought to establish in England. A further visit to Italy in the autumn of 1933 confirmed for him that 'here was a great new conception of civilization'.[35]

In general, at the beginning of the 1930s, Mosleyite fascists described the German experiment as a Teutonic form of fascism. Not as perfect as the Italian Corporate State, it was nonetheless a step forward toward European fascism. In 1933 British fascists seemed concerned by the fact that the issue of fascism had been obscured in Germany by the 'irrelevant Jewish question,' which complicated the access to power of the Nazis: 'anti-Semitism is no issue of Fascism, and is unknown to Fascism outside the Teutonic races. In Germany, anti-Semitism is a symptom, not of Fascism, but of Germany.'[36] On the contrary, the 'Jewish issue' was unknown to the Italian, perfect form of fascism: 'let us recall the single-mindedness of the Italian leader, who avoided conflict with Jews, with Church, with sectional interests of any kind, and thus established on unshakeable basis the Power of Fascism in Italy.'[37]

James Drennan confirmed this belief in his history of the BUF, saying that Mussolini had been able to invoke the myth of Rome 'to obliterate the memories of centuries of Italian disunity'. On the contrary, 'the Nazis can only turn upon the nearest aliens in the streets to find consolation for the past and assurance for the future'.[38] Germany, unlike Italy and Britain, was not granted a Roman past. Still, choosing fascism, it chose to belong to a European tradition: 'Fascism – National Socialism – whatever we like to call it, is essentially a European movement – a political and spiritual transformation, having its roots and taking its expression from the oldest seats of European culture.'[39]

The sense of being part of a unique new spirit was indeed stronger than national distinctions. Friendship between men who had in common 'a vast conception and a great ideal' raised 'no question of subordination,' since fascism would one day 'unite Europe in a new civilization'.[40] Robert Gordon-Canning described the imagined future Europe as follows:

> Before you can build a nation, you must have villages, districts and towns, each with their local patriotisms. Out of these one welds a unified country where these local patriotisms give way before the greater patriotism to the unified country. Similarly, before building a united Europe or a united world, it is necessary to create a series of nations, each of whose basis are sound and well-balanced from the economic point of view.[41]

If Mosley claimed such an egalitarian alliance between fascist nations in 1933 and 1934, his views appear to have changed a good deal between 1934 and 1939, when he stated that although the 'National Socialist and Fascist creed' were both universal, the British did not borrow ideas from foreign countries. They had no models abroad because, wrote Mosley, 'we are proud enough of our own people to believe that, once Britain is awake, our people will not follow, but will lead mankind'.[42] Only Germany would retain a complementary role, due to the fact that it did not need an empire, since the new German believed that 'racial deterioration will result from such racial intercourse;' the new German had 'another mission in the world rather than to elevate savages'.[43] The Germans were not called by nature to this 'noble duty,'[44] which came from the Romans to both Britain and Italy. Germany had another duty, the Germanization of Eastern Europe and the elimination of Jews.

The question of hierarchies within the hypothetical European new fascist order, which became fundamental during the years of the Second World War, was already perceptible, despite the frequent appeals to fascist solidarity in the first half of the 1930s. In fact it had been present since the first attempts to constitute a fascist international at the Congress in Montreux in December 1934, and at the three following meetings in Paris, in Amsterdam, and again in Montreux, in 1935. The most striking fact was perhaps that neither the British nor the Germans joined the congresses.[45]

An Italian universalist sent to the BUF headquarters in London on behalf of the Committees of Action for the Universality of Rome (CAUR), Pier Filippo Gomez, thought that the BUF was considering its shift from Italy to Nazi Germany as early as June 1934. His mission was to acknowledge the possibility of establishing a group of the CAUR in Britain and whether this could be done with the help of the

BUF. Mosley told the CAUR official that the BUF at that moment could not easily join an organization for the 'universality of Rome', since this would have been viewed as foreign by public opinion. He added that the use of the black shirt by the BUF did not mean imitation of the Italians, but represented the symbol of 'pure fascism' as 'the idea of the twentieth century'. He understood that Mediterranean fascist movements joined the CAUR, since they were Roman in race, but for the British, who had their own Empire, it was a different matter. The following vague attempts to say that he still preferred Rome to Berlin did not appear convincing. The map of Europe with two 'fascisms', a northern European and a Mediterranean one, had already been drawn.

The so-called 'Jewish question' was also taken up by the BUF in October 1934. Beyond the usual anti-Semitic reasons, it must be borne in mind that the Jews came to be regarded as the enemy basically because they were viewed as anti-German; in this case, the BUF did not consider the Jews simply as an internal enemy, but as a European anti-fascist enemy, the core of the anti-fascist international. In 1935 *Blackshirt* reminded its readers that the first occasion of a breach with the Jews in Britain occurred when, in 1933, a film interview sympathetic to Hitler could not be shown because the Jews, alleged owners of most London cinemas, imposed a ban on it. Only in 1939 did the BUF accept the German biological racist explanation that the Jew was a 'foreigner', simply because he 'comes from the Orient and physically, mentally and spiritually, is more alien to us than any Western nation'.[46]

The Italian and German examples were never entirely transposed by the BUF. The BUF always offered an anglicized version of European fascism. In 1936 the BUF created a Fascist Youth organization, after a careful study of the Italian and German ones. While the German organization differed from the British because of its 'tradition of open air life', it was mainly the Italian one that was not suited to the English youth. The latter was 'marked by a self-consciousness which prevents him from those open expressions of patriotism so easy to the Latin temperament'.[47] In the education of youth the BUF also emulated the Italian institution of fascist summer camps for children, one of the most successful organizations of the Italian regime in the fascistization of children both in Italy and of Italians living abroad. According to the BUF, these camps 'lay the foundation for the Fascist future', when the womanhood and manhood of Britain would 'live in the same spirit'. The meaning of the camps was also to visit 'the countryside we love', which was allegedly exploited by rich Jews, while children of poor English families had to spend their lives in polluted city streets. In the accounts of *Blackshirt*, time in the camps was spent in playing games, and had nothing of the Italian paramilitary and rhetorical aspects. The photographs published by the newspaper showed Mosley during a visit: he was smiling, surrounded by children in shirts and ties. Very little was reminiscent of a fascist atmosphere if compared to the photographs of Italian summer camps published every summer by *L'Italia Nostra*. Articles in *Blackshirt* focused mainly on the poverty of those children and on how they benefited from the camps.[48]

The shift from Italophilia to Naziphilia was associated with two main issues: the role of British pride in the attempt to establish a fascism 'better' than the Italian, and the shift from a Roman to a Teutonic model of fascism, linked with the new concept of Anglo-German complementarity in the New European Order. Mussolini had made clear that the new European civilization was Mediterranean, since it had developed from Rome and was made universal again by Rome. The entry on 'Fascismo nel mondo', in *Il fascismo nella Treccani* of 1938 stated that differences existed between Italian Fascism and German Nazism due to individual traditions, geographical conditions, social structure and mentality, of which the main example was the German identification of nation with race.[49] By that year, it was clear that, for the BUF, European fascism was no longer a Roman form of fascism but rather a Teutonic one, led by Germany and Britain.

The BUF had had contacts with Germany even before 1935, through visitors from Britain and permanent residents there. They had a liaison officer at the Nuremberg Nazi Congress, and BUF members frequently travelled to Germany.[50] Moreover, as MI5 records reveal, the BUF in Britain had contacts not only with the Italian *Fasci* abroad, but also with the German *Auslandsorganisation*.[51]

However, during the Abyssinian War Mosley did his best to support the Italian cause, and in the conflict between the British and the Italian governments he chose the latter, a position that appeared incoherent for a movement that claimed to hold as its main principle 'Britain first'. Grandi was impressed by the choreography of Mosley's speeches: fascist hymns, a vast display of flags and guidons, the use of drums, and the sudden appearance of the leader surrounded by a group of stewards, walking amid rows of Blackshirts demonstrating their reverence with the Roman salute.[52]

Yet BUF meetings were never simply pro-Italian. Their banners explained the reasons why the BUF supported the Abyssinian campaign: 'Sanctions and unemployment' and 'Seven million pounds wasted': for Britain rather than for Italy. Additional banners demanded 'Peace with Germany'.[53] The main question for the BUF was that of sacrifices made by British workers due to sanctions, rather than the rights of Italy in Abyssinia.[54] BUF support for the Abyssinian campaign was thus politically and culturally a pro-British fight rather than a pro-Italian one: the BUF believed that a threat to British prestige in Africa from Italian ambitions was less serious than the threat posed by the possibility of African success over Europeans. At a deeper level, the BUF thought that the Italian cause was also a British cause. The Abyssinian one was not.[55]

In October 1935, while Italy was unleashing an aggressive anti-British propaganda campaign and Anglo-Italian relations were worsening, the BUF decided to shut down all its offices in Italy.[56] Life for British citizens in Italy became difficult during those months of intense anti-British propaganda. Pro-Italian articles in *Blackshirt* were now very few if compared to the number of articles on German culture and on Nazism. German discipline was admired as it reflected life in a supposedly happy country. Photographs of German parades were published. Robert Gordon-Canning participated in the 1935 Nazi Party rally at Nuremberg, and, although 'an Englishman proud of the heritage and tradition' of his country, when Hitler passed by he said 'without any hesitation' and from the depth of his heart 'Heil Hitler'.[57]

The shift to Naziphilia was followed by the reorganization of the BUF, accompanied by the growing influence, from May 1935, of the 'radical element' represented by Joyce, Beckett, Chesterton and Raven-Thomson.[58] It was later emphasized in June 1936, with a change of name to the 'British Union of Fascists and National Socialists'. That decision followed a period of uncertainty and reorganization, reflected by several changes in the first pages of *Blackshirt*: in February 1936 the sub-title 'Britain First' took the place of the previous 'For King and people', and the symbol of the flash in the circle, the specific British contribution to fascist symbolism in the BUF, appeared for a few issues next to the title. From March, the subtitle changed again, now 'The patriotic workers' paper'.

The only active efforts to continue the organization of Anglo-Italian fascism were made by British fascists resident in Italy. In 1935, after BUF offices in Italy were closed, these British subjects founded a new group called the 'British Union of Friends of Italy'. The organizers were the same people, the most active of whom was still John Celli. Other leaders included Captain Ernest Platt, Harry Brittain, and the universal fascist James Strachey Barnes. Even during the anti-British propaganda at the time of the Abyssinian War, these Britons continued to criticize British foreign policy publicly, an attitude which the British Foreign Office regarded as a form of treason: it was permissible behaviour for Englishmen living in Britain, but it savoured of disloyalty when conducted by Englishmen in the enemy's country.[59] Given the rationalist outlook of the BUF, it was likely that the British fascists shared this view.

Despised by the Foreign Office and abandoned by the BUF, the Friends of Italy were left with little initiative. Yet they received support from the Italian regime, in particular from the ministry of popular culture and from the CAUR, which participated in their events. It is significant that they organized lectures and conferences together with the CAUR when Mosley had already refused co-operation with the Italian universalists. Their support for Italy in Abyssinia was culturally completely different from that of the BUF. This was evident, for example, at a party they gave in Milan in January 1937 for the CAUR of Lombardy and for various fascists and soldiers returned from East Africa. The speakers, among whom were Celli and Platt, emphasized the gratitude Britain owed to Italy, and the 'sanctity of brotherly and civic ties'. Their message ended with an exhortation 'to embrace the generous Italian soldiers and Italians in general'.[60] At a dinner they hosted in a Milan restaurant in December 1937, the Italian authorities, CAUR members, and British Italophiles were present.[61]

General John Frederick Fuller, who was both an Italophile and a BUF member, and Muriel Currey, an Italophile journalist who sometimes participated in the Friends of Italy's events, reflected such admiration for the Italian soldiers in the diaries they wrote after having followed Italy's troops in East Africa.[62] Currey's narration of the Abyssinian War was imaginative and idealized. She reported on Italian soldiers leaving for Africa and singing the songs of the revolution, building roads in Asmara and cleaning up the town, resting and talking about their own regions and the different ways of making macaroni.[63] Fuller's account described the Italian army as 'a huge melodramatic troupe; a Fascist demonstration; a gathering of armed men in which each group possessed a discipline or lack of discipline of its own'. It was an 'Army of the Exodus which crossed the Red Sea in search of the Promised Land'.[64] Their leaders were selected not always because they were of military worth, but because they were 'poets, orators, or futurist artists'.[65] Fuller emphasized that Italy won thanks to the peculiar Fascist organization of the war. It was a new idea of war, unknown to British colonization. The Italians allegedly 'fought like Crusaders', they were 'a revolutionary army imbued with the spirit of the army of Huss and those who fought in the religious wars of the sixteenth century'.[66] Such a tribute to the Italians made Fuller an exception among BUF members after 1935, and characterized the British Italophiles who lived in Italy rather than the Mosleyites.

The British Union of Friends of Italy was able to achieve the support of several distinguished Italophiles in Britain, including Charles Petrie and Leo Amery. Such support was facilitated by a change of name in 1938 from 'British Union of Friends of Italy' to the 'Anglo-Italian Cultural Association'. The reason for this change, in Celli's opinion, was that Anglo-Italian understanding was now an accomplished fact and therefore required activities of a purely cultural nature. They organized public meetings, most of them in Milan. The ministry of popular culture and the CAUR again backed these events. At a crowded public meeting held in Milan in 1938, Celli described the British press as not really free because it was owned by big finance and by the Jews. A British Foreign Office informer reported that Celli depicted the British people as 'good honest folk who had been led terribly astray but who were gradually beginning to see the light'. In contrast,

> Fascist Italy, secure in her great glory, was begged to be long-suffering and to exercise magnanimity towards a friend who had erred and astrayed (largely as a result of the pernicious influence of 'one of the most dangerous men that had ever appeared on the European stage ...') but who was well-meaning at heart and deserving of pity and good-will.[67]

The Anglo-Italian Cultural Association continued to organize conferences, meetings and social events in the hope of strengthening political friendship between British Fascists resident in Italy and the Italian authorities. The Italian regime, despite the interruption in its relationship with the BUF, was still interested in co-operation with international fascist movements, provided that they were pro-Italian. However, the initiatives of the Anglo-Italian Cultural Association were difficult to organize, because the Association received no support from either the BUF or from the British authorities, who naturally wanted to keep British cultural activities in a foreign country under control. In May 1938, Platt wrote to Grandi that his mission was 'to cement this friendship and a real understanding between ourselves and your great and beautiful country, and your distinguished Statesman Leader'.[68] Unlike the BUF, the Association included Britons whose patriotism was matched by a profound love for Italy and by admiration for the Duce. They also organized social encounters, mostly in an upper-class environment, which achieved a great success among British Italophiles living in Italy or temporarily travelling to Italy. Similarly, this had the result of strengthening friendship between themselves and Italian Universal Fascists. The change of name to Anglo-Italian Cultural Association therefore indicates both the attempt to attract more educated British fascist sympathizers and the intention of organizing cultural events, which was, however, frustrated by the British authorities, since the Association did not dare, or intend, to promote any activity without consular consent. The British embassy and the consulates described the Association's meetings as simply exaltations of Italy and of Mussolini, and concluded that neither Italo-British society nor British cultural activity existed in Italy in 1938. Following the lack of success of the Anglo-Italian Cultural Association, one of its founders, Colonel Rocke, made a further attempt to form an 'Anglo-Italian Fellowship' towards the end of 1938, and asked for Chamberlain's support. As usual, the British government considered that such a proposal had to be left to private initiative, and the Fellowship never materialized.[69]

After Italy had conquered Abyssinia, Anglo-Italian fascist relations never revived. In 1937 A. K. Chesterton published in *Blackshirt* a series of articles on 'aspects of the German revolution', which revealed the extent of the cultural shift and of the BUF's radicalization. He rejected British individualism and egotism, which allegedly led to intellectual sterility, and claimed that the main purpose of National Socialist education was 'to eradicate all the bourgeois values centring around "Self" and replacing them with ... "Service"'.[70] The 'British Council Against European Commitments', created in 1938 by some BUF members, took the view that Britain and Germany were the two countries responsible for bringing world civilization forward. A war between Britain and Germany, they believed, meant 'Bolshevism in both countries, and the loss of everything for which both countries stand ... It is worth fighting to save civilization, but not to kill it.'[71]

In 1939, Mosley's propaganda increasingly insisted on the idea of the need to rescue the 'European spirit' against both so-called 'money power' and communism. While Mosley's autobiography tended to explain his support for Germany as merely a question of foreign policy (Germany could expand into the East and Britain could reinforce its empire without need for war), the idea of a common British and German civilization had at this stage become a central aspect. Unity Mitford, Mosley's sister-in-law, gave the most dramatic example of such feelings of loyalty to an Anglo-German fascist ideal when she shot herself after Britain had declared war on Germany in September 1939.[72]

Another Form of Fascism:
The Cultural Impact of the French 'Radical Right' in Britain

Richard Griffiths

Discussions of the impact of foreign influences upon the British Right in the twentieth century have tended, in the case of political movements, to concentrate on Italian Fascism and German Nazism. When it comes to more general political ideas, a convincing case has been made for the impact of Nietzsche's ideas upon sections of the intelligentsia, and on certain fringe political movements.[1] What has not sufficiently been realized, however, is the influence of sections of the French radical Right on a number of English (and American) artistic and political thinkers in the first half of the twentieth century, and also on an emerging political movement in Wales.

One of the major characteristics of the French Right, from the 1880s onwards, was that political activism often went hand in hand with literary creation – many of the political activists being major writers and literary critics in their own right. Part of the attraction of such figures, for sections of the British intelligentsia, was the way in which their political tenets and their artistic ideals appeared each to influence the other. In that sense, the impact of the French Right was probably the most striking *'cultural* expression of the far Right' to be found in twentieth-century Britain.

It would be wrong to see the French Right of the late nineteenth and early twentieth centuries as being a coherent whole. There were various quite separate strands, each of which, in its way, affected British thinkers and activists.

The most straightforward manifestation of the Right in the period 1870–1940 was the traditional Catholic Right.[2] In the early years of the Third Republic, as the anti-clerical attitudes of many Republican politicians became clear, attitudes had hardened among Catholic thinkers and politicians, and Catholic politics had become inextricably entwined with monarchism. A spate of prominent conversions in the 1880s and 1890s brought to the fore a number of intransigent thinkers and writers, who consistently took the opposite standpoint from the tenets of liberal republicanism. For Liberty, they substituted Discipline and Order (together with a 'Caesarist' longing for dictatorial government); for Equality, they substituted the need for Hierarchy; for Fraternity, they substituted Charity.[3] Their views were violent, their hatreds unforgiving. As Léon Bloy said: '(Rule without any exception). Concede nothing to the enemy, nothing, nothing, NOTHING'.[4]

These people had an obsession with 'the modern world' ('le monde moderne'), which they saw as responsible for most of the evils around them. As they looked back with nostalgia to a more perfect world, which in fact had never existed, they contrasted the virtues of a rural agrarian society, in which everyone had known their place and where religion had been the basis of the community, with the evils created by the industrial society: class divisions, unrest, disorder, poverty, neglect, atheism. It was but a short step from this to an attack on the international capital that had created this situation. And it was a yet shorter step, in the atmosphere created by the writings of Édouard Drumont in the 1880s,[5] to an association between the powers of capital, and the Jews. Anti-Semitism became a leading feature of the Catholic Right.

It was against the background of this Catholic Revival that a radical form of right-wing politics emerged, which has been characterized as 'the revolutionary Right'.[6] In contrast to the conservatism of mainline Catholic reaction, these people, in varied ways, produced radical policies that often vied with the Left on its own ground. Their anti-capitalism was far from the nostalgic vision we have seen; it was grounded in positive doctrines for change, looking to a re-ordering of society, rather than a simple return to the past. Their opposition to democracy was absolute. In their policies an appeal to the Catholic public was central, even if the two major figures with which we will be concerned, Maurice Barrès and Charles Maurras, were in fact agnostics.

Maurice Barrès (1862–1923) was a major novelist and essayist. Much of his fiction was devoted to the promulgation of his political ideas. He stood for an authoritarian republicanism based on the idea of a dictator, for a strong nationalism and (initially) for an anti-capitalist desire for social reform. In the 1890s he developed his philosophy of 'the land and the dead' ('la terre et les morts'), whereby the essence of the French nation lay in the land on which Frenchmen were born, and their forebears who had lived there. This was expounded in the trilogy of novels called Le Roman de l'énergie nationale, of which the first, Les Déracinés (1897), which depicted the tribulations of a number of young Lorrainers in Paris, coined in its title the word which summed up this policy, 'the uprooted'. Barrès was not just a French nationalist; he was also a regionalist, continually harking back to his roots in Lorraine; and a number of his other works (including the novel Colette Baudoche) dealt with the 'lost provinces' of Alsace-Lorraine, taken by Germany in 1870, and with the need to regain them for France. Barrès's anti-Semitism (which came to the fore particularly at the time of the Dreyfus Affair) stemmed directly from his view of the nature of the French nation, which had no place for outsiders.

Charles Maurras (1868–1952) was a politician of a very different kind. He was a political activist, whose activities were essentially extra-parliamentary. The movement he headed, 'Action Française', was, from the Dreyfus Affair until the end of the Second World War, one of the most successful mass political movements in French history. The movement's policies were royalist, nationalist, authoritarian, Catholic, anti-Semitic, anti-masonic and (at the start) anti-capitalist.

The position of Action Française in the spectrum of movements of the Right has been a matter of some discussion. Many political scientists have stressed its more 'traditional' aspects, and described it as 'conservative' rather than 'fascist'. The movement itself shared, however, many of the characteristics of the international fascism of the inter-war period.[7] The violent street-action of its shock-troops certainly does not belie that impression. The movement often seems to have had a double life. On the one hand there was its cult of violence. On the other, there was Maurras's presentation of it as an intellectual movement, in which ideas predominated.

Maurras's ideas on politics and literature were closely related. As a major writer and literary critic, he stressed the importance of 'classicism', and abhorred the 'romanticism' that had, in his view, destroyed the excellence of French literature, and at the same time been politically the basis for the French Revolution. 'Classicism' stood for order and discipline both in literature and politics. In literature, Maurras believed in the need for a return to classical values and forms. In politics, he proposed an escape from the liberal legacy of the 'romantic' Rousseau.[8] The Catholic Church was in his view the bastion of social order, and therefore, even though he was himself an agnostic, he made his movement a Catholic one. Action Française was, however, above all sustained by hatred: hatred of the capitalist Jews and of the freemasons whom Maurras saw as subverting the state; hatred of republicans, and of foreigners of all kinds (but particularly the Germans and the British); hatred of all manifestations of the 'modern world'.

There is a further strand of the French radical Right that was to have some effect in Britain. This was the work of Georges Sorel (1847–1922), whose book *Réflexions sur la violence* (1908) was later to be acclaimed by Mussolini as one of the major influences upon the development of Italian Fascism. Sorel himself came from a completely different stable from those we have so far been examining. A product of the Left, a revolutionary syndicalist, he developed gradually into a 'neither Right nor Left' situation typical of proto-fascism. He had been strongly influenced (as had many other radical Rightists) by the philosophy of Henri Bergson (1859–1941), sharing Bergson's mistrust of the rational, and his belief in intuition (and at the same time having a Nietzschean desire for a healthy society, based on a new set of values). A healthy society, for Sorel, was one of conflict. The modern concern for arbitration and peace-making, as opposed to social conflict, had been pursued by a cowardly middle class that continued to pursue the chimera of social peace. Violence was important in itself, whether it pursued a practical end or not, because it provided the 'extreme moments' which sustained the class struggle, and through that the health and vigour of society as a whole. Progress, humanitarianism etc., were bourgeois myths which merely helped to sustain a weak and illusory semblance of society. What the proletariat needed were powerful 'myths' (whether real or not) that would stir them to action.

Sorel's pessimistic view of human nature, his hatred of democracy, and his puncturing of the myth of 'progress' brought him for a time, just before the First World War, into the ambit of Action Française and the nationalist Right; but, while he shared these essentially negative ideas with them, the main thrust of his philosophy was a combination of left-wing aims and authoritarian, illiberal means.

*　　*　　*

In Britain, there was certainly some impact of the general Catholic French Right, above all on the circles surrounding Belloc and Chesterton. Hilaire Belloc (1870–1953) was, through his background, particularly open to this trend (he was born in France, was part-French and was educated in England at the Oratory School, becoming a British citizen in 1902). His anti-Semitism was clearly a product of this background; as Dean Inge said in 1922, of Belloc's book *The Jews*:

> Nearly every page reminds us that during the Dreyfus agitation Mr Belloc was almost the only man in England who did not take the part of the unfortunate prisoner … The fact is that Mr Belloc, as a Frenchman and a Roman Catholic, takes the Continental rather than the English view of what he calls the Jewish problem.[9]

That anti-Semitism spilled over, too, into the main organs of the Distributist movement headed by Belloc and G. K. Chesterton (1874–1936), where it took on the typical form of an association of the Jews with the 'international capitalist forces' that were being attacked. Opening *G. K.'s Weekly* (edited by G. K. Chesterton) for one year in the 1920s at random, one finds, for example, reminiscences of the Marconi scandal, in which, said G. K., he and his fellow-attackers of Lloyd George and Sir Rufus Isaacs had been supported by 'our anti-Semitic sympathisers'; an attack on the prominent industrialist Sir Alfred Mond, so 'solitary and foreign' at English social gatherings that 'perhaps he would feel more at home if he wore a gabardine'; and a number of other attacks against Jews.[10]

Chesterton and Belloc's Distributism, their alternative to the 'usurous' capitalist system, is in many respects similar to the theories of the French economist Frédéric Le Play, which were so influential on the French Right, and particularly on Action Française.[11] But it is dangerous to try to ascribe everything to one cause or to one influence; there were many attempted alternatives to capitalism in this period, including of course Major Douglas's Social Credit, which, too, had much in common with Distributism; and many of the Social Crediters and other people concerned with monetary reform (such as Arthur Kitson and the Duke of Bedford) were equally prone to associate the evils of capitalism with the Jews. For this reason, the major part of this chapter will concern itself with the *avowed* and *specific* influence of the French Right upon individuals and movements in Britain; we will find the major force in this influence to have been the Action Française movement.

Now, it is true (as with fascist doctrines) that the main body of Englishmen was not influenced by Action Française ideas, to the extent that Lucien Dubech, in 1938, was able to state that the country in which Action Française was least known was England.[12] But there was a significant minority that was so influenced; and it presents us with a very interesting series of cases (with the influence extending into artistic as well as political ideas).

The most profound Action Française influence in England centred on the literary group known as the 'Imagists', and in particular on its philosophical mentor T. E. Hulme and its later disciple T. S. Eliot. The Imagists flourished between about 1909 and 1917, and included a number of English and American poets, including Ezra Pound, Ford Madox Ford and Amy Lowell. The movement is generally accepted to have been based upon 'the aesthetic theories of T. E. Hulme'.[13]

T. E. Hulme (1883–1917) described himself as a 'philosophical amateur'. In his short life (he was killed at the front in 1917) most of his written output (apart from translations of Bergson and Sorel) consisted of articles in Orage's *New Age*; yet he gained a reputation and an influence far wider than might have been expected. His ideas both on literature and on politics appeared revolutionary in an age that had still not emerged from the liberal and romantic consensus of the eighteenth and nineteenth centuries; T. S. Eliot famously described him as 'classical, reactionary and revolutionary'. His originality stemmed, however, in large part from the appropriation of Action Française doctrines, and in particular the ideas of Lasserre and Maurras.

Hulme had been attracted to Bergson's philosophy, and had already written about him in the *New Age*, when he passed through France in 1911, on his way to Italy. There he met two significant people, with whom he had already been in contact by correspondence: Jules de Gaultier and Pierre Lasserre. Jules de Gaultier was a philosopher (about whom Hulme had already written in the *New Age*) who was also a prominent Barrèsian;[14] Lasserre was a major Action Française theorist, whose theories on Romanticism and Classicism, as put forward in his book *Le Romantisme français* (1907) had done much to clarify Maurras's own views on this subject. In this book Lasserre had pilloried Rousseau as the embodiment of Romanticism, and as one of the principal agents of the French Revolution.

Hulme was to refer with admiration to 'the brilliant set of Neo-Royalist writers grouped around *L'Action Française*'.[15] More importantly, in both his aesthetic and his political writings, he was continually to stress in Action Française terms the classical–Romantic dichotomy. In his essay 'Romanticism and Classicism'[16], he states that he is using these terms to 'conform to the practice of the group of polemical writers who ... have almost succeeding in making them political catchwords. I mean Maurras, Lasserre, and all the group connected with L'Action Française.' He stresses the *political* importance of the terms: suggesting that you can deduce, from the use made of them, what a man's politics are. Romanticism, he asserts, is 'in both Britain and France ... associated with certain political views'. Like Maurras and Lasserre, he contrasts Rousseau, who taught 'that man was by nature good, and that it was only bad laws and customs that had suppressed him', that 'something positive could come out of disorder', and that the individual was all-important, with the classical view that 'man is an extraordinarily fixed and limited animal' who can only be of any use through 'tradition and organisation'.

While much of this article is taken up by the *literary* importance of returning to classicism (with Horace, the Elizabethans and the writers of the Augustan age being contrasted with Hugo, Lamartine, Byron, Shelley, Swinburne etc.), there is also a stress on Romanticism as 'disorder', as the foundation for revolution. Hulme mentions with approval the violent riots that Action Française thugs had carried out in order to disrupt a professor's lectures on Racine (in which he had disparaged Racine's works):

> These people interrupted because the classical ideal is a living thing to them ... That is what I call a real vital interest in literature. They regard romanticism as an awful disease from which France has just recovered. ... It was romanticism that made the revolution. They hate the revolution, so they hate romanticism.

Hulme put forward the same ideas in a more politically-orientated way in a series of articles he wrote under the pseudonym 'Thomas Grattan' in the *Commentator* in 1912. Typically (like T. S. Eliot after him) he equates Maurrasism with 'Toryism'.[17] (Like Eliot, however, he also saw Toryism as needing to go beyond 'conservatism'. 'I am more than a conservative' he once said to a friend. 'I am a reactionary.')[18] His aim in these articles, he says, is to explain 'why I can't stand romanticism, and why I am a certain kind of Tory'. 'Lasserre, Maurras, etc' are the people who 'have done most work on this particular aspect of political theory'. Hulme elaborates on the theme of Original Sin. Man is incapable of perfection.

> The best results can only be got out of man as the result of a certain discipline which introduces order into this internal anarchy ... Nothing is bad in itself except disorder; all that is put in order in a hierarchy is good. The classical attitude, then, has a great respect for the past and for tradition ... It does not expect anything radically new, and does not believe in any real progress.

Though Hulme's ideas have sometimes been compared with Nietzsche's, he quite clearly dissociates himself in these articles from that author, whom he sees (perhaps because of his association with Hulme's *bête noire* Anthony Ludovici)[19] as having completely distorted what were otherwise sound principles:

> Most people have been in the habit of associating these views (order, discipline, tradition, etc) with Nietzsche. It is true, they do occur in him, but he made them so frightfully vulgar that no classic would acknowledge them. In him you have the spectacle of a romantic seizing on the classic point of view because it attracted him purely as a theory, and who, being a romantic, passed his slimy fingers over every detail of it. Everything loses its value. The same idea of the necessary hierarchy of the classes, with their varying capacities and duties, gets turned into the romantic nonsense of the two kinds of morality, the slave and the master morality, and every other element of the classic position gets transmuted in a similar way into something ridiculous.[20]

Hulme proposes, in these articles, to deal with the political question under various headings.[21] Each heading consists of two opposites: 'Constancy and Progress' (in which the idea of progress will be seen as 'a pernicious and disastrous influence on political thought and action'; 'Order, Authority and Liberty'; 'Equality and Hierarchy' (which will include 'an account of the French syndicalist, Georges Sorel, who, strangely enough, takes the Tory view'); and 'Nationalism and Universalism'.[22]

The mention of Sorel is a significant one. Here, Hulme seems to be regarding him as a mere adjunct to what is entirely a list of Action Française categories. By the time of his translation of Sorel's *Reflections on Violence*, which appeared in 1916, he was stressing, however, (in his Introduction)[23] what he saw as certain major differences between Sorel and Action Française, to the advantage of the former. Indeed, it has been suggested that in that work he was 'seeking, apparently, to dissociate Sorel from the thinkers of the Action Française for whom he was for a while in sympathy'.[24] While Sorel has clearly come to the forefront of Hulme's concerns by this time, the picture is in fact far more complicated, with Hulme continuing to base himself in Action Française philosophies, while stressing Sorel's conception of 'justice asserting the equality of men', and contrasting it with those who 'play with the idea of inequality'.

Hulme's picture of Sorel, in this Introduction, is a strangely limited one. One does not find the detailed exposition of Sorel's doctrine that one would expect. Instead, Hulme stresses how puzzling Sorel must be to most observers, because he combines a 'classical, pessimistic' anti-democratic ideology with the 'working-class or revolutionary movement'. Hulme then goes on to examine with approval (and with Action Française terminology) the anti-democratic nature of Sorel's ideology, which has been put to the service of the working-class cause. In other words, eschewing a proper account of Sorel's ideas, Hulme attempts to put him in the straitjacket of the simple classical–Romantic dichotomy we have already seen. In his footnotes he even gives Action Française chapter and verse for his sources:

> All Romanticism springs from Rousseau, and the key to it can be found even in the first sentence of the *Social Contract* – 'Man is born free, and he finds himself everywhere in chains'. [*Footnote reads:* 'For a history of the romantic movement in French Literature from this point of view, see Pierre Lasserre's excellent *La* [sic] *Romantisme française* [sic].]

Sorel, says Hulme, puzzles most observers because he 'denies the essential connection' which simple thinkers believe to exist between the working-class movement and democratic, progressive principles: 'It is difficult for them to understand a revolutionary who is anti-democratic, an absolutist in ethics, who … speaks contemptuously of modernism and *progress*.' Their only answer is to try to discredit him.

Hulme points to the elements in Sorel's philosophy which bring him near to Action Française, and to the major area in which he differs from them:

> The belief that pacifist democracy will lead to no regeneration of society, but rather to its decadence, and the reaction against romanticism in literature, is naturally common to many different schools. This is the secret, for example, of the sympathy between Sorel and the group of writers connected with *L'Action Française*, which is so eagerly fastened on by those anxious to discredit him. His *ideology* resembles theirs. Where he differs is in the application he finds for it. He expects a return to the classical spirit through the struggle of the classes. … There are many who begin to be disillusioned with liberal and pacifist *democracy*, while shrinking from the opposed *ideology* on account of its reactionary associations. To these people Sorel, a revolutionary in economics, but classical in ethics, may prove an emancipator.

Hulme retains all the lessons he had learned from the Action Française, therefore and (very simplistically) projects them onto his new hero, Sorel. There is only one difference: while adhering to the reactionary nature of those doctrines, Hulme rejects the one issue of 'hierarchy', and sees Sorel as putting his anti-democratic doctrines to the cause of human equality. This is essentially a misreading of Sorel; but it tells us much about Hulme, who retains his 'classical' disdain for all the products of romanticism and of the French Revolution: the beliefs in progress, democracy, liberty and 'disorder'.

*   *   *

Hulme's influence upon the Imagists was profound; it was his philosophy's application to *literature*, however, which had the most effect upon them (even though the political odyssey of Ezra Pound – with his espousal of Social Credit, anti-Semitism and Mussolinian Fascism – was to be an extreme version of the 'shift to the radical Right' adumbrated by Hulme). In a revolt against Romanticism, the Imagists specialized in conciseness of expression, concreteness of imagery, the avoidance of abstraction. Hulme had predicted a new era of 'dry, hard, classical verse',[25] eschewing the excesses of Romantic self-indulgence, and this is what the Imagists provided. In this they were (possibly inadvertently) following, via Hulme, the 'cultural' agenda of Action Française.

It is with a later disciple of the Imagists, the young Anglo-American poet T. S. Eliot, that these cultural concerns once more became bound up with political ones, attached to Action Française. He appears to have come to Action Française completely independently from Hulme. Among the early influences upon him, in his Harvard days (1906–9 and 1911–14), had been the reactionary thinker Irving Babbitt. Babbitt was later, in the 1920s, to become a leader of the New Humanism, 'a philosophical and critical movement' which 'fiercely criticized Romanticism, stressing the value of reason and restraint';[26] he admired Maurras, finding him 'romantically anti-romantic'.[27] It was at one time thought that it was Babbitt who introduced Eliot to Maurras's works; but the truth appears to have been the other way around. In 1910–11 Eliot had paid a long visit to Paris, and was, after a reading of Maurras's *L'Avenir de l'intelligence*, strongly affected by Action Française thought. Later in 1911, he returned to Harvard for a further three years. It is more than likely that he conveyed his enthusiasm for Maurras and for his anti-Romanticism to Babbitt, whose first mentions of Maurras post-date this period, as does the New Humanism movement.

Eliot's enthusiasm for Action Française was political as well as literary. He can hardly have been unaware of the violence perpetrated by

Action Française in the same period as his Paris visit, or of the revolutionary rhetoric adopted by the movement. But he appears to have accepted all this, seduced as he was by the intellectual image of Charles Maurras, the agnostic who had nevertheless seen the Catholic Church as an integral part of the nation's traditions, and as a 'force for order' within the nation.

When Eliot settled in England from 1914 onwards (he became a British subject and a member of the Church of England in 1927), he set about creating his own tradition. He took on a new persona – the most English of personae. He decided to become a Tory. From such a young man it is fascinating to hear, as early as 1923, the statement: 'I am, as you know, an old-fashioned Tory'.[28] What did he mean, however, by 'Toryism'? As we have seen, a number of people, from Hulme to Ludovici, had in the 1920s associated 'Toryism' with a variety of foreign doctrines of a far more radical kind. It is hardly surprising to find that Eliot saw Action Française as a kind of 'toryisme français'.

In Eliot's 1928 volume *For Lancelot Andrewes* (which was significantly sub-titled *Essays in Style and Order*) he summed up his position, as expressed in the volume, thus: 'The general point of view ... may be described as classicist in literature, royalist in politics and anglo-catholic in religion.'[29] The combination is clearly Maurrasian (with Anglo-Catholicism taking the place of the Catholic Church). Eliot saw Anglicanism as taking the same place in the 'Tory' tradition as Catholicism took in French royalism. It was part of the 'English tradition'. Indeed, he fiercely attacked Anthony Ludovici for suggesting in his book *A Defence of Conservatism* (1927) that Roman Catholicism could be a potential inspiration to Toryism, stressing that Toryism was, and must remain, Anglican:

> His cardinal point seems to be that Toryism should discard the Church of England in favour of a better organised and more firmly hieratic church, the Church of Rome. In this I believe ... that he is wrong in principle and betrays some ignorance of history. Toryism is essentially Anglican ... The problem of Toryism should be rather to make the church of Laud survive in an age of universal suffrage ...[30]

Like Catholicism for the French, Anglicanism was seen by Eliot as having a social and political role; he believed that 'if there is one idea ... by which Toryism may be tried, it is the idea, however vague, represented by the phrase "Church and State"'.[31] It is significant that he chose as his great model within that church its most reactionary form, the Anglicanism of the seventeenth century, in the tradition of Archbishop Laud. He wrongly, however, associated this conservative form of Anglicanism with modern Anglo-Catholicism, which though reactionary in its theology has, politically, often been associated with the Left.[32]

In the 1920s, Eliot frequently referred to his admiration for Maur-ras. After Action Française's papal condemnation in 1926, for example, he found himself defending his master against prominent English Catholics, and in the process expressing some of the things that attracted him to him. In 1928, for example, he wrote: 'If anyone is attracted by Maurras's political theory, and if that person has as well a tendency toward interior Christianity, that tendency will be quickened by finding that a political and a religious view can be harmonious.'[33]

The Maurrasian influence on Eliot is made even clearer by his com-ment on what he meant by 'royalist in politics': 'I am aware that the ... term is at present without definition, and easily lends itself to what is worse than clap-trap, I mean temperate conservatism.'[34] Here, by dis-sociating Toryism (in his definition) from 'temperate conservatism', he is also showing that his 'Toryism' has little to do with the indigenous Conservative tradition, and has far more in common with the radical Right. Yet, in the situation of the 1920s, with Mussolini's Fascism hit-ting the European headlines, Eliot appears to have been unaware of the fact that Action Française spokesmen saw strong similarities between the two movements, claiming that it was Action Française's doctrines that had inspired those of Italian Fascism. Indeed, Eliot seems to have seen the Italian experiment, a 'well-meaning revolt against "capitalism"' that 'did not appear to get to the bottom of the matter', as being sentimental and wishy-washy in comparison with Action Française, which was an effective and logical opposition to capitalism, as he had seen in Paris in 1910–11 (at the time of Action Française's most radical anti-capitalist phase): 'If anything ... is to pre-serve us from a sentimental Anglo-Fascism, it will be some system of ideas which will have gained much from the study of Maurras.'[35]

The strength of Eliot's commitment to Maurras's ideas is shown by the fact that even after the Second World War, when Maurras had been condemned to life imprisonment for wartime collaboration, and when Action Française had been disbanded, he was still prepared to write in Maurras's praise, in a new journal entitled *Aspects de la France et du monde*. He wrote, of Maurras, that 'his idea of monarchy and hierarchy is closer to mine than to most others; he is close to those English conservatives whose ideas remain intact despite the modern world.'[36]

Note the reference to 'the modern world'. Eliot's views remained essentially continental in tone. And over and above his concepts of 'classicism in literature', 'Church and State', hierarchy and tradition, anti-capitalism, Eliot owed something else to Action Française: his anti-Semitism, the natural corollary of this nexus of reactionary opin-ions. Once you blame everything on 'the modern world' and on 'capitalism' it is but a step to seeing those forces as being almost entirely caused by the Jews. It is also true to say that in the discourse

of the inter-war period, it was common to find the Jew equated to capitalism, and that Action Française was merely one among the many
influences on this belief.[37] Eliot's anti-Semitism is based on a nostalgia
for things past, and on a belief that the Jews were responsible for the
destruction of European civilization. As in so much anti-Semitic writing, Eliot also stresses a caricature of the behavioural characteristics of
the Jew, as in the character of the international Jew Bleistein in 'Burbank with a Baedeker: Bleistein with a cigar'. Here the decline of
civilization is shown by the influence of the Jew, and of money. The
Jew cannot understand culture, his money undermines it all. Princess
Volupine the Venetian aristocrat entertains Sir Ferdinand Klein. The
lion of Venice has been clipped. Note how even the shade of Shylock
is raised, in a 'collage' effect from Shakespeare's *Merchant of Venice*:

> But this or such was Bleistein's way:
>   A saggy bending of the knees
> And elbows, with the palms turned out,
>   Chicago Semite Viennese.
>
> A lustreless protrusive eye
>   Stares from the protozoic slime
> At a perspective of Canaletto.
>   The smoky candle end of time
>
> Declines. On the Rialto once.
>   The rats are underneath the piles.
> The Jew is underneath the lot.
>   Money in furs. The boatman smiles,
>
> Princess Volupine extends
>   A meagre, blue-nailed, phthisic hand
> To climb the waterstair. Lights, lights,
>   She entertains Sir Ferdinand
>
> Klein. Who clipped the lion's wings
>   And flea'd his rump and pared his claws?
> Thought Burbank, meditating on
>   Time's ruins, and the seven laws.[38]

*   *   *

In England, the ideas of the French Right appealed to intellectuals, but
had no appreciable impact on political movements and activists.
Indeed, it is interesting to note that there was no perceivable French
influence upon British fascism, whether it be upon the British Union
of Fascists or the other, minor movements such as the British Fascists
and the Imperial Fascist League. This was no doubt in large part
because of the practical political success of Mussolinian Fascism, and
later German Nazism (as opposed to the comparative lack of practical
success of the French radical Right).

There was, however, one area of practical politics in Britain which was strongly influenced by the French radical Right. This was a new movement in Wales, founded in the 1920s, Plaid Cymru, the Welsh Nationalist Party. Why was there this influence here? In large part, it seems to have been because it was above all intellectuals who were involved in the foundation of the new movement, so that Action Française's appeal to intellectuals was here, as opposed to in England, likely to lead to practical political involvement. It may also have been partly due to the emotional attachment felt by many Welshmen to France.

Far from being insular and inward-looking, Welsh nationalism has always kept a window open to Europe, and has seen Wales as part of a universal European tradition. Wales stretches out its hand, over England, to Europe. Indeed, Welsh nationalism has been one of the few nationalist movements consistently to support European union. In the 1920s, interest in France was very strong in Welsh intellectual circles, and, as Prys Morgan puts it, 'Wales had broken out of its cocoon – the twenties were a time of books about the continent, and of many translations from continental languages.'[39] In the inter-war period, Dafydd Glyn Jones tells us, 'it became something of a tradition ... that the Welsh nationalist should adopt France as his second country.'[40]

There were many articles on French literature in the Welsh journals of the early 1920s. One of the most striking, in the first number of the new intellectual journal Y Llenor in 1922, was R. T. Jenkins's 'Yr Adwaith yn Llenyddiaeth Ffrainc yn yr Oes Bresennol' ('Reaction in French Literature of the Present Day'), which dealt with the main writers and thinkers of the French Catholic Revival: Bourget, Brunetière, Barrès, Lemaître, de Vogüé, Huysmans, Claudel, Jammes, Péguy, Maurras etc. While this article showed a strong interest in the literature of the French Right, it was, however, a very balanced piece of work, and Jenkins himself, despite his intense Francophilia, was in no way part of the 'reactionary' French-influenced wing of the Welsh Nationalists.

The same can not be said of an article in the second number of the same journal, by Ambrose Bebb (1894–1955),[41] who was to become one of the founder-members of the Welsh Nationalist Party. Bebb, a graduate in Welsh and history from Aberystwyth, was at this time in Paris, teaching Welsh and lecturing on Welsh literature at the Sorbonne. There he had come under the strong influence of Maurras and Action Française, and also 'fell in love with the doctrine, liturgy and architecture of the Catholic Church, and came to regard it as one of the main pillars of civilisation.'[42] Bebb's article in the 1923 Y Llenor shows just how infatuated he was with Maurras. He referred to him as 'one of the wise men of Greece who has risen again in our day',[43] and, in a play of words upon the 'immortals' of the Académie Française, pronounced that: 'If it can be said of anybody that he is immortal, it can be said of him … Charles Maurras will not die.'[44] Maurras, he said, had given a new direction to the thinking of the age: 'He defends order, tradition and inheritance, authority and intelligence'.[45] He would, said Bebb, be quoted and referred to in every major discussion that humanity would have in the future.

Bebb had been working closely with the Breton Nationalists, and calling, in their journal *Breiz Atao*, for a similar movement in Wales. In 1924 Bebb, on a visit to Wales, met Saunders Lewis and co-founded with him and Griffith John Williams the group 'Y Mudiad Cymreig' (the Welsh Movement), which a year later was to grow into 'Plaid Genedlaethol Cymru' (the Welsh Nationalist Party), of which Saunders Lewis was to be president until 1939.

Saunders Lewis (1893–1985) was another figure who had been strongly influenced by the French Right. In his case the major influence was Maurice Barrès. Born in Wallasey, Cheshire, Lewis had studied English and French at Liverpool University, his studies being interrupted by the outbreak of war. He served as an officer in the South Wales Borderers, and while in France made the discovery of Barrès's writings. Years later, he was to describe this as being the influence of Barrès's *Culte du moi*, an early cycle of non-political novels. But the way in which he described this influence shows that it must have been the novels of the *Roman de l'énergie nationale*, and above all *Les Déracinés*, that had inspired in him the view that 'the only way to cultivate your personality … is to go back to your roots.'[46] Another of Barrès's books that influenced him strongly was *Colette Baudoche*, the depiction of a young girl in German-occupied Alsace-Lorraine. In 1924, writing of the recently-deceased Barrès, Lewis wrote:

> I cannot hear of this man's death without openly acknowledging my debt to him. Discovering his work had the effect of changing the course of my life … It was through him that I discovered Wales, and that the hedonism of my youth was transformed into something else. My play, *Noble Blood*, is no more than an attempt at turning *Colette Baudoche* into Welsh and into a Welsh setting.[47]

So Barrès's regionalism affected Saunders Lewis, as did his ideas on 'la terre et les morts', and on nationalism. But Lewis's writings show that he was in addition affected by other aspects of the French radical Right in this period. These aspects include:

1. The dislike of the 'modern world' that has destroyed old values.
2. The hatred of the forces of capitalism, which hold the world in thrall.
3. The close relationship between religion and politics (the religion being Catholicism, to which Lewis was to convert in 1933).
4. A hatred of aliens, including Jews.

Like many on the Right in the inter-war period, Saunders Lewis saw capitalism and communism as being two sides of the same coin; what was needed was something between the two.[48] In Lewis's case, this third way was nationalism. Opposed to this were the forces of international finance; and in various writings, including his poetry, Lewis made it clear that by this he meant the Jews. In a poem entitled 'Y Dilyw 1939' (The Deluge 1939) Lewis starts by describing, in the nostalgic tones of the international Right, the desecration of an imagined former Utopia, a desecration which has been produced by the capitalist society. 'Here once was Wales', he wrote, describing the desolation of the mining valleys amid the effects of the slump. The description of the urban poor is, however, singularly lacking in sympathy; they, too, are an example of the decline caused by the 'modern world'.

> The dregs rose from the empty docks
> Over the dry ropes and the rust of cranes,
> Their proletarian flood crept
> Greasily civil to the chip shops,
> It crawled as blood about the feet of policemen
> And spread into a pool of silicon spittle
> Through the faceless valleys of the industry of the dole.

Soon, amid 'the sniggering of Basle and its foul usurers', we have a depiction of those who have created all this misery, the Jewish capitalists:

> Then, on Olympus, in Wall Street, nineteen-twenty-nine,
> At their infinitely scientific task of guiding the profits of fate,
> The gods decreed, with their feet in the Aubusson carpets,
> And their Hebrew snouts in the quarter's statistics,
> That the day had come to restrict credit in the universe of gold.[49]

Lewis's anti-Semitism has other affinities with that of Barrès, however: the dislike of 'aliens' who do not share one's roots. In this the Jews share the fate of all those who are not Welsh, and who impinge on Welsh life. In a poem entitled 'Golygfa mewn Caffe' (Scene in a Café), written in 1940, Lewis described the unwelcome presence of alien English evacuees in Welsh Aberystwyth:

> Amid the motley horde,
> The sad horde that had lost the goodness of intellect,
> The living dead,
> Amid the cheerless cackle and red claws of females,
> Their brute lips like a wanton nightmare rending the sleep of their
> > gorilla faces,
> Amid the horde in flight …

There are elements in this unflattering description which point to a different kind of racism, however. Lewis is clearly targeting Jews when, amid the alien herd of evacuees, we find 'Whitechapel's lard-bellied women, Golders Green Ethiopians' (Blonegesau Whitechapel, Ethiopiaid Golders Green).[50]

Such anti-Semitism was a facet of a small, but vociferous, part of the Welsh Nationalist movement in its early days. In an article in *The Welsh Nationalist* in 1932, for example, J. Alun Pugh wrote the following scornful criticism of Welsh non-Nationalists: 'The Anglo-Welshman is always running after English politicians, English Jews or English Trade Union leaders.'[51]

Lewis's general debt to the French Right can be seen, also, in some of the 'Ten Points of Policy' of Plaid Cymru, published in *Y Ddraig Goch* (*The Welsh Dragon*) in 1933; they stated that 'for the moral well-being of Wales, and for the health, moral and physical, of its people, there must be a de-industrialization of South Wales', and 'agriculture should be the main industry of Wales and the basis of its civilization'.[52]

Saunders Lewis's vision of a Catholic Europe attaches him to a far wider strain of the French Catholic Right than that advocated by Bebb. Indeed, in 1927, in the face of attacks on the 'neo-Catholic' tendency within Plaid Cymru, Lewis, distancing himself from Bebb and Action Française, proclaimed his Catholic mentors as Paul Claudel (the dramatist and poet), François Mauriac (the regionalist novelist), Étienne Gilson (the Thomist philosopher) and Jacques Rivière (editor of the *Nouvelle Revue Française*, and disciple of Claudel). The name of Claudel is significant, in that the list claims to be one of philosophical influences, rather than poetic ones. Paul Claudel (1868–1955), while being an innovative and 'modern' dramatist-poet to whose work Lewis's has much affinity, was at the same time one of the most intransigent and reactionary figures in the Catholic revival: traditional, anti-democratic, anti-Semitic, and violent in his hatreds.[53] In other words, Saunders Lewis, despite denying Action Française, was not aligning himself with 'modernist' Catholicism, but with the Catholic Right. In Dafydd Glyn Jones's view, Lewis's writings 'place him squarely, with Claudel and Bernanos, in the tradition of Léon Bloy, and in line with the "Condemnation of Modernism" issued by Pius X in 1906.'[54] Some writers have, by stressing Lewis's debt to Maritain, suggested that this brought Lewis in line with a more 'liberal' wing of French Catholicism; but Maritain was a profoundly ambiguous figure, a member of Action Française whose connection with that movement was only to be severed in 1926 at the time of the papal condemnation of the movement; his 'liberal' tendencies were not to emerge until later. His influence on Lewis, like that of Gilson, appears to have been based on his neo-Thomism. Indeed, it has been argued that Lewis's desire to re-create a society that would be analogous to the medieval model, embodying the human values of the ages of faith, owed much to the Maritain of this early period.[55]

What of Action Française? Lewis, it is true, shared in the Action Française cult of neo-classicism, abhorring the 'romantic' tradition, and drawing a relationship between literary and political attitudes.[56] This may have come from Action Française, but could easily have come from elsewhere – Hulme and the Imagists or Eliot, for example, with whom some of his literary writing has common characteristics. Dafydd Glyn Jones has pointed out how typical he was of certain trends in Britain in the first decades of this century (note how many of the writers mentioned have already figured in this chapter):

> He is the broad representative of that broad international movement which, rather oddly, straddles the First World War, and which includes, among its leading figures, Ezra Pound, T. E. Hulme, W. B. Yeats, Wyndham Lewis, T. S. Eliot, G. K. Chesterton, H. Belloc, Irving Babbitt and even (in some respects) D. H. Lawrence.[57]

Even if Lewis shared many of the *cultural* characteristics of Action Française, we find no specific favourable references to that movement's politics in his writings before 1927, and thereafter we find him distancing himself from it.

What *is* clear is that, for a time, certain elements in the new party founded in 1925 were strongly interested by Action Française. As Diekmann has noted,[58] there was a great deal of discussion of Action Française in Plaid circles in the late 1920s, as witness the letter-columns of journals[59] and the comments by contemporary observers, such as this one in 1930:

> In France ... politically the nationalist party is a cipher: intellectually it dominates. It is the creation of one man, Charles Maurras, whose influence has spread to many lands not excluding Wales. There are some among our younger Welshmen to whom Maurras means a great deal.[60]

Action Française was described as 'the fount of inspiration for some modern nationalist movements in other countries and not least in Wales.'

Saunders Lewis and Ambrose Bebb, in their different ways, remained in debt to the French Right. In the 1930s, both became involved in support for continental 'fascist' movements. Mussolini, of course, had received much admiration in the British press in general, and not least in Wales; but Bebb was to go completely over the top in an article with the almost blasphemous title 'Gwr Dolurus, Cynefin a Dolur' ('A Man of Sorrows, and Acquainted with Grief'),[61] in which Mussolini was described as having 'borne the cross of his nation'. Meanwhile Saunders Lewis was engaging in controversies relating to his support for Portugal's dictator Salazar (whose Catholic dictatorship owed so much to the doctrines of Action Française),[62] and was declaring his support for other leaders such as Léon Degrelle, the Action-Française-influenced Belgian Rexist leader, and Jacques

Doriot, the head of the French Parti Populaire Français, who, he said, were 'neither Socialists nor Capitalists', and 'spokesmen of large numbers of their fellow-countrymen.'[63]

Lewis, it is true, contrasted such leaders with 'that State-Capitalism which is the hallmark alike of the Nazi, Fascist and Communist state', which he deplored. As war approached, however, he became convinced that Wales should stay out of a fight between two equally deplorable empires. In Ulster, he said, 'there has been a dictatorship as cruel and cowardly as anything Welshmen believe to exist in Germany and Italy'.[64] Note the words 'Welshmen *believe*'. Lewis felt, with many other 'fellow travellers of the Right' in Britain, that the Press and the BBC controlled people's opinions, and unjustly led them to see the dictators as monsters:

> Welsh Socialists cry out against the terrible cruelties of Hitler and his oppression of all the German people. They speak with conviction. They believe they have knowledge. They simply and helplessly cannot distinguish between propaganda and violence.[65]

The English papers, in his view, were 'prepared to advocate war on a European scale in defence of the capitalist-democratic system of the 19th century which made England the richest country in the world'.[66] At the time of the Munich crisis, Lewis described the Welsh as 'a national minority that has every cause to appreciate the rights of the Sudeten minority in Czechoslovakia, and has also the strongest reasons for desiring to avoid armed conflict.' The Welsh nation, he said, 'must not be conscripted for war in defence of the unjust frontiers established by the Treaty of Versailles.'[67]

Paradoxically, it was Bebb who opposed Plaid Cymru's policy of neutrality. He believed, on the basis of what he had learned from Maurras's writings about the German threat, that the Welsh should side with France and England against Germany in order to protect French civilization from the 'German barbarians'. Before the fall of France, Bebb described Maurras as someone 'who detested Germany's barbarity so much, who served his goddess, France, ... with the passion and purity of a Saint, and who warned his nation of the wrath which would spew over it from the east'.[68] It is not recorded what Bebb's reaction was when his hero welcomed the fall of France and the accession of Pétain as head of the Vichy State, with the words 'Quelle divine surprise!'

What has been looked at here is merely, because of the specific interests of this volume, one aspect of that many-faceted movement, Plaid Cymru. Many members of the party were in no way connected with such views. The vast majority, for example, were Nonconformists, even if in the popular view Plaid Cymru was 'The Pope's Party'. Many abhorred fascism in all its forms. Others, while left-wing in sympathies, found much to attract them in the leadership's anti-capitalist policies. And, of course, the post-war Plaid Cymru was to see itself as a primarily left-wing movement. What is of interest, however, is the extent to which the philosophies of the French Catholic Right could reach into the highest echelons of the leadership of a political party within these islands, during the inter-war period. Where one can dismiss the dabbling with French 'radical Right' ideas by people such as Hulme and Eliot as mere dilettantism, the Welsh experience presents us with a political manifestation of such ideas which extends into the practical arena.

*   *   *

What was the cultural, as opposed to political, impact of the French Right in Britain? The cult of 'classicism' paradoxically led, both in the Imagists and in the writings of T. S. Eliot, not to a backward-looking, nostalgic form of literature, but to revolutionary, 'modern' forms of expression. The rejection of the legacy of 'romanticism' cleared the way for something new, rather than leading back to earlier literary forms. This may in part have been because the Romantic cult of 'imagination' was replaced not by 'reason' (which was equally discredited because of its eighteenth-century manifestations), but, via Hulme, by a Bergsonian and Sorelian concentration on the 'intuition'. So it was that Hulme could, on the one hand, describe poetry as being no more than 'accurate, precise and definite description' and, on the other hand, see the creation of a poem, in Bergsonian terms, as being 'a constant struggle with language, a ceaseless search for metaphors, a bringing together of very different levels of experience in order to reproduce in the consciousness of the reader the original intuition of the poet.'[69]

It is important to realize how much, in the twentieth century, political reaction has gone hand-in-hand with artistic innovation. Marinetti, Eliot, Pound, Céline, Pessoa – the list is endless.[70] To some extent the acceptance of modernism, on the part of the Right, can be explained negatively by the fact that, unlike the communists, the Right felt no need to dismiss such literature as being irrelevant to the class struggle. But there is more to it than that: the 'flight from Reason' that, in the wake of Bergson and Nietzsche, has characterized so much of modern politics, is a far more convincing explanation of this literary trend.

So it is that Eliot, with his insistence on 'classicism', nevertheless completely revolutionized poetry in the English language, building on the ironic, tortured, logic-destroying techniques of the French poet Laforgue, refining them into poetry which becomes ever richer, ever more meaningful, through the rejection of simple 'meaning', and the subtle injection of powerful, suggestive ideas through a new manipulation of language. Similarly the poetry and drama of Saunders Lewis, who was in part influenced by the early work of Pound and Eliot,[71] is a meeting-ground of some of the most vital poetic traditions and trends of the twentieth century.

It has sometimes been suggested that there was a 'fascist aesthetic' that transcended national borders and national cultures. In relation to literature, it would be hard to make a case for this. Modernism was not exclusive to fascists – they were merely a number among the many writers who espoused this literary trend. Also, there were a great many 'fascist' or radical Right writers (including those associated with the British Union of Fascists, such as the novelist Henry Williamson) who wrote in a far more traditional way. What *can* be said is that, in Britain, the liaison between 'Fascism' and modernism was above all to be found in the circles that had been influenced either by the French Right and its aesthetic theories, or, in the case of Wyndham Lewis, by Marinetti and the Italian Futurists. And these are the writers whose reputation has lasted.

The Far Right and the Back-to-the-Land Movement[1]

Dan Stone

> The movement back to nature proves itself contrary to nature a thousand times over, because development is part of nature and turning back is against nature.
>
> Victor Klemperer, Diary entry, 10 January 1939.[2]

Introduction

In February 1942, T. S. Eliot wrote in his capacity as editor at Faber and Faber to Viscount Lymington, praising the drafts of his forthcoming book *Alternative to Death* (1943): 'I was rather pleased, incidentally, to find your suggesting something that has occurred to me independently, which is that a real aristocracy can only be founded or revived on a relationship between right social organization and values and the land.'[3] Although we know that Eliot was no progressive thinker, it would also not do to label him a fascist. What was it that Eliot saw in Lymington's back-to-the-land ideas? And why were these ideas the clearest cultural expression of Lymington's own far right ideology, an ideology that was manifested in his running of the English Array (earlier the English Mistery) and his bankrolling of the British Council Against European Commitments? What were the connections before 1945 – and for a few even after – between aristocracy, agricultural reform, the landscape, racism and 'national revival'?

The back-to-the-land movement was by no means confined to only one side of the political spectrum. Yet in the inter-war period representations of the landscape were crucial to the development of a specifically British far Right ideology. These representations comprised two poles, a 'negative' and a 'positive' one. The former concentrated on the threat to the landscape presented by foreigners, especially Jews (*rootless* refugees and internationalist financier-cosmopolitans) concentrated in dirty cities, and the second on a celebration of the health and vitality of the threatened English landscape, and the rootedness of the people in it.

The far Right back-to-the-land movement cannot simply be condemned as a kitschy, Wandervögel-type movement. Rather, the concerns of many 'back-to-the-landers' – from rural revivalists such as H. J. Massingham and Rolf Gardiner to fully-fledged fascists such as Viscount Lymington and Robert Saunders – in many ways adumbrate the post-war environmentalist movement, particularly in its concern for organic farming. Dissecting such movements as Lymington's Kinship of Husbandry helps us to understand why it was that such concerns as mechanization, the industrialization of agriculture and the increasing use of chemicals were seen as a political and a cultural threat in terms of racial degeneration, rather than as purely health or nutrition issues.

This chapter will stress two points: first, the indigenous nature of British fascism, which is too often dismissed as an imitative movement (one has in mind solely the black-shirted British Union of Fascists (BUF)); second, to show that this fascism is not 'other', some kind of political aberration, but emerged out of longstanding concerns. In the first instance, the concerns of Lymington and his circle are traced to a heritage of English writers earlier in the century who promoted aristocratic revivalism and the Diehard movement against reform of the House of Lords and Home Rule in Ireland. And in the second, it will be shown how many of the back-to-the-landers' ideas were in fact taken seriously by the wartime government and helped inform post-war planning where nutrition was concerned, thereby scotching the myth of their isolation from mainstream ideas. Furthermore, at the beginning of the twenty-first century, their ideas about organicism (now largely divorced from crude forms of racism) are more influential than ever, though their real value remains disputed.

Finally, it will be argued that the back-to-the-land movement presents an interesting methodological challenge to notions of cultural and political history. The political aspirations of the back-to-the-landers were fully integrated with their cultural expressions of them. This organo-fascist vision of a culturally homogeneous nation or race, dependent on the soil and deriving identity and meaning from it, means that the cultural and political aspects of this type of fascism are inseparable. The anthropological bent in cultural history that stresses representations and the creation of meaning through symbolic landscapes is illustrated clearly in the context of a movement that derived its political strategy and symbolic action from (putatively) real landscapes.

Roots and Soil

The idea of rootedness is a powerful cultural force. For all the talk of fragmented, nomadic, hybrid, postmodern identities, the stability conjured up in the idea of a home in which one has one's roots remains a staple of everyday conversation and yearning.[4] A 'family tree' is more than mere metaphor; when actually drawn it is clear that the family literally grows out of the soil. The 'modern iconography of kinship' is, Uli Linke asserts, still based on 'deeply rooted cultural assumptions about nature, health, fertility, and abundance'. According to these assumptions, 'metaphoric models of ancestry and blood origin placed the social body into the semantic field of nature. ... Genealogical models appropriated images of nature – blood, soil, and tree – as markers of descent, symbolising the natural order of things.'[5]

From the turn of the twentieth century onwards, the cultural pessimism that gripped most of Europe meant that these widely cherished assumptions about the basis of social and cultural life were perceived to be under threat. Their defence manifested itself in many ways, not all of them easily explicable. From concerns with racial degeneration that contributed to the wide-scale creation of hiking and athletics groups to fears of rapid social change that engendered fully-fledged fascist movements, the first half of the twentieth century was a period of ideological turmoil in which fascism was by no means an option solely of social outcasts, but seemed to many people to be the most dynamic way both of defending tradition and responding to the modern world. This dynamism seemed especially attractive in the wake of the Bolshevik Revolution and the Europe-wide crisis of parliamentary democracy.[6]

One of the most complex responses to these circumstances was the British back-to-the-land movement, itself part of a wider neo-Romanticist trend across Europe.[7] On the one hand, this movement's association with the far Right is entirely unsurprising. Given the strength of notions of rootedness, their radicalization in times of uncertainty is to be expected, and thus the veritable outpouring of works both scientific and popular extolling the virtues of soil and propounding a philosophy of roots in the 1930s and 1940s is quite understandable. Yet the back-to-the-land movement was not comprised solely of fascists. Such a caricature would all too easily avoid the real challenge of this movement: the fact that the same people who argued for a 'blood and soil' organo-fascism were simultaneously putting forward arguments about organic farming and environmental protection that are not just still considered pioneering but are gaining influence with each passing year and each new food crisis. The problem then is explaining how a group of people who could put forward such visionary ideas about farming, food and care of the environment could at the same time – and not as a random corollary to these ideas but as fundamental to their articulation – argue for a holistic philosophy of nature which embraced concepts of race, culture and gender that are immediately recognizable today as fascistic. For the organo-fascist element of the back-to-the-land movement questions of health, nutrition and environmental science may not even have been their prime concern; instead these issues followed from their fears of racial degeneration and cultural annihilation.[8]

Many of these concerns were shared across the political spectrum; concepts of returning to wholesome nature to escape polluting and degrading cities and alienating industrial labour were of course just as common on the Left as on the Right. Therefore it is necessary to try and isolate the specific elements that allow one to speak of the far Right or even 'organo-fascism' without either condemning the back-to-the-land movement *tout court* or stretching the concept of fascism so far as to make it devoid of meaning. Since the back-to-the-land discourse is so similar on the Left and the Right – both appealing to notions of purity and liberation from speculation and middlemen – this chapter will focus on the strategic employment of landscape imagery as a means of encouraging 'stock breeding' of human beings, aristocratic leadership, and racial homogeneity as the ways in which an organo-fascist vision may be distinguished from a Ruskinian, Arts and Crafts, guild socialist, or even Baldwinian back-to-the-land vision.

On the Left the Romantic ideas of Morris and Ruskin competed for socialist sympathies even in the days of Fabianism and technocratic socialism, when H. G. Wells, for example, could complain that 'A population of small agriculturalists that has really got itself well established is probably as hopelessly immovable a thing as the forces of progressive change will have to encounter.'[9] On the right, Fr Vincent McNabb, one of the leading ideologues of Distributism – a movement that sought the equal distribution of property on the premise that this would force a return to an authentic, pre-industrial era – wrote that '[t]here is no hope for England's salvation except on the land. But it must be the land cultivated on a land basis and not on an industrial basis. Nothing but religion will solve the land question. And nothing but a religious order seeking not wealth but God will pioneer the movement from town to land.' Distributism is an example of the ideological instability of the back-to-the-land movement, since it was an ideology 'oscillating between the extreme possibilities of fascism on the one hand and a kind of anarcho-syndicalism on the other'.[10] Most famously, the Conservative Prime Minister Stanley Baldwin conjured up an unchallenging rural vision in which 'England is the country, and the country is England'.[11]

But on the far Right, fascism in Britain never really achieved the 'reactionary modernist' synthesis that characterized Nazism, and stayed essentially a nostalgic, reactionary movement.[12] Although both Left and Right could have argued for the freedom from the homogenizing tendencies of industrial culture to be found on the land, and even anti-Semitism was to be found on the Left (the Jews as representatives of international capital), the Left was less likely than the Right to appeal to a eugenic vision of social hierarchies in which a pure and vigorous stock of peasants or yeomen would work in harmony with an aristocracy of race devoted to the concept of service.

In other words, the writings of far Right back-to-the-landers cannot simply be labelled 'fascist', even though they often tend in that direction. They are in fact a strange mixture of ideas, and are rather different from Italian Fascism or German National Socialism. Along with the same fears about degeneration and racial purity, and the same celebration of the 'folk', the British organicists also advocated local organization, resisted centralization and decried the populism and vulgarity of continental fascist movements. This does not mean that British organicists cannot be seen as proto-fascists, as some have claimed,[13] simply because they did not fall in line with the BUF. Rather, it means that British organo-fascism developed in its own way, based on notions of British cultural characteristics. It is of course correct to note that there was no *necessary* connection between the organicist movement and blood and soil racism; nevertheless, some of the most influential and high-profile members of the organicist movement in the 1930s and 1940s to a large degree were blood and soil racists, so it is wrong to argue that the fundamentalism that typified the German *Bündische Jugend* was absent in England.[14] This fundamentalism was not present across the whole spectrum of English neo-romantic and back-to-the-land thought; but in some variation it was behind the ideas of Rolf Gardiner (1902–71), Viscount Lymington (1898–1984), Arthur Bryant (1899–1985) and H. J. Massingham (1888–1952), the most influential of this school. In these writers' work the blend of anti-modernism and cultural pessimism unmistakably gave rise to a cultural expression of the far Right.

The writings of Sir George Stapledon (1882–1960), a leading agricultural scientist and Professor of agricultural botany at Aberystwyth, indicate the similarity of left-wing and right-wing organicist visions, and point to the difference. Opening his 1935 book *The Land Now and To-morrow*, Stapledon explained that his initial intention to confine the subject to purely agricultural implications had become impossible: 'To-day, however, that is not enough, for the land must be considered in relation to the nation as a whole.'[15] Since the land was the place closest to nature, its protection meant the best guarantee for the future of the nation's health: 'unless rural England is provided with the amenities and facilities necessary rural England and rural psychology are doomed – and then the driving force behind the English character would be lost'.[16] The problem, as Stapledon saw it, was that this threat was very real indeed:

> We take trouble to produce stock seeds and stock animals. The country is the place in which stock men are produced, or, alas! now we can only

say in which stock men can and should be produced. ...The era of industrialization and urbanization has nearly killed rural Britain, and it is the deep-going psychological influences that count for aye or nay. Let rural Britain die completely, and the whole superstructure will totter to ruin. It is just and only just not too late to stop the rot, but only heroic endeavour will suffice.[17]

Similarly, the organicist dietician Lionel Picton argued that '[t]he very soil is often degenerate, exhausted by the non-return of the natural waters and the substitution of chemicals'.[18] This eugenicist vision combined with a vitalist call to action on behalf of the sacred bond between nation and land was no doubt what lay behind the decision of Stapledon and Picton, as well as other leading agriculturalists such as Albert Howard, to associate with, if not actually to join, the Kinship in Husbandry group. Yet outside that context, their writings remain only suggestive of far-right ideas, and could hardly be labelled 'fascist'.

Kinship in Husbandry was founded in April 1941 by Rolf Gardiner, the rural revivalist, H. J. Massingham, the countryside's most prolific eulogist, and Gerald Wallop, Viscount Lymington (later the ninth Earl of Portsmouth), the latter the most openly fascist of the prominent back-to-the-landers. Their aim was to initiate a forum in which members could share their experiments in organic farming. Its members kept a notebook in which they recorded the results of their farming activities, and they met periodically to discuss them, usually in Edmund Blunden's rooms in Oxford. Apart from Gardiner, Massingham, and Lymington, its members were: C. Henry Warren, Edmund Blunden, Lord Northbourne, J. E. Hosking, Arthur Bryant, Adrian Bell, Douglas Kennedy, Philip Mairet, and Robert Payne. They were joined later on by Laurence Easterbrook, Michael Graham, Ronald Duncan and Jorian Jenks. Stapledon, Howard, Picton and Robert McCarrisson were associated with the group though not actually members.[19]

When the most influential organicist campaigning group, the Soil Association, was founded in 1945, its council included Gardiner, Lymington and Massingham. Eve Balfour, still held in high regard by proponents of organic farming, wrote in *The Living Soil* (1943), which David Matless calls 'effectively the founding document of the Soil Association',[20] that 'Society, like a house, does not start at ground level, but begins quite literally beneath the surface of our planet, within the soil itself. For out of the soil are we fashioned, and by the products of the soil is our earthly existence maintained.'[21] Balfour shared this quasi-mystical reverence for the soil with many leading organicist authorities on soil science, including Northbourne and compost theorist Maye Bruce, all of whom argued in favour of the vital powers of humus as opposed to artificial chemical fertilizers. It certainly helped attract them to the more *outré* beliefs of the Kinship's members. Jenks, for example, the editor of *Mother Earth*, the journal of the Soil Association, was also a prominent member of the BUF, speaking for them on agricultural matters. Just as fascists repudiated mainstream politics as stultifying, ossifying, and degenerative, so organicist farmers in the 'epoch of fascism' reviled mainstream farming methods for 'killing the soil'[22] on which all life depends, and for killing *British* soil in particular, for this especially fertile soil nurtured the now-threatened racial characteristics of the British.

The Threat to the Landscape

What then were the specific fears and aims of the organo-fascists? The writings of all of them reveal the same distaste for modern farming methods, combined with a romanticized image of the landscape and a fear of its pollution by urban cosmopolitans and unhealthy immigrants. Their attitude rests on a fundamentally aesthetic concept of society, a notion of 'sound taste', 'right values', and 'good breeding' that tolerates no notion of difference, and rests on a belief in the need for aristocratic leadership, cultural homogeneity and racial purity. Their panegyrics to the English landscape brought all of these themes together.

These followed a trajectory from themes shared with the romantic Left to specifically far Right concerns. Massingham, for example, revealed his guild socialist background in his introduction to a collection of essays on the *English Country* in which he attacked the modern world for breaking the authentic bond between people and land:

> The loss of personal values and of an individual particularity is certainly a major evil of our times. Arbitrary government that creates and is created by herd-mentality; mass-production that so blindly produces as deliberately to destroy part of its own product; the vast automatism of contemporary life whose diversions are as mechanical as its labour; the authority of abstractions like the State, are all hostile in grain to the spirit of place and to the sensitive human vision which discloses and interprets it.[23]

This passage is typical in combining a blanket condemnation of 'modernity' with an unquestioned belief in the author's better knowledge. In particular, the appeal to the 'spirit of place' was a very common trope: Massingham produced a series of books celebrating the particularities of the landscape of the English counties. And he broke with his earlier guild socialism – and with socialism altogether – by taking refuge in anti-modern dreamscapes and romanticized medievalism rather than in trying to fight the inequities of the modern world, whether rural or urban.

But Lymington went further, indicating the grounds that separate generally-held back-to-the-land ideas and organo-fascism. His vision of the land was one in which social order was upheld by a rigorously maintained hierarchy that bound the classes to one another through the idea of service. 'The land,' said Lymington, 'is not only a reservoir for health but for leadership'; it was 'still the nucleus of a true aristocracy' in which a landlord who fails to live up to his duties should be 'ruthlessly deprived of his individual rights'.[24] But this was not simply a book about an agriculture developed in the context of organic farms and organic societies. It was also a discussion of the role of race in the health of the British Empire. Arguing that the best way of ensuring 'a healthy future' in Britain was to export the domestic 'population problem' (most of these writers took it for granted that there was such a thing[25]) to the white settlements, making the Empire self-supporting, Lymington wrote that:

> From the Dominion point of view there can be very little hope for the white Empire, as distinct from its aboriginal inhabitants, if we try to develop it by international immigration. We will be heir to all the ills from which the United States is now suffering owing to its pre-War policy of indiscriminate immigration. We have only to look at the results of Irish immigration into the Clydeside to find an example at our doors of the results of mongrelism.

The conclusions were obvious for Lymington: '[m]iscegenation of culture is as evil as miscegenation of blood.'[26] Lymington's writings connected an aesthetic concept of the land with a vigorously expressed sense of race-belonging and national/natural order.

How these concerns tied in with a broader fascist philosophy can be seen with reference to the English Mistery (later the English Array), the small radical Right group of which Lymington was the leading member. Its whole outlook was founded on aesthetic notions of taste and breeding, in which the defence of national homogeneity meant the safeguarding of 'sound' traditions and healthy physical types. It upheld a monarchist organic vision of an ethnically pure society in which class warfare would be unknown, gender divisions would be strictly upheld and the concept of 'service' would govern behaviour. Although these ideas meant that the Mistery was formally at odds with the statist populism of Mosley, in practice the two groups had contacts, and shared more than it might first appear, especially their diagnosis of society's ills.[27] The English Mistery and the BUF were also in contact over agricultural issues, with Neil Francis-Hawkins, the BUF's main administrator, writing to Lymington to ask for advice.[28]

In the ranks of the Mistery, Anthony Ludovici shared Lymington's interest in the links between the land and the health of the nation. Ludovici (1882–1971), a Nietzschean scholar (one of the translators of the first English edition of Nietzsche's *Collected Works*, and a close friend of its editor, Oscar Levy[29]), was a prodigious author, ranging from anti-feminism to art criticism (he had an art column in the *New Age*) to eugenics and anthropology. He advocated incest, inbreeding, 'controlled sacrifice', and pre- and post-natal selection (that is, selective infanticide) as means of ensuring racial purity. He was also obsessed with health, and convinced of the link between 'right posture', 'right use of the self', physical well-being, and mental worth. He lectured on the Alexander Technique to the St James's Kin of the English Mistery,[30] and regularly bemoaned the negative effects of processed food, white bread and cheap beer. He was not only a key figure in the early Nietzsche movement in Britain, but went on to become a major theorist of fascism in Britain, acting as the English Mistery's 'intellectual', and eventually becoming a Nazi fellow-traveller. His influence, though it has been overlooked, was profound, and can be detected in the writings of Lymington, Gardiner, and others.[31]

In a letter to C. P. Blacker, chairman of the Eugenics Society, in 1932, Ludovici wrote that 'England, poor old England is going down in a stew of female sentimentality.'[32] The attempt to save 'poor old England' and all the cultural associations called up by that phrase was what motivated the organo-fascists – especially Ludovici and Lymington – to blend their back-to-the-land ethos with radical politics. So when Ludovici was invited by the BBC to take part in a debate about 'Efficiency and Liberty in England' in 1938, he assiduously wrote to Lymington asking for advice. Lymington provided Ludovici with information relating to the spraying of potatoes, and 'the sickness of plants, animals and man through the impoverishment of the soil'. How these agricultural statistics related to politics is immediately clear from such dramatic vocabulary, equating the mechanical 'mistreatment' of the land with racial decline, and is even more clear in Ludovici's next question to Lymington: 'Now then, can I correlate the whole lot, as I am going to do in regard to other facts, with the factor *freedom*? In other words, is it possible in any way to correlate the facts you have given me with the "freedom" and the "right of private judgment" which have prevailed in England for over a century? If so, how?'[33] The answer – echoing Ludovici's anthropological claims – is to be found in the writings of Lymington, Massingham, Gardiner, Blunden and the rest of the Kinship in Husbandry group, as they contrasted the 'green and pleasant land' with the ravages of modernity:

> In loving service to the soil men see each season how death may be cheated and learn how they must always protect the sound seed from the weeds, and how close breeding makes fine types of stock. ... if the best are to survive it must be by careful tending and protection from

weeds and parasites. If only to relearn this ancient lesson, regeneration of the soil must come before national revival.[34]

If, on the one hand, the organo-fascists celebrated an ethnically homogeneous England whose people were rooted in the soil, so, on the other hand, they condemned those population groups that seemed to threaten that vision. It should come as no surprise that special distaste was reserved for the Jews, and for the ill-effects they had allegedly brought to the nation. For the organo-fascists, as for fascists generally, the Jews were the main agents of modernity, and thus constituted one of the gravest threats to national and cultural purity. For many of the organo-fascists anti-Semitism was expressed only through a standard, coded language, including attacks on machinery, international finance, banking, speculation and middlemen. Lymington, for example, wrote that 'In no case should the land be sport of dealers or speculators.'[35] And Gardiner, retrospectively describing the activities of his youth, wrote: '[c]ould England develop the creative dynamism of the continent without sacrificing her native traditions? That was the sort of question which some of us posed at the attempts of would-be leaders like Mosley and Hargrave to stir English youth into revolt against Edwardian money-power.'[36]

Ludovici, however, went further, although only under the pseudonym of 'Cobbett', a name calculated to call to mind William Cobbett's *Rural Rides* (1830), a book which combined political radicalism and evocations of the English landscape with the threat posed to the Englishman's liberty by middlemen and speculators, in particular the Jews. Tracing the racial heritage of the Jews back to the twelve tribes, Ludovici argued that 'it may be that it is precisely these few stubborn and primitive desert traits in the Jews which have repeatedly moulded their history, in spite of the thousands of years which now separate them from desert life'.[37] Those traits included 'that complex of mental habits, emotions, gifts and tastes, which necessarily forms in the nomad State – such, for instance, as the inability to become, or feel, rooted to any territory, hence the lack of appreciation and capacity for a territorial national's attachment to a particular soil and environment'. Ludovici warned against mixed English-Jewish breeding, but also noted that the influence of Jewish values was already so deep that a general transvaluation of values was necessary, and not just the exclusion of Jews from positions of power.[38] For Ludovici, the Jews' brash mercantile values were synonymous with rootlessness, and so the threat to authentic English values was also a threat to English property and land. In Ludovici's writings we see how organicist ideas merged with British fascist ideology.

By contrast with Ludovici, whose career trajectory took him into the ranks of pro-Nazi fellow travellers, the case of Rolf Gardiner is a difficult one, as other scholars have noted.[39] His ideas reveal most clearly the difficulties of using the term 'organo-fascism'. An inspirational figure, whose inter-war cultural links with German youth groups and whose Springhead Trust in Dorset gave many of his followers a genuine taste of an alternative lifestyle, Gardiner's ideas on the environment and organic farming were way ahead of his time. Nevertheless, they were articulated through a framework of cultural pessimism, anti-modernism, and apocalypticism that brought him into the orbit of the far Right. Gardiner had been instrumental in establishing links with German organicist groups since the early 1920s, when he was an undergraduate at Cambridge and a member of John Hargrave's Kibbo Kift Kindred, a kind of paranoid-style scout movement which was later part of the Social Credit movement.[40] If one defines 'fascist' as someone belonging to a self-designated fascist movement, then Gardiner was no fascist. Indeed, the cultural expressions of folk dance, organicist rural revivalism, agricultural autarky, male hiking groups, and anti-modernism were elements in a wider cultural malaise of the inter-war period, one common to the Left and the Right. Even so, that Gardiner was not a fascist does not mean that scholars should overlook the obviously far Right aspects of his thought and behaviour. For Gardiner, organicism was a cultural expression of a far Right political strategy that involved extreme 'one-nation' ideas mixed with notions of aristocratic revivalism, a masculine renaissance, and racial hygiene. Their shared organicist vision explains why in a paper delivered to the English Mistery in October 1933 (which he wrote after discussions with Ludovici), Gardiner could claim that a nation's health could be judged by its attitude to music. His argument that the modern state neglected the importance of music meant that 'a progressive barbarisation of taste has set in' (a very Ludovician formulation) led him to assert that the only 'way out from this decadence' was 'the resumption by masculine leadership and by state-building forces of the musical life of the people'.[41] Similarly, when he agreed in March 1938 to review Lymington's *Famine in England* for the English Array's *Quarterly Gazette*, applauding 'the daring and swiftness and conviction' of the Nazi actions, and praising collaboration between his Springhead Ring and the Array, he surely knew what he was saying.[42]

An Indigenous Organo-Fascism

Much of the literature on fascism in Britain, perhaps because it has until recently concentrated on the BUF, suggests (either implicitly or explicitly) that British fascism was really an imitative movement, taking its inspiration from its more successful continental counterparts. Yet fascism in Britain, even when one refers only to those movements that used the name, has a history dating back before 1932. Rotha Lintorn-Orman founded the British Fascisti in 1923, and there were many smaller groups in the inter-war years – such as the English Mistery – who can only be described as fascistic – who did not subscribe to many of the views of the BUF.

Besides, there is much more to the far Right in Britain than its strictly fascist elements. The intellectual provenance of these elements reveals the extent to which Britain produced its own native far Right, perhaps not of the statist variety as in Italy or Germany, but certainly racist, nostalgic, eugenicist, and aiming at what Roger Griffin calls 'palingenesis', or national rebirth.[43] The English Mistery/Array was, in its membership, linked both to the BUF and to the Conservative Party. Lymington, for example, was Conservative MP for Basingstoke 1929–34, and Reginald Hugh Dorman-Smith was Minister of Agriculture 1939–40 and subsequently Governor of Burma (1941–6). It is important to bear in mind, however, that British fascism remained, for the most part, at a theoretical level, and barely developed further than the creation of fairly small fascist movements, such as the British Fascisti, National Fascisti, and the British Empire Fascists. In the BUF a movement was born that attempted to root itself in the political arena, but ultimately failed. Only in the most limited sense, then, can fascism in Britain be seen as having got beyond a stage of theoretical articulation and grown into a form of political *action*.[44] But when one talks of cultural expressions of the far Right, a far broader vista opens up.

There is a danger that talk of a 'native' far Right sounds like a replication of the back-to-the-landers' own language, a passionate defence of all things British. Yet certain intellectual currents of the late Victorian and Edwardian period did fuel a domestic form of fascism: the Boer War and the fear of 'racial degeneration', the 'national efficiency' campaign, the popular leagues for conscription and military expenditure, the rise of the feminist and labour movements, the rise of mass democracy, the Home Rule crisis in Ireland, constitutional reform of the House of Lords and the role of the 'Diehards'. In other words, the ideas of the back-to-the-landers did not come from nowhere.[45]

The back-to-the-land movement began to make its presence felt at the same time as the first wave of anti-immigrant clamour and the rise of the 'national efficiency' campaign. In 1893 one writer exclaimed that 'At the present time no cry is more popular than "Back to the Land"; it is taken up on all sides.'[46] At the same time Arnold White, the influential jingoist journalist, was starting to publish his anti-asylum, eugenicist and nationalist views which were among the founding documents of an indigenous British fascism. They were strongly connected to fears about the land: '[t]he destruction of private property in land and the loss of security hitherto given by the State to the owners of land marks degeneration in the capacity of the ruling caste.'[47] Accompanying them was an Edwardian aristocratic revivalism, articulated largely by those who made up the Diehards in the constitutional crises of 1909–14. Lord Willoughby de Broke, for example, who came close to advocating civil war over the issue of Irish Home Rule, formulated a theory of National Toryism, and celebrated traditional rural sports. His volume devoted to fox-hunting was expensively bound and lavishly illustrated, as befitted such a noble pursuit.[48] And the organic, aristocratic, land-oriented society he espoused was precisely what Lymington was advocating two decades later, although now in the context of fascism and heightened international tension.

This widespread backing for the back-to-the-land movement was not without its critics, however. The two co-authors of one such critique astutely noted that 'It was said of the allotments provided by the Guardians a hundred years ago that they enabled the destitute to grow their own poor rates. It must not be said of any new land settlement schemes that they have enabled the workless to grow their own doles.'[49] But this kind of 'hard-headed' criticism was exactly the sort of technocratic thinking that the organo-fascists were resisting. Their diagnoses of society's ills led them to quite different conclusions, ones suffused with apocalyptic imagery. Gardiner, for example, spoke of a 'new dark age' and 'the approaching winter of Western Civilisation', and all set up their discussions in dualistic terms, as a zero-sum game: '[I]t might well be the business of our own age to decide whether it is to be a record of abiding things, or beautiful epitaph.'[50]

The Effects of the War

One can rapidly dispense with the notion that the organicist far Right was primarily an inter-war movement as soon as one considers the sudden increase in publications by Massingham, Blunden, Lymington and others during the war years. Indeed, Kinship in Husbandry was only founded in 1941, in response, as Gardiner put it, to '[w]artime emergencies [that] were being used as an excuse for enforcing inorganic methods of production, for sacrificing quality for the sake of quantity'.[51] It is important to take note of this wartime literary production, for it furthered the longstanding arguments of the organo-fascists whilst simultaneously bolstering their claims to be British ultra-patriots rather than pro-Nazi traitors. Few people connected to the rural revivalist movement were interned under Defence Regulation 18B that saw Mosley and his circle imprisoned. Yet the intensification of the organo-fascists' claims, with their representations of the landscape becoming ever more shrill during these years, was a continuation of the same themes of cultural protectionism, ethnic homogeneity, and rural preservation that had always been their stock-in-trade.

The prose used by the rural revivalists to describe the bucolic idyll that was the British countryside became more and more purple, revealing the fact that this was more a mental landscape than a real one. Celebrating the virtues of the small-holder, the 'countryman', the nostalgic element of the back-to-the-land movement came to the fore. As an antidote to wartime industrial production and rationing, it is easy to see why such depictions of the landscape – 'the culture of pre-industrial England, the wonder of landscapes haunted by the ghosts of a remote past'[52] – became so popular. In contrast to the modern world, the traditional 'country community' was 'an unostentatious, a good-tempered tradition, a work of sturdy character content with native fields and the honour of a local achievement'.[53] It sought to remind people that the 'modern world, with its drab, industrial cities, discontented workers, dole queues, mass hatreds, and wars of industrial destruction, is ... the result of an attempt to realise an ideal which views man as a consumer only, and forgets that he is equally a producer'.[54] The contrast was important; rural England could only be viewed through a suitably rosy hue as long as one remembered that '[c]ivilisation has brought us to a pass of mechanised savagery which nothing will cure perhaps except famine and disease'.[55] Rather cunningly, Gardiner turned the accusation of fascism on his opponents, saying that the bureaucratic imposition of culture of countryside was already underway: 'This is a surreptitious or unconscious form of cultural Fascism, in which the fatal elements of centralisation and mechanisation of method have full play.'[56] This appeal reminds us that the appeal to landscape was not necessarily a fascist strategy, and that in fact these representations of the landscape must be seen in a broader context of far Right politics.

Even so, for all Gardiner's attempts to turn the tables, the organo-fascists were not unequivocally dedicated to the Allies' cause. As Lymington wrote to Lt Commander Malcolm Le Mare, stationed on HMS Royal Arthur at Skegness, on 21 December 1939: '[t]he only sensible Ministry is the Ministry of Agriculture – up to a point. The others are so over organized by urban mentalities that the best thing that could happen for this country would be for Hitler to bomb each Ministry in turn! And then we could get real decentralisation and get on with our job.'[57] Remarkably, Lymington was not interned during the war, presumably because of his aristocratic status, though had this letter been intercepted perhaps things would have been different. It gives the lie to the implication that the back-to-the-land circle around Lymington was not fascist, and that it willingly fought for the Allied cause.[58] Its members did fight, but reluctantly, more out of a dutiful sense that it was better to keep Britain unoccupied than from a firm belief in the evils of Nazism, and certainly with the belief that '[w]hoever won the battles in a European war, it would be a victory only for the Jews and Bolsheviks'.[59] Or, in the case of Bryant, patriotism was advocated to stave off the impending threat of internment. His *English Saga* (1940) was famously penned in a matter of weeks in 1940 as a kind of apology for his previous book, the unashamedly pro-Nazi *Unfinished Victory* (1940). Where in the earlier work, Bryant had enthusiastically written that the 'native Germans' were confronting the problem of 'rescuing their indigenous culture from an alien hand and restoring it to their own race', he now wrote that the Englishman's war against the same Germans, 'however tragic, was a noble one: he was fighting against evil things and a cruel, unappeasable aggressor who tortured racial minorities, who tore up treaties, who ranted and shouted and bullied and, when he was thwarted, rained death and destruction on peaceful millions.'[60] Besides, the war presented the group with the first real opportunity to find a wide audience for its organicist beliefs, as it helped orchestrate the government's wartime food policy of self-sufficiency, aided by the land-girls.

The war then actually helped strengthen organo-fascist claims. Henry Williamson, for example (another author whose fascism is underestimated by his hagiographers[61]) felt able to combine an appeal to wartime sentiment with 'harder' organicist views:

> It has taken a war to put British farming on its feet, and to bring back to us generally the idea that work is the true basis of life in the world. A nation that neglects its land, and its peasants – which are its root-stock – will perish. The idea of living by easy money is no good. Napoleon said that toil produced a hard and virile race, while trade produced a soft and crafty people; and that is true. We British are hard and virile, and we must have overseas trade in order to build up a high standard of life; but the cut-price, get-rich-quick idiom was beginning to spoil that hardness and virility. The by-products of that past epoch were over-intellectualism, spiciness and hyper-stimulation of feeling: too many cocktails, too-glamorous movies, a rootlessness showing itself in artistic distortion; pavementism. These things were an emanation of the same system that produced the dole-queues, slums, malnutrition, the 'class-war'. The war has brought us back to the fundamentals of life; and when it is over, on the basis of our new, hard economy, we shall build a fine civilisation in this country, and its Empire, on the simple virtues of life.[62]

Their views even began to receive some attention in official circles. Advocating self-sufficiency, or at least growing as much of one's own food as possible, was a wartime measure advocated by, if not adopted from, the organicists, and the Ministry of Food's 'National Wholemeal Loaf' was partly inspired by organicists' attacks on white bread.[63] Even so, despite these organicist successes, their inroads into government wartime policy could hardly compete with the rather larger orthodox emphasis on modernizing agriculture, and the role of the organicists was minor in comparison with that of planning technicians.

After the war very little changed. A subtle shift in language took place that (almost) concealed the anti-Semitism and racism that was implicit in pre-1945 back-to-the-land attacks on international finance, trade and middlemen. But although rural nostalgia now took prominence, the claims were the same. The example of Jenks is informative here. The same eulogy to the land was present as before the war, Jenks espousing 'a truly native and essentially kindly way of living', for '[i]ndigenous roots, well bedded in a fertile soil, have provided constant resources, both spiritual and material, of national validity'.[64] As Matless notes, 'Antisemitism is absent from Jenks's 1950 *From the Ground Up*, but a philosophy of roots asserting that "Husbandry is Fundamental" and critiquing the world economy from a position still associated with British fascism risks being accused of not entirely declaring its hand.'[65] When other back-to-the-landers were still saying that '[t]he whole conception of dominant money is ... foreign to the soil',[66] it becomes even harder to deny Matless's point.

Conclusions

Studying cultural history provides an insight into the nature of fascism in Britain that one cannot gain from focusing solely on political history. In this case, studying the impact of organicist thought on the British right means that it becomes clear to what extent one can talk of *British* fascism in the sense of an indigenous movement emerging out of longstanding socio-cultural concerns, rather than a fascist movement *in Britain*, denoting simply an imitation of more successful parties in continental Europe.

In this history, the continuity of ideas is important. Organo-fascism did not account for the whole gamut of organicist or back-to-the-land thinkers in Britain, but it tied in with an influential strand of thought that had emerged out of Edwardian radical Right concerns of national efficiency, constitutional reform, mass democracy, gender divisions, aristocratic revivalism, military conscription and racial degeneration. All of these ideas – which gained in radicalism after the First World War – stressed the need for an 'organic' society, in the sense of being a holistic, unitary, racially pure body, and in the sense of being rooted in the soil, and led by a hereditary landed aristocracy that instinctively performed its leadership role. Hence, to some extent, the organo-fascist concerns of Lymington, Ludovici, Massingham, Gardiner et al. were the culmination of a specifically British form of fascism. That it was subsequently overshadowed by the populism of the BUF should not blind us to the fact that an important part of the organic movement in Britain began life largely tied to fascist concerns. Nor should it blind us to the fact that such concerns were very widely shared.

In other words, in reality it is not possible to distinguish cultural from political aspects of British fascism. The dual threat to the land posed by soil erosion, the result of modern agricultural techniques, and to the race, the result of alien infiltration, meant that the representation of the landscape was bound up with political extremism even as it was situated in longstanding tropes of Britishness. Of course, such representations were symbolic in the sense that they were not 'real' places (Blunden's and Massingham's 'English Villages' did not exist isolated from the rest of the country). But the same was true in reverse: the real environment was perceived to be threatened by symbolic representations of Jews and other 'aliens'. Similarly, the representation of the landscape as a site of pristine nationhood remains powerful, and no more so than when it is 'under threat', as of course it always is according to publications such as *This England*.[67] The brown-green alliance is still with us, as an undercurrent in green politics, as a way in which extreme Right groups attempt to appear respectable, and as a subtext of wilderness philosophy.[68] Attempts by the BNP to infiltrate the Countryside Alliance may be seen not simply as a cynical ploy to win 'respectable' votes, but as part of an ongoing cultural project of the British radical Right. Organo-fascist ideas have a history, and that history is not yet at an end. The all-pervasive symbolism of organicist ideas means that the line between reality and representation is hard to discern. Cultural history, at the same time that it broadens and deepens our understanding of fascism, also complicates it, that is to say, historicizes it as a phenomenon, thereby making its portrayal more convincing, for it shows that the idea of fascism as an aberration in British political life must be called into question.

Notes

Introduction

1 What follows is merely a sample of historical works that should provide a guide for further reading, rather than an exhaustive bibliographical survey. Studies of the membership patterns and local support for the BUF include, in order of publication: W. F. Mandel, 'The Leadership of the British Union of Fascists', *Australian Journal of Politics and History*, 12 (1966), pp 360–83; Michael Billig, *Fascists: A Social Psychological View of the National Front* (London, 1978); N. Fielding, *The National Front* (London, 1981); John D. Brewer, *Mosley's Men: The British Union of Fascists in the West Midlands* (London, 1984); S. Rawnsley, 'Fascism and Fascists in Britain in the 1930s. A Case Study of Fascism in the North of England' (unpublished PhD dissertation, University of Bradford, 1981); Gerry C. Webber, 'Patterns of Membership and Support for the British Union of Fascists', *Journal of Contemporary History*, 19, 4 (1984), pp 575–606; S. M. Cullen, 'The British Union of Fascists, 1932–1940: Ideology, Membership and Meetings' (unpublished MLitt thesis, University of Oxford, 1987); David Turner, *Fascism and Anti-Fascism in the Medway Towns 1927–1940* (Rochester, 1993); Thomas Linehan, *East London for Mosley: The British Union of Fascists in East London and South-West Sussex, 1993–1940* (London, 1996); David Renton, *Red Shirts and Black: Fascists and Anti-Fascists in Oxford in the 1930s* (Oxford, 1996); Richard Grifitths, *Patriotism Perverted: Captain Ramsey, the Right Club and British Anti-Semitism, 1939–40* (London, 1998); Philip Coupland, 'The Blackshirts in Northampton, 1933–1940', *Northamptonshire Past and Present*, 53 (2000), pp 71–82.
2 See Richard Thurlow, *Fascism in Britain: A History, 1918–1985* (Oxford, 1987); Gerry C. Webber, *The Ideology of the British Right, 1918–1939* (London, 1986); Barbara Storm Farr, *The Development and Impact of Right-Wing Politics in Britain 1903–1932* (New York, 1987); S. Cullen, 'The Development of the Ideas and Policy of the British Union of Fascists, 1932–1940', *Journal of Contemporary History*, 22, 1 (1987), pp 115–36; David Stephen Lewis, *Illusions of Grandeur: Mosley, Fascism and British Society, 1931–81* (Manchester, 1987); David Baker, *Ideology of Obsession: A. K. Chesterton and British Fascism* (London, 1996).
3 See Robert Benewick, *The Fascist Movement in Great Britain* (London, 1972); P. Cohen, 'The Police, the Home Office and Surveillance of the British Union of Fascists', *Intelligence and National Security*, 1, 3 (1986), pp 416–34; J. Hope, 'British Fascism and the State 1917–1927: A Re-examination of and Impact of the Documentary Evidence', *Labour History Review*, 57, 3 (1992), pp 53–77; Panikos Panayi (ed.), *Minorities in Wartime: National and Racial Groupings in Europe, North America and Australia during the Two World Wars* (Oxford, 1993); Stephen M. Cullen, 'Political Violence: The Case of the British Union of Fascists', *Journal of Contemporary History*,

28, 3 (1993), pp 245–67; Richard Thurlow, *The Secret State: British Internal Security in the Twentieth Century* (Oxford, 1994); Alfred William Brian Simpson, *In the Highest Degree Odious: Detention without Trial in Wartime Britain* (Oxford, 1992); David Renton, *Fascism, Anti-Fascism and Britain in the 1940s* (London, 2000); N. Hillman, '"Tell me chum, in case I got it wrong. What was it we were fighting during the war?": The Re-emergence of British Fascism, 1945–58', *Contemporary British History*, 15, 4 (2001), pp 1–34.

4 A ground-breaking account along this line of enquiry is Richard Griffiths, *Fellow Travellers of the Right: British Enthusiasts for Nazi Germany, 1922–39* (London, 1980). Unable to speak for herself, David Pryce Jones's *Unity Mitford: A Quest* (London, 1976) provides many clues as to the informal foreign relations between Unity and the Nazi elite. See also William J. West, *Truth Betrayed* (London, 1987), and Adrian Weale, *Renegades* (London, 1994).

5 Studies in this genre range from the scholarly and high political, such as Robert Skidelsky's controversial biography, *Oswald Mosley* (London, 1975), to the more personal and to journalistic and popular accounts. Following on from Oswald Mosley's *My Life* (London, 1968), other autobiographies followed suit: Diana Mosley, *A Life of Contrasts* (London, 1977) and *Loved Ones: Pen Portraits* (London, 1985). Nicholas Mosley's *Rules of the Game* (London, 1982) and *Beyond the Pale* (London, 1983) combined original material gleaned from exclusive access to family papers with personal recollections, and enlivened by the dynamic literary style of one of Britain's important post-war novelists. Other Mosley relations have also contributed their own tomes: Jonathan and Catherine Guinness, *The House of Mitford: Portrait of a Family* (London, 1984). Nicholas Mosley's family memoir was the basis for the 1998 Channel 4 biopic, *Mosley*, and this type of popular fascination has been further fed by such works as Jan Dalley, *Diana Mosley: A Life* (London, 1999), and Anne De Courcy, *The Viceroy's Daughters: The Lives of the Curzon Sisters* (London, 2000). Trevor Grundy, *Memoirs of a Fascist Childhood: A Boy in Mosley's Britain* (London, 1998) offers an inside account of the Union Movement from the perspective of the son of rank-and-file members, and Francis Beckett's biography of his father, *The Rebel Who Lost his Cause: The Tragedy of John Beckett, MP* (London, 1999), is another good example of the next generation's coming to terms with the deeds and misdeeds of the fathers.

6 During the 1980s, and especially the 1990s, the Home Office has released a wealth of documentary evidence relating to official responses to extremist political activity during the 1920s, 1930s and the Second World War, with the result that the collection at the Public Record Office in Kew is an indispensable archive for historians. With the guiding light of Professor Colin Holmes and Richard Thurlow, based at the University of Sheffield, the University of Sheffield Library, Special Collections, has amassed an impressive archive of published and unpublished primary material on the extreme Right. Other important collections for the study of the extreme Right include the Weiner Library, the LSE Library, the Parkes Library at the University of Southampton, and the University of Birmingham Special Collections. Further, since the 1980s, former BUF members have broken their silence, been more willing to be interviewed by historians, and been the source of a growing body of published mat-

erial. Arguably motivated by the attention conferred on Mosley's apologia of 1968 – *My Life* – among his Blackshirt followers to follow suit with their own version of events have been John Christian (ed.), *Mosley's Blackshirts: The Inside Story of the British Union of Fascists 1932–1940* (London, 1986), and John Charnley, *Blackshirts and Roses* (London, 1990), as well as the unpublished autobiographies by R. R. Bellamy, 'The Memoirs of a Fascist Beast' (University of Sheffield, British Union Collection), and N. Driver, 'From the Shadows of Exile' (J. B. Priestley Library, University of Bradford).

7 See Roger Eatwell, 'Why has the Extreme Right Failed in Britain', in P. Hainsworth (ed.), *The Extreme Right in Europe and the USA* (London, 1992) and Mike Cronin (ed.), *The Failure of British Fascism* (London, 1996).

8 See Thomas Linehan, *British Fascism, 1918–1939: Parties, Ideology and Culture* (Manchester, 2000) and Philip Coupland, 'Blackshirt Utopians', *Journal of Contemporary History,* 33, 2 (1998) pp 255–72.

9 See Tony Kushner and Kenneth Lunn (eds), *The Politics of Marginality: Race, Radical Right and Minorities in 20th Century Britain* (London, 1990); Martin Durham, *Women and Fascism* (London, 1998); Tony Collins, 'Return to Manhood: The Cult of Masculinity and the British Union of Fascists', *International Journal of the History of Sport*, 16, 4 (1999), pp 145–61; R. M. Douglas, *Feminist Freikorps: The British Voluntary Women Police, 1914–1940* (Westport, 1999); Julie V. Gottlieb, *Feminine Fascism: Women in Britain's Fascist Movement, 1923–1945* (London, 2000); Julie V. Gottlieb, '"Motherly Hate": Gendering Anti-Semitism in the British Union of Fascists', *Gender and History,* 14, 2 (2002), pp 294–320.

10 See Elazar Barkan, *The Retreat of Scientific Racism: Changing Concepts of Race in Britain and the United States between the Wars* (Cambridge, 1992); Richard Griffiths (ed.), *The Pen and the Sword: Right-Wing Politics and Literary Innovation in the Twentieth Century* (London, 2000); and Dan Stone, *Breeding Superman: Nietzsche, Race and Eugenics in Edwardian and Interwar Britain* (Liverpool, 2002). At present, intellectual historians are bringing new verve to an existing historiography. For a longer perspective on the development of the historiography on the intellectual, literary and high cultural history of the British far Right also see J. R. Harrison, *The Reactionaries* (London, 1966); A. Hamilton, *The Appeal of Fascism: A Study of the Intellectual and Fascism, 1919–45* (London, 1971); Martin Green, *Children of the Sun: A Narrative of 'Decadence' in England After 1918* (London, 1976); J. Carey, *The Intellectuals and the Masses: Pride and Prejudice among the Literary Intelligentsia, 1880–1939* (London, 1992).

11 Roger Griffin, 'The Primacy of Culture: The Current Growth (or Manufacture) of Consensus within Fascist Studies', *Journal of Contemporary History,* 37, 1 (2002), pp 21–43.

12 See, for example, Griffin, 'The Primacy of Culture'; Walter Adamson, *Avant-Garde Florence: From Modernism to Fascism* (Cambridge, Mass., 1993); Mark Affron and Mark Antliff (eds), *Fascist Visions: Art and Ideology in France and Italy* (Princeton, 1997); Mabel Berezin, *Making the Fascist Self: The Political Culture of Fascist Italy* (Ithaca, 1997); Günter Berghaus (ed.), *Fascism and Theatre* (Oxford, 1996); Emilio Gentile, *The Sacralisation of Politics in Fascist Italy* (Cambridge, Mass., 1996).

13 The BUF's 'organic' version of culture is discussed at greater length in Thomas Linehan's contribution to a recent debate on the relevance of

culture to fascist studies. See David Roberts, Alexander De Grand, Mark Antliff and Thomas Linehan: 'Comments on Roger Griffin, "The Primacy of Culture: The Current Growth (or Manufacture) of Consensus within Fascist Studies"', *Journal of Contemporary History*, 37, 2 (2002), pp 259–74.

14 George Mosse, 'Fascist Aesthetics and Society: Some Considerations', *Journal of Contemporary History*, 31, 2 (1996), pp 245–52.

Women and the Nation

1 The author would like to acknowledge financial assistance given to support research for this chapter by the Social Sciences and Humanities Research Council of Canada and the Northrop Frye Centre at Victoria University in the University of Toronto. He would also like to thank Professors Trevor Lloyd, Richard Rempel, Stephen Heathorn and the editors of this book for their comments on this chapter.

2 For just a small selection see Martin Durham, *Women and Fascism* (London and New York, 1998); Claudia Koonz, *Mothers in the Fatherland: Women, the Family and Nazi Politics* (New York, 1987); Jost Hermand, 'All Power to the Women: Nazi Concepts of Matriarchy', *Journal of Contemporary History*, 19, 4 (1984), pp 649–67; Victoria de Grazia, *How Fascism Ruled Women, Italy 1922–1945* (Berkeley and Los Angeles, 1992); Robin Pickering-Iazzi (ed.), *Mothers of Invention: Women, Italian Fascism and Culture* (Minneapolis and London, 1995); Barbara Spackman, *Fascist Virilities: Rhetoric, Ideology and Social Fantasy in Italy* (Minneapolis and London, 1996); Paul Corner, 'Women in Fascist Italy: Changing Family Roles in the Transition from an Agricultural to an Industrial Society', *European History Quarterly*, 23, 1 (1993), pp 51–68.

3 Julie V. Gottlieb, *Feminine Fascism: Women in Britain's Fascist Movement, 1923–1945* (London and New York, 2000); Julie V. Gottlieb, 'Women and Fascism in the East End' in Tony Kushner and Nadia Valman (eds), *Remembering Cable Street: Fascism and Anti-Fascism in British Society* (London, 2000), pp 31–47; Martin Durham, *Women and Fascism*; Martin Durham, 'Women and the British Union of Fascists' in Tony Kushner and Kenneth Lunn (eds), *The Politics of Marginality* (London, 1990), pp 3–18; Martin Durham, 'Gender and the British Union of Fascists', *Journal of Contemporary History*, 27, 3 (1992), pp 513–27.

4 For example, Oswald Mosley, the leader of the BUF used 'constant vituperation against old men, old women and fathers' (both real and imagined), Gottlieb, *Feminine Fascism*, p 111.

5 For the crucial emphasis on hypermasculinity in the BUF see Tony Collins, 'Return to Manhood: The Cult of Masculinity and the British Union of Fascists', *International Journal of the History of Sport*, 16, 4 (1999), pp 145–62, and Gottlieb, *Feminine Fascism*, esp. pp 106–12. On the link between masculinity and violence for the fascists see Stephen M. Cullen, 'Political Violence: The Case of the British Union of the Fascists', *Journal of Contemporary History*, 28, 3 (1993), pp 245–67 and Martin Pugh, 'The British Union of Fascists and the Olympia Debate', *Historical Journal*, 41, 2 (1998), pp 529–42.

6 Martin Pugh, *The Tories and the People* (Oxford, 1985), pp 12–13.

7 Ibid., pp 28–31. Another interesting though unpublished study is Diane Sheets, 'British Conservatism and the Primrose League: The Changing

Character of Popular Politics, 1883–1901', (PhD dissertation, Columbia University, 1986). On the Primrose League and new versus old Conservatives see E. H. H. Green, *The Crisis of Conservatism: The Politics, Economics and Ideology of the British Conservative Party, 1880–1914* (London and New York, 1995), p 107.

8 Andrew J. Davies, *We, the Nation: The Conservative Party and the Pursuit of Power* (London, 1995), p 138; Frans Coetzee, 'Villa Toryism Reconsidered: Conservatism and Suburban Sensibilities in Late-Victorian Croydon', *Parliamentary History,* 16, 1 (1997), p 44.

9 One of the best overall treatments is Martin Pugh, *Electoral Reform in War and Peace 1906–1918* (London, 1978). Recent works include Sandra Stanley Holton, *Suffrage Days: Stories from the Women's Suffrage Movement* (New York, 1996); Angela V. John and Claire Eustace (eds), *The Men's Share? Masculinities, Male Support and Women's Suffrage in Britain, 1890–1920* (New York, 1997) and Martin Pugh, *The March of the Women: A Revisionist Analysis of the Campaign for Women's Suffrage, 1866–1914* (Oxford, 2000). Historians on the opposition to women's suffrage are not as wide ranging: Brian Harrison, *Separate Spheres: The Opposition to Women's Suffrage in Britain* (London, 1978) still remains one of the best-known works though it has been by supplemented by biographical studies such as John Sutherland, *Mrs. Humphry Ward* (Oxford, 1990).

10 G. E. Maguire, *Conservative Women: A History of Women in the Conservative Party, 1874–1997* (Basingstoke, 1998); For the impact of female enfranchisement on the Conservatives see David Jarvis, 'The Conservative Party and the Politics of Gender, 1900–1939', in Martin Francis and Ina Zweiniger-Bargielowska (eds), *The Conservatives and British Society, 1880–1980* (Cardiff, 1996), pp 172–93.

11 One of the few exceptions was over the Ulster issue. Conservatives sometimes tried to mobilize Britannia to rouse opposition to the supposedly traitorous impulses of the Liberal government. See 'No Ulster Medal!' National Union of Conservative and Unionist Associations (hereafter referred to as NU) No. 1790, Conservative Party Archives Pamphlet Collection (hereafter referred to as CPA) 1914/117. On general histories of the origins of Britannia as a symbol see Madge Dresser, 'Britannia', in Raphael Samuel (ed.), *Patriotism: The Making and Unmaking of British National Identity,* Volume III – National Fictions (London and New York, 1989), pp 26–50 and Roy T. Matthews, 'Britannia and John Bull: From Birth to Maturity', *The Historian*, 62, 4 (2000), pp 799–820.

12 A figure of Britannia represented imperial unity to commemorate the Colonial Conference of 1907, 'Britannia's Throne', *Primrose League Gazette*, XIV, 5 (May 1907), p 1. An image of Britannia in a living tableau of Empire performed at a Primrose League gathering in Lincolnshire appeared in July 1907, 'The Flag', *Primrose League Gazette*, XIV, 7 (July 1907), p 9. In June 1911, the League recommended that League habitations organize a floral march of children with banners representing all parts of the Empire filing past a figure of Britannia. 'A Floral March', *Primrose League Gazette*, XIX, 21 (June 1911), pp 10, 15.

13 'Mrs. Free Trade Cobdenism Objects to Colonial Preference', *Primrose League Gazette*, XIX, 17 (February 1911), p 12; 'A New Year's Gift to the Empire', *Primrose League Gazette*, XXI, 40 (January 1913), p 1.

14 Judy Giles, *Identity and Private Life in Britain, 1900–50* (Houndmills and London, 1995), p 2.

15 Ibid.

16 Martin Pugh, 'Women, Food and Politics, 1880–1930', *History Today,* 41 (March 1991), p 19.

17 Jon Lawrence, 'Class and Gender in the Making of Urban Toryism', *English Historical Review,* CVIII, 428 (July 1993), pp 629–52.

18 As Alison Light has said, Baldwin's England became 'a nation of gardeners and housewives', Alison Light, *Forever England: Femininity, Literature and Conservatism Between the Wars* (London and New York, 1991), p 211.

19 Frans Coetzee, *For Party or Country: Nationalism and the Dilemmas of Popular Conservatism in Edwardian England* (New York and Oxford, 1990), p 3.

20 Matthew Hendley, '"Help us to Secure a Strong, Healthy, Prosperous and Peaceful Britain": The Social Arguments of the Campaign for Compulsory Military Service in Britain, 1899–1914', *Canadian Journal of History,* XXX, 2 (August 1995), pp 261–88.

21 Joni Lovenduski, Pippa Norris and Catriona Burness 'The Party and Women', in Anthony Seldon and Stuart Ball (eds), *Conservative Century: The Conservative Party Since 1900* (Oxford, 1994), p 619.

22 Richard Thurlow, *Fascism in Britain: A History, 1918–1985* (Oxford, 1987), pp 1–2.

23 Gottlieb, *Feminine Fascism,* pp 11, 13.

24 Gottlieb has cited Ernest Nolte's definition of a fascist minimum as including 'anti-communism, anti-liberalism, anti-conservatism, leadership principle, party army and the aim of totalitarianism', Gottlieb, *Feminine Fascism,* p 33.

25 Thomas Linehan, *British Fascism, 1918–1939: Parties, Ideology and Culture* (Manchester and New York, 2000), p 69.

26 Bonar Law speaking at Blenheim in July 1912 argued that 'force in Ulster would overthrow parliamentary majorities if necessary and he assured the party's support in advance with no limitations.' John Ramsden, *The Age of Balfour and Baldwin, 1902–1940* (London and New York, 1978), p 78. On Bonar Law's political strategy towards Ulster see Jeremy Smith, 'Bluff, Bluster and Brinkmanship: Andrew Bonar Law and the Third Home Rule Bill', *Historical Journal,* 36, 1 (1993), pp 161–78.

27 Pugh, *The Tories and the People,* p 90.

28 Ibid., p 174.

29 'The Primrose League and Sir Edward Carson', *Primrose League Gazette,* XXII, 52 (January 1914), p 8; Miss Graham Hope, the organizing secretary of the Women's Unionist Association and Mr Gerald Arbuthnot, the Vice Chancellor of the Primrose League served as Hon. Secretaries for the joint organization. 'Help the Ulster Women Committee', *Primrose League Gazette,* XXII, 52 (January 1914), p 3.

30 'Vice Chancellor's Letter', *Primrose League Gazette,* XXII, 53 (February 1914), p 7.

31 Pugh, *The Tories and the People,* p 165.

32 'Vice Chancellor's Monthly Letter', *Primrose League Gazette,* XXII, 59 (August 1914), p 7. Other historians have noted the 'very elaborate scheme' which had been drawn up, A. T. Q. Stewart noted that the wives and families of the Ulster Volunteer Force as well as women and children

in vulnerable outlying areas were given priority for evacuation: A. T. Q. Stewart, *The Ulster Crisis* (London, 1968), pp 231–2.

33 'Ulster's Appeal to the British Public', CPA 1913/76; 'Ulster's Appeal', CPA 1914/120.

34 'A Vote for the Radical Means a Widow in Ulster', NU No. 1776, CPA 1914/120.

35 'The Wives of Ulster: Rally for the Struggle', *Daily Mail*, 21 January 1914, p 5.

36 Lady Edward Cecil and Mrs Rudyard Kipling both assisted with the Ulster women refugee scheme and both had similar experiences during the South African war. See 'Vice Chancellor's Monthly Letter', *Primrose League Gazette*, XXII, 59 (August 1914), p 7. For other accounts see The Viscountess Milner, *My Picture Gallery, 1886–1901* (London, 1951), pp 137–8.

37 Other work included needlework, the sale of special commemorative stamps for war relief and collections of funds to purchase ambulances.

38 This type of domestic patriotism became wide-ranging throughout British society during the war. See Paul Ward, '"Women of Britain Say Go": Women's Patriotism in the First World War', *Twentieth Century British History*, 12, 1 (January 2001), pp 31–3.

39 On National Insurance see Derek Fraser, *The Evolution of the British Welfare State: A History of Social Policy since the Industrial Revolution* (second edition, Basingstoke, 1984), pp 163–76; Bentley Gilbert, *The Evolution of National Insurance in Great Britain: The Origins of the Welfare State* (London, 1966).

40 'The National Insurance Bill, 1911 – Do you Keep a Servant?', NU No. 1465, CPA 1911/13; 'The National Insurance Bill, 1911 – Have You a Child in Service?', NU No. 1464, CPA 1911/14. Fraser notes that the press focused on the bureaucratic elements of the scheme and 'stirred up public opposition, especially among mistresses and their servants, against the "monstrous scheme of stamp licking"', Fraser, *The Evolution of the British Welfare State*, p 167.

41 Green, *The Crisis of Conservatism*, pp 193, 240–1, 206, 260–3.

42 Alan Sykes, *Tariff Reform in British Politics, 1903–1913* (Oxford, 1979), p 56.

43 'The Child's Appeal', NU No. 1245, CPA 1910/28.

44 'Dearer Living and Less Comfort', NU No. 693, CPA 1908/6.

45 'Ask Your Wife', NU No. 1349, CPA 1910/127.

46 'The Dear Loaf Lie – an Exposure', NU No. 1296, CPA 1910/76.

47 'The Woman and the Canvasser', NU No. 1261, CPA 1910/44.

48 'What Line does the Primrose League Take on the Fiscal Question?', *Primrose League Gazette*, XI, 2 (February 1904), p 10.

49 Pugh, *The Tories and the People*, pp 160–2, 168–71.

50 'Picture Politics for the Man in the Street', *Primrose League Gazette*, XI, 10 (October 1904), p 5; 'Mrs. Free Trade Cobdenism Objects to Colonial Preference', *Primrose League Gazette*, XIX, 17 (February 1911), p 12.

51 Conservative Party, *Fighting Notes. With a Few General Directions Upon Canvassing*, p 5; CPA 1912/8.

52 Anthony Howe, *Free Trade and Liberal England, 1846–1946* (Oxford, 1997), p 275.

53 Lawrence, 'Class and Gender', p 646.

54 Ibid., p 646; 'The Socialist Catechism: The Working-Man and Socialist', *Primrose League Gazette*, XV, 1 (January 1908), p 12.

55 'Under Socialism – Mr. Keir Hardie in the State Nurseries', *Primrose League Gazette*, XV, 10 (October 1908), p 7.

56 'When the Socialist Millennium Arrives', NU No. 696, CPA 1908/9; 'Socialism and the Family', NU No. 682, CPA 1907/49; NU No. 992, CPA 1909/257; 'What Socialism Means', NU No. 681, CPA 1907/48; NU No. 991, CPA 1909/256; 'Socialism and your Children', NU No. 1044, CPA 1914/3; NU No. 1044, CPA 1909/309; 'Socialism and Irreligion', NU No. 898, CPA 1909/163.

57 Lawrence, 'Class and Gender', p 651.

58 Pugh, *The Tories and the People*, p 184.

59 Ramsden, *The Age of Balfour and Baldwin*, pp 250–1; Neal R. McCrillis, *The British Conservative Party in the Age of Universal Suffrage: Popular Conservatism, 1918–1929*, (Columbus, Ohio, 1998), pp 21, 46–82; Pugh, *The Tories and the People*, pp 178–83. Although there are no total post-war membership figures, the strength of the League can be seen by post-war annual enrolments. These reached a post-war peak in 1924 with the election of the first ever Labour government with 28,030. After 1924, the numbers began to decline with a momentary rise in the year of the General Strike and reached a low point in 1929 with 11,425 new members enrolled. See Matthew Hendley, 'Patriotic Leagues and the Evolution of Popular Patriotism and Imperialism in Great Britain, 1914–32', (PhD dissertation, University of Toronto, 1998), pp 337–46.

60 For League concerns over educating newly enfranchised women voters see 'The Primrose League: Annual Report of Grand Council to Grand Habitation, 1927–28', Bodleian Library, Oxford. Primrose League Papers. MSS Primrose League 6/1. No. 16. 1914–32. Leafs 1003–5. See also Mrs Ian Malcolm, 'Speaker's Classes', *Primrose League Gazette*, XXVII, 115 (May 1919), p 1.

61 'The whole attitude of the Conservative Party is childish. Hours of valuable time is spent in idle talk, social parties, whist drives, and games for the young members of the Primrose League.' Quoted from 'Why I Left the Tories: A Woman Explains', *Action*, 28 May 1938, in Gottlieb, *Feminine Fascism*, p 135. Anne Brock Griggs attended a Primrose League rally at the Royal Albert Hall and found nothing to praise in the political activism of Conservative women. Griggs grew tired to 'see woman after woman pass, to see the same face eternally repeated: the face of the woman conservative worker', quoted from 'Baldwin's Lips Unsealed: Anne Brock Griggs Reports His Speech to the "Primroses"', *Blackshirt*, 13 May 1936, in Gottlieb, *Feminine Fascism*, p 135.

62 For example, Linda Colley has shown the use of gendered images to satirize the political activities of the Duchess of Devonshire in the eighteenth century. 'The Devonshire Amusement, 1784' in Linda Colley, *Britons: Forging the Nation, 1707–1837* (New Haven and London, 1992), p 245.

63 'The Happy Radical Family – Hopeless Disagreement', CPA 1905/30, NU No. 374; 'A Happy Family' – Picture Leaflets, 1905 # 18. CPA 1905/85.

64 'Mrs. Bannerman's Cabinet Pudding', 1905, Conservative Central Office No. 387, CPA 1905/43.

65 'The Empty Cupboard', NU No. 730, CPA 1908/42.

66 'John Bull's Kitchen (Too Many Cooks)', NU No. 732, CPA 1908/44.

67 'The Fallen Idol', *Primrose League Gazette*, XXI, 46 (July 1913), p 5; 'The Detected Smugglers' and 'A Slight Rally', *Primrose League Gazette*, XXI, 51 (December 1913), p 5; 'This Month's Cartoon', *Primrose League Gazette*, XXX, 38 (November 1912), p 5.

68 'Home (rule) Made', *Primrose League Gazette*, XIX, 21 (June 1911), p 6; 'In Mid-Stream', *Primrose League Gazette*, XIX, 23 (August 1911), p 1.

69 'The Fallen Idol', *Primrose League Gazette*, XXI, 46 (July 1913), p 5; 'John Bull and the Lady', *Primrose League Gazette*, XXII, 52 (January 1914), p 6.

70 'The Dress Exhibition', *Primrose League Gazette*, XV, 3 (March 1908), p 5.

71 'In Leading Strings: The Penalty of being Little', *Primrose League Gazette*, XVIII, 5 (February 1910), p 1; 'An Unwelcome Partner', *Primrose League Gazette*, XIX, 15 (December 1910), p 10; 'Untitled', *Primrose League Gazette*, Election Supplement – December 1910; 'More than He Bargained For', *Primrose League Gazette*, XIX, 23 (August 1911), p 10; 'The Cold, Cold Tub!', *Primrose League Gazette*, XX, 30 (March 1912), p 8.

72 On British comedians who used cross-dressing see Robert Ross, *Benny Hill – Merry Master of Mirth* (London, 1999) and Robert Ross, *Monty Python Encyclopedia* (London, 1979).

73 Jarvis, 'The Conservative Party and the Politics of Gender', p 184.

74 'Women's Suffrage', *Primrose League Gazette*, XIV, 3 (March 1907), p 20; 'The Primrose League and Women's Suffrage', *Primrose League Gazette*, XVII, 2 (November 1909), p 6.

75 Hendley, 'Patriotic Leagues and the Evolution of Popular Patriotism', pp 160–2.

76 'Women's Suffrage', NU No. 708. CPA 1908/21.

77 Lisa Tickner, *The Spectacle of Women: Imagery of the Suffrage Campaign* (Chicago, 1988), pp 192–205.

78 Unlike the organizations supporting female suffrage like the Artists Suffrage League and the Suffrage Atelier, there was no organization with large numbers of Conservative female artists providing images to use as propaganda, Tickner, *The Spectacle of Women*, pp 13–26.

79 On the Conservative fears of losing male members to the BUF see Jarvis, 'The Conservative Party and the Politics of Gender', p 181.

80 Gottlieb notes that it attracted a number of older Conservative women such as Mercedes Barrington (who had assisted the Conservatives in elections since 1918) and Viscountess Downe who were adopted as prospective parliamentary candidates for the BUF in 1936, Gottlieb, *Feminine Fascism*, pp 70–4.

Reactionary Spectatorship

1 Arthur Kenneth Chesterton, *Oswald Mosley. Portrait of a Leader* (London, n.d.), p 114.

2 For the purposes of this chapter, 'contemporary cinema' refers to both the domestic film industry and the corpus of motion pictures arriving in Britain from overseas, particularly from the United States, Nazi Germany and Fascist Italy.

3 Peter Miles and Malcolm Smith, 'The British Film Industry and the Hollywood Invasion', in Peter Miles and Malcolm Smith, *Cinema, Literature and Society: Elite and Mass Culture in Interwar Britain* (Beckingham, 1987), p 166.

4 The quota was set initially at five per cent, rising to twenty per cent by 1935.
5 *Action*, 22 April 1939; *Action*, 24 July 1937 on Chesterton.
6 *Action*, 24 July 1937.
7 *Blackshirt*, 13 July 1934.
8 *Action*, 2 October 1937.
9 On the 'culture industry' theory, see Andreas Huyssen, *After the Great Divide. Modernism, Mass Culture and Postmodernism* (London, 1986), pp 19–25.
10 Anthony Aldgate and Jeffrey Richards, *Best of British. Cinema and Society from 1930 to the Present* (London, 1999), p 6.
11 Miles and Smith, 'The British Film Industry and the Hollywood Invasion', p 163.
12 Ibid., p 164.
13 Stephen Shafer, *British Popular Films 1929–1939* (London, 1997), p 2.
14 John Stevenson, *British Society 1914–1945* (Harmondsworth, 1984), p 396.
15 John Ellis, *Visible Fictions* (London, 1982), p 81.
16 Aldgate and Richards, *Best of British*, p 4.
17 Aldous Huxley, *Brave New World* (London, 1932).
18 John Frederick Charles Fuller, *The Dragon's Teeth. A Study of War and Peace* (London, 1932), p 37.
19 *Blackshirt*, 11 January 1935; and *New Pioneer*, February 1939.
20 *Action*, 23 July 1936.
21 *Action*, 27 August 1936.
22 *Blackshirt*, 4 January 1935.
23 *Blackshirt*, 28 September 1934.
24 *Action*, 29 January 1938.
25 *Blackshirt*, 28 September 1934.
26 *Fascist Bulletin*, 20 February 1926.
27 *Action*, 14 November 1936.
28 *Action*, 13 August 1936.
29 *Fascist Week*, 20–6 April 1934.
30 *Blackshirt*, 11 January 1935.
31 *Blackshirt*, 21 November 1936.
32 *Blackshirt*, 28 September 1934.
33 *Action*, 29 January 1938.
34 Ibid.
35 Jonathan Munby, *Public Enemies. Public Heroes. Screening the Gangster From Little Caesar to Touch of Evil* (Chicago, 1999), p 13. On the Horatio Alger myth, see E. Mitchell, 'Apes and Essences: Some Sources of Significance in the American Gangster Film', in Barry Grant (ed.), *Film Genre Reader 11* (Austin, 1995), pp 203–12.
36 On fascist responses to the city, see Thomas Linehan, *British Fascism, 1918–1939: Parties, Ideology and Culture* (Manchester, 2000), pp 245–57.
37 See Thomas Schatz, *Hollywood Genres* (New York, 1981), pp 82–5, and Munby, *Public Enemies. Public Heroes*, pp 45–6.
38 Ibid., p 45.
39 Ibid.
40 Andrew Bergman, 'Frank Capra and Screwball Comedy, 1931–1941', in Gerald Mast and Marshall Cohen (eds), *Film Theory and Criticism* (Oxford, 1979), pp 769–70.

41 *Action*, 27 August 1936.
42 Ibid.
43 *Action*, 24 April 1937.
44 *Patriot*, 26 August 1926.
45 *Action*, 3 September 1936.
46 *Blackshirt*, 21 November 1936.
47 *Action*, 31 October 1936.
48 Ibid.
49 *Action*, 26 March 1936.
50 *Patriot*, 26 August 1926.
51 Ibid.
52 Ibid.
53 *Action*, 3 September 1936.
54 *Fascist Week*, 20–6 April 1934.
55 *Action*, 3 September 1936.
56 *Blackshirt*, 21 September 1934.
57 Ibid.
58 *Action*, 13 August 1936.
59 *Patriot*, 29 March 1928.
60 Ibid.
61 Ibid.
62 *Patriot*, 24 March 1927 and 19 January 1928.
63 See Linehan, *British Fascism*, pp 16, 95.
64 *Patriot*, 1 December 1927.
65 *Blackshirt*, 9 November 1934.
66 Ibid.
67 Ibid.
68 *The Fascist*, April 1934.
69 *Patriot*, 23 April 1925.
70 *Blackshirt*, 21 November 1936.
71 Ibid.
72 On this theme, see Edward Said, *Orientalism* (London, 1978).
73 *Action*, 2 October 1937.
74 *Action*, 27 March 1937.
75 Ibid.
76 Ibid.
77 *Action*, 18 February 1939.
78 Chesterton, *Oswald Mosley*, p 159.
79 *Patriot*, 25 February 1925.
80 *Action*, 17 April 1937.
81 *Action*, 2 December 1937.
82 Ibid.
83 *Action*, 17 April 1937.
84 *Action*, 2 December 1937.
85 *Action*, 17 April 1937.
86 Ibid.
87 *New Pioneer*, April 1939.
88 *Action*, 30 December 1937.
89 *Action*, 2 December 1937. *The White Squadron* won the Mussolini Cup in Venice in 1936.
90 *British Union Quarterly*, III, 4 (October–November 1939), p 65.

91 Chesterton, *Oswald Mosley*, p 159.
92 *New Pioneer*, April 1939.
93 Eric Rentschler, *The Ministry of Illusion. Nazi Cinema and Its Afterlife* (Cambridge, Mass., 1996), p 180.
94 *Blackshirt*, 1 March 1935.
95 Ibid.
96 *Action*, 9 January 1937.
97 *Action*, 6 March 1937.
98 Ibid.
99 See above and *Action*, 3 September 1936 on *Mary of Scotland*.
100 *New Pioneer*, May 1939.
101 *Action*, 17 April 1937.
102 See the review in *Blackshirt*, 17 May 1935.
103 Rentschler, *The Ministry of Illusion*, p 75.
104 On this theme, see Linda Schulte-Sasse, *Entertaining the Third Reich: Illusions of Wholeness in Nazi Cinema* (Durham, 1996), pp 132–3, and pp 62–7, on an interesting application of the horror narrative to Nazi anti-Semitic films like *Jew Süss*.
105 *Blackshirt*, 17 May 1935.
106 Ibid.
107 *Action*, 3 July 1937 and *Action*, 11 September 1937.
108 *Fascist Week*, 20–6 April 1934.
109 Morando Morandini, 'Italy From Fascism to Neo-Realism', in *The Oxford History of World Cinema* (Oxford, 1996), p 355.
110 Eric Rentschler, 'Germany: Nazism and After', in *The Oxford History of World Cinema*, p 377.
111 Ibid.
112 *Action*, 24 April 1937.
113 Walter Benjamin , 'The Work of Art in the Age of Mechanical Reproduction', in Mast and Cohen, *Film Theory and Criticism*, pp 848–70; Siegfried Kracauer, *From Caligari To Hitler: A Psychological History of the German Film* (Princeton, 1947).
114 Rentschler, 'Germany: Nazism and After', p 379.
115 Ibid., p. 378.

'This Fortress Built Against Infection'

1 It will soon become clear that this chapter is concerned primarily with the ideological matrix underlying the BUF's diagnosis of the state of the theatre and musical arts. It is thus not concerned with the biographical profiles of individual artists and intellectuals who devoted their creative or critical skills to the BUF, nor with actual performances of theatrical or musical works put on by BUF members or under the aegis of the BUF. I hope that a student of fascism is waiting in the wings to fill this lacuna.
2 The closest to such a monograph is Alexander Raven-Thomson's *Civilisation as Divine Superman* which was published in 1932 just before the creation of the BUF and at least a year before Raven-Thomson fell under Mosley's spell. It nonetheless expounds the (slightly adapted) Spenglerian philosophy of history which informed all his subsequent ideological productions for the BUF including his important corporatist theory. It also displays fascinating parallels and contrasts with the numerous cyclic

theories of history elaborated by other fascist ideologues (Arthur Rosenberg, Adolf Hitler, Julius Evola, Giovanni Gentile, Francis Yockey and Oswald Mosley himself). The most probing account of Raven-Thomson's philosophy of history to date is Peter Pugh, 'A Political Biography of Alexander Raven Thomson' (unpublished PhD thesis, University of Sheffield, 2001) which I hope will one day appear in book form. Significantly, Spengler himself, after the success of *Der Untergang des Abendlandes*, developed his own anti-tragic, counter-deterministic (and deeply fascist) vision of rebirth based on the concept of Caesarism, even though both the Nazis and Mosley continued to brand him as a 'fatalist' and a 'pessimist'.

3 'Publicism' refers to cultural production in the written media in the form of newspapers, pamphlets, and periodicals. In this case it is synonymous with the BUF press.

4 For a sense of how the present chapter fits into comparative studies of fascist culture and an example of how a relatively homogeneous cultural vision can underlie the highly heterogeneous aesthetics of another fascist movement, see Roger Griffin, 'The Sacred Synthesis: The Ideological Cohesion of Fascist Culture', *Modern Italy*, III, 1 (1998), pp 5–23. This analysis in turn is rooted in the emergent academic consensus (pioneered by George L. Mosse in the 1960s and Stanley Payne and Zeev Sternhell in the 1970s) that fascism is to be seen as a revolutionary form of nationalism whose mythic core is the vision of a total cultural (rather than economic or political) regeneration (palingenesis). On the growing acceptance of this approach to generic fascism see Roger Griffin, 'The Primacy of Culture: the Growth (or Manufacture) of Consensus in Fascist Studies', *Journal of Contemporary History*, 37, 1 (2002), pp 21–43. For an important analysis of the central preoccupation with cultural decadence and renewal within British fascism in general see Thomas Linehan, *British Fascism 1918–39. Parties, Ideology and Culture* (Manchester, 2000), chs 8–11, a book which appeared after this chapter was written but which is in full harmony with the 'new consensus' and vital for locating this chapter in the wider context of BUF ideas of cultural decadence and regeneration explored here. For a collection of pioneering essays on fascism and Nazism which prepared the ground for this approach see George L. Mosse, *The Fascist Revolution* (New York, 1999).

5 Partly under Raven-Thomson's influence, Oswald Mosley devised his own eclectic cyclic theory of the rise and fall of civilizations, equally influenced by Oswald Spengler's *Decline of the West*. For Mosley's own account of his own 'anti-determinist' version of Spenglerism, which he unveiled in a major speech given to the English Speaking Union in March 1933, see ch. 17, 'The Ideology of Fascism. Science and Caesarism', in his autobiography *My Life* (London, 1968). See also Richard Thurlow, 'Destiny and doom: Spengler, Hitler and "British" Fascism', *Patterns of Prejudice*, 15, 4 (1981).

6 A. L. Glasfurd, 'Fascism and the English Tradition', *Fascist Quarterly*, 1, 3 (July 1935), pp 360–4.

7 Mosley, 'The Ideology of Fascism', p 330.

8 *Action*, 17 August 1934.

9 In this text 'fascism' refers to generic fascism, while 'Fascism' refers specifically to the fascism of the BUF, or where the context makes it clear, Italian Fascism.

10 Alexander Raven-Thomson, *The Coming Corporate State* (London, 1937), p 45.
11 A. K. Chesterton, 'The Cancer of Jewish Art', *Action*, 24 July 1937.
12 E. D. Randall, 'Fascism and Culture: The True Place of Creative Genius', *Blackshirt*, 23 March 1934.
13 Theo Lang, 'Britain's Leadership and Britain's Culture: Fascism Lends its Strength to the Eternal Realities of Man', *Blackshirt*, 9 January 1937.
14 Mosley, 'The Ideology of Fascism', pp 316–17.
15 Ibid., p 330.
16 H. A. Harvey, *Blackshirt*, 4 October 1934.
17 *Action*, 31 July 1937.
18 Glasfurd, 'Fascism and the English Tradition', p 363.
19 Mosley, 'The Ideology of Fascism', p 328.
20 *Blackshirt*, November 1938, Editorial.
21 It is to be stressed that the jeremiads on contemporary society so familiar in fascist ideology are only to be seen as expressions of 'cultural pessimism' if we accept that the 'despair' is dialectically related to hope in imminent rebirth, in other words is an integral component of the palingenetic mind-set.
22 Arthur Reade, 'The Defence of Western Civilization, Part 1', *British Union Quarterly*, III, 3 (July–September 1939), p 16.
23 A. K. Chesterton, 'Our Cultural Inheritance Debased by Aggressive Cosmopolitans', *Action*, 31 October 1936.
24 Chesterton, 'The Cancer of Jewish Art', pp 10–11.
25 Henry Gibbs, 'Crisis in the English Theatre', *Action*, 6 January 1938.
26 Raven-Thomson, *The Coming Corporate State*, p 43.
27 Ezra Pound, 'A Cultural Level', *British Union Quarterly*, II, 2 (April–June 1938), p 41.
28 Reade, 'The Defence of Western Civilization, 1', p 16.
29 Ibid.
30 Raven-Thomson, *The Coming Corporate State*, p 45.
31 Ibid.
32 Chesterton, 'The Cancer of Jewish Art', p 11.
33 K. T. Duffield, '"Fascintern" or "Pan-Europa"?', *British Union Quarterly*, III, 3 (July–September 1939), pp 58–9.
34 Chesterton, 'The Cancer of Jewish Art', p 11.
35 E. D. Randall, 'Fascism and Culture', *Blackshirt*, 23 March 1934.
36 Anne Cutmore, 'Assumed and Deliberate Barbarism is Decadence', *Blackshirt*, 17 August 1934.
37 A. K. Chesterton, *Blackshirt*, 14 September 1934.
38 John Rumbold, 'Dangers of our Film Censorship', *British Union Quarterly*, I, 3 (July–September 1937), pp 45–55.
39 The original version (1956) of this film is pervaded by the anti-communist paranoia of the McCarthy years.
40 Chesterton, 'The Cancer of Jewish Art', p 11. Samuel Goldwyn was the cinema magnate and Hore-Belisha was minister of transport at the time Chesterton was writing, and eventually secretary of state for war. They were also both Jews.
41 Alexander Raven-Thomson, 'Why Fascism', *Fascist Quarterly*, 1, 2 (1935), p 235.
42 Randall, 'Fascism and Culture', p 1.

43 Raven-Thomson, *The Coming Corporate State*, p 46.

44 There was indeed a huge state-sponsored Dante cult under Mussolini. Other candidates for fascist appropriation, such as Manzoni, Calderon, Goethe, Nietzsche, Wagner, Racine, Corneille, Homer, all required even more selective editing to become part of the nation's 'usable past' or long pre-existed its emergence as a modern state.

45 *Action*, 6 August 1936.

46 A. K. Chesterton, *Blackshirt*, 5 October 1934.

47 *Blackshirt*, 18 April 1935.

48 Anne Cutmore, 'The Drama's Reawakening', *Fascist Quarterly*, 1, 4 (October 1935) pp 490–1.

49 *Blackshirt*, 13 September 1935.

50 *Action*, 4 June 1938.

51 Martin Adeson, Jr, *Blackshirt*, 11 July 1936.

52 *Blackshirt*, 6 March 1937.

53 *Action*, 26 August 1939.

54 *Blackshirt*, 6 March 1937.

55 *Blackshirt*, 27 March 1937.

56 S. W. Wilkinson, 'Save the Music Halls', *Action*, 1 May 1937.

57 Gibbs, 'Crisis in the English Theatre'.

58 *Action*, 17 December 1938.

59 *Blackshirt*, 17 May 1935.

60 Chesterton, 'Our Cultural Inheritance Debased', p 7.

61 John F. Porte, 'Rescue British Music', *Fascist Week*, 9–15 February 1934.

62 Selwyn Watson, 'The Future of Music', *Blackshirt*, 21 December 1934.

63 I am using this phrase loosely to refer to the most articulate and educated of the many ideologues of fascism (Raven-Thomson, A. K. Chesterton etc.) who contributed to the BUF's publicistic production of propaganda and doctrine, which was prodigious given the size of the BUF membership.

64 Reader's letter to *Blackshirt*, 15 March 1935.

65 Porte, 'Rescue British Music'.

66 John Porte, 'Merrie England. A Lovable Opera of National Music', *Fascist Week*, 25–31 May 1934.

67 Captain Cuthbert Reavely, 'Hotch-potch of Garvin and Beachcomber', *Blackshirt*, 25 April 1935.

68 Reade, 'The Defence of Western Civilization, 1', p 16.

69 *Action*, 30 October 1937.

70 *Blackshirt*, 7 December 1934.

71 *Blackshirt*, 16 May 1936.

72 *Action*, 2 April 1936.

73 *Blackshirt*, 24 July 1937.

74 George Baker, 'The Tragedy of the Concert Hall', *Blackshirt*, 12 October 1934.

75 *Blackshirt*, 7 August 1937.

76 *Action*, 4 June 1936.

77 *Action*, 16 July 1932.

78 Watson, 'The Future of Music'.

79 Cutmore, 'The Drama's Reawakening', pp 489–95.

80 Reader's letter, *Blackshirt*, 15 March 1935.

81 Porte, 'Rescue British Music', p 7.

82 *Action*, 30 October 1937.
83 Oswald Mosley, *The Greater Britain* (first edition, London, 1932), pp 31–2.
84 Oswald Mosley, *The Greater Britain* (second edition, London, 1934), p 41.
85 Oswald Mosley, *Fascism: 100 Questions Asked and Answered* (London, 1936), Qu. 25, pp 23–5.
86 Randall, 'Fascism and Culture', p 1.
87 Raven-Thomson, *The Coming Corporate State*, pp 43–6.
88 Cutmore, 'The Drama's Reawakening'.
89 Raven-Thomson, *The Coming Corporate State*, pp 43–6.
90 Wilkinson, 'Save the Music Halls'.
91 Cutmore, 'The Drama's Reawakening'.
92 Another BUF commentator, writing in *Blackshirt*, 30 January 1937, was particularly impressed by the way the Nazi Strength through Joy organized local variety shows and the People's Stage (*Volksbühne*) put on plays at affordable prices.
93 Raven-Thomson, *The Coming Corporate State*, p 45.
94 Leigh Vaughan-Henry, 'Fascist Culture', *Blackshirt*, 18 January 1935.
95 Raven-Thomson, *The Coming Corporate State*, p 48.
96 Vaughan-Henry, 'Fascist Culture', p 6.
97 Edwin Cornforth, *Action*, 17 August 1934.
98 *Action*, 14 May 1936.
99 *Blackshirt*, 29 June 1934.
100 See the detailed scheme proposed in Wilkinson, 'Save the Music Halls'.
101 For the typically palingenetic text of this song see Roger Griffin, *Fascism* (Oxford, 1995), pp 177–8.
102 *Action*, 11 June 1936.
103 See, for example, the advertisement for the Blackshirt Dance Band playing at the Surrey Blackshirt Ball in *Blackshirt*, 15 March 1935, or for 'Jazz without Jews' in *Blackshirt*, 4 September 1937. For a brilliant analysis of the ideological complexities and tensions within the Nazi jazz scene see Michael Kater, *Different Drummers. Jazz in the Culture of Nazi Germany* (Oxford, 1992).
104 'Cornish Opera's Success at the Lyceum', *Blackshirt*, 12 July 1935.
105 Porte, 'Merrie England'.
106 Porte, 'Rescue British Music'.
107 On the complex relationship between Nazism and Modernism in music see Michael Kater, *The Twisted Muse. Musicians and their Music in the Third Reich*, (Oxford, 1997); for the anti-modernist law which operates in the painting of totalitarian regimes see Igor Golomstock, *Totalitarian Art in the Soviet Union, the Third Reich, Fascist Italy, and the People's Republic of China*, (London, 1990).
108 Selwyn Watson, 'Enthusiastic Audience at B.U.F. Concert', *Blackshirt*, 27 December 1935.
109 Albert Lynden, 'Why Germany Banned Jewish Culture', *Blackshirt*, 25 July 1936.
110 *Action*, 31 July 1937.
111 *Blackshirt*, 15–22 July 1933.
112 'The Cleansing Flame', *Blackshirt*, 22 August 1936.
113 Eveline Marlow, 'Jewish Theatrical Agencies', *Blackshirt*, 4 December 1935.
114 'Bluebird', 'The Death of Tunefulness', *Action*, 30 October 1937.

115 Arthur Reade, 'The Defence of Western Civilisation, Part 2', *British Union Quarterly*, III, 1 (October–December 1939), p 61.
116 Duffield, '"Fascintern" or "Pan-Europa"?', pp 44–60.
117 See Philip Coupland, 'The Blackshirted Utopians', *Journal of Contemporary History*, 33, 2 (1998).
118 Marla Stone, 'The State as Patron. Making Official Culture in Fascist Italy', in Matthew Affron and Mark Antliff (eds), *Fascist Visions. Art and Ideology in France and Italy*, (Princeton, 1997).
119 Oswald Mosley, 'Wagner and Shaw: A synthesis', *The European*, 17 March 1956, p 61.

The Developing British Fascist Interpretation of Race, Culture and Evolution

1 Robert Skidelsky, *Oswald Mosley* (London, 1975), pp 317–33.
2 Gisela Lebzelter, *Anti-Semitism in England 1918–1939* (Basingstoke, 1978), pp 49–109.
3 Richard Thurlow, *Fascism in Britain: From Oswald Mosley's Blackshirts to the National Front* (revised edition, London, 1998), pp 61–131.
4 Anthony James Gregor, *The Ideology of Fascism* (London, 1969), pp 257–8.
5 Ibid., pp 245–82; R. Thurlow, 'Fascism and Nazism – No Siamese Twins', *Patterns of Prejudice*, 14, 1 (1980), pp 5–16.
6 John Morell, 'Arnold Leese and the Imperial Fascist League: the Impact of Racial Fascism', in Kenneth Lunn and Richard Thurlow (eds), *British Fascism* (London, 1980), pp 57–75.
7 Oswald Mosley, 'The World Alternative', *Fascist Quarterly*, 2, 3 (July 1936), p 384.
8 Oswald Mosley, *Mosley, Right or Wrong* (London, 1961) pp 125–6, Oswald Mosley, 'The World Alternative', *Mosley Newsletter*, 3 (January–February 1947), p 391.
9 Richard Thurlow, 'The "Jew-Wise": Dimensions of British Political Anti-Semitism 1918–1939', *Immigrants and Minorities*, 6, 1 (1987), pp 44–65.
10 Public Records Office (PRO), Home Office (HO) 144/21377/28 Special Branch report.
11 *The Britons Patriotic Society* (founded 1918), pamphlet (London, n.d.). On the history of the Britons see Lebzelter, *Anti-Semitism in England*, pp 49–67, and Colin Holmes, *Anti-Semitism in British Society* (London, 1979), pp 141–60.
12 G. P. Mudge, 'Pride of Race', *The Hidden Hand or The Jewish Peril*, V, 2 (February 1924).
13 G. P. Mudge, 'Pride of Race', *The Hidden Hand or The Jewish Peril*, V, 3 (March 1924).
14 G. P. Mudge, 'Pride of Race', *The Hidden Hand or The Jewish Peril*, V, 4 (April 1924).
15 George L. Mosse, *The Crisis of German Ideology* (London, 1966), pp 1–125; G. C. Field, *Evangelist of Race: The Germanic Vision of Houston Stewart Chamberlain* (New York, 1981), pp 199–244.
16 John Morell, 'The Life and Opinions of A. S. Leese' (unpublished MA thesis, University of Sheffield, 1974), pp 6–51.
17 Thurlow, *Fascism in Britain*, pp 47–51.
18 PRO, HO 45/24967/105 MI5 report on IFL, 1942.

19 Arnold Spencer Leese, 'Communism and Race', *Fascist*, October 1931 and June 1932.
20 Arnold Spencer Leese, 'The Nordics', *Fascist*, February 1933.
21 Arnold Spencer Leese, 'The Colour Problem in Great Britain', *Fascist*, June 1932.
22 Arnold Spencer Leese, 'Some Questions and Answers', *Fascist*, March 1933.
23 Arnold Spencer Leese, 'Death from Poison', *Gothic Ripples*, 14 (11 April 1946).
24 Hans Guenther, *The Racial Elements of European History* (London, 1927), p 517; Madison Grant, *The Passing of the Great Race* (New York, 1970), p vii; Lothrop Stoddard, *The Revolt against Civilisation* (London, 1925), p 12.
25 Roger Eatwell, *Fascism: A History*, (London, 1995), pp 259–75, D. Prowe, '"Classic Fascism" and the New Radical Right in Western Europe: Comparisons and Contrasts', *Contemporary European History*, 3, 3 (1994), pp 289–313.
26 John Tyndall, *Six Principles of British Nationalism* (London, 1965); John Tyndall, *The Eleventh Hour* (London, 1989).
27 John Tyndall, 'The Creed of a Nationalist', *Spearhead*, December 1978.
28 John Tyndall, 'In the case of Anglo-Saxondom', *Spearhead*, October 1979.
29 John Tyndall, 'Tyndall Speaks. Our Anglo-Saxon Heritage' (tape, New National Front 1982).
30 John Tyndall, 'Decline of the Briton', *Spearhead*, March 1982.
31 Oswald Mosley, *The Greater Britain* (London, 1932, 1934); Oswald Mosley, *The Alternative* (Ramsbury, 1947).
32 A. L. Glasfurd, 'Fascism and the English Tradition', *Fascist Quarterly*, 1, 3 (July 1935), pp 360, 363.
33 David Baker, *Ideology of Obsession. A. K. Chesterton and British Fascism* (London, 1996), pp 91–120.
34 James Drennan, *BUF, Oswald Mosley and British Fascism* (London, 1934), p 30.
35 Mosley, *The Alternative*, p 76.
36 Oswald Mosley, 'The Philosophy of Fascism', *Fascist Quarterly*, 1, 1 (January 1935), p 43; Eric Bentley, *The Cult of the Superman*, (Gloucester, Mass., 1946).
37 Oswald Mosley, *Tomorrow We Live* (London, 1938), pp 25, 289.
38 R. Thurlow, 'Destiny and Doom: Spengler, Hitler and British Fascism', *Patterns of Prejudice*, 15, 4 (1981), pp 17–33.
39 Francis Hitching, *The Neck of the Giraffe* (London, 1982), pp 143–5.
40 George W. Stocking, Jr, *Race, Culture and Evolution* (New York, 1968), pp 234–69.
41 Marvin Harris, *The Rise of Anthropological Theory* (London, 1969), pp 81f.
42 Mosley, *Tomorrow We Live*, p 72.
43 Mosley, *The Alternative*, p 311.
44 Mosley, 'The Philosophy of Fascism', p 43; Oswald Mosley, *My Life* (London, 1968), p 311.
45 Mosley, *Tomorrow We Live*, p 70; George Bernard Shaw, *Back to Methuselah* (London, 1922), pp ix–lxxxv.
46 Skidelsky, *Oswald Mosley*, p 512.
47 For the Mendelian-Biometrician controversy on genetic inheritance see Robin Marantz Henig, *A Monk and Two Peas* (London, 2000), pp 192–218.

48 Ulrika Segerstrale, *Defenders of the Truth* (Oxford, 2000), pp 177–84; Andrew Brown, *The Darwin Wars* (London, 1999).
49 R. Verrall, 'Karl Marx's Piltdown Men', *Spearhead*, February 1978.
50 R. Verrall, 'Sociobiology: the Instincts in our Genes', *Spearhead*, March 1979.
51 R. Verrall, 'Science is Championing our Creed of Social Nationalism', *New Nation*, 1 (Summer 1980).
52 Edward Wilson, *Sociobiology* (London, 1975); Richard Dawkins, *The Selfish Gene* (Oxford, 1989); Stephen Rose, Richard Lewontin and Leonard Kamin, *Not in Our Genes* (Harmondsworth, 1990); Stephen Gould, *The Mismeasure of Man* (London, 1986); Martin Barker, *The New Racism* (London, 1981).

Britain's New Fascist Men

1 Oswald Mosley, *The Greater Britain* (London, 1932), p 40.
2 See Martin Durham, *Women and Fascism* (London, 1998), and Julie V. Gottlieb, *Feminine Fascism: Women in Britain's Fascist Movement, 1923–1945* (London, 2000).
3 Walter Benjamin, 'The Work of Art in the Age of Mechanical Reproduction', in *Illuminations* (London, 1992), p 234.
4 Tony Collins, 'Return to Manhood: The Cult of Masculinity and the British Union of Fascists', *International Journal of the History of Sport*, 16, 4 (December 1999), pp 145–62.
5 J. A. Mangan (ed.), *Shaping the Superman: Fascist Body as Political Icon – Aryan Fascism* (London, 1999), p xi.
6 George Mosse, *The Image of Man: The Creation of Modern Masculinity* (New York, 1996), pp 156–60.
7 George L. Mosse, 'Fascist Aesthetics and Society: Some Considerations', *Journal of Contemporary History*, 31, 2 (1996), pp 245–52.
8 Barbara Spackman, *Fascist Virilities: Rhetoric, Ideology and Social Fantasy in Italy* (Minneapolis, 1996), p xii.
9 A. K. Chesterton, 'Return to Manhood', *Action*, 9 July 1936.
10 Joanna Bourke, *Dismembering the Male: Men's Bodies, Britain and the Great War* (London, 1996), p 19.
11 'Youth and Physical Training: Where Fascism Attracts', *Manchester Guardian*, 7 June 1934.
12 See Hugh Ross Williamson, 'Youth's Alternative: Fascism or Communism', *Everyman*, 4 April, 1934; 'Youth Versus Age a False Issue', *Nottingham Guardian*, 2 February 1934.
13 The BUF organized in defence of the memory of the First World War dead, but the construction of manhood that accompanied this fascist war commemoration was far more complicated than those rather obvious images of fascist machismo that catalysed youth gang violence. In the late 1930s the BUF's metamorphosis from a hoard of hooligans into a party advocating international peace, and this redirection of ideological priorities, also modified their memories of the First World War dead.
14 'Come, All Young Britain', in *Songs of British Union: Twelve Songs* (London, n.d.).
15 'A Marching Song', in *Songs of British Union*.

16 Hannan Swaffer, 'I Heard Yesterday: Pricking the Great Fascist Bubble', *Daily Herald*, 11 April 1934. He reported on a case where a member, upon resigning in indignation over the 'smash-and-grab' violence of the Black-shirt stewards, was summoned to attend a court martial at BUF headquarters. He was tried, condemned and expelled.

17 'What this Paper Stands For', *Action*, 8 October 1931.

18 Oswald Mosley, 'Ancient Gentlemen at War', *Action*, 15 October 1931.

19 *The New Times*, June 1932.

20 E. Hamilton Piercy, *The New Times*, July 1932.

21 See also 'Mosley Party to Have Storm Troops', *Daily Herald*, 20 August 1932.

22 Public Records Office (PRO), Home Office (HO) 144/19070/50–60.

23 'Fascists' New Citadel: A "Brown House" in Chelsea', *Daily Telegraph*, 30 August 1933.

24 'Where London Gangsters are Trained', *Daily Worker*, 24 July 1934.

25 The whole question of drilling was legally contentious, and as a result the BUF frequently made public statements to clarify their position. See 'The Fascist Army', *Manchester Guardian*, 5 July 1934.

26 G. E. de Burgh Wilmot, 'Fascism: Rights to Free Speech', *Yorkshire Post*, 2 June 1934.

27 Alexander Raven-Thomson, *The Coming Corporate State* (London, 1937) The pamphlet evokes the decline of the British empire and makes the analogy with the decline of the Roman. Raven-Thomson complains that British men are spectators and not participants at football games, and this is an indication of the physical and spiritual degeneration of youth. He observed the same difference between Greece and Rome, between the athlete and the gladiator.

28 Collins, 'Return to Manhood'.

29 'Why Sir Oswald Mosley Cancelled a Meeting', *Sunday Dispatch*, 24 June 1934.

30 Blackshirt weddings included those of Unit-Leader Baxter and Miss Flor-ence Brown, both of the Islington branch in May 1934; the 'first deo-Fascist wedding' in Liverpool of Fascist Elizabeth Price and U/L Charles Nurse, and Fascist De O'Farrel and Fascist John Morris (*Blackshirt*, 25–31 May 1934); another Blackshirt wedding in Hull between B. O. Robert J. Piper Officer i/c Hull Branch and Marjorie McDonald of the Women's Section: 'The bride was attended by four bridesmaids, the two adults being dressed in white costume with red, white and blue cravats.' ('Blackshirt Wedding in Hull', *Blackshirt*, 29 June 1934); and the Fascist wedding of Mr A. C. V. Bristol, Inspecting Officer of the London Branches of the BUF to Lillias Francis-Hawkins, sister of the Officer-in-Command, London Area in June 1934. There was a Fascist funeral in May 1934, and Fascist christenings were common, such as that of the daughter of Mr and Mrs (Gandhi) Kershaw in May 1934.

31 'Miss Vivien Mosley Opens Bazaar', *Fascist Week*, 22–8 December 1933.

32 'Fascist Architecture: A Reply to a Question to Sir Oswald Mosley', *Architects Journal*, 17 April 1934.

33 'Blackshirts at Battersea', *Manchester Guardian*, 2 September 1935.

34 'Blackshirt Meeting in East End', *Daily Mail*, 8 June 1936.

35 'The Blackshirts Have Definite Remedies for Unemployment', *Evening News*, 16 April 1934.

36 Viscount Rothermere, 'Hurray for the Blackshirts', *Daily Mail*, 15 January 1934.

37 Ibid.

38 J. S. Alan, 'What the Blackshirts are Doing', *Sunday Dispatch*, 17 June 1934.

39 W. J. Leaper, 'Eighty Percent of our Young Men Below C.3 Standard', *Fascist Week*, 15–21 December 1933.

40 Ann Page, quoted in John Christian (ed.), *Mosley's Blackshirts: The Inside Story of the British Union of Fascists*, (London, 1986), p 16.

41 See Gottlieb, *Feminine Fascism*, ch. 2.

42 Oswald Mosley, *My Life* (London, 1968), p 344.

43 See 'Fascist Fiction: Official Membership', *News Chronicle*, 6 February 1934.

44 'Why so Many Women Support the Blackshirt Movement', *Evening News*, 18 April 1934.

45 'Mussolini – The Man', *Action*, 28 February 1936.

46 'Searchlight over Britain: Action Challenges the Mood of Defeat', *Action*, 21 February 1936.

47 One of the most poisonous indictments Mosley could make against his left-wing opponents was that they allowed women to do the men's work of political rabble-rousing. At a meeting at the city hall in Sheffield: 'Later, when a woman kept interrupting, Sir Oswald said, amid laughter, "She is getting a little excited. They have not much control over them in the Socialist Party. Women run the whole party. They do it very well."' 'Sir O. Mosley's Great Rally', *Daily Mail*, 29 June 1934.

48 From the 'Blackshirt Marching Song'.

49 While the BUF glorified male violence, violence engineered by their own kind and for their own purpose, a change in direction was discernable by the outbreak of the Second World War, and when the BUF launched its peace campaign. Under these circumstances, the movement evoked images of the mutilated male body, mutilated by a war machine gone astray. See Capt. R. Gordon-Canning, MC, *Mind Britain's Business: British Union Foreign Policy,* (c. 1939) Gordon-Canning also evokes the apocalypse, Revelations etc. as the BUF's aesthetic sensibility became increasingly messianic with they outbreak of a war they opposed.

50 A. K. Chesterton, 'Return to Manhood: Regiment of Old Women Routed', *Action*, 9 July 1936.

51 Quoted in Christian (ed.), *Mosley's Blackshirts*, pp 4–5.

52 'The East London Shopkeeper, Leonard Wise', in Christian (ed.), *Mosley's Blackshirts*, p 4.

53 Raven-Thomson, *The Coming Corporate State*.

54 Charles Greenwood, 'Sex Appeal to Bloomsbury Bacilli', *Blackshirt*, 2 May 1936.

55 'Exhibition – or Exhibitionism: The Surrealists', *Action*, 2 July 1936.

56 'Lucifer', 'The Intellectual Noxiousness of Bloomsbury Socialists', *Fascist Week*, 17–23 November 1933.

57 A. K. Chesterton, 'To the Intellectuals: You Shall Cater for a Sane and Virile Nation', *Fascist Week*, 5–11 January 1934.

58 Blackshirt anti-Semites held the Jew himself, and the Jew alone, responsible for fomenting anti-Semitism; see, especially, A. K. Chesterton, *Apotheosis of the Jew: From Ghetto to Park Lane* (London, n.d.).

59 'As soon as Fascism was born in Britain, however, the Jews saw an excellent opportunity of currying favour with our race. Playing upon the old idea of the Englishman, sportsman and lover of fair play, they pretended that those terrible Fascists were persecuting them for no reason at all ...', E. G. Clarke, *The British Union and the Jews* (Nuneaton, n.d.). The Jew was imagined as a vampire, a cancer, a degenerate force in the body politic and the body of British manhood. His socio-biological profile was anathema to the Englishman soldier type.

60 This contention that the Blackshirts were only responding to violence was a point Mosley emphasized time and again: see Sir Oswald Mosley, 'The Blackshirts are Advancing: And the People of Britain are With Us', *Sunday Dispatch*, 11 February 1934.

61 'The Man Who Keeps Order', *Sunday Dispatch*, 18 February 1934.

62 At the Quartermaster Stores of the BUF, located at Madeira Hall in Streatham, the following could be purchased: badges, bathing costumes, belts, brass ware (ash trays, bells, brushes, forks, knockers, pokers), blouses, caps, cuff links, Blackshirt dolls, jackets, notepaper, pencils, pennants, pullovers, shoes, shirts, skirts, ties and trousers. See Robert Saunders Collection, University of Sheffield, file A. 1.

63 Winifred Holtby and Norman Ginsbury, *Take Back Your Freedom* (London, 1939), p 41.

64 'Mosley!', in *Songs of British Union*.

65 Oswald Mosley, 'More Freedom in Private Life', *Sunday Dispatch*, 27 May 1934.

66 From a speech delivered on 8 May 1937, quoted in *Mosley: The Facts*, p 91.

67 Oswald Mosley, 'Steel Creed of an Iron Age', *Fascist Week*, 17 November 1933. 'It is right to build this new movement of the modern age, to bring to Britain this tremendous expression of the very soul of post-war manhood in this urge to achieve its salvation.' 'Building a Great Home Market', *Daily Mail*, 2 June, 1934 – Mosley speaking at Usher Hall in Scotland.

68 Mosley, *The Greater Britain*, p 39.

69 A. K. Chesterton, 'Return of Manhood: Regiment of Old Women Routed', *Action*, 9 July 1936.

70 Chesterton, *Oswald Mosley: Portrait of a Leader*, p 164.

71 Mosley, *My Life*, p 303.

72 Ibid., p 305. In his post-war thinking, Mosley developed a somewhat modified typology of men, with three categories: the 'Will to Comfort' man (democracy), the 'Will to Power' man (self-serving authoritarianism), and the 'Will to Achievement' man or the 'Thought Deed' man. The latter was the ideal type and would bring to being his new European idea. See Mosley, *The Alternative*, pp 289–95.

73 Gerald Barry, 'No Private Armies!', *News Chronicle*, 21 June 1934.

74 A. J. Cummings, 'The Political Peep-Show', *News Chronicle*, 13 June 1934.

75 Birch described three or four Blackshirt types, all of whom shared 'a conviction that they themselves are the custodians of the manly tradition and that tolerance is a feminine virtue'. Lionel Birch, *Why They Join the Fascists* (London, 1937), p 9.

76 'A New Phase of Fascism', *British Free Press*, 2 February 1934.

77 J. A. Spender, 'The Bravo in Politics', *News Chronicle*, 7 February 1934.

78 Swaffer, 'I Heard Yesterday'.

79 'Where London Gangsters are Trained'.
80 'Another Fascist Resigns', *Jewish Chronicle*, 27 May 1938.
81 'Mosley is an orator, possibly the most effective in England. He has what is known as "magnetism", and a manner which acquaintances find personally charming. He has sex-appeal of a sort. For some people his appearance resembles that of a traditional cavalry officer, for others that of a traditional gigolo.' Lionel Birch, *Why They Join the Fascists*, p 38.
82 Quoted in Brian Harrison, *Prudent Revolutionaries: Portraits of British Feminists between the Wars* (Oxford, 1987), p 97.

The Black Shirt in Britain

1 Walter Benjamin, 'The Work of Art in the Age of Mechanical Reproduction', in *Illuminations* (London, 1973), pp 219–44, esp. pp 243–4.
2 The best description of BUF uniforms is still Colin Cross, *The Fascists in Britain* (New York, 1963; first published 1961), pp 75–6. Although including some useful illustrations of fascist insignia, the pamphlet by the collector Jamie Cross is very sketchy in its treatment (*British Fascist Regalia from the 1920s to 1940* (Newmarket, 1994)). Aside from brief mentions in passing, historians of dress have not explored the meaning of British fascist uniform. The most detailed treatment to date is in John Harvey's study of the use of black in the history of male dress (*Men in Black* (London, 1997; first published 1995), pp 239–43). Simonetta Falasca-Zamponi's study of Italian Fascism not only indicates the general utility of what might be called the 'new cultural history' to studies of fascism, but also to the investigation of the place of uniform in fascist political culture (*Fascist Spectacle: The Aesthetics of Power in Mussolini's Italy* (Berkeley, CA, 1997), pp 100–5).
3 'Plain Dealer', 'Blackshirt Ballyhoo', *Truth*, 115 (13 June 1934), pp 940–1.
4 On the semiotics of dress see Roland Barthes, *The Fashion System* (Berkley, CA, 1990, first published 1967); theoretical approaches to the interpretation of dress are discussed in Fred Davies, *Fashion, Culture, and Identity* (Chicago, 1992); and the historiography of dress history is dealt with in Christopher Breward, 'Cultures, Identities, Histories: Fashioning a Cultural Approach to Dress', *Fashion Theory*, 2, 4 (1998), pp 301–14. For the specific topic of uniform see Nathan Joseph, *Uniforms and Nonuniforms: Communication Through Clothing* (New York, 1986).
5 Geoffrey Gorer, *Nobody Talks Politics: A Satire with an Appendix on Our Political Intelligentsia* (London, 1935), p 93.
6 Oswald Mosley, *My Life* (London, 1968), p 302.
7 C. S. Sharpe (Assistant Director-General of Organisation), letter to Robert Saunders, 20 May 1936, Robert Saunders Papers, University of Sheffield (RSUS), MS119/A2/288 (i–ii).
8 Harold Nicolson, *Diaries & Letters 1930–39* (1969), p 89.
9 'James Drennan' [W. E. D. Allen], *BUF, Oswald Mosley and British Fascism* (London, 1934), p 243.
10 *Action*, 30 January 1937.
11 'Should Blackshirts Be Banned?', *Spectator*, 152 (15 June 1934), p 910.
12 *Daily Mail*, 22 January 1934.
13 Winifred Holtby, *Women and a Changing Civilisation* (London, 1934), p 3.

14 Beverley Nichols, *A Thatched Roof* (London, 1936; first published 1933), p 109.
15 *Punch or The London Charivari*, 6 September 1933, p 257.
16 Robert Bernays, 'The Future of British Fascism', *Spectator*, 157 (18 December 1936), p 1075.
17 'Why We Wear the Black Shirt', *Sunday Dispatch*, 21 January 1934, p 11.
18 A. K. Chesterton, *Oswald Mosley: Portrait of a Leader* (London, 1937), pp 119–20.
19 Nicolson, *Diaries & Letters*, p 89; *TNT: The New Times*, 1 (June 1932), p 2; 2 (July 1932), p 2; 3 (August–September, 1932), p 6.
20 The author of the 'Greyshirt Anthem', Malcolm Moir, placed Mosley's fascist movement in the succession of Italian Fascist and Nazi movements, the song's chorus began: 'First the Blackshirt, then the Brownshirt, now the Greyshirt legions stand' (University of Birmingham, Special Collections, Oswald Mosley papers, Box 8).
21 Harvey, *Men in Black, passim.*
22 Lewis Broad and Leonard Russell, *The Way of the Dictators* (London, n.d., c. 1935), p 289.
23 Oswald Mosley, 'Old Parties or New?', *Political Quarterly*, 3 (1932), p 28.
24 Oswald Mosley, *Fascism: 100 Questions Asked and Answered* (London, 1936), Qu. 5.
25 Ivor Brown, 'War's New Ally: Fascism', in Philip Noel Baker, et al., *Challenge to Death* (London, 1934), pp 139–53, esp. p 145.
26 Oswald Mosley, *The Greater Britain* (London, 1932), pp 150–1.
27 'Dormouse', 'Maxton on the Spot', *New Clarion*, 2, 39 (4 March 1933), p 246.
28 *Hansard*, 317 (16 November 1936), col. 1388.
29 'The Goose Step', *G. K's Weekly*, 19 (14 June 1934), pp 225–6.
30 Cited in Cross, *The Fascists in Britain*, p 53.
31 E[ric] C. P[eake], letter to G. T. Wiltshire, 23 January 1936, RSUS, MS119/A1/322(ii).
32 *Action*, 17 October 1936.
33 Robert Gordon-Canning, 'What the Black Shirt Means', *Fascist Week*, 18–24 May 1934.
34 *Action*, 6 March 1937.
35 *Fascist Week*, 8–14 December 1934.
36 *Blackshirt*, 9–15 December 1933.
37 *Action*, 10 July 1937.
38 *Blackshirt*, 9–15 September 1933.
39 Ibid.
40 *Blackshirt*, 1 February 1935.
41 *Fascist Week*, 22–8 December 1933.
42 *Fascist Week*, 2–6 February 1934.
43 'Fascinating Fascism', in Susan Sontag, *Under the Sign of Saturn* (New York, 1980), pp 73–105, esp. p 94.
44 Phoebe Fenwick Gaye, 'Mosley à la Mode', *Time and Tide*, 15 (16 June 1934), pp 764–5; 'Sir Oswald Beats the Band', *Truth*, 115 (25 April 1934), p 646.
45 *New Leader*, 3 March 1933.
46 Mosley, *Fascism: 100 Questions*, Qu. 5.
47 *Daily Herald,* 18 April 1934; 20 April 1934; 26 April 1934.

48 *Daily Worker*, 6 October 1936.
49 Philip Gibbs, *England Speaks* (London, 1937), p 232.
50 *Sunday Chronicle*, 22 October 1933.
51 *Hansard*, 317 (16 November 1936), col. 1445.
52 *Hansard*, 286 (1 March 1934), col. 1249.
53 P. G. Wodehouse, *The Code of the Woosters* (London, 1978, first published 1938), p 51.
54 *Blackshirt*, 16 May 1933; *Fascist Week*, 25–31 May 1934; *Hansard*, 289 (16 May 1934), col. 1768; Edward Upward, *In The Thirties* (London, 1978), p 236.
55 *Church Times*, 27 April 1934, p 512.
56 'Review of the Week', *Time and Tide*, 15 (28 April 1934), pp 529–31.
57 K. Collett, 'Fascists in Action', *The Liberal Woman's News*, July 1934, p 99.
58 *Hansard*, 314 (10 July 1936), col. 1606.
59 'The Goose Step', pp 225–6.
60 E. M. Forster, 'Notes on the Way', *Time and Tide*, 15 (16 June 1934), p 765.
61 *The Spotlight on the Blackshirts* (Labour Party, 1934); *Fascism: The Enemy of the People* (Labour Publication Department, 1934), University of Warwick Modern Records Centre (MRC), MSS 127/NU/GS/3/7A.
62 National Council of Labour, *What is this Fascism?* (n.d., c. 1934), p 11.
63 *Fascism: The Enemy of the People*.
64 *New Leader*, 2 March 1934.
65 Arthur Wragg, 'Gentlemen's Outfitter', *Time and Tide*, 15 (23 June 1934), p 794.
66 'Rainbow-Coloured Politics', *Truth*, 115 (28 February 1934), p 31; see also Wyndham Childs, 'We Want no Private Armies!', *Labour*, 1, 6 (February 1934), p 136.
67 *Hansard*, 314 (10 July 1936), col. 1606.
68 *New Leader*, 6 January 1933; 3 March 1933; 9 March 1934; 4 June 1934; 3 August 1934; Public Record Office (PRO), Home Office (HO) 144/20158/114–16, cutting from *Daily Mail*, 21 February 1934; *Daily Telegraph*, 5 October 1936; PRO, HO 45/24999/1.
69 PRO, HO 45/25386/309; HO 45/25386/21; HO 45/25386/376; HO 144/20158/117; HO 144/20158/137; HO 144/20158/238.
70 Nancy Mitford, *Wigs on the Green* (London, n.d., c. 1935). '[R]ed, white and blue shirts' were also the attire of the 'Sons of Empire' in Kenneth Allott and Stephen Tait, *The Rhubarb Tree* (London, n.d., c. 1937), p 1.
71 Broad and Russell, *The Way of the Dictators*, p 280; my emphasis.
72 Linda Colley, *Britons: Forging the Nation, 1707–1837* (London, 1996; first published 1992), pp 385–98; on patriotism and the 'left' see Paul Ward, *Red Flag and Union Jack: Englishness, Patriotism, and the British Left, 1881–1924* (Woodbridge, Suffolk, 1998).
73 *Hansard*, 317 (16 November 1936), col. 1369.
74 Ibid., col. 1461.
75 'Plainshirt', 'Fascism in England: Can Mosley do it?', *Everyman*, 262 (2 February 1934), pp 9, 30.
76 *Hansard*, 286 (16 May 1934), col. 1766.
77 *Hansard*, 314 (10 July 1936), col. 1574.
78 *Daily Worker*, Supplement, 3 October 1936.
79 'Vicky', 'Breaches of the Peace?', *Time and Tide*, 27 (10 October 1936), p 1379.

80 Malcolm Muggeridge, *The Thirties: 1930–1940 in Great Britain* (London, 1940), p 211, n. 1.
81 *Hansard*, 317 (16 November 1936), col. 1440.
82 *Blackshirt*, 9–15 September 1933; original emphasis.
83 'Shamus Frazer' [James Arbuthnot], *A Shroud as well as a Shirt* (London, 1935), pp 111–12.
84 *Fascist Week*, 23 February–1 March 1934.
85 Cited in Jan Dally, *Diana Mosley: A Life* (London, 1999), p 188.
86 *Fascist Week*, 18–24 May 1934.
87 Oswald Mosley, 'Our Policy – Britain First!', *Saturday Review*, 157 (10 February 1934), pp 154–5.
88 *Action*, 14 November 1936.
89 For example, *Blackshirt*, 12 July 1935; 19 July 1935; 23 August 1935.
90 Mosley *Fascism: 100 Questions*, Qu. 5; see also Oswald Mosley, *Fascism in Britain* (London, n.d., *c.* 1933), pp 10–11.
91 *Blackshirt*, 9–15 March 1934; *Fascist Week*, 6–22 March 1934.
92 *Blackshirt*, 6 September 1935; 11 October 1935.
93 Mass Observation Archive, TC: Political Attitudes, 10/A, *Greater Britain Publications*, 11 (Autumn 1939).
94 Mosley, *Fascism: 100 Questions*, Qu. 6.
95 Mosley: *The Greater Britain*, p 40.
96 Oswald Mosley, *Blackshirt Policy* (n.d., *c.* 1934), p 16.
97 *Blackshirt*, 27 July 1934.
98 Chesterton, *Oswald Mosley*, pp 119–20.
99 'Leonard Banning Looks at the Old School Tie', *Blackshirt*, 12 October 1934, p 6.
100 *Blackshirt*, 24 August 1934.
101 *Daily Mail*, 22 January 1934.
102 H. G. McKechnie [Administrative Office (National Meetings)], letter to Robert Saunders, 14 April 1936, RSUS, MS119/A1/208; 'Badges of Rank – BUF Headquarters Staff', MRC, MSS 127/NU/GS/3/5A.
103 *Fascist Headquarters Bulletin*, 2 (n.d., *c.* 1933), PRO, HO 144/19070 56; British Union of Fascists and National Socialists (BUFNS), *Constitution and Regulations* (London, 1936), p 21.
104 'The Development of the British Union of Fascists', p 4, MRC, MSS127/NU/GS/3/5A.
105 *Fascist Headquarters Bulletin*, 2 (n.d., *c.* 1933), p 6, PRO, HO 144/19070; *Fascist Week*, 2–8 February 1934; BUFNS, *Constitution and Regulations*, p 17.
106 *Blackshirt*, 18 January 1935; BUFNS, *Constitution and Regulations*, p 36.
107 *Blackshirt*, 18 January 1935. It has been suggested that entitlement to wear the uniform progressed, garment by garment, according to the sales performance of the member. See Harvey, *Men in Black*, p 241. This is a misreading of an innovation whereby blackshirts could earn uniform items as 'prizes' in a sales incentive scheme. For example, the sale of 320 papers in four weeks entitled the member to a belt or shirt, 400 in five weeks to a uniform mackintosh, 800 in ten weeks to boots, breeches, or a greatcoat. See *Blackshirt*, 11 October 1935.
108 Robert Saunders, letter to Eric Burch, 12 February 1936, RSUS, MS119/A5/115(i).
109 BUFNS, *Constitution and Regulations*, p 26.
110 *Blackshirt*, 18 January 1935.

111 Nellie Driver, 'From the Shadows of Exile' (unpublished MS, n.d.), p 29, Nelson District Library.

112 Labour Party, *Report of the 36th Annual Conference held in The Usher Hall, Edinburgh, October 5th–October 9th 1936* (London, n.d., *c.* 1936), p 165.

113 BUF Quartermaster's Stores Price List (n.d., *c.* 1935), RSUS, MSS 119/A1/ 296; *Fascist Headquarters Bulletin*, 2 (n.d., *c.* 1933), p 6, PRO, HO 144/19070; *Blackshirt*, 28 February 1936, p 2; F. G. Palmer (General Manager, Abbey Supplies), letter to Robert Saunders, 10 June 1936, RSUS, MS119/A2/4.

114 Anonymous [Kay Fredericks], untitled (unpublished MS, n.d., *c.* 1937), MRC, MSS292/743/11/2.

115 Storm Jameson, *In the Second Year* (London, 1936), p 176.

116 'A. Freeman' [pseud.], *We Fight For Freedom* (London, 1936), p 61.

117 Martin Durham, *Women and Fascism* (London, 1998); Julie V. Gottlieb, *Feminine Fascism: Women in Britain's Fascist Movement, 1923–1945* (London, 2000).

118 Elizabeth Ewing, *Women in Uniform: Through the Centuries* (London, 1975), p 106; Richard Thurlow, *Fascism in Britain: A History, 1918–1985* (Oxford, 1987), photograph between pp 142–3.

119 *Hansard*, 290 (30 May 1934), col. 168.

120 Colin McDowell, *Hats: Status, Style and Glamour* (London, 1997; first published 1992), pp 25, 30–1, 97–9.

121 *Blackshirt*, 17 January 1936.

122 BUFNS, *Constitution and Regulations*, p 36.

123 *Blackshirt*, 21 December 1934.

124 Malcolm Muggeridge, 'Mosley Tries to go East', *Time and Tide*, 27 (10 October 1936), pp 1378–9.

125 *Blackshirt*, 16–22 February.

126 Driver, 'From the Shadows of Exile', p 20.

127 *Blackshirt*, 18 January 1935.

128 *Blackshirt*, 22 March 1935.

129 *Blackshirt*, 23 November 1934.

130 *Blackshirt*, 7–13 October 1933.

131 *Action*, 28 August 1937.

132 Philip Coupland, 'The Blackshirted Utopians', *Journal of Contemporary History*, 33, 2 (1998), pp 255–72, esp. pp 263–5.

133 *Fascist Week*, 24–30 November 1934.

134 *Blackshirt*, 18 January 1935.

135 Archibald Crawford, *Tartan Shirts* (London, 1936), pp 156, 267.

136 *Blackshirt*, 8 June 1934.

137 BUFNS, *Constitution and Regulations*, pp 18–19.

138 Ibid., p 30.

139 Mosley, *Fascism in Britain*, p 10.

140 *Blackshirt*, 5–11 January 1934.

141 Robert Saunders, personal statement on the 'Spirit of Fascism', 23 June 1934, p 8, RSUS, MS119/F2/3.

142 Robert Saunders, 'A Tiller of Several Soils' (unpublished MS), my thanks to Friends of Oswald Mosley for this reference.

143 Robert Saunders, letter to Eric Burch, 25 October 1936, RSUS, MS119/A6/ 165 (ii–iii).

144 *Fascist Week*, 4–10 May 1934.

145 Mosley, *Blackshirt Policy*, p 16.

146 *Blackshirt*, 7 September 1934.

147 John Hone, letter to Luttman-Johnson, 23 October 1935, Luttman-Johnson Papers, Imperial War Museum; Richard Reynell Bellamy, 'We Marched With Mosley: A British Fascist's View of the Twentieth Century' (undated MS, University of Sheffield Library), p 191.

148 Richmal Crompton, *William – The Dictator* (London, n.d., c. 1938), p 36 (my thanks to Charles Wilson, Just William Society for this reference).

149 H. G. Wells, *Experiment in Autobiography* (London, 1934), vol. 2, p 782.

150 H. G. Wells, *The Holy Terror* (London, 1939).

151 George Lancing, *Fraudulent Conversion: A Romance of the Gold Standard* (London, 1935), p 99.

152 *Left Review*, 2, 12 (September 1936), p 627.

153 *Guardian*, 4 March 1978, p 11.

154 Aldous Huxley, 'Notes on the Way', *Time and Tide*, 15 (3 March 1934), reproduced as 'The Prospects of Fascism in England', in David Bradshaw (ed.), *The Hidden Huxley* (London, 1995), pp 135–41, esp. pp 136–7.

155 *Blackshirt*, 2–8 March 1934.

156 'Hamadryad', 'Featuring Fascism', *Saturday Review* 157 (5 May 1934), p 500.

157 Viscountess Rhondda, *Notes on the Way* (London, 1937), p 111; original emphases; J. R. Clynes, *Memoirs: 1924–1937* (London, 1937), p 247.

158 Joseph, *Uniforms and Nonuniforms*, p 4.

159 Huxley, 'The Prospects of Fascism', pp 136–7.

160 [Kenneth C. G.] Dower and [William J.] Riddell, *Inside Britain: An Internal Scrapbook* (London, 1937), p 77.

161 Director-General of Organization, letter to All Districts, Special Instruction, 30 December 1936, RSUS, MSS119/A2/289; Special NHQ Instruction, 22 January 1937, RSUS, MSS119/A2/295.

162 Labour Party, *Report of the 36th Annual Conference*, p 165; 'Notes of a Deputation from the Manchester Watch Committee to the Home Secretary on Friday, 23rd October, 1936', PRO, HO 144/20159/13.

163 *The Tribune*, 9 July 1937.

164 For example, George Thayer, *The British Political Fringe: A Profile* (London, 1965), p 39.

165 The ambivalent effect of the Act is suggested in the responses of former fascists when questioned on this point. My gratitude goes to Stephen Cullen for very generously providing me with extracts from the oral history material he gathered for 'The British Union of Fascists, 1932–1940; Ideology, Membership and Meetings' (unpublished MLitt thesis, Oxford University, 1987).

166 *Blackshirt*, 2 January 1937.

167 Robert Saunders, letter to H. J. H. Bartlett, 14 December 1937, RSUS, MS119/A6/43, original emphasis.

168 Ronald Crisp, BUF Member West Ham (1936–7) and Epping (1937–9); taped interview, 8 August 1991 (I am grateful to Andrew Mitchell for kindly making this and other extracts from his interview transcripts available to me).

169 *Action*, 30 January 1937.

170 PRO, HO 45/25702 cited in 'The Leader's Birthday, 1942', *Comrade*, 9 (October/November 1987), p 5.

171 J. A. Booker, *Blackshirts-on-Sea: The story of the British Blackshirt Summer Camps in West Sussex, 1933–38* (London, 1999), p 110. See also the photograph of S. Grundy wearing the black shirt in Trevor Grundy, *Memoir of a Fascist Childhood: A Boy in Mosley's Britain* (London, 1998), between pp 116–17.

172 *Comrade*, 52 (November/December 1999), p 10.

173 See, for example, Francis Wheen, 'The chequered career of Max Mosley', *Guardian*, 26 November 1997; Jan Dally, 'Beauty and the Blackshirts', *Guardian, Saturday Review*, 11 September 1999; Richard Griffiths, 'When Blackshirts Were the Rage', *The Times Higher*, 2 March 2001. Late references also include as the name of a neo-Nazi, skinhead band (Sam Vitofsky, 'Blackshirts', *Searchlight*, 304 (October 2000), p 11); in radio drama (Bonnie Greer, *Louis – The Lonely Days*, BBC Radio Four (23 March 2001)); in Richard Loncraine's filmic version of Shakespeare's *Richard III* set in the 1930s (Andy Medhurst, 'Dressing the part: British costume drama', *Sight & Sound*, 6 (June 1996), pp 28–30) and as the subject of scurrilous humour ('Oswald Mosley – The Blackshirt Funnyman', *Viz*, 95 (1999), p 14).

The Blackshirts at Belle Vue

Newspaper references that do not contain a page number can be found in National Museum of Labour History, Press Cuttings on Fascism, Fas 1/1–210 and Fas 6/1–90.

1 *Manchester Guardian* used 'The Blackshirts at Belle Vue' as the headline for a number of articles on the rally discussed in this chapter during September and October 1934.

2 Stuart Rawnsley, 'The Membership of the British Union of Fascists', in Kenneth Lunn and Richard C. Thurlow (eds), *British Fascism. Essays on the Radical Right in Inter-War Britain* (London, 1980), pp 151–3.

3 Oswald Mosley, *Fascism: 100 Questions Asked and Answered* (London, 1936), Working Class Movement Library (WCML) Uncatalogued Fascism Box 4, p 61.

4 William Rust, *Mosley and Lancashire* (London, 1934), [Labour Monthly Pamphlet No. 5], WCML F25 Box 4, p 3. Bill Williams also sees Lancashire's 'dismal economic climate' as the reason that Oswald Mosley made Manchester an 'important focus' for the BUF; Bill Williams, *Manchester Jewry: A Pictorial History 1788–1988*, (1988), cited in Sharon Gerwitz, 'Anti-Fascist Activity in Manchester's Jewish Community in the 1930s', *Manchester Region History Review*, IV, 1 (1990), p 19.

5 For a comprehensive bibliography of studies on British fascism, see Thomas Linehan, *British Fascism, 1918–1939. Parties, Ideology and Culture*, (Manchester, 2000).

6 *The BUF by the BUF*, (Tiptree, Essex, c.1939), WCML Uncatalogued Fascism Box 4, p 4.

7 Rust, *Mosley and Lancashire*, p 1. Oswald Mosley referred to his family's wealthy position in Lancashire in his autobiography claiming that he had been 'reproached in political life for the rough part the family played in repressing the Chartist riots in Manchester'. See Oswald Mosley, *My Life* (London, 1968), pp 3–4.

8 For example, David Stephen Lewis, *Illusions of Grandeur: Mosley, Fascism and British Society, 1931–81* (Manchester, 1987). Kenneth Lunn and Richard C. Thurlow draw our attention to 'two well-argued themes, anti-Semitism and political violence', in Kenneth Lunn and Richard C. Thurlow, 'Introduction', in Lunn and Thurlow, *British Fascism*, p 11.
9 Reinhard Kuhnl, 'The Cultural Politics of Fascist Governments', in Gunter Berghaus (ed.), *Fascism and Theatre. Comparative Studies on the Aesthetics and Politics of Performance in Europe, 1925–1945*, (Oxford, 1996), p 30.
10 The term 'theatricality' in relation to 'public displays in fascist States' is taken from Gunter Berghaus, 'Introduction', in Berghaus, *Fascism and Theatre*, p 4. Roger Griffin has argued that although there were only two 'fully' fascist regimes, if we use his model of palingenetic ultra-nationalism to approach fascism, we can analyse the 'over-abundance of theatricality'. See Roger Griffin, 'Staging the Nation's Rebirth: The Politics and Aesthetics of Performance in the Context of Fascist Studies', in Berghaus, *Fascism and Theatre*, pp 13–18, 26.
11 For work on the 'fascination' of fascism see Gunter Berghaus, 'The Ritual Core of Fascist Theatre. An Anthropological Perspective', in Berghaus, *Fascism and Theatre*, p 66. For reflection on the 'failure' of British fascism see Mike Cronin (ed.), *The Failure of British Fascism. The Far Right and the Fight for Political Recognition*, (Basingstoke, 1996). This perspective is in keeping with Mike Cronin's comments on Roger Griffin's work that seeks to look at British society rather than fascism to ask 'what conditions would allow fascism to succeed in Britain?' See Mike Cronin, 'Introduction: 'Tomorrow We Live' – The Failure of British Fascism?', in Cronin, *The Failure of British Fascism*, p 10.
12 Gerwitz, 'Anti-Fascist Activity', p 23.
13 For example, in 1869 these attractions included a music hall, tea room, monkey house, menagerie, museum, lake, hot houses and flower gardens, bear den, maze and aviary, see *Guide to the Belle Vue Zoological Gardens*, (Manchester, 1869).
14 Ibid.
15 For the inter-war changes at Belle Vue see Helen Pussard, '"A mini-Blackpool": Belle Vue and the cultural politics of pleasure and leisure in inter-war Manchester', (unpublished MA thesis, University of Manchester, 1997).
16 Belle Vue (Manchester) Ltd, *The Greatest Centre in the Country for Exhibitions, Shows, Sports and Meetings*, (Manchester, 1933).
17 Belle Vue (Manchester) Ltd, *Belle Vue Official Guide*, (Manchester, 1928), p 26.
18 Joan Leighton, 'Power Elites and the British Union of Fascists 1932–1940' (unpublished MPhil thesis, University of Manchester, 1993), p 241.
19 A. K. Chesterton, *Oswald Mosley: Portrait of a Leader* (London, 1937), p 125.
20 *The Times*, 1 October 1934.
21 *Daily Herald*, 1 October 1934.
22 Gerwitz, 'Anti-Fascist Activity', p 22.
23 Trade Unions Council and Mark Buckley, *All to Belle Vue*, (Manchester, 1934), WCML F62 Box 10.
24 Kuhnl, 'The Cultural Politics', pp 30, 35.
25 Chesterton, *Oswald Mosley*, p 121.

26 Chesterton, *Oswald Mosley*, p 126.
27 *Daily Worker*, 15 September 1934, p 3.
28 Ibid.
29 Leighton, 'Power Elites', pp 241–5.
30 *Daily Worker*, 15 September 1934, p 3.
31 Ibid.
32 Leighton, 'Power Elites', p 241.
33 Gerwitz, 'Anti-Fascist Activity', p 23.
34 *Manchester Guardian*, 28 September 1934.
35 *Daily Worker*, 21 September 1934, p 3.
36 *Daily Worker*, 18 September 1934, p 3.
37 *Daily Worker*, 19 September 1934, p 3.
38 The fascist press, for example, claimed advances in recruitment from Manchester and in sales of *Blackshirt*. See Leighton, 'Power Elites', pp 245–6.
39 *Daily Worker*, 17 September 1934, p 1.
40 *Daily Worker*, 15 September 1934, p 3.
41 Trade Unions Council and Buckley, *All to Belle Vue*.
42 *Daily Worker*, 20 September 1934, p 3.
43 *Daily Worker*, 18 September 1934, p 3.
44 Mike Jenkins, 'Fighting Fascism in the 30s', *Comment Communist Fortnightly Review*, X, 18 (1972), p 282 and Bernard Rothman, 'The Mosley Rally, King's Hall Belle Vue, February 1933', *North West Labour History*, 18 (1993/4), p 52.
45 *Daily Worker*, 20 September 1934, p 3.
46 Alice Bellamy, '"Contesting the Nation": Fascism and Anti-Fascism in Britain in the 1930s' (unpublished MA thesis, University of Manchester, 1997).
47 For this point on the transitory nature of spectacle see Berghaus, 'Introduction', p 8.
48 Chesterton, *Oswald Mosley*, p 119.
49 *Daily Herald*, 1 October 1934.
50 Jenkins, 'Fighting Fascism', p 283.
51 *Manchester Guardian*, 1 October 1934.
52 Ibid.
53 Jenkins, 'Fighting Fascism', p 283.
54 *The Times*, 1 October 1934.
55 *Manchester Guardian*, 1 October 1934.
56 Ibid.
57 Ibid.
58 The *Daily Herald* reported that 800 Blackshirts and 500 police were present, but other estimates from the *Manchester Guardian* and *The Times* cited the number of Blackshirts at 500–600 and *c.* 1,000 respectively. See *Daily Herald*, 1 October 1934; *Manchester Guardian*, 1 October 1934 and *The Times*, 1 October 1934. The *Manchester Guardian* estimated the number of people outside the square enclosure at 3,000, while the *Daily Worker* recorded the number of anti-fascists as 1,000. See *Manchester Guardian*, 1 October 1934 and *Daily Worker*, 1 October 1934. Retrospective accounts placed the number of people present at 10,000 with 3,000 'members of the public'. See Leighton, 'Power Elites', p 245.
59 *Manchester Guardian*, 1 October 1934.

60 *Manchester Guardian*, 1 October 1934.
61 Ibid.
62 *Daily Worker*, 1 October 1934.
63 Ibid.
64 *Manchester Guardian*, 1 October 1934.
65 *Daily Herald*, 1 October 1934.
66 *Manchester Guardian*, 1 October 1934.
67 Jenkins, 'Fighting Fascism', p 283.
68 *Manchester Guardian*, 1 October 1934.
69 Ibid.
70 Ibid. and *Daily Worker*, 2 October 1934, p 4. See also Richard Griffiths, *Fellow Travellers of the Right. British Enthusiasts for Nazi Germany 1933–9* (London, 1980), pp 105–6.
71 *The Times*, 1 October 1934.
72 See above, n. 11.

Purifying the Nation

1 Richard Verrall, 'Art and Nationalism', *Spearhead*, September, 1972, p 12.
2 Ibid.
3 Ibid.
4 Ibid.
5 Ibid.
6 Adolf Hitler, speech on opening the House of German Art, Munich, 18 July 1937, in David Welch, *The Third Reich: Politics and Propaganda* (London, 1995), pp 170–4.
7 For general discussion of possible comparisons between the inter-war and post-1945 far Right, see Roger Griffin, *The Nature of Fascism* (London, 1991), pp 161–81; Diethelm Prowe, 'Classic Fascism and the New Radical Right in Western Europe: Comparisons and Contrasts', *Contemporary European History*, 3, 3 (November 1994), pp 289–313; Roger Eatwell, 'The Rebirth of the "Extreme Right" in Western Europe?', *Parliamentary Affairs*, 53, 3 (July 2000), pp 407–25.
8 Tyndall was replaced as leader of the BNP by Nick Griffin in 1999. See Nick Lowles, 'Griffin Consolidates Grip on British National Party', *Searchlight*, November 1999, p 6.
9 On the 'conservative revolutionaries' see Roger Woods, *The Conservative Revolution in the Weimar Republic* (Basingstoke, 1996). For the influence of Spengler and other conservative revolutionaries on post-1945 neofascism, see Kevin Coogan, *Dreamer of the Day: Francis Parker Yockey and the Postwar Fascist International* (Brooklyn, 1999); Richard Thurlow, *Fascism in Modern Britain* (Stroud, 2000) pp 121, 126.
10 On the BUF and its attitude to Spengler, see Richard Thurlow, 'Destiny and Doom: Spengler, Hitler and "British" Fascism', *Patterns of Prejudice*, XV, 4 (1981), pp 17–33.
11 Robert Colby, 'The End of History?', *Spearhead*, July 1996, p 17.
12 Ball, for example, called for a 'total national revolution, a veritable rebirth of our nation rather than minor cosmetic surgery'. He called for a 'great national purge' and argued: 'We must not be afraid to use the word "purge"; after all, its dictionary definition is "make physically or spiritually clean"', David Ball, 'The Assault on Tradition', *Spearhead*,

April 1984, p 15. Another BNP writer referred to the 'sickness and decay' eating away at the nation and to the 'atomised society' in which white people had been cut off from their 'culture and heritage'; the BNP embodied 'cleanliness and Life'. Richard Swain, 'A Future for White Children', *Spearhead*, July 1996, p 24.

13 Richard Thurlow, *Fascism in Britain: From Oswald Mosley's Blackshirts to the National Front* (London, 1998) p 22.

14 On Chesterton's post-BUF career, see D. L. Baker, 'The Making of a British Fascist – The Case of A. K. Chesterton' (unpublished PhD thesis, University of Sheffield, 1982); David Baker, *Ideology of Obsession: A. K. Chesterton and British Fascism* (London, 1996).

15 M. E. Romanovitch, 'Henry Williamson as a Romantic Fascist? The Origins, Context and Applications of Henry Williamson's Aesthetic and Political Ideas' (unpublished PhD thesis, Kingston University, 1992) p 3.

16 Ibid., p 73.

17 Cited in Special Branch Report on the '18B Detainees (British) Aid Fund', 16 December 1945, in Public Records Office (PRO), Home Office (HO) 45/24467. For background, see also Special Branch Report of 21 December, 1945 in PRO, HO 45/24467.

18 Cited in extract from Special Branch Fortnightly Summary no 124 for the period ending 31 December 1945, in PRO, HO 45/24467. For background, see also Special Branch Report of 21 December 1945, in PRO, HO 45/24467.

19 Oswald Mosley, 'Disrupt "Old Gang" by Permeation', *Union*, 8 May 1948; Thurlow, *Fascism in Modern Britain*, p 132.

20 Oswald Mosley, *My Answer* (Ramsbury, 1946), p 44.

21 Oswald Mosley, *The Alternative* (Ramsbury, 1947) pp 23, 292, 298.

22 Ibid., p 287.

23 Ibid., p 299.

24 Oswald Mosley, 'The State of Britain: England on the Dole', *Mosley Newsletter*, 4 (February/March 1947), pp 1–4, in PRO, HO 45/24469.

25 'G. C.', 'The Debacle of Soviet Culture', *Mosley Newsletter*, 4 (February/March), 1947, p 10, in PRO, HO 45/24469.

26 Ibid., p 12.

27 Thurlow, *Fascism in Modern Britain*, p 127.

28 David Pryce-Jones, *Unity Mitford: A Quest* (London, 1995, first published 1976) p 78.

29 Alexander Raven-Thomson, 'Britain's Part in Europe's Struggle', *Union*, 27 November 1948. Another UM writer, B. C. Kemp, however, was less cautious and continued to emphasize that the 'Extension of Patriotism' included the whole of the European family united by a common culture. He argued that the next step in evolution would involve 'nations of similar cultural inspiration' coming together as a 'supernational organism' which would include yet 'transcend' national differences. B. C. Kemp, 'Patriotism is Not Enough', *Union*, 22 January 1949.

30 Raven-Thomson, 'Britain's Part in Europe's Struggle', p 2.

31 Ibid.

32 Ibid.

33 Ibid.

34 Jeffrey Hamm, 'Heritage of Europe', *Union*, 8 October 1949.

35 Ibid., p 2.

36 Hamm, 'Heritage of Europe'.

37 Ibid.

38 Ibid.

39 Ibid.

40 Ibid.

41 'D. A. S.', 'Degradation of Taste', *Union*, 8 July 1950. Note also John Bean's critique of 'rootless culture' when describing his reasons for joining the UM in 1950; John Bean, *Many Shades of Black: Inside Britain's Far Right* (London, 1999) p 59.

42 Ibid., p 3.

43 Ibid.

44 'Disturbances by Union Movement during Film of "Sword In the Desert" (1949–50)', in PRO, HO 45/25596.

45 See, for example, 'E. O.', 'The Glory That Was Europes', *Union*, 27 August 1949; Alexander Raven-Thomson, 'Jewish Racialism', *Union*, 5 April 1952; William Whalley, 'The People's Music: European Records', *Action*, 18 October 1957; Michael MacUre, 'Records', *Action*, 24 January 1958; Michael Harald, 'D'Annunzio: Patriot and Prophet', *Action*, 14 March 1959; Michael Harald, 'Ancient Sunlight: the New Henry Williamson', *Action*, February 1960; Michael Harald, 'Call me Ishmael', *Action*, August/September 1960.

46 Mosley, *The Alternative*, p 305.

47 Ibid., pp 62–3.

48 Ibid., p 63.

49 Ibid.

50 Oswald Mosley, *Mosley – Right or Wrong?* (London, 1961), p 282.

51 Ibid.

52 Ibid., p 283.

53 Trevor Grundy, *Memoir of a Fascist Childhood: A Boy in Mosley's Britain* (London, 1998), p 93. Hamm stated that the *European* was launched to 'correct' the impression that the words 'intellectual' and 'communist' were synonymous. Jeffrey Hamm, *Action Replay* (London, 1983), pp 170–1.

54 Robert Skidelsky, *Oswald Mosley* (London, 1990, first published 1975), p 493. Mosley's wife, Diana, edited the *European* during its six-year existence.

55 William Harris, 'A Garden Green: an Examination of Britain's Traditional Cultural Heritage', *Lodestar*, 1 (Winter 1985/6), pp 20–3. Edited by Jeffrey Hamm and Robert Row, *Lodestar* was published quarterly from 1985 to 1992 and lasted for twenty issues.

56 Harris, 'A Garden Green', pp 21–3.

57 'The Education of a Nationalist', *Spearhead*, February 1970, pp 8–9.

58 Ibid., p 9.

59 John Bean, 'The Assault on Western Culture', *Spearhead*, November/December 1968, p 7.

60 Ibid.

61 Ibid.

62 Ibid.

63 Ibid.

64 John Bean, 'Nationalism and the Meaning of History', *Spearhead*, September 1970, p 16.

65 Ibid.

66 Eddy Morrison, 'Sub-culture', *Spearhead*, November 1969, p 10.
67 Ibid.
68 Ibid.
69 'Wanted: a Renaissance of Western Man', *Spearhead* (Special Issue), January/February 1972, p 14.
70 Ibid.
71 Ibid.
72 Ibid.
73 Ibid.
74 Ibid.
75 Thurlow, *Fascism in Britain*, p 254; Thurlow, *Fascism in Modern Britain*, p 152; Richard Verrall, 'Left-Wing Shift in the National Front', *Spearhead*, December 1975/January 1976, pp 10–12.
76 Verrall, 'Art and Nationalism', p 12. Note also Verrall's claim that liberal intellectuals had presided over the 'fragmentation of Western culture'. Richard Verrall, 'Reflections on the Liberal Intellectual', *Spearhead*, May 1976, pp 8–9.
77 Verrall, 'Art and Nationalism', p 12.
78 Ibid.
79 Ibid.
80 Ibid., p 13.
81 Ibid.
82 Ibid., p 14.
83 Ibid.
84 Ibid.
85 Anthony M. Ludovici, 'The Revolution in Art Examined', *Spearhead*, March 1973, pp 8–9; Nigel Fielding, *The National Front* (London, 1981) ch. 5. During the 1980s, the NF split into rival factions but the 'cultural' message remained broadly the same. Note the view of a young Nick Griffin in *New Nation* that Britain had been corrupted by the 'alien' influences of Marx, Freud and Hollywood; he called for the 'rediscovery of British culture'. Cited in Richard Dowden, 'Which Face for the National Front?', *The Times*, 11 April 1985.
86 'Our "High Noon" Approaches', *Spearhead*, January 1979, p 15; 'The British Film: Prescription for Revival', *Spearhead*, July 1980, p 4.
87 'Why Britain Needs a Revolution', *Spearhead*, February 1980, p 4.
88 'Kulture Vultures', *Searchlight*, June 1979, p 14.
89 Cited in 'The Shock Troops of Racism', *Newsweek*, 27 May 1985.
90 For the influence of Leese on Tyndall and Colin Jordan, see Denis Eisenberg, *The Re-Emergence of Fascism* (London, 1967) ch. 1; George Thayer, *The British Political Fringe: A Profile* (London, 1965) p 27; 'Fascist Traditions 2: Arnold Leese', *Searchlight*, October 1982, p 16; Thurlow, *Fascism in Britain*, pp 228–9, p 231; Thurlow, *Fascism in Modern Britain*, pp 120–1, 152. Tyndall has tried to gloss over this in recent years, claiming he was influenced more by A. K. Chesterton's 'balanced' racial ideas.
91 John Tyndall, 'More about Mosley', *Spearhead*, January/February 1969, p 12. See also John Tyndall, 'Continental Journey', *Spearhead*, October 1984, p 10; John Tyndall, 'Mosley: Record No Straighter After Latest Television Series', *Spearhead*, April 1998, pp 6–9.
92 Cited in Martin Walker, *The National Front* (Glasgow, 1977), p 69.

93 Tyndall has retained editing control over *Spearhead* during most of its existence, although Richard Verrall was formal editor from 1976–80, Thurlow, *Fascism in Modern Britain*, p 152. Nick Griffin was effective editor from 1996–9, but Tyndall resumed the editorship in August, 1999, when it became apparent that Griffin was going to challenge him for the leadership of the BNP.

94 One of the firmest advocates of the 'cultural war' strategy in far Right politics was Nick Griffin, who referred to the need for a 'cultural struggle'. Nick Griffin, 'Time to go to the ball', *Spearhead*, January 1997, p 15. His past writings borrowed from wider European neo-fascist ideas concerning the need for a cultural 'War of Position', particularly French attempts to formulate a 'Gramsciism of the Right'. Nick Griffin, 'Populism or Power', *Spearhead*, February 1996, pp 11–13; Nick Griffin, 'When the Wall Comes Down', *Spearhead*, March 1997, pp 14–16. Another advocate of this approach was Mark Deavin, who emphasized the importance of cultural hegemony prior to the attainment of political power. Mark Deavin, 'Politics of Persuasion', *Spearhead*, May 1998, pp 14–17; Mark Deavin, 'A Light from the Shadows', *Spearhead*, June 1998, pp 8–9. For the BNP's definition of cultural war, see 'A Nationalist Vocabulary', *Spearhead*, September 1997, p 13.

95 Thomas Linehan, *British Fascism 1918–39: Parties, Ideology and Culture* (Manchester, 2000), ch. 11.

96 John Tyndall, 'The Kind of Britain I Want', *Spearhead*, March 1981, p 12. In the same article, Tyndall reflected on the 'creation and protection of beauty', a discourse similar to Mosley's ideas noted earlier. However, Tyndall made it clear that 'beauty' would be firmly linked to deterministic conceptions of 'race'. In general, the words 'race' and 'culture' were often conflated and interchangeable in far Right texts. On Tyndall's more general attitudes to culture, see also Eamonn McCann, 'Dedicated Follower of Old-Fashioned Fascism', *New Statesman and Society*, 13 May 1994.

97 John Tyndall, *The Eleventh Hour: A Call For British Rebirth* (1988) (Welling, 1998), p 1.

98 Ibid., p 3.

99 Ibid., p 342.

100 Ibid.

101 Indeed, although Tyndall recognized the importance of seeking political power, he also called for an 'artistic, musical and literary counter-revolution', Tyndall, *The Eleventh Hour*, p 513. His supporters echoed this view. See, for example, Eddy Butler, 'A Call to Arms', *Spearhead*, March 1992, pp 12–13, 19.

102 John Tyndall, 'The Twentieth Century: an Historical Aberration', *Spearhead*, March 1990, p 5.

103 Ibid., p 8.

104 Ibid., p 9.

105 Ibid.

106 Ibid.

107 See, for example, articles in *Spearhead*, 266, 276, 277, 299, 302, 337, 346, 347 and 382.

108 See, for example, articles in *Spearhead*, 307, 337, 340, 341, 342, 343, 344, 353, 363, 372, 380, 382 and 384.

109 Ian Buckley, 'Wallowing in Filth', *Spearhead*, November 1997, p 5; N. G. Charnley, 'The Decline and Fall of Excellence', *Spearhead*, August 1999, pp 14–15; Colin Vernon, 'Another Myth of the 20th Century?', *Spearhead*, November 2000, pp 12–13.

110 John Tyndall, 'When Two Worlds Collide', *Spearhead*, January 1990, pp 4–6; Laurence Johnson, 'Wanted: an Architectural Renaissance', *Spearhead*, February 1992, pp 12–13; Arthur Rix, 'Cultural Diversity versus Liberal Globalism', *Spearhead*, February 1998, pp 16–17; Dominic Purcell, 'The Ugliness of New Britain', *Spearhead*, July 2000, p 15.

111 Tyndall, *The Eleventh Hour*, p 284.

112 Ibid.

113 John Tyndall, 'Recovering the National Character', *Spearhead*, October 1989, p 7.

114 Ibid.

115 John Tyndall, 'Outlook Favourable!', *Spearhead*, October 1992, p 5.

116 David Ball, 'A Case of Vandalism', *Spearhead*, March 1984, pp 4–5; John Tyndall, 'Wanted: a Resurgence of the City', *Spearhead*, September 1994, pp 5–7; Rix, 'Cultural Diversity versus Liberal Globalism', pp 16–17; Michael Ingrams, 'Things We Can Learn from the Greeks', *Spearhead*, December 1999, p 17; Tyndall, *The Eleventh Hour*, pp 336–7.

117 Tyndall, *The Eleventh Hour*, p 534.

118 George L. Mosse, 'Towards a General Theory of Fascism', in George L. Mosse (ed.), *International Fascism: New Thoughts and New Approaches* (London, 1979) pp 1–41; Richard J. Golsan (ed.), *Fascism, Aesthetics, and Culture* (London, 1992); Stanley G. Payne, *A History of Fascism 1914–45* (London, 1995) pp 450–4; Reinhard Kuhnl, 'The Cultural Politics of Fascist Governments', in Gunter Berghaus (ed.), *Fascism and Theatre: Comparative Studies on the Aesthetics and Politics of Performance, 1925–1945* (Oxford, 1996), ch. 2; Simonetta Falasca-Zamponi, *Fascist Spectacle: The Aesthetics of Power in Mussolini's Italy* (London, 2000); Linehan, *British Fascism 1918–39*, ch. 8.

119 Philip V. Cannistraro, 'Mussolini's Cultural Revolution', *Journal of Contemporary History*, 7, 3–4 (July–October 1972), p 115.

120 D. S. Lewis, *Illusions of Grandeur: Mosley, Fascism and British Society, 1931–81* (Manchester, 1987), p 7; Mark Neocleous, *Fascism* (Buckingham, 1997), pp 66–74; Steven Woodbridge, 'The Nature and Development of the Concept of "National Synthesis" in British Fascist Ideology, 1920–1940' (unpublished PhD thesis, Kingston University, 1998), pp 391–3; Mike Hawkins, 'The Foundations of Fascism: the World Views of Drieu la Rochelle', *Journal of Political Ideologies*, 5, 3 (October 2000), pp 321–41.

121 See, for example, the editorial comments by Roger Scruton on 'high culture' in the *Salisbury Review*, 16, 3 (Spring 1998), p 3. Right-wing cultural journals such as the *Scorpion* and *Right Now* attempted during the 1980s and 1990s to create common ground between the neo-conservative new Right and the neo-fascist far Right.

122 In spring 1979, for example, party chairman Tyndall issued a warning to NF members after a large number attended a screening of the Nazi film *Triumph of the Will*, arranged by the League of St George, an organization proscribed by the NF. 'NF Members Pack Nazi Film Show', *Searchlight*, June 1979, p 4.

123 The tensions between the 'suited' and the 'booted' are captured well in Barnaby Ore, 'Don't Forget our Roots', *Spearhead*, September 1998,

pp 12–13; Richard Molesworth, 'Is Rock Music White Music?', *Spearhead*, November 1999, pp 15–16.

124 'Camp Excalibur 2001, Birth of the Young BNP!', *Identity*, October 2001. *Identity* was created to replace *Spearhead* as the BNP's official magazine after Griffin became party leader.

125 See http://www.bnp.org.uk/britishheritage.html.

126 'RWB 2001 a Success!', *Identity*, September 2001. The BNP sent regular delegations to the French Front National annual equivalent festival during the 1990s.

Anglo-Italian Fascist Solidarity?

1 William Shakespeare, *Cymbeline*, V. v, in *Complete Works of William Shakespeare* (Glasgow, 1994), p 1295. Quoted in a pamphlet by the British Union of Friends of Italy (1938), Archivio Storico Ministero Affari Esteri (ASMAE), Archivio De Felice (DeF), Carte Dino Grandi (CG), b. 53, f. 126.

2 Robert Benewick, *Political Violence and Public Order. A study of British Fascism* (London, 1969), p 134; see also Mike Cronin (ed.), *The Failure of British Fascism. The Far Right and the Fight for Political Recognition* (London and Basingstoke, 1996); Andrew Thorpe (ed.), *The Failure of Political Extremism in Inter-War Britain* (Exeter, 1989); Julie V. Gottlieb, *Feminine Fascism. Women in Britain's Fascist Movement, 1923–1945* (London, 2000); Thomas Linehan, *British Fascism 1918–39. Parties, Ideology and Culture* (Manchester, 2000).

3 Richard Thurlow, *Fascism in Britain. A History, 1918–1985* (Oxford and New York, 1987), p 107.

4 'Tours to Fascist countries', *Blackshirt*, 1 April 1933.

5 'Duecento insegnanti inglesi ricevuti dal Duce', *L'Italia Nostra*, 6 April 1933, p 270.

6 'Pellegrinaggio operai inglesi disoccupati', Grandi to Italian foreign ministry, 24 October 1933, ASMAE, Ambasciata di Londra (AL), b. 800.

7 BUF to Italian Embassy, 3 November 1933, ASMAE, AL, b. 800, f. 2.

8 On the London *Fascio* see Roberta Suzzi Valli, 'Il fascio italiano a Londra. L'attività politica di Camillo Pellizzi', *Storia Contemporanea*, XXVI, 6 (1995), pp 957–1001; Claudia Baldoli, 'Ho cambiato il cielo ma non l'animo … I fasci italiani all'estero e l'educazione dell'italiano in Gran Bretagna, 1932–1934', *Studi Emigrazione. International Journal of Migration Studies*, XXXVI, 134 (1999), pp 243–81 and, forthcoming, 'Il caso inglese', in Emilio Franzina and Matteo Sanfilippo (eds), *Fascismo e emigrazione*, (Bari and Rome, 2002).

9 Camagna to Parini, 6 November 1933; see also Parini to Grandi, 15 November 1933, ASMAE, (AL), b. 805, f. 2.

10 'Una iniziativa del GUF per lo "Scambio d'ospitalità"', *L'Italia Nostra*, 11 August 1933, p 4; 'Gli universitari fascisti rendono omaggio al milite ignoto e sono passati in rivista da Sir Oswald Mosley', *L'Italia Nostra*, 18 August 1933, p 5; 'British Union of Fascists and Italian Fascist Students in London', Public Record Office (PRO), Home Office (HO) 144/19069 (486825/51).

11 'Blackshirts meet Fascisti', *Blackshirt*, 1 June 1934.

12 'Olympia had to come sooner or later. It is the real beginning of the struggle for political supremacy in Britain' (*Blackshirt*, 15 June 1934). See also other articles in the following issue: 'The truth about the Olympia disorder – Communist determination to kill Mosley'; 'Reason's triumph – Red terror smashed at Britain's biggest meeting'; 'Leader's great appeal to Olympia audience – The people demand a new creed'. See also Stephen Cullen, 'Political Violence: the Case of the British Union of Fascists', *Journal of Contemporary History*, 28, 2 (1993), pp 245–67; 'Vindicator', *Fascists at Olympia: a Record of Eye-Witnesses and Victims* (London, 1934).

13 Grandi to foreign ministry, 21 February 1933, ASMAE, Affari Politici (AP), Gran Bretagna (GB), b. 6, f. 1, sf. 1.

14 *Rheinisch-Westfälische Zeitung*, 6 March 1933, in ASMAE, AP, GB, b. 6, f. 1, sf. 1.

15 Grandi to Fulvio Suvich, 16 May 1933, *Documenti diplomatici italiani* (*DDI*), XIII, 615, pp 675–7.

16 'Il primo convegno romano dei fascisti britannici', *L'Italia Nostra*, 15 June 1934, p 2; Eric Drummond to John Simon, 8 June 1934, PRO, Foreign Office (FO) 371/18436, R3343/1929/22.

17 British Consul in Genoa to Drummond, 20 March 1934, PRO, FO 371/18436, R1929/22.

18 Ibid.

19 James Drennan, *BUF: Oswald Mosley and British Fascism* (London, 1934); Arthur Kenneth Chesterton, *Oswald Mosley: Portrait of a Leader* (London, 1937).

20 Chesterton, *Oswald Mosley*, p 127.

21 Italo Balbo, *Diario 1922* (Milan, 1932); Roberto Farinacci, *Squadrismo. Dal mio diario della vigilia* (Rome, 1933); G. A. Chiurco, *Storia della rivoluzione fascista, 1919–1922* (Florence, 1929); Luigi Villari, *The Awakening of Italy: the Fascista Regeneration* (London, 1924); Luigi Villari, *The Fascist Experiment* (London, 1926); Luigi Villari, *Italy* (London, 1929).

22 Chesterton, *Oswald Mosley*, p 108.

23 'Mosley!', *Blackshirt*, 15 June 1934.

24 'Two Years of Hitler', *Blackshirt*, 1 February 1935.

25 'Mussolini – a Man of the Twentieth Century', *Blackshirt*, 8 February 1935.

26 *Rheinisch-Westfälische Zeitung*, 6 March 1933, in ASMAE, AP, GB, b. 6, f. 1, sf. 1.

27 Mosley, *The Greater Britain* (London, 1932), p 13. My italics.

28 Oswald Mosley, *Fascism: 100 Questions Asked and Answered* (London, 1936). My italics.

29 See in particular *My Answer* (Ramsbury, 1946); *The European Situation: the Third Force* (Ramsbury, 1950); *Automation: Problems and Solution. The Answer of European Socialism* (London, 1956). See also 'The Post-War European Idea', in Oswald Mosley, *My Life* (London, 1968), ch. 23, pp 432–46, when he wrote about Europe 'as a nation'.

30 Richard Reynell Bellamy, *We Marched with Mosley*, (Holt, Norfolk, 1968, 4 vols typescript, xeroxed copy), Sheffield University Library (SUL), Special Collections and Archives, BU Collection, Memoirs of Members of the BUF, 5/6.

31 Ibid.

32 'Mary Richardson Writes on – New Rome and Old', *Blackshirt*, 28 September 1934.

33 Francis J. Burdett, 'A Modern Statesman and His Work. Il Duce' (unpublished essay), SUL, Special Collections and Archives, BU Collection, Memoirs of Members of the BUF, 5/10 (b).

34 Francis J. Burdett, 'Giovinezza … Giovinezza', *Blackshirt*, 16 November 1934.

35 John Beckett, *After My Fashion: Twenty Post-War Years* (London, 1940, typescript), SUL, Special Collections and Archives, BU Collection, Memoirs of Members of the BUF, 5/1, p 345.

36 'Editorial', *Blackshirt*, 16 May 1933.

37 *Blackshirt*, 1 April 1933.

38 Drennan, *BUF*, p 220.

39 Ibid., p 16.

40 'Visit to Rome – The "Immense Majesty" of Fascist Peace', *Blackshirt*, 1 May 1933.

41 'The Authority of Fascism – Blackshirts Principles that Lead to World Peace', *Blackshirt*, 29 June 1934.

42 Oswald Mosley, *Tomorrow We Live* (London, 1939), p 2.

43 Ibid., p 72.

44 As defined by Asvero Gravelli, *Il fascismo inglese* (Rome, 1933), p 71.

45 Italy, Holland, Switzerland, Ireland, Denmark, Norway and France did. See Gisella Longo, 'I tentativi per la costituzione di un'internazionale fascista: gli incontri di Amsterdam e di Montreux attraverso i verbali delle riunioni', *Storia Contemporanea*, XXVII, 3 (1996), pp 475–570.

46 Mosley, *Tomorrow*, p 65.

47 B. D. E. Donovan, 'The Fascist Youth Movement in England. Loyalty – Service – Principle', *Blackshirt*, 28 November 1936.

48 'Blackshirt Bognor Holiday Camp', *Blackshirt*, 1 August 1936; 'Three Hundred Kiddies were Happy', *Blackshirt*, 15 August 1936; 'The Greyshirts in Camp at Bognor Regis', *Blackshirt*, 22 August 1936.

49 Guido Bartolotto, 'Il fascismo nel mondo' (1938), in Giorgio Galli (ed.), *Il fascismo nella Treccani* (Milan, 1997), pp 218, 228.

50 Murray Stuart to Foreign Office, 11 September 1934, PRO, FO 371/18436, R5040/1929/22.

51 PRO, MI5, KV4/1, *The Security Service. Its Problems and Organisational Adjustments 1908–1945*, vol. I (March 1946), part 2, *The Nazi Threat, 1933–1939*, (a), *The NSDAP and its Ausland Organisation*, p 77.

52 Grandi to foreign ministry, 23 March 1936, ASMAE, AL, b. 912, f. 1, sf. 1.

53 'Comizio fascisti britannici all'Albert Hall', Grandi to foreign ministry, 23 March 1936, ibid.

54 'Settimanale 'Action' – campagna anti-sanzionista', Grandi to foreign ministry, 2 May 1936, ibid.

55 Daniel Waley, *British Public Opinion and the Abyssinian War, 1935–6* (London, 1975), p 76.

56 Italian ministry of interior to foreign ministry, 4 October 1935, ASMAE, AP, GB, b. 12, f. 2.

57 Robert Gordon-Canning, 'The New Germany rejoices', *Blackshirt*, 27 September 1935.

58 See Thomas Linehan, *British Fascism 1918–39*, pp 99–101.

59 'Activities of Mr John Celli', Foreign Office minutes as comments to a letter by Perth to British Foreign Office, 5 May 1938, PRO, FO, 371/22434, R5157/395/22.

60 Rome Chancery to Southern Department, 1 January 1937, PRO, FO, 371/ 21169, R75/75/22.

61 'The British Union of Friends of Italy', photographs of the dinner in which 110 Italians and 38 Britons took part, 15 December 1937, PRO, FO 371/22434, R395/395/22.

62 John Frederick Charles Fuller, *The First of the League Wars. Its Lessons and Omens* (London, 1936); Muriel Currey, *A Woman at the Abyssinian War* (London, 1936).

63 Currey, *A Woman at the Abyssinian War*, p 76.

64 Fuller, *The First of the League Wars*, pp 58, 60.

65 Ibid, pp 61, 62.

66 Ibid, p 63.

67 British Embassy to Foreign Office, 22 April 1938, PRO, FO 371/22434, R4622/395/22.

68 Platt to Grandi, 4 May 1938, ASMAE, DeF, CG, b. 53, f. 129.

69 'Proposal to form Anglo-Italian Fellowship', Treasury to Foreign Office, 28 November 1938, PRO, FO 371/22417, R9601/23/22.

70 A. K. Chesterton, 'Aspects of the German Revolution – Educational Advance', *Blackshirt*, 26 June 1937; see also 'Aspects of the German Revolution – Hitler Jugend', *Blackshirt*, 5 June 1937; 'Aspects of the German Revolution – Public Enlightenment', *Blackshirt*, 3 July 1937; 'Aspects of the German Revolution – Increase of Joy', *Blackshirt*, 10 April 1937.

71 Viscount Lymington, *Should Britain Fight?* (London, 1938), SUL, BU Collection, 3/LYM.

72 Mosley, *My Life*, p 366; *Mosley: the Facts* (London, 1957), p 10; Diana Mosley, *A Life of Contrasts: the Autobiography of Diana Mosley* (London, 1977), p 159.

Another Form of Fascism

1 See, in particular, Dan Stone, *Breeding Superman. Nietzsche, Race and Eugenics in Edwardian and Interwar Britain* (Liverpool, 2002).

2 See Richard Griffiths, *The Reactionary Revolution: The Catholic Revival in French Literature, 1870–1914* (London, 1966).

3 Paul Bourget, a leading Catholic author, suggested in his novel *L'Étape* (Paris, 1902), p 394, that the national motto should be changed from 'Liberté, Égalité, Fraternité' to 'Discipline, Hiérarchie, Charité'. Vichy France, of course, changed it to 'Travail, Famille, Patrie'.

4 Léon Bloy, letter to Bernaert, 5 October 1899. Quoted in Joseph Bollery, *Léon Bloy: Essai de biographie* (Paris, 1947), vol. 3, p 302: '(Règle sans exception). Il ne faut jamais rien accorder à l'ennemi, rien, rien, RIEN'.

5 See, in particular Édouard Droumont, *La France juive* (Paris, 1886); *La Fin d'un monde* (Paris, 1889) and *Le Testament d'un antisémite* (Paris, 1891).

6 For a brilliant exposition of this tendency, see Zeev Sternhell, *La Droite révolutionnaire: les origines françaises du fascisme, 1885–1914* (Paris, 1978).

7 In my book *An Intelligent Person's Guide to Fascism* (London, 2000), I have suggested that Action Française was far more a part of the 'international fascism' of the period than has often been presumed.

8 'Romanticism is Revolution. This child of Rousseau puts down everything that was high, and vice versa.' ('Romantisme est Révolution. Cet enfant de Rousseau met en bas ce qui etait en haut, et inversement').

Charles Maurras, *Romantisme et Révolution*, reprinted in *Oeuvres Capitales* (Paris, 1954), vol. II, pp 31–59.

9   The Very Revd William R. Inge, *'The Jews': Are They so Radically Different from Ourselves?* (London, 1922).

10 *G. K.'s Weekly*, 1926: G. K. Chesterton, 'The Mystery of Mussolini', 24 April, p 113; W. R. Titterton, 'Moritz Mond', 2 January, p 398; G. K. Chesterton, 'Profanity and Proportion', 1 May, p 129; G. K. Chesterton, 'The Poison of Plutocracy' 10 July, pp 292–3.

11 For an examination of these ideas and their influence, see Griffiths, *An Intelligent Person's Guide to Fascism*, pp 15–16, 23–4.

12 *L'Action Française*, 20 March 1938, quoted in Eugen Weber, *Action Française: Royalism and Reaction in Modern France* (Stanford, 1962), p 480.

13 *The Cambridge Guide to Literature in English* (Cambridge, 1988), p 495; *The Oxford Companion to English Literature* (Oxford, 1985), p 492.

14 In a letter to Barrès at the time of the Dreyfus Affair, Gaultier praised Barrès's attitudes, and contrasted them with those of the 'university teachers, anarchists, Protestants, men of letters … who think they are free and progressive, and believe in rational substances, Truth, Justice, before which they prostrate themselves, full of faith and foolishness, and who are ignorant of the fact that these things are fictions by means of which strong physiological realities impose themselves on weak physiological realities.' (Letter from Jules de Gaultier to Maurice Barrès, 29 October 1899, quoted in Barrès, *Mes cahiers*, ed. Guy Dupré (Paris, 1899), pp 128–9).

15 Quoted in Sam Hynes (ed.), *Further Speculations of T. E. Hulme*, (Minneapolis, 1955), p xxx.

16 'Romanticism and Classicism', reprinted in Thomas Ernest Hulme, *Speculations: Essays on Humanism and the Philosophy of Art*, ed. Herbert Read (London, 1924), pp 113–40.

17 A number of unlikely creeds were being equated with Toryism in the first half of the twentieth century. Thus the Nietzschean Anthony Ludovici put forward his ideas (treated by Dan Stone elsewhere in this volume) in *A Defence of Conservatism* (1927), and Lord Lymington, of the 'back-to-the-land' school, wrote a book entitled *Ich Dien: the Tory Path* in 1931.

18 Quoted in Sam Hynes's introduction to *Further Speculations of T. E. Hulme*, p xxx.

19 Though they both contributed in the same period to the *New Age*, Hulme violently attacked Ludovici both for his artistic views (he had, among other things, attacked Hulme's friend Epstein), and for his 'ridiculous' Nietzscheanism.

20 'Thomas Grattan', 'A Tory Philosophy', *Commentator*, 3 April 1912, pp 294–5.

21 Unfortunately the series became discontinued, so all we have are the headings and his comments on them.

22 'A Tory Philosophy', *Commentator*, 1 May 1912, p 362.

23 'Reflections on Violence' reprinted in Hulme, *Speculations*, pp 249–60.

24 Anthony Quinton, 'Introduction', in Michael Roberts, *T. E. Hulme* (Manchester 1982), p v.

25 Hulme, 'Romanticism and Classicism', in *Speculations*, p 133.

26 *Oxford Companion to English Literature*, p 56.

27 Weber, *Action Française*, p 480.
28 *Transatlantic Review*, 1923.
29 T. S. Eliot, *For Lancelot Andrewes: Essays in Style and Order* (London, 1928), p ix.
30 T. S. Eliot, 'Recent Books', *Criterion*, 6, 1 (1927), p 70.
31 T. S. Eliot, 'A Commentary' (review of Lord Lymington's *Ich Dien: The Tory Path*), *Criterion*, 11, 52 (1931), p 69.
32 In the nineteenth century Anglo-Catholics, though reactionary in their religion, were often social reformers, heavily involved in founding churches in the poorest areas of the big cities of the industrial revolution. It is no surprise that many leading Labour Party figures in the twentieth century, from George Lansbury to Eric Heffer, have been Anglo-Catholics.
33 T. S. Eliot, 'A Reply to Mr Ward', *Criterion*, 7, 4 (1928), p 87.
34 Eliot, *For Lancelot Andrewes*, p ix.
35 T. S. Eliot, 'The Action Française', *Criterion*, 7, 3 (1928), pp 196–7.
36 *Aspects de la France et du monde*, 25 April 1948.
37 See Richard Griffiths, *Fellow Travellers of the Right: British Enthusiasts for Nazi Germany, 1933–39* (London, 1980), and *Patriotism Perverted: Captain Ramsay, the Right Club and British Anti-Semitism 1939–40* (London, 1998).
38 T. S. Eliot, 'Burbank with a Baedeker: Bleistein with a Cigar', *Poems* (London, 1920).
39 Prys Morgan, 'R. T. Jenkins – The Historian as Author', in Sam Adams and Gwilym Rees Hughes (eds), *Triskel One*, (Llandyssul, 1971), p 150.
40 Dafydd Glyn Jones, 'His Politics', in Alun R. Jones and Gwyn Thomas (eds), *Presenting Saunders Lewis*, (Cardiff, 1973), p 54.
41 Much of my information on Bebb comes from a remarkable article by Gareth Meils, entitled 'Ambrose Bebb' in the journal *Planet*, 37/38 (1977), pp 70–9.
42 Ibid., p 71.
43 Ambrose Bebb, 'Trythro gydag Athrylith', *Y Llenor*, II (1923), pp 177–80; 'Un o ddoethion Groeg gynt wedi ei godi yn ein dyddiau ni.'
44 Ibid., 'Os gellir dywedyd am neb sydd byw heddyw ei fod un anfarwol, amdano ef y gellir hynny. … Ni bydd marw Charles Maurras.'
45 Ibid., 'Amddiffyn trefn y mae, a thraddodiad, ac etifeddiaeth, awdurdod a deall.'
46 'Saunders Lewis: A Television Interview', *Planet*, 53 (1985), pp 3–12, the text of a BBC interview with Aneirin Talfan Davies on 19 May 1960, translated into English by Caryl Davies.
47 Quoted in Jones, 'His Politics', p 24.
48 See, for example, various articles by Saunders Lewis in the *Welsh Nationalist*: 'The Bankers and the Socialists', March 1934; 'Capitalism and Communism United', February 1934; 'Capitalism and Socialism', May 1935; etc.
49 Saunders Lewis, 'The Deluge 1939', translated into English by Gwyn Thomas, in Jones and Thomas, *Presenting Saunders Lewis*, p 177–9.
50 Saunders Lewis, 'Scene in a Café', in *Saunders Lewis: Selected Poems*, trans. Joseph Clancy (Cardiff, 1993).
51 *Welsh Nationalist*, July 1932.
52 Quoted in Jones, 'His Politics', p 37.

53 See Richard Griffiths, 'Three "Catholic" Reactionaries: Claudel, T. S. Eliot and Saunders', in Richard Griffiths (ed.), *The Pen and the Sword: Right-Wing Politics and Literary Innovation in the Twentieth Century* (London, 2000), pp 57–80.
54 Ibid., p 45.
55 Ibid., p 50.
56 'The ideal of the classical poets must remain our ideal as well. We too must endeavour towards order, wholeness and synthesis in life'. Saunders Lewis, *Williams Pantycelyn* (London 1927), Jones, 'His Politics', p 50.
57 Jones, 'His Politics', p 46.
58 Knut Diekmann, *Die Nationalistische Bewegung in Wales* (Paderborn, Munich, Vienna and Zurich, 1955), p 265.
59 See, for example, the letter, quoting Maurras approvingly, by J. Arthur Price in *Welsh Outlook*, XV, 6 (June 1928).
60 The Revd Gwilym Davies, 'Wales and the World', *Welsh Outlook*, XVII, 3 (March 1930).
61 *Y Ddraig Goch*, August 1935.
62 See *Welsh Nationalist*, September–October 1936.
63 Saunders Lewis, 'Notes and Comments', *Welsh Nationalist*, October 1936.
64 Saunders Lewis, 'In Ulster Now: a Blackguard Dictatorship', *Welsh Nationalist*, July 1936.
65 Ibid.
66 Saunders Lewis, 'On Hitler', *Welsh Nationalist*, August 1938.
67 Saunders Lewis, 'Where we Stand', *Welsh Nationalist*, October 1938.
68 Quoted in Meils, 'Ambrose Bebb', p 75.
69 A. R. Jones, *The Life and Opinions of Thomas Ernest Hulme* (London, 1960), pp 46–7.
70 See Griffiths, *The Pen and the Sword*, for an examination of this phenomenon in a variety of countries.
71 Saunders Lewis, 'Welsh Writers of To-day', BBC Welsh Home Service, April 1961. Reprinted in Jones and Thomas, *Presenting Saunders Lewis*, pp 164–70.

The Far Right and the Back-to-the-Land Movement

1 My thanks to Richard Griffiths for suggesting that I write this chapter, and to Scott Ashley for his assistance in the process of doing so.
2 Victor Klemperer, *I Shall Bear Witness: The Diaries of Victor Klemperer 1933–1941*, trans. Martin Chalmers (London, 1999), p 355.
3 Eliot to Lymington, 13 February 1942. Hampshire Record Office, Wallop Collection, 15M84/F165 (individual folios unpaginated). I am grateful to Lord Portsmouth for permission to cite from his grandfather's papers (henceforth cited as HRO and the file number).
4 On the concept of 'home' see my 'Homes without Heimats? Jean Améry at the Limits', *Angelaki*, II, 1 (1995), pp 91–100.
5 Uli Linke, *German Bodies: Race and Representation after Hitler* (New York, 1999), p 15. See also, on the notion of 'organic purity', Scott Straus, 'Organic Purity and the Role of Anthropology in Rwanda and Cambodia', *Patterns of Prejudice*, 35, 2 (2001), pp 47–62.
6 See Richard Griffiths, *An Intelligent Person's Guide to Fascism* (London, 2000).

7 See David Mellor (ed.), *A Paradise Lost: The Neo-Romantic Imagination in Britain 1935–55* (London, 1987); Frank Trentmann, 'Civilization and its Discontents: English Neo-Romanticism and the Transformation of Anti-Modernism in Twentieth-Century Western Culture', *Journal of Contemporary History,* 24, 4 (1994), pp 583–625. But see also the work of Peter Mandler: 'Against "Englishness": English Culture and the Limits to Rural Nostalgia, 1850–1940', *Transactions of the Royal Historical Society,* 6th series, VII (1997), pp 155–75; 'The Consciousness of Modernity? Liberalism and the English National Character, 1870–1940' in Martin Daunton and Bernhard Riegner (eds), *Meanings of Modernity: Britain from the Late-Victorian Era to World War II* (Oxford, 2001), pp 119–44.

8 I use the term 'organo-fascist' to mean that section of the back-to-the-land movement that saw the issues shared by organicists — rural decline, rural life as the essence of the nation, the mechanization of agriculture, soil erosion, the threat posed by fertilizers, the need for self-sufficiency — as being at one with issues that are characteristically fascistic: the question of racial purity, the quest for national 'revival', the need for social order, rootedness in the national soil, autarky, 'deliverance' from middlemen and speculators.

9 H. G. Wells, 'Developing Social Elements' in *The Works of H. G. Wells: The Atlantic Edition, vol. IX: Anticipations and Other Papers* (London, 1924, first published 1902), pp 82–3.

10 Elizabeth Ward, *David Jones Mythmaker* (Manchester, 1983), p 27. McNabb is cited on p 28.

11 Stanley Baldwin, *On England* (London, 1926), p 5.

12 Jeffrey Herf, *Reactionary Modernism: Technology, Culture and Politics in Weimar and the Third Reich* (Cambridge, 1984).

13 See especially Trentmann, 'Civilization and its Discontents', p 614.

14 Ibid., p 603.

15 R. G. Stapledon, *The Land Now and To-morrow* (London, 1935), p vii.

16 Sir George Stapledon, 'Agriculture and the Countryside' in *The Way of the Land* (London, 1943), p 92 (originally delivered as a lecture to the Council for the Preservation of Rural England, Chester, 14 October 1938).

17 Stapledon, 'The Land and the Nation', in ibid., p 94 (originally a paper read to the Autumn School of the National Labour Organization, Eastbourne, 6 November 1938).

18 Dr L. J. Picton, 'Diet and Farming' in Harold John Massingham (ed.), *England and the Farmer: A Symposium* (London, 1941), p 111.

19 For more on Kinship in Husbandry see David Matless, *Landscape and Englishness* (London, 1998), pp 104f; and, for a more appreciative view, R. J. Moore-Colyer, 'Back to Basics: Rolf Gardiner, H. J. Massingham and "A Kinship in Husbandry"', *Rural History,* XII, 1 (2001), pp 85–108. The fact that most of these men cannot unproblematically be called 'fascists' (Bell especially) suggests the validity of Griffiths's argument (above, n. 6).

20 Matless, *Landscape and Englishness*, p 106.

21 E. B. Balfour, *The Living Soil: Evidence of the Importance to Human Health of Soil Vitality, with Special Reference to Post-War Planning* (London, 1943), p 13.

22 Cf. ibid., p 17; Lord Northbourne, *Look to the Land* (London, 1940). Although the Soil Association has been effectively purged of fascist

affiliations, it still has a tendency to promote some rather 'mystical' books on the land. See the books for sale at its website: www.soilassociation.org.

23 H. J. Massingham, 'Introduction', in *English Country: Fifteen Essays by Various Authors* (London, 1934), p ix.

24 Viscount Lymington, *Horn, Hoof and Corn: The Future of British Agriculture* (London, 1932), p 59.

25 Cf. George Pitt-Rivers, 'Is there a Population Problem?', *The New Age*, XXVII, 5 (3 June 1920), pp 69–71.

26 Lymington, *Horn, Hoof and Corn*, pp 106, 121. Compare the comments on race of Harold Peake, *The English Village: The Origin and Decay of its Community. An Anthropological Interpretation* (London, 1922), pp 37–46.

27 See the writings of the English Mistery's founder, William Sanderson, *Statecraft* (London, 1927), and *That Which was Lost: A Treatise on Freemasonry and the English Mistery* (London, 1930). On the English Mistery/Array and its relationship with fascism see my article 'The English Mistery, the BUF, and the Dilemmas of British Fascism' (forthcoming).

28 HRO 15M84/F195. Francis-Hawkins to Lymington.

29 On whom see my *Breeding Superman: Nietzsche, Race and Eugenics in Edwardian and Interwar Britain* (Liverpool, 2002), ch. 1.

30 Anthony M. Ludovici, *Health and Education Through Self-Mastery* (London, 1933).

31 For more on Ludovici see my *Breeding Superman*, ch. 2. On Ludovici as a Nazi fellow-traveller see his three-part article 'Hitler and the Third Reich', *English Review*, LXIII, 1–3 (1936), pp 35–41, 147–53, 231–9, in which he discusses his visits to Germany, the Nuremberg rally and his meetings with leading Nazis.

32 Ludovici to Blacker, 25 January 1932. Eugenics Society Archive, SA/EUG/C.212/3 (Eugenics Society. 'People' – A. M. Ludovici 1927–1947). Cited by permission of the Galton Institute and the Wellcome Trustees, Contemporary Medical Archives Centre, Wellcome Institute for the History of Medicine, London.

33 HRO 15M84/F195. Ludovici to Lymington, 5 February 1938 and 8 February 1938.

34 Viscount Lymington, *Famine in England* (London, 1938), p 118. Unfortunately, I have been unable to locate Lymington's reply to Ludovici's letter.

35 L. [Lymington], 'Notes on Rural Life and Land Tenure' in Edmund Blunden (ed.), *Return to Husbandry* (London, 1943), p 18.

36 Rolf Gardiner, *England Herself: Ventures in Rural Restoration* (London, 1943), pp 9–10.

37 'Cobbett' [Anthony M. Ludovici], *Jews, and the Jews of England* (London, 1938), pp 65–6. Ludovici's inspiration was William Cobbett, *Rural Rides* (Harmondsworth, 1985, first published 1830).

38 'Cobbett', *Jews, and the Jews of England*, pp 67, 115, 116–17.

39 Matless, *Landscape and Englishness*, pp 110f; Malcolm Chase, 'This is No Claptrap, This is our Heritage' in Christopher Shaw and Malcolm Chase (eds), *The Imagined Past: History and Nostalgia* (Manchester, 1989), pp 128–46; Malcolm Chase, 'Rolf Gardiner: an Inter-War, Cross-Cultural Case Study' in Barry J. Hake and Stuart Marriott (eds), *Adult Education Between Cultures: Encounters and Identities in European Adult Education since 1890* (Leeds, 1992), pp 225–41; Patrick Wright, *The Village that Died for England: The Strange Story of Tyneham* (London, 1995).

40 See J. L. Finlay, 'John Hargrave, the Green Shirts, and Social Credit', *Journal of Contemporary History*, 5, 1 (1970), pp 53–71.

41 Rolf Gardiner, 'Reflections on Music and Statecraft' in Andrew Best (ed.), *Water Springing from the Ground: An Anthology of the Writings of Rolf Gardiner* (Fontmell Magna, 1972), pp 99, 100. 'Masculine renaissance' was one of Ludovici's most-loved ideas.

42 HRO 15M84/F195. Gardiner to Lymington. See also Georgina Boyes, *The Imagined Village: Culture, Ideology and the English Folk Revival* (Manchester, 1993), pp 154f.

43 Roger Griffin, *The Nature of Fascism* (London, 1991). On Lintorn-Orman see Julie V. Gottlieb, *Feminine Fascism: Women in Britain's Fascist Movement 1923–1945* (London, 2000), pp 11–42.

44 See Robert O. Paxton, 'The Five Stages of Fascism', *Journal of Modern History*, LXX, 1 (1998), pp 1–23.

45 See for example G. R. Searle, 'Critics of Edwardian Society: the Case of the Radical Right' in Alan O'Day (ed.), *The Edwardian Age: Conflict and Stability 1900–1914*, (London, 1979), pp 79–96; Arnd Bauerkämper, *Die "radikale Rechte" in Großbritannien: Nationalistische, antisemitische und faschistische Bewegungen vom späten 19. Jahrhundert bis 1945* (Göttingen, 1991).

46 Harold E. Moore, *Back to the Land* (London, 1893), p xiii.

47 Arnold White, 'The Inevitable', in *The Views of 'Vanoc': An Englishman's Outlook* (London, 1910), p 65. See also *The Modern Jew* (London, 1899), and *Efficiency and Empire* (London, 1901).

48 Lord Willoughby de Broke, 'National Toryism', *National Review*, LIX, 351 (May 1912), pp 413–27; Lord Willoughby de Broke (ed.), *The Sport of Our Ancestors* (London, 1921). See Gregory D. Phillips, 'Lord Willoughby de Broke: Radicalism and Conservatism', in J. A. Thompson and Arthur Mejia (eds), *Edwardian Conservatism: Five Studies in Adaptation*, (London, 1988), pp 77–104.

49 Charles Stewart Orwin and William Francis Drake, *Back to the Land* (London, 1935), p 9.

50 R. G. [Rolf Gardiner], 'When Peace Breaks Out: Tasks of Youth in a Post-War World' in Edmund Blunden (ed.), *Return to Husbandry*, (London, 1943), p 24; R. G. [Rolf Gardiner], 'Youth and Europe' in *Water Springing from the Ground*, p 20; J. C. Squire, 'Introduction' to Edmund Blunden, *The Face of England: In a Series of Occasional Sketches* (London, 1932), p vii. Matless correctly observes (in *Landscape and Englishness*, p 126) that 'There is a sense in organicist work of the melancholy pleasure inherent in documenting something doomed.'

51 Gardiner, 'Can Farming Save European Civilisation? in *Water Springing from the Ground*, p 197.

52 Gardiner, *England Herself*, p 62.

53 Edmund Blunden, *English Villages* (London, 1941), p 20.

54 A. B. [Adrian Bell], 'Husbandry and Society' in Blunden (ed.), *Return to Husbandry*, pp 5–6.

55 R. G. [Rolf Gardiner]. 'When Peace Breaks Out', p 21.

56 Rolf Gardiner, *England Herself*, p 146.

57 Lymington to Le Mare, HRO 15M84/F238.

58 Trentmann, 'Civilization and its Discontents', p 613.

59 'Notes of the Month: the Probable Results of War', *New Pioneer*, I, 6 (May 1939), p 139. This journal was run by Lymington.

60 Arthur Bryant, *Unfinished Victory* (London, 1940), p 141; Arthur Bryant, *English Saga (1840–1940)* (London, 1940), p 313.

61 Anne Williamson, *A Patriot's Progress: Henry Williamson and the First World War* (Stroud, 1998), p 153.

62 Henry Williamson, 'Introduction', in Sir John Russell, *English Farming* (London, 1941), p 10.

63 See Matless, *Landscape and Englishness*, pp 159–60. See also Philip Conford, 'A Forum for Organic Husbandry: the *New English Weekly* and Agricultural Policy, 1939–1949', *Agricultural History Review*, XLVI, 2 (1997), pp 197–219.

64 Jorian Jenks, *From the Ground Up: An Outline of Rural Economy* (London, 1950), p 215. See also Jorian Jenks, *The Country Year* (London, 1946); Jorian Jenks, *British Agriculture and International Trade* (London, 1948); Jorian Jenks, *The Stuff Man's Made Of: The Positive Approach to Health through Nutrition* (London, 1959) by which point the stress was much more firmly 'ecological'.

65 Matless, *Landscape and Englishness*, p 308, n. 83.

66 Guy Theodore Wrench, *Reconstruction by Way of the Soil* (London, 1946), p 85.

67 See J. E. Tunbridge and Gregory John Ashworth, *Dissonant Heritage: the Management of the Past as a Resource in Conflict* (Chichester, 1996); Brian Graham, G. J. Ashworth and J. E. Tunbridge, *A Geography of Heritage: Power, Culture and Economy* (London, 2000); and the essays in Brian Graham, (ed.), *Modern Europe: Place, Culture, Identity* (London, 1998). The countryside is always under threat because, of course, the England that is portrayed in magazines such as *This England* 'is not a country that really exists or ever existed except in literature.' Steve Silver, 'That England', *Searchlight*, 305 (November 2000), p 20.

68 See Max Oelschlaeger, *The Idea of Wilderness: From Prehistory to the Age of Ecology* (New Haven, 1991).

Index